MW00790922

DUMBARTON OAKS
MEDIEVAL LIBRARY

Jan M. Ziolkowski, General Editor

OLD ENGLISH SHORTER POEMS

VOLUME I

DOML 15

Old English
Shorter Poems

VOLUME I

RELIGIOUS AND DIDACTIC

Edited and Translated by

CHRISTOPHER A. JONES

DUMBARTON OAKS
MEDIEVAL LIBRARY

HARVARD UNIVERSITY PRESS
CAMBRIDGE, MASSACHUSETTS
LONDON, ENGLAND
2012

Library of Congress Cataloging-in-Publication Data
Old English shorter poems / edited and translated by Christopher A.
Jones.

    p. cm.—(Dumbarton Oaks medieval library ; DOML 15)
   Includes bibliographical references and index.
   ISBN 978-0-674-05789-0 (alk. paper)
   1. English poetry—Old English, ca. 450–1100. I. Jones, Christopher A.
(Christopher Andrew)
   PR1508.O55 2012
   829'.1—dc23   2011036260

Contents

Introduction   ix

POETIC ALLEGORIES OF NATURE
The Panther   2
The Whale   8
The Partridge   16
The Phoenix   18

POEMS OF WORSHIP AND PRAYER
The Lord's Prayer (I)   66
The Lord's Prayer (II)   68
The Lord's Prayer (III)   78
The Apostles' Creed   82
The Gloria patri (I)   88
The Gloria patri (II)   94
The Kentish Hymn   96
Cædmon's Hymn   100
Godric's Hymn   102
A Prayer   104
Resignation (A)   110

POEMS ON CHRISTIAN LIVING
Almsgiving 118
Homiletic Fragment (I) 120
Homiletic Fragment (II) 124
Aldhelm (A Verse Preface to His Treatise
De virginitate) 126
Thureth (Commemorative Verses in a
Bishop's Book) 128
The Rewards of Piety 130
Instructions for Christians 138
Seasons for Fasting 156
The Menologium 174

POEMS ON THE LAST THINGS
Soul and Body 192
The Soul's Address to the Body (from the
Worcester Fragments) 204
The Grave 230
Judgment Day (I) 232
Judgment Day (II) 242

Epilogue: A Lament for the English Church 264

CONTENTS

Appendix A: The Judgment of the Damned
(A Late Old English Sermon with Embedded Verse) 269
Appendix B: Bilingual Materials from the Divine Office 284
Note on the Texts 344
Abbreviations 346
Notes to the Texts 347
Notes to the Translations 375
Bibliography 439
Index 451

Introduction

The modern stereotype of Old English poetry as a distant realm of warriors and mead halls betrays how far a single work, *Beowulf*, has molded expectations of an entire literature. Readers closer to the Anglo-Saxons than we are, by contrast, invoked an entirely different standard in measuring what was valuable. When an anonymous poet, active at Worcester perhaps a century after the Norman Conquest, looked back to his Anglo-Saxon forebears, what he found admirable about them had nothing to do with legends such as *Beowulf*. The heroes who loom large in his vernacular poem, here called *A Lament for the English Church*, are all ecclesiastics, such as Saint Cuthbert, the Venerable Bede, and Ælfric of Eynsham, whose common glory lay in one achievement: their use of Old English to transmit Christian teachings. In the poet's eyes, this was the defining virtue of an Anglo-Saxon culture recently supplanted by "others" *(opre leoden)*, presumably Norman-French clergy who neither knew Old English nor cultivated it for pastoral ends.

Historians will caution that the Worcester poet's nostalgia says less about the past than about his worries as an Anglophone cleric under the Norman regime. It is true that most Norman prelates did not value Old English as their predecessors had. But manuscript evidence reveals that popular preaching in English continued well into the Norman period. Likewise, the poet's view of the Anglo-Saxon pastorate is probably too generous. Some of the figures he praises are indeed known to have championed vernacular ministry, while for others there is no evidence for such a practice.

Even so, the Worcester poet's characterization of the Anglo-Saxon past is, broadly speaking, a defensible one, at least for the period from ca. 900 to ca. 1100. From those centuries, when Latin remained the principal language of the western church, evidence of Old English in everyday ecclesiastical affairs survives to an extent unequaled by any other European vernacular. The most admired examples of the trend are sophisticated Old English sermons, biblical translations, and pedagogical works by the monk Ælfric of Eynsham (d. ca. 1010). But Ælfric was far from alone. His colleague Wulfstan, archbishop of York from 1002 until 1023, composed artful sermons and law codes in the people's language. The monk Byrhtferth of Ramsey (fl. ca. 1000) wrote a treatise, partly in Old English, on the science of computus (the reckoning of the calendar). And those are just the named authors. When anonymous translations, sermons, saints' lives, penitentials, prayers, and other texts are taken into account, the volume and diversity of Old English writing from the later Anglo-Saxon period are staggering, and most of it pertains to ecclesiastical subjects. Given this record, the Worcester poet can hardly be blamed for his perception that accomplished teaching and writing in the vernacular had always been part of Anglo-Saxon Christianity.

When praising his ancestors' cultivation of Old English, the Worcester poet was probably thinking first of prose writings that he had come across, especially homilies, sermons, and saints' lives.[1] But he may well have had in mind religious poems, too, which had long occupied a respected place alongside prose. Two of the most celebrated figures of the early Anglo-Saxon church, Aldhelm and Bede, were renowned as authors both of Christian prose and of Latin and vernacular poetry on religious themes. Anonymous Anglo-Saxon authors retold at length stories from the Bible and the lives of saints adapted to the conventions of traditional Old English heroic verse, producing sophisticated narrative poems such as *Genesis, Exodus, The Dream of the Rood, Andreas, Elene, Guthlac,* and many more.[2]

In addition to such famous works, dozens of other religious poems survive in Old English. The present volume gathers together many of these nonnarrative poems on overtly Christian themes. As usual with Old English verse — and, indeed, many medieval writings — all the texts collected here are anonymous.[3] They vary greatly in length, ambition, and date, though many of them were probably composed in the later Anglo-Saxon period.[4] Only a few items included here, such as *Cædmon's Hymn,* enjoy any celebrity today. Most others will be unfamiliar to a general audience; indeed, some are rarely read now even by specialists. Several of the compositions — namely *Instructions for Christians, Seasons for Fasting, The Menologium, The Lord's Prayer (II), The Gloria patri (I), The Kentish Hymn, A Prayer, Homiletic Fragments (I)* and *(II), Aldhelm,* and the Worcester Fragments — have long wanted accessible, up-to-date translations.

At the same time, it would be disingenuous to imply that the aforementioned poems and others like them have suffered neglect by chance only. In truth, their style and subject matter have often struck modern readers as comparatively unimaginative and unsubtle—in short, unpoetic. In those very features, however, also lies one significance of such texts in the history of Old English literature: in form and content, many of them are as closely related to prose, especially to late Old English sermons, as they are to other verse. In general, the boundary between poetry and prose grows harder to define in late Old English writings. Discrete poems and prose texts occasionally intermingle, as in the tenth-century manuscript known as the Vercelli Book. Also into individual prose works authors would occasionally splice lines or whole passages of Old English poetry, so that it can be hard to know whether a given segment was intended as poetry, prose, or something in between.[5] The criterion of meter, which might seem an objective standard for distinguishing verse from prose, only complicates the issue. Late Old English poems show frequent departures from the "classical" meter of *Beowulf.* Verse and prose could also diverge or blend in their diction, with the result that certain poems are now labeled "prosaic" if their vocabulary contains a high proportion of words normally excluded from verse.[6]

In sum, by the tenth century there apparently existed no rigid definition of Old English poetic form but rather a spectrum, with "classicizing" poetry at one end, more prose-like verse near the other, and, perhaps at the farthest end, "rhythmical" or "mixed prose."[7] Not all the poems included in the present book are "postclassical" or "prosaic" in the strict senses, but many of them do broaden our understanding of what constituted poetry for the Anglo-Saxons and what functions they considered appropriate for verse.

The remainder of this introduction surveys the individual

poems under four headings: allegories on nature, poems re-
lated to prayer and worship, poems on Christian morality
and custom, and poems on the last things (death, judgment,
heaven, and hell). Before the overview, however, a prelimi-
nary word is necessary concerning the titles assigned to in-
dividual works. Because Old English poems almost never
bear titles in the surviving manuscripts, modern editors
have had to invent them.[8] The results—often bland and
strange-looking names like *Resignation (A)* or *The Lord's
Prayer (III)*—appeal to no one, but neither have various
alternatives proposed from time to time. It has therefore
seemed preferable to retain titles established by convention,
especially since some of these texts are so little known to
begin with.[9]

POETIC ALLEGORIES OF NATURE

The belief that nature encodes moral lessons for those who
know how to read them is found in classical antiquity and
near the beginnings of Christianity. Saint Paul taught that
all people could discern through creation the existence of a
just God who condemns some ways of living and rewards
others (Romans 1:19–25). Extending those ideas, one anony-
mous early Christian text that came to be called the *Phys-
iologus* applied to details of the natural world the kinds of
allegorical interpretation that contemporary exegetes prac-
ticed on sacred scriptures. Each chapter in the *Physiologus*
examines some creature in order to explain what its attri-
butes reveal about the qualities of God or the devil or the
morals of humanity. Translated into many languages and
often expanded, the *Physiologus* enjoyed a wide dissemina-

tion, becoming the basis for an even more popular medieval genre, the bestiary.

Originally written in Greek, the *Physiologus* was known in the early medieval west through two different Latin prose versions. One of these, or portions of it, must have reached Anglo-Saxon England, where an anonymous author translated three of its chapters into Old English verse. The three poems (or one poem in three parts) survive adjacent to one another within a famous tenth-century poetic miscellany known as the Exeter Book. The first two poems discuss the panther, allegorized as a figure of Christ, and the whale, explained as a symbol of the devil. Neither allegory is systematic, and it is impossible to be certain that departures from the Latin *Physiologus* reflect the poet's own creativity and not simply variants in his now-lost copy of the source.[10] There are nevertheless hints that the poet had a flair for accentuating details in the original: his comparison of the panther's fur to Joseph's coat of many colors (lines 20b–30a), for example, seems to have blossomed from a quite brief reference in one of the Latin versions. Similarly, in *The Whale* the poet heightens an eschatological emphasis by amplifying a few comparatively brief mentions of damnation and hell in the Latin (38–47a and 67b–81).

Much less can be said with certainty about the third part of the Old English *Physiologus*. Its opening lines mention "a certain bird," but thereafter a leaf has been lost from the Exeter Book, and scholars do not agree whether the text that resumes following the lacuna belongs to the same poem or not. Several clues nevertheless support a circumstantial case that the "certain bird" is a partridge. What remains of the third poem in the Old English *Physiologus* is at least consistent with such an allegory (see the notes to the translation).

The last work in this section also descends from ancient traditions of animal lore. *The Phoenix,* a long and celebrated poem, also survives in the tenth-century Exeter Book. The text divides roughly in half. Over the first part (1–380), the poet describes the habitation of the mythical bird, its appearance (291–319), and its amazing resurrection at the end of a thousand-year life cycle. It has long been recognized that this first part of *The Phoenix* amounts to an expanded translation of a Latin poem, *De ave phoenice* ("On the Phoenix"), attributed to the church father Lactantius (d. ca. 325).[11] At the point where *De ave phoenice* ends, however, the Old English author supplies an entire second part (381–677), for which few Latin sources have been discovered. The souls of the faithful, the poet explains, resemble the phoenix as they suffer the pains of death in order to rise to new life (381–92). Just as fire consumes the bird and its nest, the Last Judgment will purify and renew the righteous (491–545). The poet's allegorical method resembles that in early Christian homilies as well as in the *Physiologus.*[12] Whatever generic influences shaped *The Phoenix,* its subject matter gave the author plenty of opportunity to explore the eschatological themes of death and resurrection, which appear widely in Old English sermons and poems alike.

POEMS OF WORSHIP AND PRAYER

In the next group are poems associated with prayer and worship—both public, in the communal liturgies of the medieval church, and private, in the many types of devotional and penitential prayer that medieval piety fostered. The Old English poetic versions of the Lord's Prayer may serve to illustrate the general character of this "liturgical" verse and some questions that it raises. Two of the gospels recount that Jesus, when asked by his disciples how they ought to pray, gave them what would become known as the Lord's Prayer (*Oratio dominica* in Latin, or the *Pater noster* after its opening words). The versions at Matthew 6:9–13 and Luke 11:2–4 differ slightly from each other, but a conflation of the two became the essential Christian prayer: "Our Father who are in heaven, hallowed be your name. Your kingdom come, your will be done on earth as it is in heaven. Give us today our daily bread, and forgive us our debts, as we forgive our debtors. And lead us not into temptation, but deliver us from evil."

It is not surprising that the Lord's Prayer and other basic Christian texts were translated into simple Old English prose. Catechists taught the Christian message through these formulas, and every believer was supposed to know them by heart.[13] Stranger to modern tastes is the enthusiasm of medieval poets for subjecting the *Pater noster* to sometimes exuberant literary embellishment. Three Old English verse translations of the prayer survive. The fragment known as *The Lord's Prayer (I)*, preserved in the Exeter Book anthology, is a simple translation. A more ambitious effort is *The Lord's Prayer (III)*, in which the poet moves phrase by phrase through the Latin *Pater noster*, expanding each segment into three to five lines of Old English verse. By far the most interesting, however, is *The Lord's Prayer (II)*, which resembles *The Lord's Prayer (III)* in bilingual format but goes much farther in the range of its elaborations. The author of this poem treats the Latin as a sequence of prompts for meditation on doctrines merely implicit in the prayer. Thus the simple words "Our Father" lead the poet to invoke God in his role as both creator and loving redeemer (1–9); "Who are in heaven" introduces an imagined scene of angelic beings praising God in the words of the Eucharistic hymn known as the *Sanctus* (10–19). And so the poet continues in this vein, reserving his most expansive elaboration for the clause "And forgive us our debts," which becomes a vivid seventeen-line meditation on the Last Judgment (93–110).

The Lord's Prayer was not the only basic text to receive such treatment. A verse paraphrase also survives of the short confession of faith known as the Apostles' Creed. The Old English verse *Apostles' Creed* resembles *The Lord's Prayer (II)*, both by its intercalation of partial phrases from the Latin and by its imaginative expansions of the very terse creedal statements.[14] Thus where the Latin says only that Christ "was conceived by the Holy Spirit, [and] born of the Virgin Mary," the poet adds other details concerning the annunciation by the angel Gabriel and the "marriage" of the Virgin to the Holy Spirit (10–26). The section of the creed that refers briefly to Christ's death turns into a more dramatic account of Christ's burial and harrowing of hell (27–35). Likewise the short statement "I believe in the Holy Spirit" gives way to a reflection on the doctrine of the Trinity (45–53).

Two poetic renditions of the *Gloria patri* survive in Old English. This short doxology ("Glory be to the Father, and to the Son, and to the Holy Spirit: as it was in the beginning, is now, and ever shall be, forever and ever. Amen") occurred frequently in medieval worship. One of the verse translations, *The Gloria patri (II),* adds nothing of substance to the source. But the other, *The Gloria patri (I),* more nearly resembles *The Lord's Prayer (II)* and *The Apostles' Creed.* In fact, similarities of style and vocabulary suggest that the same author wrote both *The Gloria patri (I)* and *The Lord's Prayer (II).*[15] *The Gloria patri (I)* exhibits the same expansive, dual-language format as *The Lord's Prayer (II),* turning the brief Latin formula into an Old English poem of over sixty lines. The focus often wanders far from the original: the phrase "as it was in the beginning," for example, yields seventeen lines on the creation of the cosmos and the importance of keeping Sunday a holy day (16–33).

A final poem in this group bears the modern title *The Kentish Hymn* because its language shows many Kentish dialect features, but its content is mainly a paraphrase of the *Gloria in excelsis deo* ("Glory to God in the highest"), an ancient hymn based on Luke 2:14 and sung at Mass on Sundays and major feasts. While *The Kentish Hymn* does not quote the Latin text or elaborate it significantly, the poet's small expansions suggest a theologically sophisticated reading of the hymn as both an expression of worship and a quasi-creedal statement about the roles of God the Father and God the Son.

Since all the poems discussed so far in this section derive from Latin texts that had some place in the liturgy, they are sometimes called "liturgical" verse.[16] The Lord's Prayer and Apostles' Creed also figured prominently in catechesis and individual piety, however, leading some modern readers to classify the same poems as "catechetical" or "devotional." All such labels are defensible, but their implicit claims about the functions of this poetry should be regarded with caution, as should analyses based on the poems' manuscript contexts (see Appendix B). It seems safest to view the Old English poetic renditions of the Lord's Prayer, the *Gloria patri,* the Apostles' Creed, and the *Gloria in excelsis deo* as literary compositions that Anglo-Saxon readers may have adapted to any number of purposes, not necessarily those of the original composers. The very form of the poems suggests a blending of influences, from the classroom and library as much as from the choir. Latin poetic paraphrases of the Lord's Prayer and Apostles' Creed were common exercises for students learning to compose verse, and other scholastic traditions probably exerted their influences as well.[17]

The very possibility that "liturgical" poems could have served a range of functions reminds us that Old English was not just tolerated but valued as a medium of piety and of religious institutions. Confessional and devotional prayers in Old English survive in impressive numbers, especially from the later Anglo-Saxon period.[18] Latin remained the dominant liturgical language, but Old English came to be widely used for the extensive instructions (or "rubrics") accompanying Latin prayers in liturgical manuscripts and penitentials.[19] Defining the place of Old English poems relative to devotional and liturgical practices is complicated by the overlap of those two domains in the earlier Middle Ages. New liturgical forms in Latin drew inspiration from devotional prayers, while new devotions drew on the texts of the liturgy. Some of the Old English prayers classified as "devotional" probably lived in closer proximity to liturgical performance than we can now perceive. Likewise, it is clear that texts from the liturgy influenced new vernacular compositions, just as the Mass-chant *Gloria in excelsis deo* underlies *The Kentish Hymn.*

The remaining poems in this section depend less closely on familiar Latin sources but raise similar questions about the ties between Old English poetry and the domains of prayer or worship. Though not usually considered in these contexts, the famous poem *Cædmon's Hymn* perhaps should be. Bede's *Ecclesiastical History* tells how Cædmon, a seventh-century layman on a monastic estate, left a banquet one evening rather than take his turn at singing and playing the harp.[20] That night, after encountering an angelic messenger, Cædmon receives a miraculous ability "to sing verses which he had never heard before in praise of God the Creator." Bede presents the episode as a wonder but does not clarify whether the supernatural element in Cædmon's poetic gift was his sudden mastery of poetic composition or his adaptation of native verse forms to new Christian subject matter. Questions also surround the text of the *Hymn* itself. The vernacular poem that survives, in two slightly different versions, as *Cædmon's Hymn* first appears copied into the margins of early manuscripts of Bede's Latin *History,* leading some scholars to suggest provocatively that no poem by Cædmon survives and that our *Cædmon's Hymn* is an anonymous translation of Bede's Latin *into* Old English verse.[21]

Whatever its relation to the story told by Bede, the Old English *Cædmon's Hymn* does not simply renarrate Genesis 1. It is rather a biblically inspired praise-poem honoring God as creator. As such it bears a resemblance to portions of the psalms and to other poems such as *The Gloria patri (I)* and *The Kentish Hymn.* This resemblance might be easier to see if not for the constraints of Bede's frame narrative. About the

uses to which Cædmon's poems were put, Bede says only
that "in all of [his songs] he sought to turn his hearers away
from delight in sin and arouse in them the love and prac-
tice of good works."[22] This perhaps indicates that the poems
served as private reading or devotional matter, or were read
aloud at mealtimes in the monastic refectory. It has even
been suggested that poetry like *Cædmon's Hymn* could have
occupied a place within the liturgy, or at least within a litur-
gical framework.[23]

For a companion piece to the famous *Hymn* attributed
to Cædmon, I include also the relatively obscure *Godric's
Hymn*. Though both are vernacular poems that complicate
our distinctions between liturgy and private devotion, for-
mally and chronologically the two are worlds apart. The
later "hymn" is attributed to a northern English hermit-
saint, Godric of Finchale, who was born on the eve of the
Norman Conquest and lived far into the Anglo-Norman pe-
riod, dying in 1170. Indeed, the text may be more properly
considered early Middle than Old English, and its form—
quatrains of end-rhymed lines in an *aabb* pattern—shows an
ascendancy of Latin and Norman-French versification.[24] Yet
the similarities to the story of Cædmon are also striking: the
earliest copies of these short verses attributed to Godric oc-
cur in accounts of his life otherwise recorded in Latin, and
those narratives describe the poem as a supernatural gift be-
stowed on the saint in a vision.[25]

The two final poems in this section exemplify another
important strain in medieval piety, the concern with per-
sonal sinfulness. The language of penance frames the poem
known simply as *A Prayer*, which begins and ends with the
speaker's admissions of sinfulness (1–15 and 61–79). The lines

in between are a tissue of praises and professions of faith that often have a biblical or gnomic ring but cannot be traced to particular sources.[26] The major influence on the rhetorical form of the poem seems to come from contemporary Latin devotional prayers of the kind now called "affective" because of their highly emotive character. One symptom of affective rhetoric in *A Prayer* is the poet's overreliance on the ineffability topos and hyperbole (see 30–44 and 51–55).

The last poem in this group, *Resignation (A),* also illustrates a blending of penitential prayer, profession of faith, and hymn of praise. The poem is now considered to be a fragment. (On the "(A)" in its title, see the notes to the text.) While penitential in spirit, the mood of the poem is hopeful, and its rhetoric more controlled than that of *A Prayer.* Some critics have noted a more precise similarity between *Resignation (A)* and a particular kind of liturgical prayer known as the *commendatio animae* ("commendation of the soul [to God]"), associated with rituals for the dying and recently dead.[27]

Poems on Christian Living

Both *A Prayer* and *Resignation (A)* illustrate the blending of influences characteristic of devotional prayers and, behind those, of the psalms. In common with the "liturgical" verse discussed earlier, their implied voice is that of the individual Christian seeking to express or arouse a particular attitude of piety. The next group of texts works to similar ends through different means: rather than put words in believers' mouths, they adopt directly the voices of religious authorities such as preachers and confessors.

A remarkable number of these pieces survive only as fragments, perhaps excerpted as highlights from longer compositions. The poem known as *Almsgiving,* for instance, consists of little more than an extended allusion to Ecclesiasticus 3:33 ("Water quencheth a flaming fire, and alms resisteth sins"). Another incomplete text, *Homiletic Fragment (I),* merges a paraphrase of Psalm 28 (Vulgate 27):3 with a simile that likens slanderers to bees, carrying honey in their mouths but a sting in their tails. A warning against disloyal friends and false faith similarly appears at the start of the damaged *Homiletic Fragment (II).*

Also apparently fragmentary are the seventeen verses, now usually called *Aldhelm,* that preface a copy of the Latin prose treatise *De virginitate* ("On Virginity") by Aldhelm of Malmesbury (d. ca. 710).[28] This odd poem was probably composed near the date of its tenth-century manuscript, a period that saw the revival of interest in Aldhelm's difficult Latin writings. The Old English poem overflows with Latin and Greek words in tribute to the ostentatious style of Aldhelm's own works. The speaker of the verses is neither the poet nor Aldhelm but the manuscript itself or the text of the prose *De virginitate.* The talking book holds up its author, Aldhelm, as a chaste, laboring ascetic who suffered greatly as a monk weighed down by burdens of office and maligned by his enemies in the world.

Both the style and subject matter of *Aldhelm* imply a restricted audience. But much other late Old English verse treats morals pertinent to Christians at large and especially to laypeople endowed with privileges of wealth and rank. The subject of alms, for instance, comes up very frequently, not only in the fragment *Almsgiving* mentioned above but also in a number of longer texts such as *The Rewards of Piety, Instructions for Christians,* and *Seasons for Fasting* (all discussed below). The obligation to give alms was a universal one, but poems such as these perhaps sweetened the message for the particular audiences whose generous almsgiving and other forms of benefaction cost the most.[29]

Poetry could reward as well as encourage the largesse of patrons who showed disdain for earthly treasures. One layman, a wealthy noble named Thored *(Þored)*, donated the resources for a precious binding to be crafted for a bishop's liturgical book. The brief poem called *Thureth,* copied into the manuscript, commemorates his gift. Written in the voice of the richly clad codex, *Thureth* resembles other examples of prosopopoeia in Old English verse such as the aforementioned *Aldhelm,* the *Riddles* of the Exeter Book, and parts of the famous *Dream of the Rood. Thureth* stands, however, as the only surviving Old English poem dedicated to praise of an actual layperson who was neither a saint nor a royal nor a battlefield hero. The contrast with the poem *Aldhelm* is revealing: the latter extols a virginal monk and intellectual whose legacy is the *content* of a talking book. *Thureth* praises a layman whose chief virtue is his ability to protect a book and adorn it with riches; as for its contents, the book that speaks in *Thureth* identifies itself with the power of bishops, not with the lay patron.

Because gift giving loomed large in the social worlds portrayed by traditional Old English verse, alms and other forms of Christian benefaction may have seemed natural subjects for poetry, with its aristocratic airs. To portray self-abasement in penance as a mark of authentic Christian nobility posed a greater imaginative obstacle, and the poem now known as *The Rewards of Piety* suggests one way of meeting the challenge.[30] In its first section (1–81), an unidentified speaker describes many moral duties that a Christian must observe in order to attain heaven. Modern critics have compared this part of the text to a homily (indeed, some quotations of the poem turn up in at least one anonymous homily).[31] Others regard it as a stylized version of the sort of address that penitents might have heard from priests at the beginning of sacramental confession. Based on that reading, it is possible to view the second part of the poem (82–112), with its alternating Old English and Latin half-lines, as echoing the actual formulas for ritual confession and absolution.[32] The individual penitent, identified only as (singular) "you" throughout *The Rewards of Piety,* is also addressed as *har hilde-rinc* (57a). The phrase literally means "gray-haired [= old, seasoned] warrior" and gives to penance a hint of heroic glamour.[33]

To the extent that the forms of Old English poetry retained their association with elevated subjects and aristocratic audiences, the use of verse to transmit even ordinary kinds of Christian teaching probably had social resonances hard for us to detect today. They still register plainly, at least, in one sprawling work that modern editors call *Instructions for Christians,* a late Old English poem that survives only in a twelfth-century copy. A seeming jumble of pious aphorisms, the work constructs both ecclesiastical authority and its audiences in telling ways. Several of its passages concerning wealth, for example, balance an expected attitude of *con-*

temptus mundi ("contempt for the world") with fawning assurances that riches are not bad in themselves, as proven by several biblical figures who were both rich *and* favored by God (117–49). Wealth likewise permits the sort of lavish almsgiving that, the poet maintains, cancels out sins (47–54 and 184–89).[34] Other parts of the work seem designed to assure men and women living in the world that secular status is no bar to the holiness that constitutes true nobility: resolutely abandoning former sins, for example, and practicing abstinence are said to confer a merit equal to that of having remained chaste (58–62). The final measure of a "lordly man" will be how well he has served God and neighbor in his youth (235–40).

The two final poems in this section also illustrate how Old English verse could be used to teach and simultaneously define an audience that might be called a "popular elite"—that is, less educated clergy as well as those laypeople who, being of sufficient status to grant or withhold patronage, took an interest in the right ordering of the church. The poem *Seasons for Fasting* would have spoken to just such an audience. The text is essentially a sermon in verse on the importance of fasting and on the correct times for the Ember Days—special fasts observed on the Wednesday, Friday, and Saturday in four appointed weeks throughout the year (39–102).[35] As the poet explains, the fall and winter Ember Fasts occurred in the full weeks prior to the fall equinox and the feast of Christmas (63–78). The poet advocates a view, allegedly authorized by Pope Gregory the Great (43–46 and 93–102), that the spring Ember Days should fall during the first week of Lent (47–48) and the summer ones in the week after Pentecost (55–60). A different tradition prevailed on the

Continent, where the first and second fasts were observed in the first full week of March and the second week of June, respectively. This rival schedule is perhaps the poet's target when he refers to unwelcome teaching by "Bretons or Franks" (see the notes to the translation at line 88). The defensive tone briefly subsides as the poet discusses biblical precedents for Lent in the fasts of Moses, Elijah, and Christ (103–75). But the polemic returns as the poem ends (incomplete) with attacks on clergy who violate their fasts in letter or in spirit (184–230).

Where *Seasons for Fasting* is plainly homiletic in inspiration, the generic backgrounds of *The Menologium* are more complex. Didactic poems on technical subjects were familiar enough in antiquity and the Middle Ages, and Latin metrical calendars were not uncommon. *The Menologium* is not just a versified list of holy days, however, but a calendar in verse that combines—as medieval calendars typically did—several overlapping schemata for calculating time. Some of its more memorable poetry concerns the changing months and seasons, and in this feature it resembles a kind of Old Irish metrical calendar, the *félire*.[36] The poem also marks out the twelve months, giving their names in both Latin and Old English. Overlying and dominating these frameworks, however, is the Christian liturgical year made up of two interlocking cycles. Most feasts celebrating events from the lives of Christ, the Virgin Mary, and other saints fall on fixed dates. But the principal celebration of Easter and others dependent on it, such as Ascension and Pentecost, vary in calendar date from year to year. The movable date of Easter was the single most important issue in any medieval discussion of the calendar, yet it receives only passing mention in *The Menologium* (63–68a). The principal concern of the poem seems to be with the fixed feasts of the Virgin, the apostles, and a few saints of wide significance to the Anglo-Saxons, such as Gregory the Great (39–40a). Notably, *The Menologium* excludes not just those saints whose cults had only local followings; *all* native Anglo-Saxon saints are omitted, even Saint Cuthbert, whose cult had achieved virtually national standing by the later tenth century. The implied view of the poem is that the national saints of the English *are* the universal saints of the western church. The closing lines assert that the small number of universal feasts mentioned in the poem "are to be observed wherever the command of the Saxons' king extends throughout Britain in this present time" (229b–231). The reference to (West-)Saxon authority "throughout Britain" suggests that the composition of *The Menologium* should be dated no earlier than the second quarter of the tenth century, and probably later in that century.

POEMS ON THE LAST THINGS

Less educated audiences may have welcomed the sort of popularizing treatments of religious discipline that *Seasons for Fasting* and *The Menologium* provide. Yet ordinary Anglo-Saxons did not have to calculate for themselves when fasts and saints' days would occur. The inexorable ends of human existence, on the other hand, were matters of universal concern: death and resurrection, divine judgment, and life forever in heaven or hell. A large proportion of texts that survive in Old English touch on these eschatological questions to one degree or another. The sheer ubiquity of the theme bespeaks its fundamental importance in medieval Christianity; eschatology was not just one theological topic among others but a ground for all Christian teaching about morals and belief. The imminence of death and judgment made a forceful argument for repentance, faith, and the exercise of virtues here and now.

We have already encountered these themes as primary ones in *The Phoenix* and as secondary in works such as *The Lord's Prayer (II)* and *Resignation (A)*. The texts in this final section reflect Anglo-Saxon beliefs about the last things in more direct, sustained ways. The poems show scant concern to sort out the often complicated and apparently contradictory teachings in the Bible and church fathers regarding the last things. Hard theological questions—about the condition of saved souls between death and judgment, for example, or the existence of an interim Paradise or purgatorial state—are acknowledged only implicitly, if at all.[37] The poems focus instead on emotive descriptions of a few key events: the separation of soul and body at death and subsequent decay of the corpse, the final purification of the world by fire, the reunion of souls and bodies at the general resurrection, the terrifying drama of Judgment Day, and the final conditions of the blessed in heaven and the damned in hell.

Old English poems and sermons in the so-called soul-and-body tradition focus on death and its aftermath as anticipatory of the Last Judgment.[38] Typically in this literature, a complaining soul chides its decomposing body that, by implication, seems to go on feeling, knowing, and remembering even in the grave. As a result, "distinctions between living and dead bodies blur" in these texts.[39] The vestige of consciousness in the corpse makes all the more horrifying these poems' commonplace descriptions of dark, confining coffins, devouring worms, and disintegrating flesh. The fact that souls in the Old English soul-and-body literature usually describe themselves as helpless victims of their bodies' thoughts and desires during life actually accords with evidence of popular beliefs. Many Anglo-Saxons evidently persisted in associating the mind, senses, and emotions with the body, not—as Christian intellectuals insisted—with the soul (Old English *sawol* or *gæst*); the latter, according to the same popular model, had little active function during the present life.[40]

The Old English poem titled *Soul and Body* emphasizes exactly this passivity of the soul in its earthbound existence, contrasted with the body's indulgence of sinful pleasures (33–48). Similarly, the present loathsomeness and degradation of the corpse are set against its former luxuries (52–62a, 65, 74b–86). The series of contrasts culminates in a gruesome description of the decaying body, part by part (105b–127), and its provision of food to the devouring worm named *Gifer* ("Ravenous," 117a). *Soul and Body* exists in two versions, both preserved in tenth-century copies. The shorter, in the Exeter Book, consists only of the damned soul's address. The longer version, found among the sermons and poems in the Vercelli Book, contains much the same material as the shorter version but is supplemented with a second address by a redeemed soul to its body. The speech by the saved soul is incomplete because of damage to the Vercelli Book, though enough of it survives to show the poet's design that the blessed soul will simply reverse the damned soul's earlier rhetoric (136–53). Instead of emphasizing the horrors of the grave (which the bodies of the damned and saved alike must undergo), the blessed soul focuses on the temporariness of physical decay and on the joys awaiting the pair when they will be reunited at Judgment Day (154–67).[41]

To supplement the Old English *Soul and Body,* I have also included *The Soul's Address to the Body,* considered a poem by some, a rhythmical-prose homily by others. The text is preserved among the so-called Worcester Fragments alongside *A Lament for the English Church* (discussed at the beginning of this introduction). As its language and form suggest a twelfth-century date of composition, the Worcester *Soul's Address* perhaps belongs more to early Middle than to Old English. With its delight in grisly catalogs and ironic antitheses, *The Soul's Address* nevertheless relies on many of the same conventions observed in the Old English *Soul and Body.* The surviving fragments of the early Middle English poem describe with even greater relish the body's decomposition and the horrors of the grave (e.g., B40–42; C27b–32, C38–50; D1–8; E4–11). Of particular interest in the Worcester *Soul's Address* is the poet's attention to the common rituals of death in medieval society, such as the preparation of the corpse (A30–35). The poet candidly portrays the reactions — bereft, greedy, relieved, or indifferent — of those who survive the departed (e.g., A36–44; B10–16 and 37–39; C9–22 and 33–36; D10–16; F17–18). Largely absent from the Old English *Soul and Body,* these small social dramas imagined around the events of death imbue the dead man with a distinct personality: he was someone wealthy enough to inspire envy but who begrudged charity to the poor and patronage to the church (B10–16, 20–29, and 30–34; C23–27); he was powerful enough to issue corrupt "judgments" and insults without fear of reprisal (C16–22; E18–20; G11–13a). He was, in one of the poet's unforgettable similes, like a hedgehog who did not feel the sting of his own spines (F19–33). It is regrettable that *The Soul's Address* does not survive undamaged, but another late and likewise incomplete poem, titled *The Grave,* stands in close relationship to it, showing a number of verbatim correspondences. Probably *The Grave* is a fragment of a once-longer work based on a source or sources also known to the author of *The Soul's Address.*

The grotesquerie of these soul-and-body poems should not distract us from their significance in the larger scheme of medieval eschatology. The poets' erosion of boundaries between life and the grave made Judgment Day itself the real horizon of human hopes and fears.[42] And, when poets chose to address the Last Judgment as their principal theme, its scale and complexity posed special challenges. Two poems are included here to illustrate different approaches to the topic.[43] The first, called *Judgment Day (I),* also survives in the Exeter Book. Its picture of the Last Judgment is impressionistic, better suited to stirring pious fears than clarifying doctrine. The poet's descriptions move freely back and forth along a time line that never quite becomes clear, and he repeats many points in no evident order. Certain details recur, such as mentions of a purifying fire that overwhelms creation in advance of judgment (7–8a, 9a–13a, 51b, 53b–56a, 58b) and becomes, for the damned, a foretaste of their everlasting fate (18b). The sounding of a trumpet summons all to the judgment, which the poet describes with grim understatement as a *spræc* ("exchange of words," 8b–9 and 100a–101). More peculiarly, the poem also refers to a final flood sent to extinguish the flames and cool the earth in preparation for the assembly (1–2a and 37b–39).

The last poem to be considered here, titled *Judgment Day (II),* presents a more theologically sophisticated and rhetorically artful meditation, in part because the text is a free translation of an accomplished Latin poem, the *Versus de die iudicii* ("Verses on the Day of Judgment"), a work attributed to the Venerable Bede.[44] This Old English poem does not aspire any more than did *Judgment Day (I)* to reconcile conflicting traditions about doomsday. Even so, *Judgment Day (II)* manages to deliver a relatively straightforward account. Nearly the entire first third of the poem (10–91) develops a penitential commonplace that one who confesses and laments his sins in the present will have no cause to lament on the Day of Judgment. The depiction of that event begins in earnest around line 92, with a catalog of biblical portents announcing the end of the world (99–112). Accompanied by the angelic hosts, Christ arrives in terrible majesty; the whole human race is miraculously gathered so that all may be forced to divulge the secrets of their hearts (113–44). Only at this point does the poet describe the onslaught of fire, which overtakes all the assembled but burns only those still tainted by sin (145–75). The remainder of the poem dwells on the torments endured thereafter by the damned in hell (181–246) and the blessings enjoyed by the saved in heaven (247–300).

On its own terms, *Judgment Day (II)* makes plain the connection between eschatology and penitential spirituality. The link appears even stronger, some critics have noted, when the poem is considered in its manuscript context. It survives in part of an eleventh-century codex of penitential, legal, and homiletic works (Cambridge, Corpus Christi College 201). There the poem immediately precedes three others, already mentioned: *The Rewards of Piety, The Lord's Prayer (II),* and *The Gloria patri (I).* The entire sequence has been read as a meditation in verse on the elements of sacramental confession: thus *Judgment Day (II)* dramatizes how reflecting on the last things inspires contrition; *The Rewards of Piety,* as discussed already, may echo the priest's address to a penitent and the ritual formulas of confession and absolution. *The Lord's Prayer (II)* and *The Gloria patri (I)* could, by the same reading, stand in for the penances to follow absolution.[45]

Finally, *Judgment Day (II)* also illustrates in a particularly striking way the ties that existed between late Old English verse and homiletic prose. Numerous lines in the poem closely resemble passages in one late Old English sermon, suggesting that the author of the prose text has drawn on *Judgment Day (II)* as a source.[46] The connection is symptomatic not only of the general overlap between verse and prose in late Old English but also of a more precise trend: some other Old English prose sermons on Judgment Day also incorporate rhythmical, alliterative passages that modern scholars identify as fragments of actual poems. One such embedded poem, known as *The Judgment of the Damned,* is printed along with its surrounding prose as Appendix A.

This introduction has touched only briefly on some complex issues and passed over many more in silence. Readers who make their way through the texts and translations that follow will certainly notice how loose are the four divisions here imposed on the materials. Other groupings could and should be imagined: the *Physiologus* poems, for example, might just as easily be read alongside those on Christian morality, *The Phoenix* with those on eschatology. The inextricable themes of morality and future judgment run through nearly all the texts, and the language of the liturgy and the Bible, especially the psalms, is by no means restricted to poems overtly connected to genres of prayer.

A final word is in order about the principles of editing and translating in this book. The texts of the Old English works are based largely on editions already published; further details about them are provided in the Note on the Texts at the end of the volume. The facing-page Modern English versions have all been prepared new, though I have often consulted others' published translations, where available. My translations seek to balance faithfulness to the content of the original Old English with the requirements of clear, idiomatic Modern English prose. When, as often, those two considerations stood in tension, I have usually chosen to err on the side of a less literal but more readable translation. This has meant, for example, quietly supplying the occasional subject, verb, or conjunction not expressed in the original. Here and there it has been possible to suggest in Modern English the feel of Old English poetic devices such as variation and artful diction, but I do not attempt to mimic more elusive features of the verse, such as figures of repetition and wordplay.

In the editions, translations, and textual notes, ellipses (. . .) indicate gaps in the texts, evident either from damage to the manuscript or from an apparent break in the sense. (Exceptionally, in Appendix B, most ellipses mark the scribe's deliberate truncations of prayers or psalms to their opening words, a normal medieval practice when copying liturgical texts.) Latin passages of the Bible quoted within the Old English have been translated following the Douay-Rheims version, albeit sometimes lightly modernized or adapted to reflect textual variants in the Old English/Latin text across the page. Any text that appears in Latin (or, in the case of *Aldhelm,* transliterated Greek) in the original is printed in italics in the facing translation. Throughout the original-language texts, Old English and medieval Latin spellings have not been normalized, save that consonantal *u* in Latin has been silently regularized to *v,* in accordance with the policy of this series. As for capitalization, each language (Old English, Latin, and Modern English) has its own norms that I have tended to respect rather than make uniform across all three. This means that capitals appear more sparingly in the Old English and Latin than in the translations, though I do capitalize Old English *God* (the deity). Editions in this series print nominal and adjectival compounds in Old English with hyphens, though I have admitted some exceptions.

More detailed notes to the individual works in translation also appear at the end of the volume. Those notes do not pretend to be comprehensive. Their chief purpose is to explain, for a general readership, points of historical background or literary reference (especially biblical allusions) helpful for basic comprehension of the texts. An additional purpose of the notes is to acknowledge my debts to others' translations and published scholarship on particular points, especially when someone else's interpretation of a given line or passage would yield a plausible translation significantly different from my own.

Just as this book rests on the work of many past editors,

textual critics, and translators of Old English, it has also incurred debts to several scholars at present who have been generous with their time and expertise. Detailed corrections and suggestions by Katherine O'Brien O'Keeffe, Elizabeth Tyler, and Leslie Lockett improved the book in many ways, though responsibility for any mistakes still in it is mine alone. Dan Donoghue and Rob Fulk kindly advised on specific matters of presentation for the Dumbarton Oaks series. I am grateful to Charles D. Wright for suggestions concerning two difficult passages, and to Jan Ziolkowski for his warm encouragement throughout the entire project. This book is dedicated, with gratitude, to Roberta Frank and Toni Healey.

Notes

1 On the transmission of Old English after the Conquest, see the essays in Swan and Treharne, *Rewriting Old English.*

2 Some of these have already appeared in the Dumbarton Oaks Medieval Library; see Anlezark, *Old Testament Narratives.* Other biblical and hagiographic poems will appear in a volume translated by Mary Clayton, and the metrical psalms in a volume by Patrick O'Neill. Many of the pertinent texts are meanwhile available in Bradley, *Anglo-Saxon Poetry.* An accessible, wide-ranging introduction to the whole canon of Old English writing is Fulk and Cain, *History of Old English Literature.* On the interface between Christian and oral traditions in Old English verse, see Orchard, "The Word Made Flesh."

3 Portions of the so-called *Benedictine Office* have, however, been attributed to Wulfstan the homilist; see the introduction to Appendix B.

4 The choice of poems included here was largely determined by the editorial plan for the Old English subseries in the Dumbarton Oaks Medieval Library. That plan assumes a traditional definition of the Old English poetic corpus, differing little from that of the standard collected edition, the Anglo-Saxon Poetic Records (1931–1953).

5 See Letson, "Poetic Content," 140–42. At least two poems included here, *Judgment Day (II)* and *The Rewards of Piety,* were probably used as sources by anonymous homilists. For an example of poetry integrated into a late Old English prose work, see Appendix A.

6 Stanley, "Prosaic Vocabulary"; Frank, "Poetic Words"; Richards, "Prosaic Poetry."

7 The status of Ælfric's "rhythmical prose" is still contested; see most recently Bredehoft, *Early English Metre,* esp. 70–98.

8 The possible exception among poems in this volume is *Judgment Day (II),* which has a quasi-title at its beginning and end. See the notes to the text.

9 The poem here called *A Lament for the English Church* is the major exception; see the notes to that text. Other changes that I have introduced, such as *The Gloria patri (I)* for earlier *Gloria (I),* are minor and not likely to mislead.

10 The relevant parts of the Latin versions, with English translations, are printed by Squires, *Old English Physiologus,* 102–11; see also Allen and Calder, *Sources and Analogues,* 156–61. For the complete Latin text in translation, see Curley, *Physiologus.*

11 For translations of the Latin sources, see Allen and Calder, *Sources and Analogues,* 113–20. On other possible sources, see Gorst, "Latin Sources."

12 A homiletic account of the phoenix survives in late Old English alliterative prose; see Blake, *The Phoenix,* 94–96. For the analogies with the *Physiologus,* see O'Donnell, "Fish and Fowl," 164–70.

13 Bede translated these texts for the laity, though his versions do not survive; see Bede's "Letter to Egbert," in McClure and Collins, *Bede: The Ecclesiastical History,* 346. For Ælfric's translations of the Lord's Prayer and Creed, see Thorpe, *Homilies,* 2:596.

14 The verse *Apostles' Creed* also shares two lines almost verbatim with another late poem, *Seasons for Fasting* (discussed below); see Sisam, *Studies,* 47–48.

15 Ure, *Benedictine Office,* 50–51; Whitbread, "Poems of the *Benedictine Office,*" 38–40.

16 Now see the collection by Keefer, *Liturgical Verse.* Keefer's "liturgical" poems also include the so-called *Kentish Psalm,* a verse paraphrase of Psalm 51 (Vulgate 50) with lines of the Latin source intercalated.

17 See Walther, "Versifizierte Pater noster und Credo." For other possible influences, see Jones, "Performing Christianity."

18 Pulsiano, "Prayers, Glosses and Glossaries," 209.

19 On Old English in and around the liturgy, see Gittos, "Evidence for the Liturgy of Parish Churches?"; Jones, "Performing Christianity."

20 The story is found in Book 4, chap. 24. In what follows, I cite the translation from Colgrave and Mynors, *Bede's Ecclesiastical History,* 415–21.

21 On the arguments—not generally accepted—that the Old English poem depends on Bede's Latin, see the summary by O'Donnell, *Cædmon's Hymn,* 174–78.

22 Colgrave and Mynors, *Bede's Ecclesiastical History,* 419. Where they translate "his hearers," the Latin has only *homines* ("persons"); Bede actually says nothing about aural as opposed to readerly reception of the poems.

23 Holsinger, "Parable of Cædmon's Hymn."

24 On the *Hymn* and the Latin sources in which it is transmitted, see the notes to the text.

25 On the many analogues to Cædmon, see O'Donnell, *Cædmon's Hymn,* 29–59.

26 On the sapiential element, see Keefer, *Liturgical Verse,* 157 and 161.

27 Malmberg, *Resignation,* 3.

28 One critic has argued that *Aldhelm* might in fact be complete; see the notes to the text.

29 The many references to almsgiving in Anglo-Saxon writings are surveyed by Olson, "Textual Representations of Almsgiving."

30 This composition was once considered two poems (see the notes to the text). Similarities of wording and theme suggest some relationship between *The Rewards of Piety* and adjacent poems in the same manuscript; see the discussion of *Judgment Day (II),* below, and Caie, *"Judgement Day II,"* 1–24.

31 I.e., in Vercelli Homily XXI and a later composite derived from it, Napier Homily XXX; see the notes to the text.

32 Förster, "Liturgik der angelsächsischen Kirche," 38–42; cf. Frantzen, *Literature of Penance,* 181–82. See the discussion of *Judgment Day (II),* below.

33 On the sapiential associations of the phrase, see Zacher, "Rewards of Poetry," 87–88.

34 Mize, "Representation of the Mind," 77–80.

35 The remainder of this paragraph is much indebted to Richards, "Old Wine in a New Bottle."

36 On the analogues in Latin and Irish, see Hennig, "Irish Counterparts."

37 A systematic doctrine of Purgatory did not fully emerge until the twelfth and thirteenth centuries. For Anglo-Saxon beliefs about an interim state, see Kabir, *Paradise, Death and Doomsday;* and Forbes, "*Diuiduntur in quattuor.*"

38 On soul-and-body literature in Old English, see Moffat, *Old English Soul and Body,* 28–35. Latin analogues are translated in Allen and Calder, *Sources and Analogues,* 40–50.

39 Thompson, *Dying and Death,* 46.

40 Godden, "Anglo-Saxons on the Mind," 286–91; Lockett, *Anglo-Saxon Psychologies,* 25–33 and 389–95.

41 Frantzen, *Literature of Penance,* 187; Thompson, *Dying and Death,* 142–43.

42 Thompson, *Dying and Death,* 46.

43 The most developed poem on the Last Judgment, known as *Christ (III)* or *Christ in Judgment,* will be included in Mary Clayton's forthcoming volume in this series.

44 For a Modern English translation of the Latin, see Allen and Calder, *Sources and Analogues,* 208–12. On Bede's authorship, see Lapidge, "Bede and the 'Versus de die iudicii.'" On the Old English poem's relation to the Latin, see Lendinara, "Translating Doomsday."

45 Whitbread, "Notes on Two Minor Old English Poems," 126–27; Caie, "Editing Old English." But note that the last two poems (*The Lord's Prayer (II)* and *The Gloria patri (I)*) were copied by a different, later hand. Any penitential "sequence," if real, belongs to the reception-history of these poems, not necessarily to their authors' intentions.

46 On the relation of the poem to Napier Homily XXIX, see the notes to the text.

POETIC ALLEGORIES
OF NATURE

The Panther

Monge sindon   geond middan-geard
unrimu cynn,   þe we æþelu ne magon
ryhte areccan   ne rim witan;
þæs wide sind   geond world innan
5   fugla ond deora   fold-hrerendra
wornas wid-sceope,   swa wæter bibugeð
þisne beorhtan bosm,   brim grymetende,
sealt-yþa geswing.   We bi sumum hyrdon
wrætlice gecynd   wildra secgan
10   firum frea-mærne   feor-londum on
eard weardian,   eðles neotan
æfter dun-scrafum.   Is þæt deor "pandher"
bi noman haten,   þæs þe niþþa bearn,
wisfæste weras,   on gewritum cyþað
15   bi þam an-stapan.   Se is æghwam freond,
duguða estig,   butan dracan anum,
þam he in ealle tid   ondwrað leofaþ
þurh yfla gehwylc   þe he geæfnan mæg.
      Ðæt is wrætlic deor,   wundrum scyne
20   hiwa gehwylces.   Swa hæleð secgað,
gæst-halge guman,   þætte Iosephes
tunece wære   telga gehwylces
bleom bregdende,   þara beorhtra gehwylc
æghwæs ænlicra   oþrum lixte
25   dryhta bearnum,   swa þæs deores hiw,

2

The Panther

Many are the species, countless throughout the world, whose lineage we cannot reckon or numbers we cannot know; multitudes of birds and of beasts that stir on the earth are very widely established throughout this world as far as the water, the roaring sea, the surge of briny waves, encompasses this bright horizon. Regarding one of those untamed 8 creatures, we have heard tell that its exotic kind guards in distant lands a habitation, very celebrated among men, enjoys its native dwelling among caves in the mountains. That beast is called by the name "panther," according to what children of mortals, men of tried wisdom, set forth in writings about that solitary wanderer. The animal is a friend to 15 everyone, gracious in its favors except to the serpent alone, against which it lives perpetually in a state of hostility, on account of every evil that it [the serpent] can do.

The panther is an extraordinary beast, amazingly beauti- 19 ful in every one of its colors. Just as men with sainted souls recount that Joseph's tunic shimmered with hues of every color, each of which beamed to the children of men more brightly, altogether more splendidly than the next; so that beast's color, brilliant in every changing shade, shines more

blæc brigda gehwæs,   beorhtra ond scynra
wundrum lixeð,   þætte wrætlicra
æghwylc oþrum,   ænlicra gien
ond fægerra   frætwum bliceð,
30   symle sellicra.
                He hafað sundor-gecynd,
milde, gemetfæst.   He is mon-þwære,
lufsum ond leof-tæl,   nele laþes wiht
ængum geæfnan   butan þam attor-sceaþan,
his fyrn-geflitan,   þe ic ær fore sægde.
35   Symle fylle fægen,   þonne foddor þigeð,
æfter þam gereordum   ræste seceð
dygle stowe   under dun-scrafum;
ðær se þeod-wiga   þreo-nihta fæc
swifeð on swefote,   slæpe gebiesgad.
40   Þonne ellen-rof   up astondeð,
þrymme gewelgad,   on þone þriddan dæg,
sneome of slæpe.   Sweg-hleoþor cymeð,
woþa wynsumast   þurh þæs wildres muð.
Æfter þære stefne   stenc ut cymeð
45   of þam wong-stede,   wynsumra steam,
swettra ond swiþra   swæcca gehwylcum,
wyrta blostmum   ond wudu-bledum,
eallum æþelicra   eorþan frætwum.
Þonne of ceastrum   ond cyne-stolum
50   ond of burg-salum   beorn-þreat monig
farað fold-wegum   folca þryþum,
eored-cystum,   ofestum gefysde,
dareð-lacende;   deor efne swa some
æfter þære stefne   on þone stenc farað.
55   Swa is dryhten God,   dreama rædend,

4

wondrously bright and beautiful, so that each shimmers, more striking than another, more splendid yet and more beautiful, each being always more excellent [than the last].

The panther has its particular nature, gentle and moder- 30 ate. It is kind, loving and amiable, wishes to cause no harm at all to any, save to the poisonous foe, its ancient adversary, which I mentioned previously. When it partakes of food, 35 after that meal, happy from feasting, it always seeks out as a resting spot places hidden deep in caves among the mountains; there the people's champion, overcome by sleep, dozes in a slumber for the space of three nights. Then, on 40 the third day, the boldly courageous creature rises up swiftly from sleep, adorned with majesty. A melodious noise, most delightful of sounds, comes from the mouth of the untamed creature. Following that voice, an aroma issues from the place, a breath more delightful, more sweet and potent than every fragrance, than the flowering herbs or blossoms on the trees, more refined than all the treasures of earth. Then, 49 out of cities and royal households, and out of fortified halls, many a host in throngs of people, chosen companies, warriors journey the paths of earth, troops driven with haste; animals likewise travel toward the aroma in the wake of that voice.

In the same way the Lord God, ruler of joys, is kindly 55

eallum eað-mede   oþrum gesceaftum,
duguða gehwylcre,   butan dracan anum,
attres ord-fruman   (þæt is se ealda feond,
þone he gesælde   in susla grund,
60   ond gefetrade   fyrnum teagum,
biþeahte þrea-nydum);   ond þy þriddan dæge
of digle aras,   þæs þe he deað fore us
þreo-niht þolade,   þeoden engla,
sigora sellend: þæt wæs swete stenc,
65   wlitig ond wynsum   geond woruld ealle.
Siþþan to þam swicce   soðfæste men
on healfa gehwone   heapum þrungon
geond ealne ymbhwyrft   eorþan sceata.
Swa se snottra gecwæð   sanctus Paulus:
70   "Monigfealde sind   geond middan-geard
god ungnyðe   þe us to giefe dæleð
ond to feorh-nere   fæder ælmihtig,
ond se anga hyht   ealra gesceafta,
uppe ge niþre":   þæt is æþele stenc.

disposed to all other beings, to each in his retinue save to the serpent alone, the origin of poison (that is, the ancient enemy whom God sent into the abyss of torments and bound with fiery chains, buried under miseries); and [like the panther, Christ] arose from a secret place on the third day after he, the prince of angels, bestower of victories, endured death for our sake for a space of three nights: that [sc. the resurrection] was the sweet aroma, lovely and pleasant throughout all the world. Afterward, from every corner, the 66 righteous flocked in crowds to that fragrance, from across the entire expanse of the earth's surface. Thus did the wise man, Saint Paul, say: "Manifold throughout the world are the unstinted goods that the almighty Father and sole hope of all creatures above and below dispenses to us freely and for the rescue of our lives": that is the splendid fragrance.

The Whale

Nu ic fitte gen   ymb fisca cynn
wille woð-cræfte   wordum cyþan
þurh mod-gemynd   bi þam miclan hwale.
Se bið unwillum   oft gemeted
5   frecne ond ferð-grim   fareð-lacendum,
niþþa gehwylcum;   þam is noma cenned,
fyrn-streama geflotan,   *Fastitocalon.*
Is þæs hiw gelic   hreofum stane,
swylce worie   bi wædes ofre,
10   sond-beorgum ymbseald,   sæ-ryrica mæst,
swa þæt wenaþ   wæg-liþende
þæt hy on ealond sum   eagum wliten,
ond þonne gehydað   heah-stefn scipu
to þam unlonde   oncyr-rapum,
15   sælaþ sæ-mearas   sundes æt ende,
ond þonne in þæt eglond   up gewitað
collen-ferþe;   ceolas stondað
bi staþe fæste,   streame biwunden.
Ðonne gewiciað   werig-ferðe,
20   faroð-lacende,   frecnes ne wenað,
on þam ea-londe   æled weccað,
heah-fyr ælað;   hæleþ beoþ on wynnum,
reonig-mode,   ræste geliste.

8

The Whale

Through the thoughts of my mind I will now further express
in words, by poetic art, verses concerning a species of fish,
the great whale. Dangerous and cruel, it is often met by sail-
ors, by mortals against their will; the name given to that
swimmer in the ocean is *Fastitocalon*. Its appearance is like   8
scaly stone, as if a massive clump of seaweed is drifting along
an ocean shore, ringed by banks of sand in such a way that
seafarers suppose they are gazing upon a sort of island; and
then they tether with anchor-ropes their high-prowed ships
to that land which is no land, tie their sea horses at the
ocean's edge, and then, bold at heart, they make their ad-
vance onto the island; the boats stand secure at the shore,
surrounded by the current. Then weary ocean travelers   19
make camp; suspecting no danger, they kindle a fire on the
island, ignite a towering blaze; pleased with their resting

Þonne gefeleð   facnes cræftig
25 þæt him þa ferend on   fæste wuniaþ,
wic weardiað   wedres on luste,
ðonne semninga   on sealtne wæg
mid þa nowe   niþer gewiteþ
gar-secges gæst,   grund geseceð,
30 ond þonne in deað-sele   drence bifæsteð
scipu mid scealcum.
                    Swa bið scinna þeaw,
deofla wise,   þæt hi drohtende
þurh dyrne meaht   duguðe beswicað,
ond on teosu tyhtaþ   tilra dæda,
35 wemað on willan,   þæt hy wraþe secen,
frofre to feondum,   oþþæt hy fæste ðær
æt þam wær-logan   wic geceosað.
Þonne þæt gecnaweð   of cwic-susle
flah feond gemah,   þætte fira gehwylc
40 hæleþa cynnes   on his hricge biþ
fæste gefeged,   he him feorg-bona
þurh sliþen searo   siþþan weorþeð,
wloncum ond heanum,   þe his willan her
firenum fremmað;   mid þam he færinga,
45 heoloþ-helme biþeaht,   helle seceð,
goda geasne,   grundleasne wylm
under mist-glome,   swa se micla hwæl,
se þe bisenceð   sæ-liþende
eorlas ond yð-mearas.

place, the desperate men feel joy. When the cunningly 24
treacherous creature senses that travelers are dwelling se-
curely upon it, making an abode there and relishing the fine
weather, the ocean spirit then suddenly plunges down into
the briny surf, with that vessel seeks the abyss and then con-
signs ships with their crews to a hall of death by drowning.

Such is the habit of demons, the way of devils: using their 31
unseen power, they deceive the company of the living and
entice them to the ruin of good works, lure them accord-
ing to their desires, so that humans would seek support and
consolation from demons, until they permanently choose a
dwelling there with those oath breakers. As soon as the en- 38
emy, hostile and determined, perceives from his place of liv-
ing torment that any member of the human race is fixed se-
curely to his back, through that cruel trap he then becomes
the slayer of those who, by their sins, have done his will here,
the proud and the lowly alike; together with them, he [the
devil], hidden beneath a concealing cover and lacking all
good, abruptly seeks out hell, a bottomless, seething pool
beneath the oppressive dark, just like the great whale does
that drowns seafaring men and horses of the waves.

He hafað oþre gecynd,

50 wæter-þisa wlonc,   wrætlicran gien.

Þonne hine on holme   hungor bysgað
ond þone aglæcan   ætes lysteþ,
ðonne se mere-weard   muð ontyneð,
wide weleras;   cymeð wynsum stenc

55 of his innoþe,   þætte oþre þurh þone,
sæ-fisca cynn,   beswicen weorðaþ,
swimmað sund-hwate   þær se sweta stenc
ut gewiteð.   Hi þær in farað
unware weorude,   oþþæt se wida ceafl

60 gefylled við;   þonne færinga
ymbe þa here-huþe   hlemmeð togædre
grimme goman.   Swa biþ gumena gehwam,
se þe oftost his   unwærlice
on þas lænan tid   lif bisceawað,

65 læteð hine beswican   þurh swetne stenc,
leasne willan,   þæt he biþ leahtrum fah
wið wuldor-cyning.   Him se awyrgda ongean
æfter hinsiþe   helle ontyneð,
þam þe leaslice   lices wynne

70 ofer ferhð-gereaht   fremedon on unræd.
Þonne se fæcna   in þam fæstenne
gebroht hafað,   bealwes cræftig,
æt þam edwylme   þa þe him on cleofiað,
gyltum gehrodene,   ond ær georne his

75 in hira lif-dagum   larum hyrdon,
þonne he þa grimman   goman bihlemmeð
æfter feorh-cwale   fæste togædre,
helle hlin-duru;   nagon hwyrft ne swice,
ut-siþ æfre,   þa þær in cumað,

That proud water traveler has a second trait more amaz- 49
ing still. When hunger oppresses it at sea and the awful crea-
ture wants something to eat, the guardian of the ocean then
opens its mouth, its lips wide; a pleasant fragrance issues
from its insides, so that other kinds of fish in the sea are be-
guiled by it, swim confidently toward the source of the sweet
smell. In a heedless company, they enter in there until the 58
wide maw is filled up; then suddenly the cruel jaws slam shut
around the spoils. So it is for every man who too often re-
gards with insufficient care his life in this fleeting age, who
allows himself to be beguiled by a sweet aroma, an illusory
pleasure, so that he becomes guilty of sins against the king
of glory. The accursed one opens hell to receive after death 67
those who foolishly pursued vain pleasures of the body in
violation of the soul's due. When the deceiver, skilled at de-
struction, has delivered into the fiery whirlpool in that
stronghold those persons who cling to him, arrayed in their
own sins, and who hitherto obeyed his teachings readily dur-
ing life, he then, upon their death, slams those cruel jaws
tightly together, the prison doors of hell; those who enter
there will never have recourse or respite or escape any more

80   þon ma þe þa fiscas   farað-lacende
     of þæs hwæles fenge   hweorfan motan.
        Forþon is eallinga   . . .
     dryhtna dryhtne,   ond a deoflum wiðsace
     wordum ond weorcum,   þæt we wuldor-cyning
85   geseon moton.   Uton a sibbe to him
     on þas hwilnan tid   hælu secan,
     þæt we mid swa leofne   in lofe motan
     to widan feore   wuldres neotan.

than the swimming fish might return from capture by the whale.

It is therefore entirely . . . to the Lord of lords, and by 82 words and deeds oppose the devils always, that we may behold the king of glory. During this transitory age, let us always seek peace and salvation from him, that we may forever enjoy glory with so beloved a Lord, offering praise.

The Partridge

Hyrde ic secgan gen   bi sumum fugle
wundorlicne ...

       ... fæger,
þæt word þe gecwæð   wuldres ealdor:
5   "In swa hwylce tiid   swa ge mid treowe to me
on hyge hweorfað,   ond ge hell-firena
sweartra geswicað,   swa ic symle to eow
mid sib-lufan   sona gecyrre
þurh milde mod.   Ge beoð me siþþan
10   torhte tir-eadge   talade ond rimde,
beorhte gebroþor   on bearna stæl."
    Uton we þy geornor   Gode oliccan,
firene feogan,   friþes earnian,
duguðe to dryhtne,   þenden us dæg scine,
15   þæt swa æþelne   eard-wica cyst
in wuldres wlite   wunian motan.
    Finit.

The Partridge

I have heard told, moreover, a marvelous . . . concerning a
certain bird . . . beautiful, the word that the Lord of glory
has spoken: "In whatever time you turn to me in your mind,   5
by means of faith, and give up dark, hellish acts of sin, so
will I immediately turn toward you in gentle disposition,
with familial love. After that, to me you will be numbered   9
and reckoned as resplendent and gloriously blessed, radiant
brethren in my children's place."

Let us the more readily placate God, hate sin, and merit   12
protection, favor from the Lord, while day yet shines upon
us, that we may be able to dwell in so noble, so excellent a
habitation in the splendor of glory.

Here ends the work.

The Phoenix

Hæbbe ic gefrugnen   þætte is feor heonan
east-dælum on   æþelast londa,
firum gefræge.   Nis se foldan sceat
ofer middan-geard   mongum gefere

5   folc-agendra,   ac he afyrred is
þurh meotudes meaht   man-fremmendum.
Wlitig is se wong eall,   wynnum geblissad
mid þam fægrestum   foldan stencum.
Ænlic is þæt ig-lond,   æþele se wyrhta,

10   modig, meahtum spedig,   se þa moldan gesette.
Ðær bið oft open   eadgum togeanes,
onhliden hleoþra wyn,   heofon-rices duru.
Þæt is wynsum wong,   wealdas grene,
rume under roderum.   Ne mæg þær ren ne snaw,

15   ne forstes fnæst   ne fyres blæst,
ne hægles hryre   ne hrimes dryre,
ne sunnan hætu   ne sin-caldu,
ne wearm weder   ne winter-scur
wihte gewyrdan,   ac se wong seomað

20   eadig ond onsund.   Is þæt æþele lond
blostmum geblowen.   Beorgas þær ne muntas
steape ne stondað,   ne stan-clifu
heah hlifiað   swa her mid us,
ne dene ne dalu   ne dun-scrafu,

The Phoenix

I have heard that the noblest of lands, renowned among men, exists in regions of the east, far from here. That area of earth is inaccessible to many across the world who rule over peoples; rather, by the creator's power, the place is established far away from evildoers. All that plain is beautiful, 7 gladdened with joys, with the loveliest fragrances of earth. That isolated land is unique, and the maker who fashioned the region is noble, high-minded, and abundantly empowered. There the celebration of singing voices, a door to the heavenly kingdom, is often opened to the blessed. That is a delightful plain, its spacious forests green beneath the heavens. There neither rain nor snow, gust of cold nor blast of 14 flame, torrent of hail nor fall of frost, heat of the sun nor lasting cold, warm weather nor winter shower does any harm at all; rather the plain endures, blessed and free from hurt. That noble land flowers with blossoms. Neither hills 21 nor mountains stand steeply there, nor do rocky cliffs tower high, as they do here among us; nor are there glens or valleys or mountain caves, nor mounds or knolls, nor does any

25   hlæwas ne hlincas,   ne þær hleonað oo
      unsmeþes wiht,   ac se æþela feld
      wridað under wolcnum,   wynnum geblowen.
      Is þæt torhte lond   twelfum herra,
      folde fæðm-rimes,   swa us gefreogum gleawe
30   witgan þurh wisdom   on gewritum cyþað,
      þonne ænig þara beorga   þe her beorhte mid us
      hea hlifiað   under heofon-tunglum.
      Smylte is se sige-wong;   sun-bearo lixeð,
      wudu-holt wynlic.   Wæstmas ne dreosað,
35   beorhte blede,   ac þa beamas a
      grene stondað,   swa him God bibead.
      Wintres ond sumeres   wudu bið gelice
      bledum gehongen;   næfre brosniað
      leaf under lyfte,   ne him lig sceþeð
40   æfre to ealdre,   ærþon edwenden
      worulde geweorðe.   Swa iu wætres þrym
      ealne middan-geard   mere-flod þeahte,
      eorþan ymb-hwyrft,   þa se æþela wong,
      æghwæs onsund,   wið yð-fare
45   gehealden stod   hreora wæga,
      eadig, unwemme,   þurh est Godes;
      bideð swa geblowen   oð bæles cyme,
      dryhtnes domes,   þonne deað-ræced,
      hæleþa heolstor-cofan,   onhliden weorþað.
50   Nis þær on þam londe   lað-geniðla,
      ne wop ne wracu,   wea-tacen nan,
      yldu ne yrmðu   ne se enga deað,
      ne lifes lyre   ne laþes cyme,
      ne synn ne sacu   ne sar-wracu,
55   ne wædle gewin   ne welan onsyn,

rough surface protrude there; rather the noble field thrives beneath the skies, flourishing happily.

As sages, learned from their studies, reveal to us through 28 the wisdom in their writings, that radiant land is a place twelve fathoms higher than any of the mountains that looms tall and bright here among us, beneath the stars of heaven. Tranquil is that plain of victory; its sunny grove, a pleasant forest, is full of light. Its fruits, splendid yields, do not decay; rather the trees stand ever green, as God has commanded them. In winter and summer alike the wood is 37 adorned with fruits; its leaves never wither beneath the sky, nor will fire ever damage them until the end of the world occurs. When a surge of water, a pouring sea, long ago covered all the habitable world and the earth's entire compass, that noble plain, uninjured in any part, blessed and unharmed, stood protected by God's grace from the deluge of violent waves; thus flourishing will it remain until the coming of flame, the Lord's judgment, when sepulchers will be opened wide, the dark graves of men.

In that place no hated foe exists, no weeping or suffering, 50 no mark of grief, no old age or poverty, no oppressive death or loss of life, no enemy's incursion, no sin or strife or painful affliction, no struggle with want, no lack of wealth, no

ne sorg ne slæp   ne swar leger;
ne winter-geweorp   ne wedra gebregd
hreoh under heofonum,   ne se hearda forst
caldum cyle-gicelum   cnyseð ænigne.

60   Þær ne hægl ne hrim   hreosað to foldan,
ne windig wolcen,   ne þær wæter fealleþ
lyfte gebysgad,   ac þær lagu-streamas
wundrum wrætlice,   wyllan onspringað
fægrum flod-wylmum.   Foldan leccaþ

65   wæter wynsumu   of þæs wuda midle;
þa monþa gehwam   of þære moldan tyrf
brim-cald brecað,   bearo ealne geondfarað
þragum þrymlice.   Is þæt þeodnes gebod
þætte twelf siþum   þæt tirfæste

70   lond geondlace   lagu-floda wynn.
Sindon þa bearwas   bledum gehongne,
wlitigum wæstmum.   Þær no waniað o
halge under heofonum   holtes frætwe,
ne feallað þær on foldan   fealwe blostman,

75   wudu-beama wlite,   ac þær wrætlice
on þam treowum symle   telgan gehladene,
ofett edniwe,   in ealle tid
on þam græs-wonge   grene stondaþ,
gehroden hyhtlice   haliges meahtum,

80   beorhtast bearwa.   No gebrocen weorþeð
holt on hiwe,   þær se halga stenc
wunaþ geond wyn-lond;   þæt onwended ne bið
æfre to ealdre,   ærþon endige
frod fyrn-geweorc   se hit on frymþe gescop.

85   Ðone wudu weardaþ   wundrum fæger

anxiety or sleep, no dire disease; neither onset of winter nor change of weather, harsh beneath the heavens, nor cruel frost assails anyone with frigid icicles. There neither hail 60 nor frost descends to earth, nor cloud driven by wind, nor does water rain down, forced from the air; there instead wondrously beautiful flowing streams, springs issue forth in lovely, ebullient waves. Out of the midst of the wood, pleasant waters irrigate the land; once a month, from the soil of the earth, they break forth cold as the sea, course majestically at appointed times through all the forest. It is the 68 Lord's command that those delighting streams should circulate through the splendid region twelve times. The groves are hung with their yields, beautiful fruits. There those adornments of the forest, sacred beneath the heavens, never wane at all, nor do pale blossoms, the beauty of the wood, ever fall faded to earth in that place; but splendid, laden branches, fruits ever new, exist on those trees perpetually, fresh for all time on the grassy plain, the most radiant of groves pleasingly adorned by the might of the holy one. The 80 appearance of the wood will never suffer injury, so long as the holy fragrance remains throughout the joyful land; that will never change until the one who created it in the beginning puts an end to his venerable, ancient work.

A bird that is called the phoenix, wondrously beautiful 85

fugel feþrum strong,   se is fenix haten.
Þær se an-haga   eard bihealdeþ,
deor-mod drohtað;   næfre him deaþ sceþeð
on þam will-wonge   þenden woruld stondeþ.

90 Se sceal þære sunnan   sið behealdan
ond ongean cuman   Godes condelle,
glædum gimme,   georne bewitigan
hwonne up cyme   æþelast tungla
ofer yð-mere   estan lixan,

95 fæder fyrn-geweorc   frætwum blican,
torht tacen Godes.   Tungol beoþ ahyded,
gewiten under waþeman   west-dælas on,
bideglad on dæg-red,   ond seo deorce niht
won gewiteð.   Þonne waþum strong,

100 fugel feþrum wlonc   on firgen-stream
under lyft, ofer lagu   locað georne
hwonne up cyme   eastan glidan
ofer sidne sæ   swegles leoma.

        Swa se æþela fugel   æt þam æ-springe
105 wlitigfæst wunað   wylle-streamas.
Þær se tir-eadga   twelf siþum hine
bibaþað in þam burnan   ær þæs beacnes cyme,
swegl-condelle,   ond symle swa oft
of þam wilsuman   wyll-gespryngum

110 brim-cald beorgeð   æt baða gehwylcum.
Siþþan hine sylfne   æfter sund-plegan
heah-mod hefeð   on heanne beam,
þonan yþast mæg   on east-wegum
sið bihealdan   hwonne swegles tapur

115 ofer holm-þræce   hædre blice,
leohtes leoma.   Lond beoð gefrætwad,

and strong of wing, guards that wood. A solitary being, it there occupies a dwelling, lives out its life, a bold-hearted creature; so long as the world endures, death will never harm it on that happy plain. The phoenix must observe the jour- 90 ney of the sun, go forth to meet God's candle, a brilliant jewel, and keep watch eagerly for the time when the noblest of stars rises above the wavy sea, glowing in the east, the ancient work of the Father, a glorious sign from God, shimmering in its ornaments. The stars become hidden, departed 96 beneath the waves in regions to the west, cloaked at the dawn, and the dim, dark night journeys away. Strengthened for flight, magnificent in its plumage, the bird then looks eagerly across the water, toward the ocean at the horizon, to ascertain when the ray of heaven rises in the east, gliding up over the wide sea.

Thus the noble bird, its beauty unchanging, makes those 104 welling streams its home, next to the spring. There, blessed with glory, it bathes itself twelve times in the fount before the coming of that beacon, the candle of heaven; and, just as often, the bird always tastes at every plunge the ocean-cold water from those agreeable, welling springs. Later, after its 111 swim, the proud creature bears itself up onto a lofty tree, from where it can most easily observe that journey on paths in the east when the candle of heaven, the ray of light, beams brightly across the crashing sea. The lands are adorned, the

woruld gewlitegad,   siþþan wuldres gim
ofer geofones gong   grund gescineþ
geond middan-geard,   mærost tungla.
120 Sona swa seo sunne   sealte streamas
hea oferhlifað,   swa se haswa fugel
beorht of þæs bearwes   beame gewiteð,
fareð feþrum snell   flyhte on lyfte,
swinsað ond singeð   swegle togeanes.
125 Ðonne bið swa fæger   fugles gebæru,
onbryrded breost-sefa,   blissum hremig;
wrixleð woð-cræfte   wundorlicor
beorhtan reorde   þonne æfre byre monnes
hyrde under heofonum,   siþþan heah-cyning,
130 wuldres wyrhta,   woruld staþelode,
heofon ond eorþan.   Biþ þæs hleoðres sweg
eallum song-cræftum   swetra ond wlitigra
ond wynsumra   wrenca gehwylcum.
Ne magon þam breahtme   byman ne hornas,
135 ne hearpan hlyn,   ne hæleþa stefn
ænges on eorþan,   ne organan
sweg-hleoþres geswin,   ne swanes feðre,
ne ænig þara dreama   þe dryhten gescop
gumum to gliwe   in þas geomran woruld.
140 Singeð swa ond swinsað   sælum geblissad,
oþþæt seo sunne   on suð-rodor
sæged weorþeð.   Þonne swiað he
ond hlyst gefeð,   heafde onbrygdeð
þrist, þonces gleaw,   ond þriwa ascæceð
145 feþre flyht-hwate;   fugol bið geswiged.

26

world made beautiful, as soon as that jewel of glory, most illustrious of stars, shines across the expanse of the ocean and down upon the ground, throughout the habitable earth. As soon as the sun towers high above the briny waters, the pale gray bird, radiant, leaves the tree in the forest, travels aloft in flight, swift on its wings, heading toward the sun, makes a melodious noise and sings. So beautiful then is the bird's call, so inspired its heart, so exultant with joy; with a clear voice it expresses a skill at song more wondrously than any human under heaven has heard since the supreme king, the creator of glory, established the world, the heavens and the earth. The sound of that music will be sweeter and lovelier than all other displays of skill at singing and more pleasant than every other melody. Neither trumpets nor horns can match that sound, nor can the tone of the harp, nor the voice of any man on earth, nor the strain of melodious song from the organ, nor the swan's feather, nor any of the joyful noises that the Lord has created as entertainment for men in this sad world. Thus gladdened by its happy condition, the bird sings and makes melody until the sun is brought to its resting place in the southern sky. Then it falls silent and listens; bold and wise of thought, it lifts its head, and the swift-flying creature flaps its wings three times; the bird

120

125

131

140

Symle he twelf siþum   tida gemearcað
dæges ond nihtes.

            Swa gedemed is
bearwes bigengan   þæt he þær brucan mot
wonges mid willum   ond welan neotan,
150   lifes ond lissa,   londes frætwa,
oþþæt he þusende   þisses lifes,
wudu-bearwes weard,   wintra gebideþ.
Ðonne bið gehefgad   haswig-feðra,
gomol, gearum frod.   Grene eorðan
155   aflyhð fugla wyn,   foldan geblowene,
ond þonne geseceð   side rice
middan-geardes,   þær no men bugað
eard ond eþel.   Þær he ealdordom
onfehð fore-mihtig   ofer fugla cynn,
160   geþungen on þeode,   ond þrage mid him
westen weardað.   Þonne waþum strong
west gewiteð,   wintrum gebysgad,
fleogan feþrum snel.   Fuglas þringað
utan ymbe æþelne;   æghwylc wille
165   wesan þegn ond þeow   þeodne mærum,
oþþæt hy gesecað   Syr-wara lond
corðra mæste.   Him se clæna þær
oðscufeð scearplice,   þæt he in scade weardað,
on wudu-bearwe,   weste stowe
170   biholene ond bihydde   hæleþa monegum.
Ðær he heanne beam   on holt-wuda
wunað ond weardað,   wyrtum fæstne
under heofun-hrofe,   þone hatað men
fenix on foldan,   of þæs fugles noman.
175   Hafað þam treowe forgiefen   tir-meahtig cyning,

grows quiet. It constantly marks the hours of day and of
night at their twelve intervals.

So it is ordained for that keeper of the grove that it may   147
enjoy the plain there as it wishes and benefit from its abun-
dance of life and of pleasures, the adornments of the land,
until that guardian of the wooded grove has lived to see a
thousand winters in this life. Old and wise with years, the
gray-feathered creature then grows weary. The joy of birds   154
flies from the green earth, the flourishing land, and then it
seeks a spacious kingdom in the world, one where human
beings do not inhabit the land and country. Foremost in
might, the creature there receives dominion over the race of
birds, being most accomplished of their tribe, and for a pe-
riod it inhabits that solitude with them. Strengthened for   161
flight, it then departs to the west, bearing the weight of its
years, flying swiftly on wing. Birds throng about that no-
ble one; each of them desires to be follower and servant to
that illustrious prince until, in the greatest of flocks, they
reach the land of the Syrians. There the pure creature veers   167
abruptly away from the others, so that it occupies as a ref-
uge within a wooded grove a deserted place, hidden and
concealed from many. There in the forest, beneath the vault
of heaven, it occupies and inhabits a tall tree firmly fixed by
its roots; people on earth call it a phoenix tree, after the
name of the bird. The king glorious in power, the creator of   175

meotud mon-cynnes,   mine gefræge,
þæt se ana is   ealra beama
on eorð-wege   up-lædendra
beorhtast geblowen;   ne mæg him bitres wiht
180 scyldum sceððan,   ac gescylded a
wunað ungewyrded   þenden woruld stondeð.
    Ðonne wind ligeð,   weder bið fæger,
hluttor heofones gim   halig scineð,
beoð wolcen towegen,   wætra þryþe
185 stille stondað,   biþ storma gehwylc
aswefed under swegle,   suþan bliceð
weder-condel wearm,   weorodum lyhteð,
ðonne on þam telgum   timbran onginneð,
nest gearwian.   Bið him neod micel
190 þæt he þa yldu   ofestum mote
þurh gewittes wylm   wendan to life,
feorg geong onfon.   Þonne feor ond neah
þa swetestan   somnað ond gædrað
wyrta wynsume   ond wudu-bleda
195 to þam eard-stede,   æþel-stenca gehwone,
wyrta wynsumra,   þe wuldor-cyning,
fæder frymða gehwæs,   ofer foldan gescop
to indryhtum   ælda cynne,
swetest under swegle.   Þær he sylf biereð
200 in þæt treow innan   torhte frætwe;
þær se wilda fugel   in þam westenne
ofer heanne beam   hus getimbreð,
wlitig ond wynsum,   ond gewicað þær
sylf in þam solere,   ond ymbseteð utan

humankind, has granted to that tree, so I have heard, that among all the timbers that tower on the paths of earth, it alone blossoms most splendidly; nothing at all harmful can injure it by acts of malice, but it remains forever protected, undamaged so long as the world endures.

When the wind dies down, the weather turns pleasant, 182 the sacred jewel of heaven shines brilliantly, and the clouds are dispersed; when downpours of water cease to fall, every storm beneath the heavens is calmed, and the warm candle of the sky beams from the south, shines upon the companies of men; it is then that the bird begins to prepare a nest in those branches. It has great longing to be able, by the 189 ardor of its will, to turn old age swiftly back into life, to receive its vital spirit anew. From near and far it then gathers and assembles at its dwelling place pleasant spices and forest leaves, every kind of noble fragrance and of pleasant spice that the king of glory, the Father of every beginning, created on earth as the sweetest substances under heaven, excellent goods for the human race. There the creature car- 199 ries bright ornaments into that tree; there in that solitude, the untamed bird builds a house, beautiful and pleasant, at the top of the tall tree, and it dwells there in its sunbathed

205   in þam leaf-sceade   lic ond feþre
           on healfa gehware   halgum stencum
           ond þam æþelestum   eorþan bledum.
           Siteð siþes fus.   Þonne swegles gim
           on sumeres tid,   sunne hatost,
210   ofer sceadu scineð   ond gesceapu dreogeð,
           woruld geondwliteð,   þonne weorðeð his
           hus onhæted   þurh hador swegl.
           Wyrta wearmiað,   will-sele stymeð
           swetum swæccum,   þonne on swole byrneð
215   þurh fyres feng   fugel mid neste.
             Bæl bið onæled.   Þonne brond þeceð
           heoro-dreorges hus,   hreoh onetteð,
           fealo lig feormað   ond fenix byrneð,
           fyrn-gearum frod.   Þonne fyr þigeð
220   lænne lic-homan;   lif bið on siðe,
           fæges feorh-hord,   þonne flæsc ond ban
           ad-leg æleð.   Hwæþre him eft cymeð
           æfter fyrst-mearce   feorh edniwe,
           siþþan þa yslan   eft onginnað
225   æfter lig-þræce   lucan togædre,
           geclungne to cleowenne.   Þonne clæne bið
           beorhtast nesta,   bæle forgrunden
           heaþo-rofes hof;   hra bið acolad,
           ban-fæt gebrocen,   ond se bryne sweþrað.
230   Þonne of þam ade   æples gelicnes
           on þære ascan bið   eft gemeted,
           of þam weaxeð wyrm,   wundrum fæger,
           swylce he of ægerum   ut alæde,
           scir of scylle.   Þonne on sceade weaxeð,
235   þæt he ærest bið   swylce earnes brid,

spot, and in the shelter of leaves it surrounds its body and plumage on all sides with holy spices and the noblest fruits of the earth. It sits, eager to journey forth. When the jewel 208 of heaven, the sun at its hottest in summertime, fulfills its destiny and illumines the shadows, directs its gaze over the whole world, then the bird's house grows hot from the brilliant sunshine. The fragrant plants grow warm, the pleasant dwelling smokes with sweet aromas; then, gripped by fire, the bird along with its nest burns in flame.

The pyre is kindled. The burning then engulfs the house 216 of the creature, anguished in its death throes, and fiercely hastens onward; pale flame consumes, and the phoenix burns up, old after long years. Fire then devours its perishable body; its life is departing, the treasured vital spirit of the doomed one, when the flame of the pyre consumes flesh and bone. Even so, after a period of time, life will return to the bird, the animating spirit be renewed, when its ashes begin once more to bond together after the fiery onslaught, cohering in the shape a ball. The most splendid of nests will 226 be purified then, the brave one's home destroyed by fire; the corpse, a broken vessel of bones, grows cool and the burning subsides. Then among the ashes of the pyre appears in turn something resembling an apple, from which grows a wondrously beautiful worm, as if it were hatched from eggs, bright from the shell. Then it grows in its refuge so that, at 234 first, it is like an eaglet, a graceful young bird; then, later still,

fæger fugel-timber;   ðonne furþor gin
wridað on wynnum,   þæt he bið wæstmum gelic
ealdum earne,   and æfter þon
feþrum gefrætwad,   swylc he æt frymðe wæs,
240   beorht geblowen.

                Þonne bræd weorþeð
eal edniwe   eft acenned,
synnum asundrad,   sumes onlice
swa mon to ondleofne   eorðan wæstmas
on hærfeste   ham gelædeð,
245   wiste wynsume,   ær wintres cyme,
on rypes timan,   þy læs hi renes scur
awyrde under wolcnum;   þær hi wraðe metað,
fodor-þege gefean,   þonne forst ond snaw
mid ofer-mægne   eorþan þeccað
250   winter-gewædum.   Of þam wæstmum sceal
eorla ead-wela   eft alædan
þurh cornes gecynd,   þe ær clæne bið
sæd onsawen.   Þonne sunnan glæm
on lenctenne,   lifes tacen,
255   weceð woruld-gestreon,   þæt þa wæstmas beoð
þurh agne gecynd   eft acende,
foldan frætwe.   Swa se fugel weorþeð,
gomel æfter gearum,   geong edniwe,
flæsce bifongen.   No he foddor þigeð,
260   mete on moldan,   nemne mele-deawes
dæl gebyrge,   se dreoseð oft
æt middre nihte;   bi þon se modga his
feorh afedeð,   oþþæt fyrn-gesetu,
agenne eard,   eft geseceð.
265   Þonne bið aweaxen   wyrtum in gemonge

it prospers happily until it resembles a mature eagle in form, adorned with feathers just as it had been to begin with, splendidly flourishing.

Having been born again, its roasted flesh is wholly re- 240 newed, liberated from sins, rather in the way that, at harvest, someone brings home the fruits of earth for food, delightful provisions at the time of reaping before the onset of winter, lest rainfall under the open skies destroy the crops; then people find solace, joy in feasting, when frost and snow with overwhelming force blanket the earth in wintry garments. From those same fruits a rich bounty for men shall 250 be brought forth a second time, through the nature of the grain that will be sown ahead as pure seed. Then, in spring, the ray of the sun, the sign of life, rouses the riches of earth so that fruits, adornments of the soil, are born anew in accord with their natural properties. In the same way, the bird 257 old in years becomes young once more, encompassed by flesh. It partakes of no food at all, no nourishment on earth, unless it tastes a portion of the sweet dew that often falls in the middle of the night; with that the proud creature sustains its life until it seeks out once more its ancient habitation, its own abode.

Nestled among fragrant plants it will then be grown, a 265

fugel feþrum deal;   feorh bið niwe,
geong, geofona ful.   Þonne he of greote his
lic leoþu-cræftig,   þæt ær lig fornom,
somnað, swoles lafe,   searwum gegædrað
270   ban gebrosnad   æfter bæl-þræce,
ond þonne gebringeð   ban ond yslan,
ades lafe,   eft ætsomne,
ond þonne þæt wæl-reaf   wyrtum biteldeð,
fægre gefrætwed.   Ðonne afysed bið
275   agenne eard   eft to secan,
þonne fotum ymbfehð   fyres lafe,
clam biclyppeð,   ond his cyþþu eft,
sun-beorht gesetu,   seceð on wynnum,
eadig eþel-lond.   Eall bið geniwad
280   feorh ond feþer-homa,   swa he æt frymþe wæs,
þa hine ærest God   on þone æþelan wong
sigorfæst sette.   He his sylfes þær
ban gebringeð,   þa ær brondes wylm
on beorh-stede   bæle forþylmde
285   ascan to eacan.   Þonne eal geador
bebyrgeð beadu-cræftig   ban ond yslan
on þam ea-londe.   Bið him edniwe
þære sunnan segn   þonne swegles leoht,
gimma gladost,   ofer gar-secg up,
290   æþel-tungla wyn,   eastan lixeð.

      Is se fugel fæger   forweard hiwe,
bleo-brygdum fag   ymb þa breost foran.
Is him þæt heafod   hindan grene,
wrætlice wrixled,   wurman geblonden.
295   Þonne is se finta   fægre gedæled,
sum brun, sum basu,   sum blacum splottum

bird proud in plumage; its life will be rejuvenated, youthful and filled with gifts. Then the agile creature gathers out of the dust the body that fire previously destroyed, what is left after the flame; with care it assembles the crumbled bones in the aftermath of the raging fire, and then it brings bones and ashes together again, what was left from the pyre; and with aromatic plants it then encases the spoils of battle, beautifully adorned. When it is moved to seek out once 274 more its own dwelling, it grasps with its talons the remains from the fire, clutches them in its claws, and joyfully seeks once more its home, dwellings bright as the sun, its blessed native land. Its life force is wholly restored, as is its feathered form, just as it was in the beginning, when God, secure in victory, first placed it on the noble plain. There the bird 282 will then bring its own bones, which surging fire previously engulfed with flame on a funereal mound, adding ash to ashes. Resourceful in battle, it then buries all the bones and ashes together in that isolated land. The sign of the sun is ever renewed for the phoenix when the light of heaven, fairest of jewels, the joy of noble stars, shines from the east up over the deep.

In front the bird is beautiful in appearance, colored with 291 various hues about its breast. Its head at the back is green blended with purple, indescribably variegated. Next, the tail is gorgeously divided, partly russet, partly crimson, partly covered with dark spots intricately arranged. The feathers

searolice beseted.   Sindon þa fiþru
hwit hindanweard,   ond se hals grene
nioþoweard ond ufeweard,   ond þæt nebb lixeð
300   swa glæs oþþe gim,   geaflas scyne
innan ond utan.   Is seo eag-gebyrd
stearc ond hiwe   stane gelicast,
gladum gimme,   þonne in gold-fate
smiþa orþoncum   biseted weorþeð.
305   Is ymb þone sweoran,   swylce sunnan hring,
beaga beorhtast   brogden feðrum.
Wrætlic is seo womb neoþan,   wundrum fæger,
scir ond scyne.   Is se scyld ufan
frætwum gefeged   ofer þæs fugles bæc.
310   Sindon þa scancan   scyllum biweaxen,
fealwe fotas.   Se fugel is on hiwe
æghwæs ænlic,   onlicost pean,
wynnum geweaxen,   þæs gewritu secgað.
Nis he hinderweard   ne hyge-gælsa,
315   swar ne swongor   swa sume fuglas,
þa þe late þurh lyft   lacað fiþrum,
ac he is snel ond swift   ond swiþe leoht,
wlitig ond wynsum,   wuldre gemearcad.
Ece is se æþeling   se þe him þæt ead gefeð!
320   Þonne he gewiteð   wongas secan,
his ealdne eard   of þisse eþel-tyrf.
Swa se fugel fleogeð,   folcum oðeaweð,
mongum monna   geond middan-geard;
þonne somniað   suþan ond norþan,
325   eastan ond westan   eored-ciestum,
farað feorran ond nean   folca þryþum,
þær hi sceawiaþ   scyppendes giefe

38

behind are white, the neck is green below and above, the
beak shines like glass or precious stone, and the jaws are
beautiful inside and out. The nature of its eye is piercing and 301
very similar in appearance to a stone, to a lovely jewel when
placed in a golden setting by the metalworkers' skills. Plaited
of feathers around its neck is the brightest of rings, like the
circle of the sun. Below that is a beautiful underbelly, won-
drously attractive, pure-white and lovely. The crest above is
fitted with adornments extending over the bird's back. Its
thighs are covered with scales; its feet are yellow. In every 311
respect the bird is incomparable in appearance; when it has
joyously matured, it most resembles a peacock, as books
relate. It is not sluggish or frivolous, not heavy or slothful
like some birds that fly slowly through the air; rather it is
fleet and swift and very light, beautiful and pleasing, distin-
guished by its splendor. Eternal is the prince who endows it
with that abundance!

Then it departs from this country to seek the plains, 320
its dwelling of old. As the bird flies, it shows itself to peo-
ples, to the multitudes of humankind across the earth; from
south and north, from east and west, they then assemble
in companies, journey in hosts of people from far and near
to where they will glimpse the creator's lovely gifts to that

fægre on þam fugle,   swa him æt fruman sette
sigora soð-cyning   sellicran gecynd,
330   frætwe fægran   ofer fugla cyn.
Ðonne wundriað   weras ofer eorþan
wlite ond wæstma,   ond gewritum cyþað,
mundum mearciað   on marm-stane,
hwonne se dæg ond seo tid   dryhtum geeawe
335   frætwe flyht-hwates.   Ðonne fugla cynn
on healfa gehwone   heapum þringað,
sigað sid-wegum,   songe lofiað,
mærað modigne   meaglum reordum,
ond swa þone halgan   hringe beteldað
340   flyhte on lyfte;   fenix biþ on middum,
þreatum biþrungen.   Þeoda wlitað,
wundrum wafiað   hu seo wil-gedryht
wildne weorþiað,   worn æfter oþrum,
cræftum cyþað   ond for cyning mærað
345   leofne leod-fruman;   lædað mid wynnum
æþelne to earde,   oþþæt se an-hoga
oðfleogeð feþrum snel,   þæt him gefylgan ne mæg
drymendra gedryht,   þonne duguða wyn
of þisse eorþan tyrf   eþel seceð.
350   Swa se gesæliga   æfter swylt-hwile
his eald-cyðþe   eft geneosað,
fægre foldan.   Fugelas cyrrað
from þam guð-frecan   geomor-mode
eft to earde.   Þonne se æþeling bið
355   giong in geardum.

            (God ana wat,
cyning ælmihtig,   hu his gecynde bið,
wifhades þe weres;   þæt ne wat ænig

bird, since the true king of victories created its nature from the beginning to be superior, its adornment to be lovelier, surpassing other kinds of birds. Then people the world over 331 marvel at its appearance and form, and they set down in their writings, inscribe with their hands on marble, what day and hour revealed to the multitude the adornments of that swift-flying one. Then, on every side, the race of birds presses close about it in throngs, they converge from their distant paths; with song they praise the noble-minded creature with robust voices, and thus in their flight through the air they surround it, forming a circle; in their midst is the phoenix, encompassed by those troops. The nations look 341 on, marvel with amazement at how the happy retinue, one flock after another, pays homage to the untamed creature, how they skillfully proclaim and glorify as king the beloved leader of their tribe; joyously they lead the noble phoenix toward its dwelling, until that solitary creature veers off in flight, swift on wing, so that the company of celebrants cannot follow when the delight of their troops seeks a homeland away from the ground of this earth. Thus, after the hour 350 of death, the blessed creature visits once more its country of old, that lovely land. Sad at heart, the birds turn back from their captain, heading for their own abodes. Their prince is then at home, youthful.

(Only God, the almighty king, knows what the bird's sex 355 is, whether masculine or feminine; no member of the human

monna cynnes,   butan meotod ana,
hu þa wisan sind   wundorlice,
360   fæger fyrn-gesceap,   ymb þæs fugles gebyrd.)
    Þær se eadga mot   eardes neotan,
wylle-streama   wudu-holtum in,
wunian in wonge,   oþþæt wintra bið
þusend urnen.   Þonne him weorþeð
365   ende lifes;   hine ad þeceð
þurh æled-fyr.   Hwæþre eft cymeð
aweaht wrætlice   wundrum to life.
Forþon he drusende   deað ne bisorgað,
sare swylt-cwale,   þe him symle wat
370   æfter lig-þræce   lif edniwe,
feorh æfter fylle,   þonne fromlice
þurh briddes had   gebreadad weorðeð
eft of ascan,   edgeong weseð
under swegles hleo.   Bið him self gehwæðer
375   sunu ond swæs fæder,   ond symle eac
eft yrfe-weard   ealdre lafe.
Forgeaf him se meahta   mon-cynnes fruma
þæt he swa wrætlice   weorþan sceolde
eft þæt ilce   þæt he ær þon wæs,
380   feþrum bifongen,   þeah hine fyr nime.
    Swa þæt ece lif   eadigra gehwylc
æfter sar-wræce   sylf geceoseð
þurh deorcne deað,   þæt he dryhtnes mot
æfter gear-dagum   geofona neotan
385   on sin-dreamum,   ond siþþan a
wunian in wuldre   weorca to leane.
Þisses fugles gecynd   fela gelices
bi þam gecornum   Cristes þegnum

race, no one save the creator alone knows how wondrous are its ways, how gracious the ancient ordinance concerning its birth.)

There the blessed one can enjoy its abode, the welling springs in the forest, can dwell on that plain until a thousand winters have run their course. At that point the end of life arrives; with hot flame the pyre swallows it up. Even so, mysteriously revived, the bird returns to life in miraculous fashion. In perishing, it therefore does not fear death nor the grievous agony of its demise; it is constantly aware that, after the assault of flame, life will be renewed, vitality after its decease, when from out of the ashes it is vibrantly rejuvenated in the form of a bird, becomes young once more beneath the vault of heaven. That creature is both son and father to itself, and likewise ever the inheritor, in turn, of an ancient heirloom. The mighty creator of humankind granted the bird that, in so extraordinary a fashion, it should become once more the very thing it had been previously, arrayed in feathers, though fire claim it.

So too, by experience of gloomy death, does every one of the blessed arrive at everlasting life after the pain of exile, in order that he may, when the days of his life are passed, enjoy the gifts of the Lord amid perpetual celebrations and then dwell always in glory as a reward for labors. Among the people, the nature of this bird bears a great likeness to Christ's

361

368

374

381

387

beacnað in burgum,   hu hi beorhtne gefean
390   þurh fæder fultum   on þas frecnan tid
healdaþ under heofonum,   ond him heanne blæd
in þam uplican   eðle gestrynaþ.
Habbaþ we geascad   þæt se ælmihtiga
worhte wer ond wif   þurh his wundra sped,
395   ond hi þa gesette   on þone selestan
foldan sceata,   þone fira bearn
nemnað neorxna-wong,   þær him nænges wæs
eades onsyn   þenden eces word,
halges hleoþor-cwide,   healdan woldan
400   on þam niwan gefean.   Þær him niþ gescod,
eald-feondes æfest,   se him æt gebead,
beames blede,   þæt hi bu þegun
æppel unrædum   ofer est Godes,
byrgdon forbodene.   Þær him bitter wearð
405   yrmþu æfter æte   ond hyra eaferum swa,
sarlic symbel   sunum ond dohtrum.
Wurdon teonlice   toþas idge
ageald æfter gylte.   Hæfdon Godes yrre,
bittre bealo-sorge.   Þæs þa byre siþþan
410   gyrne onguldon,   þe hi þæt gyfl þegun
ofer eces word.   Forþon hy eðles wyn
geomor-mode   ofgiefan sceoldon
þurh nædran niþ,   þa heo nearwe biswac
yldran usse   in ær-dagum
415   þurh fæcne ferð,   þæt hi feor þonan
in þas deað-dene   drohtað sohton,
sorgfulran gesetu.   Him wearð selle lif
heolstre bihyded,   ond se halga wong
þurh feondes searo   fæste bityned

chosen servants, resembling how they, with the Father's
help, maintain under the heavens their shining joy during
this treacherous time, and win for themselves supreme glory
in the heavenly homeland. We have learned that the al-   393
mighty created man and woman through the power of his
wondrous acts, and then he placed them in the most excel-
lent part of the earth, which the children of men call *neorxna-
wong* [Paradise], where they had no want of wealth, so long
as they determined to uphold in their newly created happi-
ness the word of him who is eternal, the utterance of the
holy one. Hatred hurt them there, the malice of the ancient   400
enemy who offered them food, the fruit of the tree, that
both of them might foolishly taste the forbidden apple,
transgressing against God's kindness. Following that meal,
cruel affliction befell them there and their offspring as well,
a doleful feast for their sons and daughters. Their busy teeth   407
were wrathfully repaid in accord with the offense. They re-
ceived God's anger, a harsh, injurious sorrow. Their prog-
eny afterward paid in grief for their [parents'] having eaten
that morsel, against the bidding of the eternal one. And so,
sorrowful at heart, they had to abandon the joy of their
homeland on account of the serpent's hostility, when it in-
sidiously and with treacherous intent deceived our parents
in days long ago, with the result that, far from that place,
they sought in this valley of death their way of living, more
anxious abodes. The better life was hidden from them in   417
darkness, and through the enemy's scheming the sancti-
fied plain was securely shut to them for a great many years,

420   wintra mengu,   oþþæt wuldor-cyning
     þurh his hider-cyme   halgum togeanes,
     mon-cynnes gefea,   meþra frefrend,
     ond se anga hyht,   eft ontynde.

     Is þon gelicast,   þæs þe us leorneras
425   wordum secgað   ond writu cyþað,
     þisses fugles gefær,   þonne frod ofgiefeð
     eard ond eþel   ond geealdad bið.
     Gewiteð werig-mod,   wintrum gebysgad,
     þær he holtes hleo   heah gemeteð,
430   in þam he getimbreð   tanum ond wyrtum
     þam æþelestum   eard-wic niwe,
     nest on bearwe.   Bið him neod micel
     þæt he feorh geong eft   onfon mote
     þurh liges blæst,   lif æfter deaþe,
435   edgeong wesan,   ond his eald-cyðþu,
     sun-beorht gesetu,   secan mote
     æfter fyr-baðe.   Swa ða fore-gengan,
     yldran usse,   anforleton
     þone wlitigan wong   ond wuldres setl,
440   leoflic on laste,   tugon longne sið
     in hearmra hond,   þær him hettende,
     earme aglæcan,   oft gescodan.

       Wæron hwæþre monge,   þa þe meotude wel
     gehyrdun under heofonum   halgum ðeawum,
445   dædum domlicum,   þæt him dryhten wearð,
     heofona heah-cyning,   hold on mode.
     Ðæt is se hea beam,   in þam halge nu
     wic weardiað,   þær him wihte ne mæg
     eald-feonda nan   atre sceþþan,

until the king of glory, the joy of humankind, consoler of the weary and their sole hope, opened it once more by his coming forth to meet the saints.

As teachers say and writings declare, this bird's journey, when at a ripe age it gives up its dwelling and homeland and grows old, is very similar to that [sc. the fall and post-Edenic exile of humanity]. Weary at heart, weighed down with years, it departs for a place where it finds the lofty canopy of a forest in which it builds from twigs and the most noble spices a new residence, a nest in the grove. It has great desire to be able to receive back through the roaring flame its vital spirit, life after death, to be young again and be able to seek, following that fiery bath, its country of old, habitations bright as the sun. So too those ancestors, our parents, left behind them the beautiful plain and their cherished seat of glory; they made a long journey into the hands of enemies, where hateful beings, wretched adversaries, often did them harm.

There were many, nevertheless, who by their holy customs, their glorious deeds, well obeyed the creator beneath the heavens, so that the Lord, the supreme king of the heavens, was favorably minded toward them. That is the tall tree in which holy people now make their dwelling, where no ancient enemy will be able to harm them at all with poison,

424

432

443

450   facnes tacne,   on þa frecnan tid.

Þær him nest wyrceð   wið niþa gehwam
dædum domlicum   dryhtnes cempa,
þonne he ælmessan   earmum dæleð,
dugeþa leasum,   ond him dryhten gecygð,
455   fæder on fultum,   forð onetteð,
lænan lifes   leahtras dwæsceþ,
mirce man-dæde,   healdeð meotudes æ
beald in breostum,   ond gebedu seceð
clænum gehygdum,   ond his cneo bigeð
460   æþele to eorþan,   flyhð yfla gehwylc,
grimme gieltas,   for Godes egsan,
glæd-mod gyrneð   þæt he godra mæst
dæda gefremme—   þam biþ dryhten scyld
in siþa gehwane,   sigora waldend,
465   weoruda wil-giefa.

Þis þa wyrta sind,
wæstma blede,   þa se wilda fugel
somnað under swegle   side ond wide
to his wic-stowe,   þær he wundrum fæst
wið niþa gehwam   nest gewyrceð.
470   Swa nu in þam wicum   willan fremmað
mode ond mægne   meotudes cempan,
mærða tilgað;   þæs him meorde wile
ece ælmihtig   eadge forgildan.
Beoð him of þam wyrtum   wic gestaþelad
475   in wuldres byrig   weorca to leane,
þæs þe hi geheoldan   halge lare
hate æt heortan,   hige weallende
dæges ond nihtes   dryhten lufiað,
leohte geleafan   leofne ceosað

with the stigma of betrayal, in the time of danger. There, by   451
means of glorious deeds, a soldier for the Lord builds him-
self a nest against every hostility whenever he dispenses
alms to the poor, to those who lack resources, and calls upon
the Lord, the Father, for help; or when he presses onward,
extinguishes the vices of this transitory life, dark works of
evil; or when he courageously upholds in his heart the cre-
ator's law, endeavors at his prayers with pure thoughts, and
nobly bends his knee to earth; when he puts to flight every
evil, grave transgressions, for the sake of God's love, and
with a cheerful mind is eager to do as many good works as
possible—it is to such a person that the Lord, the ruler of
victories, will be a shield on every occasion, a generous re-
warder of troops.

This is what those spices are, the yields of plants that the   465
untamed bird gathers for its dwelling from far and wide un-
der heaven, where it builds a nest wondrously secure against
every hostility. So too those who soldier for their creator
now carry out his will with mind and might, perform famous
works; in return for that, the eternal, almighty one will pay
them a blessed reward. Out of those fragrant plants, dwell-   474
ings will be erected for them in the city of glory as a reward
for their labors, since they upheld the holy teaching fer-
vently in their hearts, love the Lord day and night with an
ardent mind, and through their radiant faith choose their

480   ofer woruld-welan;   ne biþ him wynne hyht
       þæt hy þis læne lif   long gewunien.
        Þus eadig eorl   ecan dreames,
       heofona hames   mid heah-cyning
       earnað on elne,   oþþæt ende cymeð
485   dogor-rimes,   þonne deað nimeð,
       wiga wæl-gifre,   wæpnum geþryþed,
       ealdor anra gehwæs,   ond in eorþan fæðm
       snude sendeð   sawlum binumene
       læne lic-homan,   þær hi longe beoð
490   oð fyres cyme   foldan biþeahte.
        Ðonne monge beoð   on gemot læded
       fyra cynnes;   wile fæder engla,
       sigora soð-cyning,   seonoþ gehegan,
       duguða dryhten   deman mid ryhte.
495   Þonne æriste   ealle gefremmaþ
       men on moldan,   swa se mihtiga cyning
       beodeð, brego engla,   byman stefne
       ofer sidne grund,   sawla nergend.
       Bið se deorca deað   dryhtnes meahtum
500   eadgum geendad.   Æðele hweorfað,
       þreatum þringað,   þonne þeos woruld
       scyld-wyrcende   in scome byrneð,
       ade onæled.   Weorþeð anra gehwylc
       forht on ferþþe   þonne fyr briceð
505   læne lond-welan,   lig eal þigeð
       eorðan æht-gestreon,   æpplede gold
       gifre forgripeð,   grædig swelgeð
       londes frætwe.   Þonne on leoht cymeð
       ældum þisses   in þa openan tid
510   fæger ond gefealic   fugles tacen,

beloved Lord over the wealth of this world; to abide long
in this transitory life is no joyful prospect for them. Thus   482
does the blessed man earn everlasting joy through courage, a
home in the heavens with the supreme king, up until the
time when the end of his allotted days arrives, when death,
a ravenous warrior fortified with weapons, seizes the life of
every person and quickly dispatches perishable bodies, be-
reft of their souls, into the earth's embrace where they will
long remain, covered with soil, until the coming of fire.

Then many from the race of men will be led to assembly;   491
the Father of angels, true king of victories, will convene a
synod, the Lord of hosts judge with justice. All people on
earth will then undergo resurrection, when the mighty king,
the prince of angels, savior of souls, issues the order over the
vast earth, at the blaring of a trumpet. For the blessed, dis-
mal death will be ended, through the might of the Lord.
They will change into noble figures, muster in companies,   500
while this sinning world burns up in shame, incinerated
on the pyre. Everyone will grow fearful at heart when fire
destroys the fleeting riches of this realm, when flame con-
sumes all possessions amassed on earth, greedily snatches
red gold away, ravenously devours treasures of the land.
At the manifest time, the beautiful and joyous symbol of   508
this bird will then come to light for all humanity, when

þonne anwald eal   up astelleð
of byrgenum,   ban gegædrað,
leomu lic somod   ond lifes gæst
fore Cristes cneo.   Cyning þrymlice
515   of his heah-setle   halgum scineð,
wlitig wuldres gim.   Wel biþ þam þe mot
in þa geomran tid   Gode lician.
    Ðær þa lic-homan   leahtra clæne
gongað glæd-mode,   gæstas hweorfað
520   in ban-fatu,   þonne bryne stigeð
heah to heofonum.   Hat bið monegum
egeslic æled,   þonne anra gehwylc,
soðfæst ge synnig,   sawel mid lice,
from mold-grafum   seceð meotudes dom,
525   forht-afæred.   Fyr bið on tihte,
æleð uncyste.   Þær þa eadgan beoð
æfter wræc-hwile   weorcum bifongen,
agnum dædum.   Þæt þa æþelan sind
wyrta wynsume,   mid þam se wilda fugel
530   his sylfes nest   biseteð utan,
þæt hit færinga   fyre byrneð,
forsweleð under sunnan,   ond he sylfa mid,
ond þonne æfter lige   lif eft onfehð
edniwinga.   Swa bið anra gehwylc
535   flæsce bifongen   fira cynnes,
ænlic ond edgeong,   se þe his agnum her
willum gewyrceð   þæt him wuldor-cyning
meahtig æt þam mæþle   milde geweorþeð.
    Þonne hleoþriað   halge gæstas,
540   sawla soðfæste   song ahebbað,
clæne ond gecorene,   hergað cyninges þrym,

God's power raises all from their graves, gathers at Christ's knee their bones, limbs and bodies together, and the animating spirit as well. From his lofty throne, the king will beam majestically upon his holy ones, a lovely jewel of radiance. It will be well for him who can prove pleasing to God in that sorrowful time.

Bodies purified from sins will with gladdened hearts make their way to that place, souls will return to their bone vessels, when the burning rises high to the heavens. That conflagration will be searing and terrible for many when, from their earthen graves, each and every person, body and soul, seeks the Lord's judgment, the righteous and the sinful both stricken with terror. The fire will advance, burn what is not virtuous. Their period of exile over, there the blessed will be surrounded by their works and their own deeds. That is what those noble, delightful spices are with which the untamed bird so encompasses its nest that it instantly burns up in the fire, shrivels beneath the sun, and the bird along with it, and then, after the burning, it receives life once more. So too every member of the human race that is clothed in flesh will be incomparable and rejuvenated, provided he acts here on his own desires in such a way that the mighty king of glory may be merciful to him at that assembly. Then the sanctified spirits will speak, righteous souls, pure and elect, will raise a song; voice upon voice, they will praise the majesty of the king; beautifully perfumed with

518

525

534

stefn æfter stefne;   stigað to wuldre
wlitige gewyrtad   mid hyra wel-dædum.
Beoð þonne amerede   monna gæstas,
545   beorhte abywde   þurh bryne fyres.
   Ne wene þæs ænig   ælda cynnes
þæt ic lyge-wordum   leoð somnige,
write woð-cræfte.   Gehyrað witedom
Iobes gieddinga.   Þurh gæstes blæd
550   breostum onbryrded,   beald reordade,
wuldre geweorðad;   he þæt word gecwæð:
"Ic þæt ne forhycge   heortan geþoncum,
þæt ic in minum neste   neo-bed ceose,
hæle hra-werig,   gewite hean þonan
555   on longne sið,   lame bitolden,
geomor gu-dæda,   in greotes fæðm,
ond þonne æfter deaþe   þurh dryhtnes giefe
swa se fugel fenix   feorh edniwe
æfter æriste   agan mote,
560   dreamas mid dryhten,   þær seo deore scolu
leofne lofiað.   Ic þæs lifes ne mæg
æfre to ealdre   ende gebidan,
leohtes ond lissa.   Þeah min lic scyle
on mold-ærne   molsnad weorþan
565   wyrmum to willan,   swa þeah weoruda God
æfter swylt-hwile   sawle alyseð
ond in wuldor aweceð.   Me þæs wen næfre
forbirsteð in breostum,   ðe ic in brego engla
forðweardne gefean   fæste hæbbe."
570   Ðus frod guma   on fyrn-dagum
gieddade gleaw-mod,   Godes spel-boda,
ymb his æriste   in ece lif,

their good works, they will ascend to glory. Then the souls of human beings will be refined, brilliantly purified through the blaze of that fire.

Let none of the race of men suspect that I am composing 546 verses from lies, writing with poetic artifice. Listen to the prophecy of Job's verses. Encouraged in his heart by inspiration from the Spirit, the man who was honored with glory spoke forthrightly, declared this utterance: "Being a man 552 weary in body, I do not scorn in the thoughts of my heart that, encompassed in clay as I am, I should seek a deathbed in my nest, should depart from here on the long journey into the soil's embrace, lamenting my past deeds; and that then, after death, like the phoenix bird I should be able to possess through God's grace a life renewed after the resurrection, possess joys with the Lord where his cherished host offers praises to their beloved. Never will I be able to experience 561 an end to that life, to its light and its joys. Though to the delight of worms my body must decay in its house of earth, the God of hosts will nevertheless free my soul after the hour of death, awaken it into glory. Never does the hope abate in my heart that I may securely possess future happiness in the prince of the angels."

Thus a sage man in days long ago, God's messenger wise 570 in mind, sang concerning his resurrection into everlasting life, so that we might more readily perceive the glorious sign

þæt we þy geornor   ongietan meahten
tirfæst tacen   þæt se torhta fugel
575   þurh bryne beacnað.   Bana lafe,
ascan ond yslan,   ealle gesomnað
æfter lig-bryne,   lædeþ siþþan
fugel on fotum   to frean geardum,
sunnan togeanes.   Þær hi siþþan forð
580   wuniað wintra fela,   wæstmum geniwad,
ealles edgiong,   þær ænig ne mæg
in þam leodscype   læþþum hwopan.
Swa nu æfter deaðe   þurh dryhtnes miht
somod siþiaþ   sawla mid lice,
585   fægre gefrætwed,   fugle gelicast,
in ead-welum   æþelum stencum,
þær seo soþfæste   sunne lihteð
wlitig ofer weoredum   in wuldres byrig.
    Ðonne soðfæstum   sawlum scineð
590   heah ofer hrofas   hælende Crist.
Him folgiað   fuglas scyne,
beorhte gebredade,   blissum hremige,
in þam gladan ham,   gæstas gecorene,
ece to ealdre.   Þær him yfle ne mæg
595   fah feond gemah   facne sceþþan,
ac þær lifgað a   leohte werede,
swa se fugel fenix,   in freoþu dryhtnes,
wlitige in wuldre.   Weorc anra gehwæs
beorhte bliceð   in þam bliþan ham
600   fore onsyne   ecan dryhtnes,
symle in sibbe,   sunnan gelice.
Þær se beorhta beag   brogden wundrum
eorcnan-stanum   eadigra gehwam

56

that the splendid phoenix represents through being burned. After the scorching fire, the bird gathers all the remnants of bones, of ashes and embers, carries them in its talons, heading toward the sun, into the dwelling of the Lord. There, 579 where none of that citizenry can weep for injuries felt, those remnants abide ever after for many years, renewed in physical form, entirely rejuvenated. So too at present, just like that bird, do souls and bodies finely adorned with rich gifts and noble fragrances journey together after death, by the Lord's power, to the place where the righteous sun shines beautifully upon the hosts inside the city of glory.

From high above the rooftops there, Christ the savior 589 beams down on righteous souls. Beautiful birds, the elect spirits, brightly restored and exulting with joys, follow him into that happy home forever. There the accursed, malign enemy cannot injure them with wicked guile; rather, like the phoenix bird, they live there forever clothed in light, beautiful in glory, placed under the Lord's protection. In that joy- 598 ous home, the work of every inhabitant shines brightly like the sun before the face of the eternal Lord, continually at peace. There the shining crown, wondrously set with

hlifað ofer heafde.   Heafelan lixað,
605   þrymme biþeahte.   Ðeodnes cyne-gold
soðfæstra gehwone   sellic glengeð
leohte in life,   þær se longa gefea,
ece ond edgeong,   æfre ne sweþrað,
ac hy in wlite wuniað   wuldre bitolden,
610   fægrum frætwum,   mid fæder engla.
    Ne bið him on þam wicum   wiht to sorge,
wroht ne weþel   ne gewin-dagas,
hungor se hata   ne se hearda þurst,
yrmþu ne yldo.   Him se æþela cyning
615   forgifeð goda gehwylc.   Þær gæsta gedryht
hælend hergað   ond heofon-cyninges
meahte mærsiað,   singað metude lof.
Swinsað sib-gedryht   swega mæste
hædre ymb þæt halge   heah-seld Godes,
620   bliþe bletsiað   bregu selestan
eadge mid englum,   efen-hleoþre þus:
"Sib si þe, soð God,   ond snyttru-cræft,
ond þe þonc sy,   þrym-sittendum,
geongra gyfena,   goda gehwylces.
625   Micel, unmæte   mægnes strengðu,
heah ond halig!   Heofonas sindon
fægre gefylled,   fæder ælmihtig,
ealra þrymma þrym,   þines wuldres
uppe mid englum,   ond on eorðan somod.
630   Gefreoþa usic, frymþa scyppend!   Þu eart fæder ælmihtig
in heannesse,   heofuna waldend."
    Ðus reordiað   ryht-fremmende,
manes amerede,   in þære mæran byrig;
cyne-þrym cyþað,   caseres lof

precious stones, towers above the head of every one of the blessed. Their heads are radiant, covered in majesty. A wondrous, princely diadem adorns with light each of the righteous in that life, where enduring joy, everlasting and always new, never fades; rather they abide in beauty, surrounded with glory and splendid adornments, together with the Father of angels. 605

In that place there will be nothing at all to cause them pain, neither hurt nor poverty nor days of struggle, neither burning hunger nor cruel thirst, neither misery nor old age. The noble king will grant them every good. There a company of souls praises the savior and celebrates the might of the heavenly king, sings praise to the creator. Around the holy, lofty throne of God, their fellowship brightly intones the greatest of melodies; together with the angels, the blessed joyfully proclaim their benediction upon the supreme prince, their voices thus in unison: "Peace and wisdom be yours, O true God, and thanks be to you, enthroned in majesty, for all new gifts, for every good. Great, boundless, exalted and holy is the strength of your power! O Father almighty, majesty above all majesties, the heavens with their angels above are beautifully filled with your glory, and so it is on earth as well. Grant us your protection, O shaper of beginnings! You are the almighty Father on high, ruler of the heavens." 611 618 625

Thus will speak the doers of good, purified from evil, in that illustrious city; as a company of the righteous, they will declare his royal majesty, will sing in heaven their emperor's 632

635   singað on swegle   soðfæstra gedryht,
þam anum is   ece weorð-mynd
forð butan ende.   Næs his frymð æfre,
eades ongyn.   Þeah he on eorþan her
þurh cildes had   cenned wære

640   in middan-geard,   hwæþre his meahta sped
heah ofer heofonum   halig wunade,
dom unbryce.   Þeah he deaþes cwealm
on rode treow   ræfnan sceolde,
þearlic wite,   he þy þriddan dæge

645   æfter lices hryre   lif eft onfeng
þurh fæder fultum.   Swa fenix beacnað,
geong in geardum,   God-bearnes meaht,
þonne he of ascan   eft onwæcneð
in lifes lif,   leomum geþungen.

650   Swa se hælend us   helpe gefremede
þurh his lices gedal,   lif butan ende,
swa se fugel swetum   his fiþru tu
ond wynsumum   wyrtum gefylleð,
fægrum fold-wæstmum,   þonne afysed bið.

655   Þæt sindon þa word,   swa us gewritu secgað,
hleoþor haligra,   þe him to heofonum bið,
to þam mildan Gode,   mod afysed,
in dreama dream,   þær hi dryhtne to giefe
worda ond weorca   wynsumne stenc

660   in þa mæran gesceaft   meotude bringað,
in þæt leohte lif.   Sy him lof symle
þurh woruld worulda   ond wuldres blæd,
ar ond onwald,   in þam uplican
rodera rice.   He is on ryht cyning

praise, to whom alone is everlasting honor forever more. He never had any beginning, nor his happiness any origin. Though he was born here on earth, brought into the habit-   638
able world in the form of a child, the holy abundance of his powers remained high above the heavens, his glory uninter- rupted. Although he had to undergo the torment of death, severe torture on the tree of the cross, on the third day after the destruction of his body he received life again through his Father's help. So too the young phoenix in its home sig-   646
nifies the power of God's Son, when from ash it awakens again into a life above every life, strengthened in its limbs. Just as the savior, by parting with his body, provided us help and life without end, so the bird, when moved to depart, loads its two wings with sweet and pleasant spices, with lovely fruits of the earth.

As writings tell us, that action signifies the words and the   655
speech of holy persons whose minds are eager to depart for heaven to their merciful God, into the joy of joys; there they will bring the pleasing fragrance of their words and deeds into that glorious state, that radiant life, as a gift to the Lord their creator. To him through all ages let there be praise con- tinually and abundance of glory, honor and dominion in the celestial kingdom of the heavens. By right he is king of earth   664

665   middan-geardes   ond mægen-þrymmes
       wuldre biwunden   in þære wlitigan byrig.
       Hafað us alyfed   *lucis auctor*
       þæt we motun her   *merueri,*
       god-dædum begietan   *gaudia in celo,*
670   þær we motun   *maxima regna*
       secan ond gesittan   *sedibus altis,*
       lifgan in lisse   *lucis et pacis,*
       agan eardinga   *almae letitię,*
       brucan blæd-daga,   *blandem et mitem*
675   geseon sigora frean   *sine fine,*
       ond him lof singan   *laude perenne,*
       eadge mid englum.   *Alleluia.*

and encompassed with the glory of majesty in that beautiful
city. The *author of light* has allowed us that, while here, we   667
may *earn* and acquire through good deeds *joys in heaven,*
where we will be permitted to seek the greatest dominions
and take our seats *on lofty thrones,* live in the bliss *of light and
peace,* possess habitations *of generous happiness,* enjoy days of
abundance, look *forever* upon the Lord of victories *as gentle
and kind,* and with *unending adoration* sing out his praise,
blessed as we will be among the angels. *Alleluia.*

POEMS OF WORSHIP
AND PRAYER

The Lord's Prayer (I)

... halig fæder,   þu þe on heofonum eardast,
geweorðad wuldres dreame.   Sy þinum weorcum halgad
noma niþþa bearnum;   þu eart nergend wera.
Cyme þin rice wide,   ond þin rædfæst willa
5   aræred under rodores hrofe,   eac þon on rumre foldan.
   Syle us to dæge   domfæstne blæd,
   hlaf userne,   helpend wera,
   þone singalan,   soðfæst meotod.
   Ne læt usic costunga   cnyssan to swiðe,
10   ac þu us freodom gief,   folca waldend,
   from yfla gehwam,   a to widan feore.

The Lord's Prayer (I)

. . . holy Father, you who dwell in heaven, honored with the
bliss of glory. May your name be sanctified by your cre-
ations, the children of humanity; you are the savior of men.
Let your kingdom come far and wide, and your wise will   4
be established beneath the vault of the sky, as well as on
the spacious earth. Helper of men, give us today a glorious
abundance, our lasting bread, O faithful creator. Do not let   9
temptations buffet us too greatly, but grant us freedom from
every evil, O ruler of peoples, forever and ever.

The Lord's Prayer (II)

Pater noster:
Þu eart ure fæder,   ealles wealdend,
cyninc on wuldre.   Forðam we clypiað to þe,
are biddað,   nu þu yþost miht
5   sawle alysan.   Þu hig sændest ær
þurh þine æþelan hand   in to þam flæsce;
ac hwar cymð heo nu,
buton þu, engla God,   eft hig alyse,
sawle of synnum   þurh þine soðan miht?
10   *Qui es in celis:*
Ðu eart on heofonum   hiht and frofor,
blissa beorhtost;   ealle abugað to þe,
þinra gasta þrym,   anre stæfne
clypiað to Criste,   cweþað ealle þus:
15   "Halig eart þu, halig,   heofon-engla cyningc,
drihten ure,   and þine domas synd
rihte and rume,   ræcað efne gehwam,
æghwilcum men,   agen gewyrhta.
Wel bið ðam þe wyrcð   willan þinne!"
20   *Sanctificetur nomen tuum:*
Swa is gehalgod   þin heah nama
swiðe mærlice   manegum gereordum,
twa and hund-seofontig,   þæs þe secgað bec,
þæt þu, engla God,   ealle gesettest

The Lord's Prayer (II)

Our Father:

You are our Father, ruler of all, a king in glory. We therefore call upon you, pray for your grace, since you can most easily set the soul free. By your noble hand you previously sent it into the flesh; but where will it go now, O God of angels, if you do not release the soul from its sins by your just power?

Who are in heaven:

You are our hope and consolation in heaven, the brightest of joys; all bow down to you, the company of your spirits; they call upon Christ with a single voice and all say thus: "Holy, holy are you, king of the heavenly angels, our Lord, and your judgments are just and far-reaching; they extend to each and every person his own deserts. It is well for the one who carries out your will!"

Hallowed be your name:

Thus is your exalted name sanctified very gloriously in many tongues, seventy-two in number, as books relate that you, the God of angels, established all custom and ways of life for

69

25 ælcere þeode   þeaw and wisan.

Þa wurþiað þin weorc   wordum and dædum,
þurh gecynd clypiað   and Crist heriað
and þin lof lædað,   lifigenda God,
swa þu eart geæþelod   geond ealle world.

30   *Adveniat regnum tuum:*

Cum nu and mildsa,   mihta waldend,
and us þin rice alyf,   rihtwis dema,
earda selost   and ece lif,
þar we sibbe and lufe   samod gemetað,

35 eagena beorhtnysse   and ealle mirhðe,
þar bið gehyred   þin halige lof
and þin micele miht,   mannum to frofre,
swa þu, engla God,   eallum blissast.

Fiat voluntas tua:

40 Gewurðe þin willa,   swa þu waldend eart
ece geopenod   geond ealle world,
and þu þe silf eart   soðfæst dema,
rice ræd-bora,   geond rumne grund.
Swa þin heah-setl is   heah and mære,

45 fæger and wurðlic,   swa þin fæder worhte,
æþele and ece,   þar ðu on sittest
on sinre swiðran healf.   Þu eart sunu and fæder,
ana ægþer;   swa is þin æþele gecynd
micclum gemærsod.   And þu monegum helpst,

50 ealra cyninga þrym,   clypast ofer ealle;
bið þin wuldor-word   wide gehyred,
þonne þu þine fyrde   fægere geblissast,
sylest miht and mund   micclum herige,
and þe þanciað   þusenda fela,

55 eal engla þrym,   anre stæfne.

every nation. With their words and deeds they honor your works, by natural impulse they call upon and laud Christ, and they tell forth your praise, O living God, because you are renowned through all the world.

Your kingdom come: 30
Come now and show mercy, O ruler of powers, and bestow on us your kingdom, the best of habitations and everlasting life, O righteous judge, where we will encounter peace and love together, brightness for our eyes and all delight, where your holy praise and your great power will be heard as a consolation for human beings, just as you, O God of angels, gladden them all.

Your will be done: 39
May your will be carried out as you are ruler, everlastingly revealed throughout all the world, and as you yourself are a righteous judge, a mighty counselor across the spacious earth. Thus your high throne is as exalted and glorious, beautiful and honorable, as your Father nobly and everlastingly fashioned it, where you yourself sit at his right side. You are Son and Father, both and one; thus is your noble nature greatly esteemed. And you, the majesty of all kings, ex-   49
tend help to many, raise your voice above them all; your glorious word will be heard far and wide, when you graciously gladden your host, give strength and protection to that great army, and the many thousands of them, the entire force of angels, give thanks to you with one voice.

Sicut in celo:
Swa þe on heofonum   heah-þrymnesse
æþele and ece   a þanciað,
clæne and gecorene   Cristes þegnas,
60   singað and biddað   soðfæstne God
are and gifnesse   ealre þeode;
þonne þu him tiðast,   tyr-eadig cyningc,
swa þu ead-mod eart   ealre worlde.
Sy þe þanc and lof   þinre mildse,
65   wuldor and willa;   þu gewurðod eart
on heofon-rice,   heah casere,
    Et in terra,
and on eorðan,   ealra cyninga
help and heafod,   halig læce,
70   reðe and rihtwis,   rum-heort hlaford.
Þu geæþelodest þe   ealle gesceafta,
and tosyndrodest hig   siððan on manega,
sealdest ælcre gecynde   agene wisan
and a þine mildse   ofer manna bearn.
75   *Panem nostrum cotidianum:*
Swa mid sibbe   sænst urne hlaf
dæg-hwamlice   duguðe þinre,
rihtlice dælest
mete þinum mannum   and him mare gehætst
80   æfter forð-siðe   —þines fæder rice,
þæt wæs on fruman   fægere gegearwod,
earda selost   and ece lif—
gif we soð and riht   symle gelæstað.
    Da nobis hodie:
85   Syle us to dæg,   drihten, þine
mildse and mihta   and ure mod gebig,
þanc and þeawas,   on þin gewil.

72

As it is in heaven: 56

Thus do the exalted powers, noble and everlasting, give
thanks to you in heaven always, pure and chosen soldiers of
Christ sing and pray to the righteous God for his favor and
forgiveness toward the entire people; you then grant that to
them, O king blessed in glory, since you are benevolent to all
the world. Thanks and praise, glory and joy be to you on ac-
count of your mercy; you are honored as exalted emperor in
the heavenly kingdom,

So too on the earth: 67

as well as on earth, being the help and head of all kings, a
holy physician, severe and righteous, a generous Lord. For
your sake you ennobled all creatures and afterward divided
them into multitudes, gave to each kind its own character
and always bestowed your mercy among the children of
men.

Our daily bread: 75

Thus to your troop you accordingly dispense our bread in
peace each day; you justly divide nourishment among your
people, and you promise them more after their death—
namely the kingdom of your Father, which was beautifully
prepared in the beginning, the best of habitations and ever-
lasting life—if we constantly do what is just and right.

Give us today: 84

Give us today, O Lord, your mercy and strength, and bend
to your will our minds, our thoughts and our habits. Enclose

Bewyrc us on heortan   haligne gast
fæste on innan,   and us fultum sile,
90   þæt we moton wyrcan   willan þinne
and þe betæcan,   tyr-eadig cyningc,
sawle ure   on þines silfes hand.

Et dimitte nobis debita nostra:
Forgif us ure synna,   þæt us ne scamige eft,
95   drihten ure,   þonne þu on dome sitst
and ealle men   up arisað
þe fram wife and fram were   wurdon acænned.
Beoð þa gebrosnodon   ban mid þam flæsce
ealle ansunde   eft geworden;
100   þar we swutollice   siððan oncnawað
eal þæt we geworhton   on world-rice:
betere and wyrse   þar beoð buta geara.
Ne magon we hit na dyrnan,   for ðam þe hit drihten wat,
and þar gewitnesse beoð   wuldor-micele,
105   heofon-waru and eorð-waru,   hel-waru þridde.
Þonne bið egsa   geond ealle world,
þar man us tyhhað on dæg   twegen eardas,
drihtenes are   oððe deofles þeowet,
swa hwaðer we geearniað   her on life,
110   þa hwile þe ure mihta   mæste wæron.

Sicut et nos dimittimus debitoribus nostris:
Ac þonne us alyseð   lifigende God
sawle ure,   swa we her forgifað
earmon mannum   þe wið us agilt.

115   *Et ne nos inducas in temtationem:*
And na us þu ne læt   laðe beswican
on costunga,   cwellan and bærnan
sawla ure,   þeah we sinna fela

74

the Holy Spirit securely in our hearts, and give us support so that we can work your will and commend our souls into your own hand, O king abounding in glory.

And forgive us our debts: 93

Forgive us our sins, so that we are not ashamed later, O our Lord, when you sit in judgment and all arise who have been born of man and woman. Those decayed bones, together with their flesh, will all be made whole again; afterward, in that place we will recognize clearly all that we did in the kingdom of this world: our better and our worse deeds will both be as present there. By no means will we be able to   103 conceal anything, because the Lord knows it, and in that place there will be a magnificent multitude of witnesses: the inhabitants of heaven and of earth, and of hell third of all. There will be terror throughout all the world when, on that day, two abodes are established for us, the favor of the Lord or enslavement to the devil, whichever we earned here in this life while our powers were greatest.

As we forgive our debtors: 111

But the living God will then set our souls free, as we at present forgive those miserable persons who sin against us.

And lead us not into temptation: 115

And by no means allow our foes to lead us by deceit into temptations, to kill and burn our souls, even though we, in our folly, committed many sins day and night, and our idle

didon for ure disige   dæges and nihtes,
120   idele spræce   and unrihte weorc,
þine bodu bræcon.   We þe biddað nu,
ælmihtig God,   are and gifnesse;
ne læt swa heanlice   þin hand-geweorc
on ende-dæge   eal forwurðan,
125   *Set libera nos a malo:*
ac alys us of yfele.   Ealle we beþurfon
Godes gifnesse;   we agylt habbað
and swiðe gesingod.   We ðe, soðfæstan God,
heriað and lofiað,   swa þu, hælend, eart
130   cyne-bearn gecydd   cwycum and deadum,
æþele and ece   ofer ealle þingc.
Þu miht on anre hand   eaðe befealdan
ealne middan-eard.   Swilc is mære cyningc!
Amen:
135   Sy swa þu silf wilt,   soðfæst dema.
We þe, engla God,   ealle heriað,
swa þu eart gewurðod   a on worlda forð.

talk and wrongful deeds broke your commands. We now pray to you, almighty God, for grace and forgiveness; do not allow the work of your hands to perish altogether, so ignominiously, on that last day,

But deliver us from evil: 125

but rather free us from evil. We are all in need of God's forgiveness; we have transgressed and sinned greatly. We praise and glorify you, righteous God, for you, O savior, are revealed to the living and dead as the royal Son, noble and eternal, set over all things. In one of your hands you might easily hold the entire world. Such is the glorious king!

Amen: 134

May it be as you yourself will, O righteous judge. We all praise you, God of angels, for you are honored forever and ever.

The Lord's Prayer (III)

Pater noster qui es in cęlis:
Fæder mann-cynnes,   frofres ic þe bidde,
halig drihten,   þu ðe on heofonum eart.
   Sanctificetur nomen tuum:
5   Þæt sy gehalgod,   hyge-cræftum fæst,
þin nama nu ða,   neriende Crist,
in urum ferhð-locan   fæste gestaðelod.
   Adveniat regnum tuum:
Cume nu to mannum,   mihta wealdend,
10   þin rice to us,   rihtwis dema,
and ðin geleafa   in lif-dæge
on urum mode   mære þurhwunige.
   Fiat voluntas tua sicut in cęlo et in terra:
And þin willa mid us   weorðe gelæsted
15   on eardunge   eorðan rices,
swa hluttor is   in heofon-wuldre,
wynnum gewlitegod   a to worulde forð.
   Panem nostrum cotidianum da nobis hodie:
Syle us nu to dæge,   drihten gumena,
20   heofena heah-cyning,   hlaf urne,
þone ðu onsendest   sawlum to hæle
on middan-eard   manna cynnes:
þæt is se clæna   Crist, drihten God.

The Lord's Prayer (III)

Our Father who are in heaven:
Father of the human race, I pray to you for comfort, O holy
Lord, who are in heaven.

Hallowed be your name:
That your name, savior Christ, now be sanctified, secure in
our thoughts, firmly fixed in the chambers of our hearts.

Your kingdom come: 8
Ruler of powers, righteous judge, let your kingdom now
come to us, and let faith in you gloriously abide in our minds
throughout the days of our life.

Your will be done on earth as it is in heaven:
And let your will be accomplished among us in the dwelling
of the kingdom of earth, just as it is, radiant, in the glory of
heaven, adorned with joys forever.

Give us today our daily bread: 18
Lord of men, supreme king of heaven, give us today our
bread, which you send to earth for salvation of the souls of
humankind: that is Christ the pure, the Lord God.

Et dimitte nobis debita nostra:

25 Forgyf us, gumena weard,   gyltas and synna,
and ure leahtras alet,   lices wunda
and man-dæda,   swa we mildum wið ðe,
ælmihtigum Gode,   oft abylgeað.

Sicut et nos dimittimus debitoribus nostris:

30 Swa swa we forlætað   leahtras on eorþan
þam þe wið us   oft agyltað,
and him wom-dæde   witan ne þencað
for earnunge   ecan lifes.

Et ne nos inducas in temptationem:

35 Ne læd þu us to wite   in wean sorge
ne in costunge,   Crist nerigende,
þy læs we arlease   ealra þinra mildsa
þurh feondscipe   fremde weorðan.

Sed libera nos a malo:

40 And wið yfele gefreo   us eac nu ða
feonda gehwylces;   we in ferhð-locan,
þeoden engla,   ðanc and wuldor,
soð sige-drihten,   secgað georne,
þæs ðe þu us milde   mihtum alysdest

45 fram hæft-nyde   helle-wites.

Amen:

Weorðe þæt.

And forgive us our debts:

Forgive us, O guardian of men, our transgressions and sins, and dismiss our offenses, wounds against the body and works of evil, as often as we offend against you, almighty God, who are kind.

As we forgive our debtors: 29

Just as we, here on earth, forgive the offenses of those who often transgress against us, and as, for the sake of earning life without end, we do not mean to hold against them their perverse deeds.

And lead us not into temptation:

Do not lead us, as a punishment, into the pain of grief or into temptation, O savior Christ, lest we impiously grow estranged from all your mercies through animosity.

But deliver us from evil: 39

And also free us now from the evil of every enemy; in our hearts, O prince of angels, true Lord of victories, we eagerly give thanks and glory for the fact that, by your powers, you have mercifully liberated us from the captivity of hell's torment.

Amen:

So let it be.

The Apostles' Creed

Credo in deum patrem omnipotentem:
Ælmihtig fæder   up on rodore,
þe ða sciran gesceaft   sceope and worhtest
and eorðan wang   ealne gesettest;
5   ic þe ecne God   ænne gecenne,
lustum gelyfe.   Þu eart lifes frea,
engla ord-fruma,   eorðan wealdend,
and ðu gar-secges   grundas geworhtest,
and þu ða menegu canst   mærra tungla.
10   *Et in Iesum Christum filium eius unicum, dominum nostrum:*
Ic on sunu þinne   soðne gelyfe,
hælendne cyning,   hider asendne
of ðam uplican   engla rice,
þone Gabriel,   Godes ærend-raca,
15   sanctan Marian   sylfre gebodode.
Ides unmæne,   heo þæt ærende
onfeng freolice,   and ðe fæder sylfne
under breost-cofan   bearn acende.
Næs ðær gefremmed   firen æt giftum,
20   ac þær halig gast   hand-gyft sealde,
þære fæmnan bosm   fylde mid blisse,
and heo cuðlice   cende swa mærne
eorð-buendum   engla scyppend,
se to frofre gewearð   fold-buendum.

The Apostles' Creed

I believe in God the Father almighty:
Almighty Father in heaven above, who fashioned and made a radiant creation and set in place the entire plain of the earth; I profess and gladly believe that you are the one, eternal God. You are the Lord of life, prince over angels, ruler of earth; you both made the depths of the sea and know the number of the brilliant stars.

And in Jesus Christ, his only Son, our Lord:
I believe in your true Son, the redeeming king, sent here from the heavenly realm of the angels, whom Gabriel, God's messenger, announced to holy Mary in person. A lady without stain, she accepted that commission freely and conceived you, her own Father, as a child within her breast. No sin was committed in that marriage, but the Holy Spirit there provided the wedding gift, filled the woman's breast with joy; and she kindly bore, for the sake of those who dwell on earth, a being so illustrious, the creator of angels, who became a consolation for the world's peoples. And in the

25 And ymbe Bethleem bodedan englas
þæt acenned wæs Crist on eorðan.

Passus sub Pontio Pilato:

Ða se Pontisca Pilatus weold
under Rom-warum rices and doma,
30 þa se deora frea deað þrowade,
on gealgan stah gumena drihten,
þone geomor-mod Iosep byrigde,
and he of helle huðe gefette,
of þam susl-hofe, sawla manega,
35 het ða uplicne eþel secan.

Tertia die resurrexit a mortuis:

Þæs þy ðriddan dæge þeoda wealdend
aras, rices frea, recene of moldan,
and he XL daga folgeras sine
40 runum arette; and ða his rice began,
þone uplican eðel secan,
cwæð þæt he nolde nænne forlætan
þe him forð ofer þæt fylian wolde
and mid fæstum sefan freode gelæstan.

45 *Credo in spiritum sanctum:*

Ic haligne gast hihte beluce,
emne swa ecne swa is aðor gecweden
fæder oððe freo-bearn folca gereordum.
Ne synd þæt þreo godas, þriwa genemned,
50 ac is an God, se ðe ealle hafað
þa þry naman þinga gerynum,
soð and sigefæst ofer side gesceaft,
wereda wuldor-gyfa, wlanc and ece.

vicinity of Bethlehem angels announced that Christ was born on earth.

Who suffered under Pontius Pilate: 27

Pilate the Pontian held authority and jurisdiction under the Romans when the precious savior suffered death, the Lord of men mounted the gallows; sad in mind, Joseph buried him, and he [Christ] carried off plunder out of hell, many souls from that hall of torture; he commanded them to seek a heavenly homeland.

On the third day he rose from the dead: 36

Three days later, the ruler of peoples, the Lord of the kingdom, rose swiftly out of the earth, and for forty days he gladdened his followers with secret teachings. And then he began to seek his kingdom, that heavenly homeland. He said that he would leave no one behind who wished to follow him beyond that point and with a faithful heart attain his friendship.

I believe in the Holy Spirit: 45

I embrace with hope the Holy Spirit, eternal in the same way as the Father or noble Son is said to be, according to human speech. They are not three gods named three ways, but 49 rather there is one God who mysteriously possesses all three names; above the broad creation, he is true and victorious, a giver of glorious gifts to his followers, a being bold and eternal.

Sanctam ęcclesiam catholicam:

55   Eac ic gelyfe   þæt syn leofe Gode
þe þurh ænne geþanc   ealdor heriað,
heofona heah-cyning   her for life.

Sanctorum communionem:

And ic gemænscipe   mærne getreowe
60   þinra haligra   her for life.

Remissionem peccatorum:

Lisse ic gelyfe   leahtra gehwylces.

Carnis resurrectionem:

And ic þone ærest   ealra getreowe
65   flæsces on foldan   on þa forhtan tid,

Et vitam ęternam,

þær ðu ece lif   eallum dælest,
swa her manna gehwylc   metode gecwemað.

In the holy catholic church: 54
I also believe that they are dear to God who, here in this life,
praise their Lord, the supreme king of heaven, with a united
mind.

In the communion of the saints:
And here during this life, I trust in the illustrious fellowship
of your saints.

In the forgiveness of sins: 61
I believe in remission of every sin.

In the resurrection of the flesh:
And I believe in the resurrection of the flesh for all people
on earth at that dread hour,

And in life everlasting,
where you will bestow life without end on all, to the degree
that each human being here pleases his creator.

The Gloria patri (I)

Gloria:
Sy þe wuldor and lof   wide geopenod
geond ealle þeoda,   þanc and wylla,
mægen and mildse   and ealles modes lufu,
5   soðfæstra sib,   and ðines sylfes dom
wuldre gewlitegod,   swa ðu wealdan miht
eall eorðan mægen   and up-lyfte,
wind and wolcna;   wealdest eall on riht.

Patri et filio et spiritui sancto:
10   Þu eart frofra fæder   and feorh-hyrde,
lifes latteow,   leohtes wealdend,
asyndrod fram synnum,   swa ðin sunu mære
þurh clæne gecynd,   cyning ofer ealle,
beald gebletsod,   boca lareow,
15   heah hige-frofer   and halig gast.

Sicut erat in principio:
Swa wæs on fruman   frea man-cynnes
ealre worulde   wlite and frofer,
clæne and cræftig.   Þu gecyddest þæt
20   þa ðu, ece God,   ana gewrohtest
þurh halige miht   heofonas and eorðan,
eardas and up-lyft   and ealle þing.
Þu settest on foldan   swyðe feala cynna
and tosyndrodost hig   syððon on mænego.

The Gloria patri (I)

Glory:

Throughout all peoples, let glory and praise be widely proclaimed to you, thanksgiving and affection, power and mercy, wholehearted love, the peace of the righteous, and your own greatness, resplendent with glory, as you are able to control all forces on earth and the air above, the wind and the clouds; you govern everything by right.

To the Father, and to the Son, and to the Holy Spirit: 9

You are the Father of consolations and guardian of our vital spirit, one who leads to life and is the ruler of light, separated from sins, as is your illustrious Son through his pure nature, a king over all, blessed and courageous, an expounder of books, an exalted comforter of hearts and a holy spirit.

As it was in the beginning: 16

Thus in the beginning the Lord of humankind, pure and mighty, was the beauty and consolation of all the world. You have revealed that you alone, eternal God, then created the heavens and the earth, the lands and the air and all things, through your holy power. You set upon the face of the earth   23 a great many species and afterward separated them into

25 Þu gewrohtest, ece God,   ealle gesceafta
on syx-dagum,   and on þone seofoðan þu gerestest.
Þa wæs geforðad   þin fægere weorc,
and ðu sunnan-dæg   sylf halgodest
and gemærsodest hine   manegum to helpe.

30 Þone heahan dæg   healdað and freoðiaþ
ealle þa ðe cunnon   cristene þeawas,
halige heort-lufan   and ðæs hehstan gebod;
on drihtnes namon   se dæg is gewurðod.

Et nunc et semper:

35 And nu and symble   þine soðan weorc
and ðin mycele miht   manegum swytelað,
swa þine cræftas heo   cyðaþ wide
ofer ealle woruld;   ece standeþ
Godes hand-geweorc,   groweð swa ðu hete.

40 Ealle þe heriað   halige dreamas
clænre stefne   and cristene bec,
eall middan-eard,   and we men cweþað
on grunde her: "Gode lof and ðanc,
ece willa,   and ðin agen dom!"

45 *Et in secula seculorum:*

And on worulda woruld   wunað and rixað
cyning innan wuldre,   and his þa gecorenan,
heah-þrymnesse   halige gastas,
wlitige englas,   and wuldor-gyfe:

50 soðe sibbe,   sawla þancung,
modes miltse.   Þær is seo mæste lufu.
Haligdomas   heofones syndon
þurh þine ecan word   æghwær fulle,
swa syndon þine mihta   ofer middan-geard

55 swutele and gesyne,   þæt ðu hy sylf worhtest.

90

THE GLORIA PATRI (I)

their multitudes. You, eternal God, fashioned all creatures in six days, and on the seventh you rested. Then your beautiful work was accomplished, and you yourself made Sunday holy and celebrated it as a relief for many. All those who 30 know Christian customs, who know holy, heartfelt love and the command of the most high, observe and safeguard that exalted day; by the Lord's name that day is honored.

Is now and ever shall be: 34

To many your true works and your great might are manifest both now and always, as they reveal your powers widely over all the world; God's handiwork stands forever and flourishes, just as you commanded it. All holy choirs praise you 40 with pure voices, as do Christian books and all the earth, and we human beings here, on the lowest plane, say, "To God be praise and thanksgiving, everlasting love and your own glory!"

Forever and ever: 45

And forever and ever, surrounded by glory, the king abides and reigns; and so do his chosen ones, sanctified spirits of the supreme majesty, beautiful angels; and so do his glorious gifts: true bonds of peace, the gratitude of souls, mercy from the heart. In that place is the greatest love. The sanctuaries 51 of heaven are filled throughout with your everlasting words, just as your powerful deeds are clear and manifest in this world, and the fact that you yourself performed them.

Amen: 56

Amen:

We þæt soðlice   secgað ealle
þurh clæne gecynd   þu eart cyning on riht,
clæne and cræftig.   Þu gecyddest þæt
60   þa ðu, mihtig God,   man geworhtest
and him on dydest   oruð and sawul,
sealdest word and gewitt   and wæstma gecynd,
cyddest þine cræftas.   Swylc is Cristes miht!

Truly we say, all of us, that through your sinless nature you are a king by right, pure and powerful. You revealed as much when you, O mighty God, created man and put in him breath and a soul, gave him language and understanding and a natural fertility, and you revealed thereby your creative powers. Such is the might of Christ!

The Gloria patri (II)

Wuldor sy ðe and wurð-mynt,   wereda drihten,
fæder, on foldan,   fægere gemæne
mid sylfan sunu   and soðum gaste.
Amen.

The Gloria patri (II)

Glory and honor be to you, Lord of hosts, to the Father [be glory] on earth, in harmonious fellowship with your own Son and the true Spirit. Amen.

The Kentish Hymn

Wuton wuldrian   weorada dryhten
halgan hlioðor-cwidum,   hiofen-rices weard,
lufian liofwendum   lifęs agend,
and him simle sio   sigefęst wuldor
5 uppe mid ænglum,   and on eorðan sibb
gumena gehwilcum   goodes willan.

    We ðe heriað   halgum stefnum
and þe blætsiað,   bile-wit fęder,
and ðe þanciað,   þioda walden,
10 ðines weorðlican   wuldor-dreames
and ðinra miclan   mægena gerena,
ðe ðu, God dryhten,   gastes mæhtum
hafest on gewealdum   hiofen and eorðan,
an ece fęder,   ælmehtig God.

15   Ðu eart cyninga cyningc   cwicera gehwilces,
ðu eart sigcfest sunu   and soð hęlend
ofer ealle gescęft   angla and manna.
Ðu, dryhten God,   on dreamum wunast
on ðære upplican   æðelan ceastre,
20 frea folca gehwæs,   swa ðu æt fruman wære
efen-eadig bearn   agenum fæder.

The Kentish Hymn

With holy utterances let us glorify the Lord of hosts, the guardian of the heavenly kingdom, let us love with affection the author of life, and to him, among the angels above, let triumphant glory be given unceasingly, and on earth peace to every man of good will.

With holy voices we praise you and we bless you, blame- 7
less Father, and we thank you, O ruler of peoples, for the estimable bliss that is yours in glory, as well as for the mysterious workings of your great powers, through which you, Lord God, almighty God, the one, eternal Father, hold in governance heaven and earth by the strength of your Spirit.

Over every living being you are the king of kings, you are 15
the victorious Son and true savior of the whole creation of angels and humans. You dwell among joys, Lord God, Lord of every people, in that noble city up above, just as you existed in the beginning, a Son equal in blessedness to his own Father.

Ðu eart heofenlic lioht   and ðæt halige lamb,
ðe ðu man-scilde   middan-geardes
for þinre arfęstnesse   ealle towurpe,
25   fiond geflæmdest,   follc generedes,
blode gebohtest   bearn Israela,
ða ðu ahofe   ðurh ðæt halige triow
ðinre ðrowunga   ðiostra senna,
þæt ðu on hæah-setle   heafena rices
30   sitest sige-hræmig   on ða swiðran hand
ðinum God-fæder,   gasta gemyndig.
Mildsa nu, meahtig,   manna cynne,
and of leahtrum ales   ðine ða liofan gescęft,
and us hale gedo,   heleða sceppend,
35   niða nergend,   for ðines naman are.
   Ðu eart soðlice   simle halig,
and ðu eart ana   æce dryhten,
and ðu ana bist   eallra dema
cwucra ge deadra,   Crist nergende,
40   forðan ðu on ðrymme ricsast,   and on ðrinesse
and on annesse,   ealles waldend,
hiofena heah-cyninc,   haliges gastes
fegere gefelled   in fæder wuldre.

You are heavenly light and the holy lamb who, for the   22
sake of your mercy, cast down all the sinful evil of this world,
put the enemy to flight, rescued your people; you redeemed
by blood the children of Israel when, through the holy tree
of your sufferings, you lifted the darkness of sins, so that,
now exultant in victory and mindful of souls, you sit on a
lofty throne in the heavenly kingdom at the right hand of
God your Father. O mighty one, have mercy now on human-   32
kind, free your cherished creation from its sins, and save us,
creator of men, savior of humanity, for the sake of the honor
of your name.

Truly, you are holy always, you alone are the eternal Lord,   36
and you alone are the judge of all the living and the dead, O
savior Christ; for you reign in majesty, in Trinity and in unity,
as ruler of all, the supreme king of heaven, splendidly filled
with the Holy Spirit in the glory of the Father.

Cædmon's Hymn

Nu scylun hergan   hefaen-ricaes uard,
metudæs maecti   end his mod-gidanc,
uerc uuldur-fadur,   sue he uundra gihuaes,
eci dryctin,   or astelidæ.
5   He aerist scop   aelda barnum
heben til hrofe,   haleg scepen;
tha middun-geard   mon-cynnæs uard,
eci dryctin,   æfter tiadæ,
firum foldu,   frea allmectig.

Cædmon's Hymn

Now we must praise the guardian of the heavenly kingdom,
the might of the creator, and the purpose of his mind, the
works of the Father of glory, when he, the eternal Lord, laid
the beginnings of every wondrous thing. A holy creator, he   5
first fashioned heaven as a roof for the children of men; then
the guardian of humankind, the eternal Lord, almighty ruler,
afterward fashioned the habitable world, the earth for men.

Godric's Hymn

Sainte Marie uirgine,
moder Iesu Cristes Nazarene,
onfo, scild, help þin Godric,
onfang, bring hehlic wið þe in Godes ric.

5   Sainte Marie, Cristes bur,
maidenes clenhad, moderes flur,
dilie mine sinne, rixe in min mod,
bring me to winne wið self God.

Godric's Hymn

Saint Mary, virgin, mother of Jesus Christ the Nazarene, receive, protect, and help your Godric, receive and bring him gloriously with you into God's kingdom.

    Saint Mary, Christ's bower, purity of virgins, flower of   5
motherhood, wipe out my sins, reign in my heart, bring me
to joy with God himself.

A Prayer

Æla, drihten leof! Æla, dema God!
Geara me, ece waldend.
Ic wat mine saule synnum forwundod;
gehæl þu hy, heofena drihten,
5 and gelacna þu hy, lifes ealdor,
forþan ðu eðest miht ealra læca
ðæra þe gewurde side oððe wyde.
Æla, frea beorhta, folkes scippend!
Gemilsa þyn mod me to gode,
10 sile þyne are þynum earminge.
Se byð earming þe on eorðan her
dæiges and nihtes deofle campað
and hys willan wyrcð; wa him þære mirigðe,
þonne he ða hand-lean hafað and sceawað,
15 bute he þæs yfeles ær geswyce.
Se byð eadig, se þe on eorðan her
dæiges and nyhtes drihtne hyræð
and a hys willan wyrcð; wel hym þæs geweorkes,
ðonne he ða hand-lean hafað and sceawað,
20 gyf he eal-teawne ende gedreogeð.
Æla, leohtes leoht! Æla, lyfes wynn!
Getiþa me, tir-eadig kyning,
þonne ic minre sawle swegles bydde,
ece are. Þu eart eaðe, God,

A Prayer

O beloved Lord! O God my judge! Make me ready, eternal ruler: I know that my soul is wounded through and through with sins; make it whole, Lord of heaven, and heal it, ruler of life, since of all physicians who ever lived, far and wide, you are the one who most easily can.

O radiant Lord, creator of your people! Make your mind 8 merciful for my benefit; bestow your favor upon your poor creature. A poor wretch is he who fights on the devil's side and does his will here on earth; woe to him for such delight when he receives and beholds its reward, unless he quits that evil beforehand. Blessed will he be who obeys the Lord day 16 and night and always does his will here on earth; it will be well for him in return for that effort, when he receives and beholds its reward, provided he carries the work through to a perfect end.

O light from light! O life's joy! When I seek heaven for 21 my soul, then grant me everlasting favor, O king blessed in glory. You are gentle, O God; alone over all the earth and

25   hæfst and waldest
       ana ofer ealle   eorðan and heofonas
       syddra gesceafta.   Ðu eart soð meotod,
       ana ofer ealle   eorð-bugende,
       swilce on heofonum up   þu eart hælend God.

30   Ne mæg þe aherian   hæleða ænig;
       þeh us gesomnie   geond sidne grund,
       men ofer moldan,   geond ealne middan-eard,
       ne mage we næfre asæcgan,   ne þæt soðe witan,
       hu þu æðele eart,   ece drihten.

35   Ne þeah engla werod   up on heofenum
       snotra tosomne   sæcgan ongunnon,
       ne magon hy næfre areccean,   ne þæt gerim wytan,
       hu þu mære eart,   mihtig drihten.
       Ac is wunder mycel,   wealdend engla,

40   gif þu hit sylfa wast,   sigores ealdor,
       hu þu mære eart,   mihtig and mægen-strang,
       ealra kyninga kyning,   Crist lifiende,
       ealra worulda scippend,   wealdend engla,
       ealra dugeþa duguð,   drihten hælend!

45   Ðu eart se æðela   þe on ær-dagum
       ealra femnena wyn   fægere akende
       on Bethleem ðære byrig   beornum to frofre,
       eallum to are   ylda bearnum,
       þam þe gelyfað   on lyfiendne God

50   and on þæt ece leoht   uppe on roderum.
       Ðyn mægen ys swa mære,   mihtig drihten,
       swa þæt ænig ne wat   eorð-buende
       þa deopnesse   drihtnes mihta,
       ne þæt ænig ne wat   engla hades

55   þa heahnisse   heofena kyninges.

the heavens you own and govern the wide creation. You are ²⁷
the true creator, alone over all who dwell on earth, and like-
wise in the heavens above you are God the savior. No one
can praise you fully; even if we people on earth were to as-
semble across its wide foundation, from over the entire
world, we could never entirely express or truly comprehend
how noble you are, eternal Lord. And even if hosts of angels ³⁵
in heaven above began to tell of it, wisely and with one ac-
cord, they could never entirely explain or know the measure
of how glorious you are, O mighty Lord. Rather it is a great ³⁹
marvel if you yourself, ruler of angels, Lord of victory, know
just how glorious you are, how powerful and strong, a king
of all kings, the living Christ, creator of all worlds, ruler of
angels, majesty of all majesties, Lord and savior!

You are the noble one to whom, long ago, the joy of all ⁴⁵
women graciously gave birth in the town of Bethlehem, to
be a consolation for men, a means of grace for all the chil-
dren of humanity who believe in the living God and in that
eternal light in heaven above. Your power is so glorious, ⁵¹
mighty Lord, that there is no one dwelling on earth who
knows the depths of the Lord's might, nor does any mem-
ber of the angelic order know the sublimity of the king of
heaven.

     Ic þe andette,   ælmihtig God,
     þæt ic gelyfe on þe,   leofa hælend,
     þæt þu eart se miccla   and se mægen-stranga
     and se ead-moda   ealra goda
60   and se ece kyning   ealra gesceafta,
     and ic eom se litla for þe   and se lyðra man,
     se her syngige   swiðe genehhe,
     dæges and nihtes   do swa ic ne sceolde,
     hwile mid weorce,   hwile mid worde,
65   hwile mid geþohte,   þearle scyldi,
     inwit-niðas   oft and gelome.
     Ac ic þe halsige nu,   heofena drihten,
     and gebidde me to þe,   bearna selost,
     þæt ðu gemilsige me,   mihtig drihten,
70   heofena heah-kyning   and se halga gast,
     and gefylste me,   fæder ælmihtig,
     þæt ic þinne willan   gewyrcean mæge,
     ær ic of þysum lænan   lyfe gehweorfe.
     Ne forweorn þu me,   wuldres drihten,
75   ac getyþa me,   tyr-eadig kyning,
     læt me mid englum   up siðian,
     sittan on swegle,
     herian heofonas God   haligum reorde
     a butan ende.   Amen.

To you I confess, almighty God, that I believe in you, be- 56
loved savior, believe that of all gods you are the great one,
powerful and benevolent, and the eternal king of all crea-
tures; and I confess that before you I am a small and insig-
nificant person, that I sin here very often, do day and night
what I ought not do, sometimes by deed, sometimes by
word, sometimes by thought—hostile intentions that I, be-
ing thoroughly sinful, act upon often and frequently. But I 67
invoke you, Lord of heaven, and pray to you, best of sons,
that you have mercy on me, O mighty Lord, supreme king
of heaven, and that the Holy Spirit would do so as well; and
that you, almighty Father, would assist me so that I may ac-
complish your will before I depart this transitory life. Lord 74
of glory, do not scorn me, but rather grant me this, O king
blessed in glory: allow me to journey upward with the an-
gels, to take my seat in heaven, to praise forever the God of
heaven with a sanctified voice. Amen.

Resignation (A)

Age mec se ælmihta God,
helpe min se halga dryhten!   Þu gesceope heofon ond eorþan
   ond wundor eall,   min wundor-cyning,
   þe þær on sindon,   ece dryhten,
5   micel ond manigfeald.   Ic þe, mære God,
   mine sawle bebeode   ond mines sylfes lic,
   ond min word ond min weorc,   witig dryhten,
   ond eal min leoþo,   leohtes hyrde,
   ond þa manigfealdan   mine geþohtas.
10   Getacna me,   tungla hyrde,
   þær selast sy   sawle minre
   to gemearcenne   meotudes willan,
   þæt ic þe geþeo   þinga gehwylce,
   ond on me sylfum,   soðfæst cyning,
15   ræd arære.   Regn-þeof ne læt
   on sceade sceþþan,   þeah þe ic scyppendum
   wuldor-cyninge   waccor hyrde,
   ricum dryhtne,   þonne min ræd wære.
   Forgif me to lisse,   lifgende God,
20   bitre bealo-dæde.   Ic þa bote gemon,
   cyninga wuldor,   cume to, gif ic mot.

Resignation (A)

May almighty God keep me, may the holy Lord help me!
You, my wondrous king, eternal Lord, fashioned heaven and
earth and all the wonders that are in them, great and mani-
fold. To you I commend, O illustrious God, my soul and   5
my own body, my words and my works; to you, wise Lord,
guardian of light, I commend all my limbs and my manifold
thoughts. Show me, O guardian of the stars, where it is best
for my soul to observe the creator's will, that I may find fa-
vor with you in everything and nurture in me what is benefi-
cial, O righteous king. Do not permit the great thief to work   15
his harm in the shadows, even though I have obeyed you as
creator, as glorious king and powerful Lord, less often than
was good for me. O living God, mercifully forgive me those
hurtful wrongs. I remember their remedy, O glory of kings,
and will draw near to it, if I am allowed.

Forgif þu me, min frea,   fierst ond ondgiet
ond geþyld ond gemynd   þinga gehwylces
þara þu me, soþfæst cyning,   sendan wylle
25   to cunnunge.   Nu þu const on mec
firen-dæda fela;   feorma mec hwæþre,
meotod, for þinre miltse,   þeah þe ic ma fremede
grimra gylta   þonne me God lyfde.
Hæbbe ic þonne þearfe   þæt ic þine seþeah,
30   halges heofon-cyninges,   hyldo getilge
leorendum dagum,   lif æfter oþrum
geseo ond gesece,   þæt me siþþan þær
unne arfæst God   ecan dreames,
lif alyfe,   þeah þe lætlicor
35   bette bealo-dæde   þonne bibodu wæron
halgan heofon-mægnes.
                            Hwæt, þu me her fela
... forgeafe.   Gesette minne hyht on þec,
forhte fore-þoncas,   þæt hio fæstlice
stonde gestaðelad.   Onstep minne hige,
40   gæsta God cyning,   in gearone ræd.
Nu ic fundige to þe,   fæder mon-cynnes,
of þisse worulde,   nu ic wat þæt ic sceal,
ful unfyr faca;   feorma me þonne,
wyrda waldend,   in þinne wuldor-dream,
45   ond mec geleoran læt,   leofra dryhten,
geoca mines gæstes.   Þonne is gromra to fela
æfestum eaden,   hæbbe ic þonne
æt frean frofre,   þeah þe ic ær on fyrste lyt
earnode arna.   Forlæt mec englas seþeah
50   geniman on þinne neawest,   nergende cyning,
meotud, for þinre miltse.   Þeah ðe ic mana fela

My Lord, grant me time and insight, patience and mind- 22
fulness concerning everything that you intend, O righteous
king, to send my way as a test. At present you discern many
sinful works in me; take me in nevertheless, O creator, for
the sake of your mercy, even though I have committed more
serious offenses than God would have permitted me. There- 29
fore I have need that I nevertheless seek your protection, O
holy king of heaven, as these days slip away, that I look and
search for a life beyond this one, so that merciful God may
afterward grant me everlasting joy there, bestow life on me,
even though I more sluggishly atoned for wrongs than the
commands of heaven's holy might required.

Behold, you have granted me much here. . . . Upon you I 36
have set my hope, my fearful expectations, that it may rest
securely fixed. Lift up my mind, O God, king of souls, to the
benefit in store for it. From this world I now hasten to you, 41
Father of humankind, since I know that I must leave it in
a very short while; receive me then, ruler of destinies, into
your glorious happiness, and allow me to depart, O Lord of
the beloved, rescuer of my soul. When too many of the cruel 46
are given over to malice, I will have consolation from the
Lord, even though in times previously I merited few of his
favors. Let angels nevertheless bear me into your presence
for your mercy's sake, O saving king, creator. Even though I 51

æfter dogrum dyde,   ne læt þu mec næfre deofol seþeah
þin lim lædan   on laðne sið,
þy læs hi on þone fore-þonc   gefeon motan
55   þy þe hy him sylfum   sellan þuhten
englas ofer-hydige   þonne ece Crist.
Gelugon hy him æt þam geleafan;   forþon hy longe sculon,
werge wihta,   wræce þrowian.
Forstond þu mec ond gestyr him,   þonne storm cyme
60   minum gæste ongegn;   geoca þonne,
mihtig dryhten,   minre sawle,
gefreoþa hyre ond gefeorma hy,   fæder mon-cynnes,
hædre gehogode,   hæl, ece God,
meotod meahtum swiþ!
                         Min is nu þa
65   sefa synnum fah,   ond ic ymb sawle eom
feam siþum forht,   þeah þu me fela sealde
arna on þisse eorþan.   Þe sie ealles þonc
meorda ond miltsa,   þara þu me sealdest.
No ðæs earninga   ænige wæron
70   mid . . .

committed many evils in the course of my days, do not ever
allow devils to lead me, a limb of your body, off on the hated
journey, lest they exult in the same expectation by which
those proud ones supposed themselves to be better than the
eternal Christ. In that belief they were self-deluding; they   57
must therefore long suffer exile as creatures accursed. De-
fend me from them and keep them at bay whenever that
storm comes against my soul; save my soul then, O mighty
Lord, protect and receive it, O Father of humankind; heal it,
anxiously preoccupied as it is, O eternal God, creator strong
in might!

Now my mind is stained with sins, and on occasion I am   64
fearful for my soul, even though you have granted me many
favors on this earth. Thanks be to you for all the rewards and
mercies that you have granted me. By no means were my
merits such, with . . .

POEMS ON
CHRISTIAN LIVING

Almsgiving

Wel bið þam eorle   þe him on innan hafað,
reþe-hygdig wer,   rume heortan;
þæt him biþ for worulde   weorð-mynda mæst,
ond for ussum dryhtne   doma selast.
5   Efne swa he mid wætre   þone weallendan
leg adwæsce   þæt he leng ne mæg
blac byrnende   burgum sceððan,
swa he mid ælmessan   ealle toscufeð
synna wunde,   sawla lacnað.

Almsgiving

It will be well for the man who, being of upright intention, has within him a generous heart; that will be his greatest mark of honor before the world and his greatest glory before our Lord. Just as he might extinguish with water a surg- 5 ing flame so that it can no longer do harm to dwellings as it burns bright, so too with almsgiving he expels all wounds of sin, provides healing for souls.

Homiletic Fragment (I)

. . . sorh cymeð
manig ond mislic   in manna dream.
Eorl oðerne   mid æfþancum
ond mid teon-wordum   tæleð behindan,
5   spreceð fægere beforan   ond þæt facen swa þeah
hafað in his heortan,   hord unclæne.
   Byð þonne þæs wommes gewita   weoruda dryhten.
Forðan se witiga cwæð:
"Ne syle ðu me ætsomne   mid þam synfullum
10   in wita forwyrd,   weoruda dryhten,
ne me on life forleos   mid þam lige-wyrhtum,
þam þe ful smeðe   spræce habbað,
ond in gast-cofan   grimme geþohtas,
gehatað holdlice   swa hyra hyht ne gæð,
15   wære mid welerum."   Wea bið in mode,
siofa synnum fah,   sare geblonden,
gefylled mid facne,   þeah he fæger word
utan ætywe.   Ænlice beoð,
swa ða beon berað   buta ætsomne,
20   arlicne anleofan,   ond ætterne tægel
hafað on hindan,   hunig on muðe,
wynsume wist.   Hwilum wundiaþ
sare mid stinge,   þonne se sæl cymeð.
   Swa bioð gelice   þa leasan men,

Homiletic Fragment (I)

... many a sorrow, and varied in kind, intrudes upon the happiness of human beings. With malice and harmful words one man slanders another behind his back, speaks pleasantly to his face and yet holds treachery at heart, a hidden, corrupt treasure.

In that instant, the Lord of hosts will be witness to the evil deed. That is why the prophet has said: "Do not dispatch me along with the sinful, O Lord of hosts, to perish in torments, nor in this present life abandon me among deceivers who have speech well polished and cruel thoughts in their minds' enclosure; with their lips they loyally promise a fidelity to which their true aspiration does not tend." In the mind of such a person will be misery, a heart stained with sins, mingled with sorrow, filled with treachery, though he make a show of fair words outwardly. They are a peculiar sort, bearing two things at once, in the manner of bees: they have excellent sustenance, honey in their mouths, a delightful food, while behind they possess a poisonous tail. Sometimes, when the opportunity arises, they wound painfully with their sting.

That is what those dishonest people are like, who with

25   þa ðe mid tungan   treowa gehataþ
       fægerum wordum,   facenlice þencaþ
       þonne hie æt nehstan   nearwe beswicaþ;
       hafað on gehatum   hunig-smæccas,
       smeðne syb-cwide,   ond in siofan innan
30   þurh deofles cræft   dyrne wunde.
          Swa is nu þes middan-geard   mane geblonden,
       wanað ond weaxeð.   Wacað se ealda,
       dweleð ond drefeð   dæges ond nihtes
       miltse mid mane,   mægene getryweð,
35   ehteð æfestra,   inwit saweð,
       nið mid geneahe.   Nænig oðerne
       freoð in fyrhðe   nimþe feara hwylc,
       þæt he soðlice   sybbe healde,
       gastlice lufe,   swa him God bebead.
40   Forþan eallunga   hyht geceoseð,
       woruld wynsume,   se ðe wis ne415 bið,
       snottor, searo-cræftig   sawle rædes.
       Uton to þam beteran,   nu we bot cunnon,
       hycgan ond hyhtan,   þæt we heofones leoht
45   uppe mid englum   agan moton
       gastum to geoce,   þonne God wile
       eorðan lifes   ende gewyrcan.

their tongues promise loyalty using fair words and yet who treacherously anticipate the soonest chance to practice cunningly their deception; in their promises they hold the sweet taste of honey, smooth words of friendship, and in their hearts secret wounds, through the devil's scheming.

Thus is this world now shot through with evil, thus it 31 wanes and waxes. The ancient one is vigilant, by day and night he diverts and confounds mercy with evil; he trusts in his own strength, persecutes the righteous, sows discord, strife in abundance. Except for a few, there is no person who 36 so loves at heart his fellow human being that he genuinely upholds friendship and spiritual affection, as God has commanded him to do.

Therefore he who is not wise, not clever or cunning in 40 seeking counsel for his soul, unreservedly chooses earthly expectation, the pleasing world. Since we know the remedy, let us pursue the better choice, aspire and hope that we may possess as our souls' consolation the light of heaven, up above with the angels, whenever God wills to set an end to our earthly life.

Homiletic Fragment (II)

Gefeoh nu on ferðe   ond to frofre geþeoh
dryhtne þinum,   ond þinne dom arær;
heald hord-locan,   hyge fæste bind
mid mod-sefan.   Monig biþ uncuþ
5   treow-geþofta,   teorað hwilum,
waciaþ word-beot.   Swa þeos woruld fareð,
scurum scyndeð   ond gesceap dreogeð.
An is geleafa,   an lifgende,
an is fulwiht,   an fæder ece,
10   an is folces fruma   se þas foldan gesceop,
duguðe ond dreamas.   Dom siþþan weox,
þeah þeos læne gesceaft   longe stode
heolstre gehyded,   helme bedygled,
biþeaht wel treowum,   þystre oferfæðmed.
15   Siþþan geong aweox
mægeð mod-hwatu   mid mon-cynne;
ðær gelicade   þa ... op
in þam hord-fate,   halgan gæste,
beorht on br ... e scan;
20   se wæs ord-fruma   ealles leohtes.

Homiletic Fragment (II)

Rejoice now at heart and, for comfort, find favor with your Lord, and so achieve glory; keep your secret thoughts inside, fetter your mind securely within the heart. Many a dear companion will turn out to be a stranger, will sometimes fail, his boasting words prove feeble. So this world goes, so it hurtles on tempestuously and endures its fate.

There is one faith, one living [Lord], one baptism, one 8 eternal Father; there is one creator of people, he who formed this earth, its excellences and its joys. Its glory later increased, although this transitory creation long stood concealed by darkness, obscured beneath a veil, fully hidden by unformed matter, encompassed with darkness. Afterward in 15 the human race there grew up a courageous young woman; there, in that vessel fit for treasure, it pleased the Holy Spirit, who . . . brightly shone in . . . ; he was the creator of all light.

Aldhelm
(A Verse Preface to
His Treatise *De virginitate*)

Þus me gesette   *sanctus et iustus*
beorn boca gleaw,   *bonus auctor;*
Ealdelm æþele sceop   *etiam fuit*
ipselos on æðele   Angol-Sexna,

5   byscop on Bretene.   Biblos ic nu sceal
ponus et pondus,   pleno cum sensu,
geonges geanoðe   geomres *iamiamque*
secgan, soð nalles leas,   þæt him symle wæs
euthenia   oftor on fylste,

10   *æne* on eðle,   ec ðon ðe se is
yfel on gesæd.   *Etiam nusquam*
ne sceal ladigan   *labor quem tenet,*
encratea,   ac he ealneg sceal
boethia   biddan georne

15   þurh his modes gemind   *micro in cosmo,*
þæt him drihten gyfe   *dinamis* on eorðan,
fortis factor,   þæt he forð simle . . .

Aldhelm
(A Verse Preface to
His Treatise *De virginitate*)

Thus did *a holy and righteous man* compose me, a nobleman
learned in books, *an estimable author;* Aldhelm, a bishop in
Britain, *was also exalted* as a glorious poet in the country of
the Anglo-Saxons. Now I, *a book,* must tell *in all their partic-*   5
ulars the toil and the burden, the lamentation of that young
man, sorrowful *at present;* I must tell not falsehood but truth,
that *lowliness* was more often a constant help to him, *hard-*
ship in his native country, and the fact as well that he is
wrongly criticized. *Even so, the self-mastery, the toil that he sus-*   11
tains, shall *never* acquit him, but in the thoughts of his mind
he must, while *in this lesser world,* always pray eagerly for *help,*
pray that the Lord, *the mighty creator,* would grant him *the*
might while on earth that he may ever henceforth . . .

Thureth
(Commemorative Verses
in a Bishop's Book)

Ic eom halgung-boc;   healde hine dryhten
þe me fægere þus   frætewum belegde.
Þureð to þance   þus het me wyrcean,
to loue and to wurðe   þam þe leoht gesceop.
5   Gemyndi is he   mihta gehwylcre
þæs þe he on foldan   gefremian mæg,
and him geþancie   þeoda waldend
þæs þe he on gemynde   madma manega
wyle gemearcian   metode to lace;
10   and he sceal ęce lean   ealle findan
þæs þe he on foldan   fremaþ to ryhte.

Thureth
(Commemorative Verses in a Bishop's Book)

I am a pontifical; may the Lord preserve him who beautifully covered me with ornaments in this way. Thus as an act of thanksgiving did Thureth command that I be crafted, in praise and honor to the one who created light itself. He [Thureth] is mindful of every virtue by which he can accomplish good on earth, and may the ruler of nations repay him for his willingness in remembering to designate many treasures for an offering to his creator; and he is bound to discover in full an everlasting reward for what he does justly on earth. 5

The Rewards of Piety

Nu lære ic þe   swa man leofne sceal.
Gif þu wille þæt blowende   rice gestigan,
þænne beo þu ead-mod   and ælmes-georn,
wis on wordum,   and wæccan lufa
on hyge halgum   on þas hwilwendan tid,
bliðe mode,   and gebedum filige
oftost symle   þær þu ana sy.
Forðan þæt halige gebed   and seo hluttre lufu
Godes and manna   and seo ælmes-sylen
and se miccla hopa   to þinum hælende,
þæt he þine synna   adwæscan wylle,
and eac oþera fela
godra weorca   glengað and bringað
þa soðfæstan   sauwle to reste
on þa uplican   eadignesse.
Wyrc þæt þu wyrce,   word oððe dæda,
hafa metodes ege   on gemang symle
(þæt is witodlice   wisdomes ord),
þæt þu þæt ece leoht   eal ne forleose.
    Þeos woruld is æt ende,   and we synd wædlan gyt
heofena rices;   þæt is hefig byrden.
And þeah þu æfter þinum ende   eall gesylle
þæt þu on eorðan   ær gestryndes
goda gehwylces,   wylle Gode cweman,

The Rewards of Piety

I will now teach you, just as one ought to teach another who is dear to him. If you wish to ascend to the prosperous kingdom, then be humble and eager to give alms, be wise in your words and, in devout thought, love vigils with a joyful mind during this fleeting time; and, so often as possible, be always about your prayers whenever you are alone. For holy prayer 8 and a pure love of God and of others, and giving alms and having great hope in your savior, that he would blot out your sins — these and many other good works will adorn the righteous soul and bring it to its resting place in heavenly blessedness. Whatever work you perform, whether words or 16 deeds, maintain among them always a fear of the creator (which is indeed the beginning of wisdom), so that you do not utterly lose the light everlasting.

This world is near its end, and we are still destitute of the 20 kingdom of heaven; that is a weighty burden. Even if, after your end, you give away all wealth of every sort that you acquired before on earth, desiring thereby to please God, you

25 ne mihtu mid þæm eallum sauwle þine
  ut alysan, gif heo inne wyrð
  feondum befangen, frofre bedæled,
  welena forwyrned. Ac þu wuldres God,
  ece ælmihtigne, ealninga bidde
30 þæt he þe ne forlæte laðum to handa,
  feondum to frofre; ac þu fleoh þanan,
  syle ælmessan oft and gelome
  digolice. Þæt bið drihtnes lac
  gumena gehwylces þe on God gelyfð.

35 Ceapa þe mid æhtum eces leohtes,
  þy læs þu forweorðe, þænne þu hyra geweald nafast
  to syllanne. Hit bið swiðe yfel
  manna gehwilcum þæt he micel age,
  gif he him God ne ondræt
40 swiðor micle þonne his sylfes gewil.
  Warna þe georne wið þære wambe fylle,
  forþan heo þa unþeawas ealle gesomnað
  þe þære saule swiðost deriað,
  þæt is druncennes and dyrne-geligere,
45 ungemet wilnung ætes and slæpes;
  þa man mæg mid fæstenum
  and forhæfdnessum heonon adrifan,
  and mid cyric-socnum cealdum wederum
  ead-modlice ealluncga biddan
50 heofena drihten þæt he þe hæl gife,
  milde mund-bora, swa him gemet þince.
  And ondræd þu ðe dihle wisan,
  nearwe geþancas, þe on niht becumað,
  syn-lustas foroft swiðe fremman
55 earfoðlice, þy þu earhlice scealt
  gyltas þine swiðe bemurnan,

will not manage with all of it to free your soul if it becomes imprisoned by demons, deprived of comfort, denied riches. Rather you should pray intently to the God of glory, ever- 28 lastingly almighty, that he not abandon you to the hands of enemies, as a consolation to demons; flee from that instead, give alms in secret often and frequently. That will be an offering to the Lord from everyone who believes in God.

Acquire for yourself that everlasting light by means of 35 your possessions, so that you do not perish when giving them away is no longer in your power. It is altogether wrong for any person to own much unless he reveres God a great deal more than his own desire. Zealously guard yourself 41 against stuffing the belly, for it brings together all the vices that most harm the soul, namely drunkenness and secret fornication, immoderate desire for food and for sleep; those vices can be driven away through fasts and abstinence, and a person can, by visiting churches in frigid weather, humbly and earnestly beg the Lord of heaven that he would, as a kind protector, grant you salvation as he thinks fitting. And 52 beware of grievously acting too often and too much on secret habits, distressing thoughts that encroach by night, sinful desires, for which you, gray-haired warrior, will have to

har hilde-rinc; hefie þe ðincaþ
synna þine!
       Forþam þu sylf ongyte
þæt þu alætan scealt læne staþelas,
60   eard and eþel. Uncuð bið þe þænne
tohwan þe þin drihten gedon wille,
þænne þu lengc ne most lifes brucan,
eardes on eþle, swa þu ær dydest,
blissum hremi. Nu þu ðe beorgan scealt,
65   and wið feonda gehwæne fæste healdan
sauwle þine; a hi winnað embe þæt
dæges and nihtes ongean drihtnes lif.
Þu miht hy gefleman, gif þu filian wilt
larum minum, swa ic lære þe
70   digollice, þæt þu on dæg-red oft
ymbe þinre sauwle ræd swiðe smeage,
hu þu þæt ece leoht æfre begytan mæge,
siðe gesecan. Þu scealt glædlice swiðe swincan
wið þæs uplican eþel-rices
75   dæges and nihtes; þu scealt druncen fleon
and þa ofer-fylle ealle forlætan.
Gif þu wilt þa upplican eard-wic ceosan,
þænne scealt þu hit on eorðan ær geþencan,
and þu þe sylfne swiðe gebindan
80   and þa unþeawas ealle forlætan
þe þu on þis life ær lufedest and feddest.
       Þænne gemiltsað þe, N., *mundum qui regit,*
ðeoda þrym-cyningc *thronum sedens*
a butan ende . . .
85   saule þinre . . .
Geunne þe on life *auctor pacis*

lament your crimes greatly and shamefully; your sins will seem burdensome to you then!

You should therefore understand that you will have to 58 give up your transitory foundations, your dwelling and native land. You will not then know to which destination your Lord wills that you be sent, when you can no longer enjoy life, no longer enjoy a dwelling in your native land as you did before, reveling in happiness. You ought to protect yourself now and preserve your soul securely against every foe; they are always striving over that prize by day and night, against 68 the Lord's life. You can put them to flight if you are willing to follow my teachings, as I secretly instruct you, that often, at dawn, you should ponder deeply what benefits your soul, ponder how you can ever obtain that everlasting light, achieve that destiny. You ought to labor hard gladly, day and 73 night, in return for the heavenly native realm; you should flee drunkenness and wholly give up gluttony. If you want to receive that heavenly dwelling, then you must give thought to it beforehand while on earth, and you must restrain yourself severely and abandon all vices that you previously loved and nourished during life.

On you *(insert name)* will he then have mercy *who governs* 82 *the world,* the majestic king of nations, *sitting on his throne,* for ever and ever . . . to your soul . . . May the *author of peace,*

sibbe gesælða,   *salus mundi,*
metod se mæra   *magna virtute,*
and se soðfæsta   *summi filius*
90   fo on fultum,   *factor cosmi,*
se of æþelre wæs   *virginis partu*
clæne acenned   *Christus in orbem,*
metod þurh Marian,   *mundi redemptor,*
and þurh þæne halgan gast.   *Voca frequenter*
95   bide helpes hine,   *clementem deum . . .*
se onsended wæs   *summo de throno*
and þære clænan   *clara voce*
þa gebyrd bodade   *bona voluntate*
þæt heo scolde cennan   *Christum regem,*
100   ealra cyninga cyningc,   *casta vivendo.*
And þu þa soðfæstan   *supplex roga,*
fultumes bidde friclo   *virginem almum,*
and þær æfter to   *omnes sanctos*
blið-mod bidde,   *beatos et iustos,*
105   þæt hi ealle þe   *unica voce*
þingian to þeodne   *thronum regenti,*
ęcum drihtne,   *alta polorum,*
þæt he þine saule,   *summus iudex,*
onfo freolice,   *factor aeternus,*
110   and þe gelæde   *lucem perhennem,*
þær eadige   *animę sanctę*
rice restað,   *regna caelorum.*

the world's salvation, the illustrious creator grant you *by his great power* the happiness of peace during this life, and may the righteous *Son of the most high* receive you with solace, he who is *fashioner of the cosmos,* who was begotten in purity, *born from a noble virgin as Christ upon earth, the world's redeemer* and its creator, brought forth through Mary and through the Holy Spirit. *Call out often,* pray to him for help, *the merciful*   94 *God . . .* who was sent *from the highest throne* and *with good will* announced that birth, *in a resounding voice,* to the chaste woman, announced that she was to give birth to *Christ the king,* king of all kings, *while abiding chaste herself.* And *humbly*   101 *beseech* that righteous woman, pray eagerly *to the loving virgin* for help, and thereafter pray with a joyful mind *to all the saints, the blessed and the righteous,* that *with one voice* they would all intercede for you before their prince, the eternal Lord, *who rules the heights of heaven as his throne;* that he, *high-*   108 *est judge, eternal creator,* would graciously receive your soul and lead you *into perpetual light,* where blessed, holy souls find rest in the kingdom, *the realms of heaven.*

Instructions for Christians

Syle ece Gode   æhta þinra
þone teoðan dæl;   he getyþað þe
and he ðe mænigfealdað   mycle þa nigone.
   Syndon feower þing   forð-steppende
5   to þæra ecan   eadignesse;
he ne missað na   ða he gemetað.
An is monnes geswinc,   oðer muðes gebede,
þridde is leornung   on lifes æ,
seo feorða is þæt fæsten   ðe we gefremmon sceolon.
10   Syndon eac swa some   oðer feower
þære woruld-þinga,   þæt gewitan mæig
man fram deofla   and beon metodes þeing.
An is ærest   þæt he ofte do
wop and hreowe   for his misdæda.
15   Þonne is þæt oðer,   þæt he æfter þan
heofanan kyninge   herige georne.
Þonne is þæt þridde,   þæt he æfre sceal,
a wilnie   eces lifes.
Þonne is þæt feorðe   þæt he fremman sceal,
20   þæt he gemettige   metas and drincas.
   Ne synd þa þrowunga   on þissera weorulda
monna ænigum   þæra meda weorð
ðe us gegearcod is   on Godes riche;
ac lytle hwile   on þissere leana dagum

138

Instructions for Christians

Give to eternal God the tenth part of your possessions; the nine left over he will grant to you and increase them greatly for you.

There are four things leading to everlasting blessedness; 4 no one will fail to notice those four when he meets them. The first is a person's effort, the second the prayers of his mouth, the third is instruction in the law of life, the fourth is the fasting that we are bound to observe.

There exist, moreover, four other means in this world by 10 which a person is able to abandon the devil and become a follower of the creator. The first of these is that a person often weep and show remorse for his wrongful actions. Next is the second, that he praise eagerly the king of heaven. Then 17 the third is that he must always long for eternal life. Then the fourth thing that he should do is observe moderation in food and drink.

To no one are sufferings in this world worth comparing to 21 the reward that is prepared for us in the kingdom of God; rather, for a short while in these fleeting days, every wise

25   witena eanig   winnað for Criste,
      and eft swa ðeah   in ecnesse
      gewunað in wuldre   mid weroda Godd.
      For þi sceal þegna gehwilc   geþylde nimon,
      forþon is þæt seo mæste   mæigen þæra saula.
30   Æla, ðu ærma   and þu eorðlica
      man ofer moldan,   hwi ne gemynas þu a
      þæs diæðes hryre   ðe us drihten gescop?
      Gif þu þisses eorðlican weles   ane gewilnost
      orsorhnesse,   ne bið þær oht betweon þe
35   and þæm neatum   ðe naht ne witen.
      Hit is idelnisse   þæt þu her on locest,
      and eal þæt þu her sceawast   hit is sceaduwa gelic;
      æll hit gewitað   swa þe wanna scur.
      Ac þu scealt þæt selre lif   symble lufian
40   and æfre fleon   unrihte gestreon,
      forþan heo hit forgyldað   þam ðe hit georna lufað
      on þam ende-dæge   mid ęce wita.
          Ne scealt þu þæt æfre   ayldan to lange
      þæt ðu behatest   heofonan kyninge,
45   forþan ðe him unþiaw   ælc mislicað
      and ealra wyrrest   yfela getreowa.
      Ne scyle wandian   witona ænig
      þæt he his ælmessan   ofte gesyllæ;
      alning deð   oðer twegea:
50   oððe þonne monnan   miclum aliseð
      wom-dæda gehwas,   oððe his wita onleoht
      her oððe on helle,   oððe huru siððan
      on domes dæge   þurh drihtnes gifu
      lissum forgyldað   þam ðe ær lustum gæf.
55   Gif we us sylfum   synna gehwylce

man experiences struggle for Christ's sake and will nonethe-
less later dwell in glory for eternity with the God of hosts.
Therefore every man must acquire patience, since that is
the greatest virtue for souls.

Alas, you wretched and worldly human being upon the 30
earth, why are you not always calling to mind the ruin of
mortality that the Lord has prescribed for us? If you yearn
only for the comfort of earthly wealth, then there will be no
difference between you and beasts that know nothing what-
soever. What you behold here is emptiness, and all that you 36
gaze upon here is like a shadow; it all vanishes like a dark
squall. But you should love unceasingly the better life and
always flee ill-gotten gains, for on the last day they will pay
him who dearly loves [acquiring them] a return of unending
torments.

You must never defer too long what you promise to the 43
king of heaven, for every evil habit displeases him, and false
loyalties most of all. No wise man should hesitate to give
alms often; doing so always accomplishes one of two ends: it
largely absolves a person of every shameful deed or lightens
his punishments, whether here or in hell; or indeed, later, on
Judgment Day, it graciously brings reward to him who for-
merly gave with willingness.

If we guard ourselves against every sin in our dealings, 55

weriað be gewyrhtum,   ne wrecað æfre ða
ealmihtig Godd   on us syððan.

Se ðe æfter synnum   swiðe lange
forhæfednesse   habben þæncað,
60   þæt beoð anlicost   swylc swa he wære
on mægðhade   metode to willan,
and for Cristes lufan   clæne gehealdan.

Swa hwilc man swa mæg   and nu nele
geleornian hwæt-hwugo,   he bið lað Gode,
65   and his saul bið   swiðe scyldig.

Ac þæm ðe wællað lufæ   on wisdome,
he hit mid þam mod gifeð,   mihtig drihten,
mid his handum twam   þurh þone halga gast.

Se forholena cræft   and forhyded gold
70   ne bið ællunga   ungelice.

Betere bið þe dusige,   gif he on breostum can
his unwisdom   inne belucan,
þonne se snotere   ðe symle wile
æt his heah-þearfe   forhelan his wisdom.

75   Ac þu scealt gelome   gelæran and tæcan,
ða hwile þe ðe mihtig Godd   mægnes unne,
þe læs hit þe on ende   eft gereowe
æfter dæg-rime,   þonne þu hit gedon ne miht.

Onlær þinum bearne   bysne goda,
80   and eac swa some   eallum leoda;
þonne ðu geearnost   ece blisse
and æfter þisse weorlda   weorðscipe mycelne.

Se ðe leornunge   longe fyligeð
halgum bocum   her on worulde,
85   heo ðone gelæredon   longe gebetað,
and þone unlærdan   eac gelæreð.

Heo geeadmodað   eghwylcne kyng,

then almighty God will never visit punishment on us for them at a later time. If, after a man sins, he resolves to practice abstinence for a very long period, the result will be as if he lived in a state of virginity, giving joy to his creator, and as if he had been preserved in purity for the sake of Christ's love.

If any person is able to learn something and does not want 63 to do so, he will be hated by God, and his soul will be greatly guilty. But to those who burn with love for wisdom, the mighty Lord will, with his own two hands, through the Holy Spirit, grant understanding along with [the desire].

Concealed skill and hidden gold are not entirely differ- 69 ent. The fool, if he manages to keep his folly shut up inside, is better than the intelligent person who always wants to hide his wisdom when he needs it most.

But you should be teaching and instructing frequently, as 75 long as mighty God grants you the strength, so that you do not eventually have regrets in the end, after your allotted days, when you are no longer able to do so.

By good example teach your child, and likewise all peo- 79 ples; then you will earn everlasting joy and great honor when this world is past.

Whoever long pursues learning among holy books here 83 in this world will long provide correction for the learned and also teach the unlearned. Learning humbles every king;

swilce þone earman   eac aræreð
and þa saula   swa some geclensað
90   and þæt mod gedeþ   mycle ðe bliðre.
And heo eac æþelne gedeð   þone ðe ær ne wæs;
eac heo þrah-mælum   þeowne gefreolsað.
Godd sceal deman   and gume þæncan;
þæt is riht gebede   rinca gewylce,
95   þæt he þence to þam   ðe he þonne cweðe.
Se ðe ear gifeð   and eft oftihð
bearna gehwylce,   bysmer he gewyrceð
furþur mycele   þonne ænig freondscipe.
Æll þæt mon alæteð   metes oððe drincas,
100   and his innoðe   riht gemetegað,
sona þæt gefylleð   fæder almihtig
mid gastlicum gifum,   God on heofonum,
þæt he for his ege   ær gewonede.
Ac gif þu nelt   naht leofes gesyllan,
105   ne miht þu na gebicgan   þæt ðe best licað.
Is se mæsse-preost   monna gehwilces
sacerd gehaten,   þæt bið siððan gereht
eft on ænglisc   þæt he eallum scyle
clæne sellan;   he bið gecoræn to þan
110   sygora wearde.   He sceal swilc wesan
þæt he gelæran cunne   his leodscype
heofon-kyninges bebod   and halige þeawas.
Þæt is for gemænan   þæt we munuc nemniað.
Ne mot ænig heora   awiht onsundran
115   habban ænlepig,   ac sceal eal wesan
munucum gemæne,   þæt heom metod leanað.
Ne scylen ge þæs wenan,   þeah ic þisne word-cwide
after Dauiðe   dihtum sette,

likewise it raises up the pauper and, in the same way, cleanses souls and makes the mind so much the happier. Also it makes a man noble who previously was not so, and sometimes it sets the handmaiden free.

It is God's place to render judgment and man's to ponder 93 it; an appropriate prayer for every man is that he think about what he might say then [at judgment].

Every human being who has previously given something 96 and then takes it back achieves disgrace much more than friendship.

To the extent that someone gives up food or drink and 99 duly imposes moderation on his belly, the almighty Father, God in heaven, will immediately fill with spiritual gifts what that person, for fear of God, had emptied.

But if you do not wish to give away anything dear to you, 104 you will by no means be able to purchase what pleases you best.

Everyone's priest is called a *sacerdos,* which is then ren- 106 dered back into English as meaning he must "give purely" to all. He is chosen for that purpose by the guardian of victories. He must be the sort of person who knows how to teach his people holy customs and the commandment of the heavenly king.

A "monk" is so called because of community. None of 113 them is allowed to possess anything of his own privately, but rather everything that the creator lends them is to be the monks' common property.

Though, after the model of David, I have composed this 117

þæt God nelle   gumena gehwylcne
120   healan and gehyran,   þeah he heah-gestreon
on eorð-rice   age mycelne
goldes and seolfres,   and eac godes fele
to habbanne   her on weorulde.
Ac we sculon gemunan   mæla gehwylce
125   þæt se apostol   Paulus ongan
geond eal cristen folc   cyðan and læran,
þæt ða weologan   for heora woruld-rice
on heora mod-sefan   men oferseagon.
Ac se ðe hine sylfne   to swiðe ahefð
130   for his ofer-mode,   he bið earm for Gode.
    Hwæt, we þæt gehyrdon   hæleða secgan,
þæt iu-dagum   Iacob hæfde
and Moyses eac   micele speda,
swylce Isaac   and Abraham;
135   and Dauide   drihten sealde
win-burgum mid   weolan unmete;
and eac Noe hæfde   weoruld-weolona genohne.
Ealle hi wæron   æðeles kynnes,
geþungen on þeod-land;   þeah hwaðere drihten heora
140   on ælcere tide   bena gehyrda.
    Ne dereð mycel wela   manna ænegum,
gif he to swiðe ne bið   sylfe beleapen
on þes feos lufan   mid feondes larum,
for þi heo synd þearflicu   þegna gehwilcum
145   to habbanne   her on weorlde:
mid þam bið þe earman   oftost geholpen
and þa mettruman   myclum gehælede
and þa nacodan eac   niowum gewerede;
of þæm cumað monige   men to heofonum.

146

admonition, you must not suppose that God is unwilling to save and listen to every man, even if he owns a great, rich treasure of gold and silver in this earthly kingdom, and owns moreover much other property that is to be had here in this world. We should rather remember always what the apos- 124 tle Paul undertook to explain and teach among all Christian people, that the wealthy, on account of their worldly power, looked down on others in the thoughts of their minds. But if someone exalts himself too much on account of his pride, he is impoverished in the eyes of God.

Behold, we have heard men say that, in days long ago, Ja- 131 cob possessed great wealth, and so did Moses, and likewise Isaac and Abraham; and the Lord endowed David with vineyards and riches beyond measure; and Noah, too, possessed worldly wealth enough. All of them were of noble stock, prosperous in their country, and yet their Lord still heard their prayers at all times.

If one does not, following the counsel of demons, devote 141 himself excessively to love of money, great wealth does harm to nobody, since those goods are necessary for every person to possess here in the world: by means of them the poor are very often assisted, the infirm greatly healed, and the naked also clothed anew; by means of riches many people arrive at heaven.

150   Sceal æghwylc man   ælne swincan
      on swylcum cræfte   swa him Crist onlænð,
      þæt willan his   gewyrce georne.
      Ne þearf he þæs gewenan   þæt hine drihten Godd
      maran monige   þonne he hine onmunde ær.

155   Spræc God geara   to Hieremie,
      þan witegan,   and þus wordum cwæð:
      "Far nu ymbe æll   eorðan rices,
      sec and smeage,   swa ðu swiðost miht,
      gif þu mage gefinden   fæst-hydigne wer,

160   þe wel wille   and gewyrcan swa,
      recce and gesmeage   soðne geleafan,
      þæt ic mage wið hine   miltse gefremman."
      Ne scealt þu beon   to sene ne to sið,
      ne to slapor ne to slaw,   gif þu sige-drihten

165   mid cræfte on gecampe   gecweman þæncest.
      Gif mon mid ealra   innancundre
      heortan gehygde   gehreowað his synna,
      and ful fæstlice þencð   þæt he forð ofer þæt
      þam æfre to   eft ne gecyrre

170   þeah he ne fæste nawiht . . .
      þonne þreora dagas,   þeah wile drihten hine
      fæderlice onfon   æt his forð-siðe.
      Swa mon ma synna   and maran forlæt
      drihtnes þancas   on his dæg-rime,

175   swa maran þær mide   mede geearnað
      and geofona ma   Godes ealmihtiges.
      Þæt her monnum þince   mæst earfeðu
      þæt him bið on ende   ealra leofest,

Everyone should labor always at whatever skill Christ has 150
entrusted to him, so that he eagerly carries out Christ's will.
No one should suppose that the Lord God will claim more
from a person than God previously thought him fit for.

God spoke earnestly to Jeremiah the prophet and said, 155
in these words: "Travel now through all the realm of earth,
search and consider, as much as you can, whether you are
able to find a resolute man—one who desires good and to do
good, who tells of and ponders the true faith—so that I may
show mercy to him."

You must not be too lazy or too late, neither too sluggish 163
nor too slow if you intend, in this struggle, to please the
Lord of victory.

If, with all the thoughts of the innermost heart, a person 166
repents of his sins and resolutely intends never to turn back
to them thereafter, though he fast no more . . . than three
days, even so will the Lord, like a father, receive him upon
his death.

As anyone, during his allotted days, gives up sins more 173
and more for the Lord's sake, the more reward he earns
thereby, and the more gifts from God almighty.

What may at present seem to people the greatest hard- 177
ship will be most precious of all to them in the end; but on

ac hit þonne ne mæg   þegna eanig
180   onwendan to wille   gif he ne wolde ær.
    Þær ðær aht ne bið   ærfoðlices
on þam earnungum,   ne bið þær æfre þonne ma
on eadleanum   eht deor-wurðes.
    Ne doð þa ærran yfel   ænegum monna
185   laðes nawiht,   gif him ne licað
þinga gehwilce   ða he þonne doð,
gif he his ælmyssan   alning dæleð.
    Nis þæt þearfan hand   þæt ðe þince her,
ac hit is madm-ceoste   Godes ælmihtges.
190   Se bið soðlice   sylfe cristen
þe ðe æfre wile   eallum gelice
mild-heortnesse   monnum gekyðan.
    Þas worda cwæð   weroda drihten,
ælmihtig Godd,   to Ysaie;
195   weroda wuldor-kyning   to þam witegan spreac:
"Þeah ic sylfe cweðe   þæt swyltan scyle
unrihtwise man,   mid ælle forwurðon,
ac gif he æfter ðan   mid alle mægne
synna geswicað,   ne þearf he swiltan for þam."
200   Nis þæs weorkes þearf   witena ænegum
þæt he geond ealla   eorðen rices
sece sigora God,   ac he symle mæg
wunian on þem wicum   ðe he wunode ær,
gif þæt he wille   þæt he wolde ær;
205   forþon geond eall is   eorðan rices,
heofon-rices gast,   hafað þe ðe God wile.
Hwæt wilt þu gesecan   geond sidne grund
feor oððe furðor   þonne ðu geforþian miht?
Ac hafa ðu geleafa   to lifes frumon;

that occasion no one will be able to change at will, if he did not wish to do so before then.

Where there is nothing difficult in the earning, so much 181 more will there never be anything of value in the rewards.

If anyone is constantly dispensing alms, his previous acts 184 of evil will do him no harm—provided that they all give him no pleasure at the time he does them.

That is not a beggar's hand, as it may seem to you here; 188 rather it is the treasure chest of almighty God.

He is truly a Christian who desires always to show mercy 190 to all people alike.

The Lord of hosts, almighty God, spoke these words to 193 Isaiah, the glorious king of hosts to the prophet: "Even though I myself declare that an unrighteous man must perish utterly, if afterward, with all his strength, he quits his sins, he need not die because of them."

No wise man need take pains to search for the God of vic- 200 tories throughout all kingdoms of the earth; rather he can remain continually in the abode that he inhabited before, provided that he desires what he desired in the past; for the Spirit of the kingdom of heaven is found throughout the whole of earth's domain and keeps those whom God wills. Why do you want to search far beyond the immense deep, 207 or farther than you are able to attain? Rather have faith in

210 gewuna þar ðu wunodest   —þæt is wislic ræd;
forþan nis mid fota stepum   frea ealmihtig
to gesecanne   sinum þegne,
þeoda wealdend,   ac mid þeawa stepum.

Ne bið þæt fula sloh   fira eanegum
215 to ondrædanne,   gif hit forbugan mæg
and þurh eanig þing   æfre forceorran,
and his synna swa some,   þeah he symle ne mage
bewacan and beweardian   and bewitan geornan.
Ac þonne diað ne mæg   ofer drihtnes gesceaft
220 ænig eorð-bugend   æfre forbugan.

Þu ful gearowe na wast   wege þines gastes,
hu heo ðe on com   oððe hwær heo æror was,
oððe on hwylce sealo   heo sceal heonon siðian;
ne miht þu æfre þonne ma   eall aspyrian
225 ures wealdendes   weorc and angin,
forþon ðe he is heah-cræftiga   heofonas and eorðan,
weoruldes waldend,   wæteres and lyfte,
and eac ælra þæra   þe ðær on wuniað.

Wisdom is leoht   wera æghwilcum
230 to habbanne   her on weoruldæ.
Hit sceal beon onæled   mid ead-modnesse;
ne mæg hit eanig mon   æfre mid oðer
tapore ontendan   þæt hit tale leohte,
for þam ofer-mettum   ðe hit ær dwæsta.

235 Næfre ic ne gehyrde   þæt wurde laford god
eft on ylde,   se ðe ær ne was
Gode oððe monnum   on iugoð þeowa,
ne huru on ylde   æfre gewurðan

the creator of life, dwell where you have dwelled—that is wise advice; for no follower is to seek the Lord almighty, the ruler of peoples, by steps of the feet but rather by steps of moral character.

No one need dread the filthy mire if he is able to avoid it 214 and always bypass it, through whatever means; the same is true of his sins, even if a person cannot always be vigilant, on guard and careful. And yet no one dwelling on earth can ever, against the Lord's decree, avoid death.

You do not very readily know the path of your soul, how 221 it came into you or where it existed before that, or at what time it must journey hence; none the more will you ever be able to trace out all of our ruler's works and his intentions, for he is supreme architect of heaven and earth, the ruler of the world, of water and air and also of all things that dwell in them.

Wisdom is a light that every man should possess here in 229 this world. It must be kindled with humility; with no other taper can anyone ever bring it to flame so that it beams well, in place of the pride that snuffed it out before.

I have never heard that a lordly man eventually turned 235 good in old age who was not in his youth a servant to God or to others; nor, indeed, of anyone ever being served well in

wel geþeignod,   þe ne wolde ær
240   on his tale mette   tale wel þeignan.
      Ne scealt þu dysilice sprecan   ne dwollice geþencan
      ymben ænigne   eorð-buendra,
      ne nið habban   wið ænigum monnum,
      ac þu scealt æighwylcum   gearwurðian,
245   and na ymb þe sylfum   na to wel lætan,
      naðer ne for cræfta,   ne for weoruld-æhta.
      Ac þu scealt æfre þin mod   geornlicę healden
      on æighwylce timan   fram ælcan unþeawa,
      þæt þu mage clænlice   Criste geþenian,
250   kyning cwycra gehweas,   swa him gecweme sy,
      wið þon ðu mote habben   ęce to medes
      heofon-rices dæl;   þæt is hihta mæst.
      Þear is hope heagost   and sibbe ealra selost,
      lif ealra leofest,   and meda ealra mærost
255   þem ðe hit se mild-heort Crist   geunnan wille.
      Undergyte ðu þis   geornlice æfre
      þæt sigefæste weogas   syndon ealle þreo
      heonan to heofonum,   swa us se halga wer
      and se apostol   Paulus gekydde.
260   An is geleafa,   and lufu oðer,
      þridde is tohope   þam ðe eallunga
      to þam uplican hame   efestlice geþencað.
      Gefylste us, *filius dei,*
      þæt we to þam earde   becumon moton.
      Amen.

old age who did not previously desire to serve rightly and well, according to his measure.

You should not speak stupidly or think foolishly about 241 anyone who dwells on earth, or have hostility against any persons; rather you should show respect to everyone and by no means think too well of yourself, either on account of your abilities or of your worldly possessions. You should in- 247 stead, at all times, constantly preserve your mind from every vice so that you can purely serve Christ as pleases him, the king of all that lives; in return for that, you will be allowed to possess forever a portion of heaven as your reward: that is the greatest of aspirations. In that place is highest hope and 253 the best peace of all, a life most precious of all and the most glorious of all rewards for those on whom Christ the merciful wishes to bestow them.

Always understand this well, that there are altogether 256 three victorious paths from here to heaven, just as the holy man and apostle, Paul, made known to us. One is faith, the second love, the third hope among those who fully and zealously aspire to the celestial home. May *the Son of God* aid us, that we may be permitted to arrive at that dwelling place. Amen.

Seasons for Fasting

Wæs on eald-dagum   Israheala folc
þurh Moysen,   mærne lareow,
anlyht and gelared.   Swa hine lifes frea,
heofna heah-cyning,   her on life
5   þurh his sylfes word   sette for leodum,
rincum to ræde,   and him runa gescead
sylfum asæde,   hu he þone soþan weg
leofum leodscipe   læran sceolde.

Þa se leoda fruma   larum fyligde
10   heofena heah-cyninges,   and þa hæleþ samod,
swa hie on leodscipe   lærede wæron.
Gyf hie wancule   weorc ongunnon,
heom þæs of heofonum   hearm to leane
asende sigora God,   and hie sona to him
15   fryþa wilnodan   and þær fundon raþe,
gif hie leohtras heora   letan gewyrpan.

Feala is mægena   þe sio mære þeod
on þam herescype   heold and worhte,
þendan hie lifes frean   lufian woldon.
20   Ac him se ende wearð   earm and þrealic,
þa hie besyredon   sylfne dryhten,
on beam setton   and to byrgenne

Seasons for Fasting

In days long ago, the people of Israel was enlightened and instructed through Moses, a famous teacher. Thus by his own words did the Lord of life, the supreme king of heaven, appoint him, Moses, for the peoples' sake, to be counsel for men during his lifetime here, and told him the meaning of mysteries, how he was to teach that beloved nation the true path.

Then that leader of peoples obeyed the teachings of heaven's supreme king, and so did the men along with him, being instructed as a part of that nation. If they wavered in undertaking their tasks, the God of victories would send a scourge from heaven against them as repayment for that, and they would immediately sue him for peace and there quickly determine whether they could mend their vicious ways. 9

Many were the strengths which that illustrious nation possessed and demonstrated on its campaign, so long as they willed to love the Lord of life. But their end was wretched and disastrous, when they betrayed the Lord himself, fixed him to a tree and condemned him . . . to a grave. There he 17

. . . gedemdon.   He þær bedigled wæs,
and þy þryddan dæge   þeodum ætywed.

25   We þæt gehyrdon   hæleþa mænige
on boc-stafum   breman and writan,
þæt hie fæstenu   feower heoldon
and þonne offredan   unmæne neat
— þæt is lamb oþþe styrc—   leofum to tacne
30   þe for worulde wæs   womma bedæled . . .

      Ac arisan ongan   rices ealdor
of byrgenne,   blæda gefylled,
and mid heofen-warum   ham gesohte,
eard mid englum,   and us eallum
35   þone hyht gehateð,   gyf we his willaþ
þurh rihtne sefan   rædum fyligan.
Na þær in cumeð   atele gefylled,
womme gewesed,   ac scal on wyrd sceacan.

      Nu we herian sceolan   her for life
40   deorne dæd-fruman,   and him dogera gerim
ælmes-dædum   ure gefyllan,
and on fæstenum,   swa se froda iu
Moyses mælde.   And we þa mearce sceolan
heoldan higefæste   her mid Anglum,
45   swa hie gebrefde us   beorn on Rome,
Gregorius,   gumena papa.

      We þæt forme sceolan   fæsten heowan
on þære ærestan   wucan lengtenes,
on þam monþe   þe man Martius
50   geond Rom-wara   rice nemneð.
And þær twelfe sceolan   torhtum dihte
runa gerædan   in þæs rican hofe,

was concealed, and on the third day he was he revealed to the nations.

We have heard many men celebrate and set down in writ- 25 ing that they [the Jews] observed four fasts, and that afterward they would sacrifice in token to their beloved [Lord] an innocent animal—that is, a lamb or young bull—one that was, in the eyes of the world, free from blemishes . . .

But the Lord of the kingdom undertook to rise up from 31 the grave, filled with glory, and he sought a home among heaven's citizens, a habitation with the angels; he promises the same hope to us all, provided that we obey his counsels with a virtuous mind. No one glutted with evil, drenched with defilement, will enter there; rather he must depart to his own destiny.

Now, for the term of our life here, we should praise the 39 beloved worker of such deeds and for his sake fill our allotted days with acts of almsgiving and with fasts, just as Moses the wise spoke of long ago. And with resolute minds we should maintain the dates [for the Ember Fasts] here among the English just as they were written down for us by that noble at Rome, Gregory, pope over men.

The initial fast we are to observe in the first week of Lent, 47 in the month that is called March throughout the realm of the Romans. And on that occasion we are to read out twelve mysteries in magnificent sequence in the court of

heofona heah-cyninges,   herian mid sange,
wlancne weorþian   wuldres bryttan.

55   Ofer þa Easter-tid   oþer fæsten
ys to bremenne   Brytena leodum
mid gelicum lofe   þe gelesu hafað,
on þære wucan   þe æfter cumeð
þam sunnan-dæge   þe geond sidne wang
60   Pentecostenes dæg   preostas nemnað,
on þam monþe,   þæs þe me þinceð,
þe man Iunius   gearum nemde.

Ðonne is þæt þrydde   þinga gehwelces
fæsten on foldan   fyra bearnum
65   dihte gelicum   on þam deoran hofe
to brymenne   beorhtum sange
on þære wucan   þe ærur byð
em-nihtes dæge   ælda beornum,
on þam monþe,   mine gefræge,
70   þe man September   side genemneð.

We þæt feorþe sceolen   fæsten gelæstan
on þære wucan   þe bið ærur full
dryhtnes gebyrde,   and we mid deornum scylan,
wordum and weorcum,   wuldres cyninge
75   in þa ylcan tid   eallum gemynde
þeodne deman   þinga gehwylces,
efne swa swa ærran,   and þone arwesan
leofne leoda frean   lifes biddan.

On þissum fæstenum   is se feorþa dæg
80   and sixta samod   seofoþa getinge
to gelæstanne   lifes ealdre
and to bremenne   boca gerynum

the mighty one, the supreme king of heaven, and we are to honor the splendid bestower of glory, praise him with song.

Following Eastertide, a second fast accompanied by simi- 55 lar worship, as it includes the readings, should be celebrated by the peoples of Britain, and this during the week following the Sunday that priests across this broad plain call the day of Pentecost, in the month that has, I believe, been given the name June, year after year.

Next, a third fast, having a similar arrangement, is to be 63 celebrated on earth among the children of men with splendid song inside the precious temple, and this in the week that falls, for the children of mortals, before the day of the equinox in the month that, I have heard, is widely named September.

The fourth fast we should observe in the full week prior 71 to the Lord's birth, and through our mysteries, in words and deeds, we should in that same period, just as in previous ones, single-mindedly render to the Lord, the king of glory, his due for each and every thing, and pray for life from the revered one, the beloved Lord of peoples.

In these fasts, the fourth day and the sixth, together with 79 the seventh immediately following, should be observed for the sake of the Lord of life and celebrated at the ninth hour

emb þa nigoþan tyd.   Nan is on eorþan,
butan hine unhæl   an geþreatige,
85   þe mot æt oþþe wæt   ærur þicgan,
þæs þe us boca dom   demeð þeodlic.

Gif þe þonne secgan   suþan cymene
Bryttan oððe Francan,   þæt þu gebann sceole
her on eorþan   ænig healdan,
90   þæs þe Moyses iu   mælde to leodum,
na þu þæs andfeng   æfre gewyrþe;
ac þu þæt sylfe heald   þæt þe suþan com
from Romana   rices hyrde,
Gregoriæ,   gumena papa.

95   Þus he gesette   sylf ond dyhte
þa þenunga,   þeod-lareow,
fæstend-tida;   we þam forþ nu gyt
geond Engla land   estum filiað,
swa he æt þæm setle   sylfa gedemde
100   sancte Petres.   Preostas syþþan
lange lifes tyd   leordun þæt sylfe,
þæt þu oþrum ne scealt   æfre filian.

Eac we feowertig daga   fæsten healden
ær þæm æriste   ures dryhtnes,
105   þæt nu lengten-tid   leoda nemnað,
and hit ærest ongan   eorl se goda,
mære Moyses,   ær he on munt styge.
He þæt fæsten heold   feowertig daga
and nyhta samod,   swa he nahtes anbat
110   ær he þa deoran æ   dryhtnes anfenge.

with the mysteries recorded in books. Unless sickness besets him, there is no one on earth who is otherwise permitted to taste food or drink before that hour, according to what the ordinance in books decrees for us universally.

If, then, Bretons or Franks arriving from the south should 87
tell you that you ought to keep any commandment here on earth based on what Moses said to peoples long ago, do not be at all receptive to that notion; rather hold to the same command that reached you from the south, from the keeper of the Romans' realm, Gregory, pope over men.

A teacher of peoples, he himself thus established and ar- 95
ranged the services for the periods for fasting; even now we willingly perform them still throughout England in the way that he himself ordained from the throne of Saint Peter. Priests ever since, through life's long age, have taught the same ordinance, that you should never follow any others.

We also keep a fast of forty days prior to our Lord's resur- 103
rection, which people now call the period of Lent, and it was that good man, the famous Moses, who first instituted it before he went up the mountain. He kept that fast for forty days and forty nights, so that he tasted nothing before he received the cherished law of the Lord.

Him þær gesealde   sylfe dryhten
bremne boca cræft,   bæle behlæned,
of his haligan   handa gescrifene,
het hine leodum þone   leoran and tæcan
115   elda orþancum,   eallum to tacne
þæt we mid fæstene magon   freode gewinnan
and þa deopan   dryhtnes gerynu,
þa þe leoran sceolan   leoda gehwylce,
gif us þære duguþe hwæt   dryhten sylleð.

120   Eft Helias,   eorl se mæra,
him on westene   wiste geþigede,
þær him symbel-bread   somod mid wætere
dryhtnes engla sum   dihte togeanes;
and se gestrangud wearð   styþum gyfle
125   to gefæstenne   feowertig-daga
and nihta samod,   swa he nahtes anbat
ær he on Horeb dun   hali ferde.

Uton þæt gerine   rihte gehicgan,
þæt se mæra þegen   mihta ne hæfde
130   to astigenne   stæppon on ypplen
ær him þæt symbel wearþ   seald fram engle.
We sint on westene   wuldres blisse
on þæm ænete   ealra gefeana;
nu is helpes tid,   halig dryhten,
135   hu we munt þinne   mærne gestygan!

Sint for englas geteald   eorþ-bugendum
þa þe dryhtnes word   dædum læraeð.
We þa andlifene   ofstum þycgen
and þone deoran wist,   dryhtnes lare;
140   uton fæstan swa   fyrene dædum

There the Lord himself, enveloped in flame, bestowed on III
Moses the celebrated knowledge of books, of writings from
his own holy hands, commanded him to teach and explain it
to the people by means of human ingenuity; this God did as
a sign to all that we who are obligated to teach every people
can, by fasting, attain to the friendship and profound mys-
teries of the Lord, provided the Lord bestows on us some
portion of virtue.

Elijah too, that famous man, received nourishment in the 120
desert where one of the Lord's angels placed feast-bread be-
fore him, and water with it; and from that sparing diet he
was given strength to fast for forty days and nights, so that
he tasted nothing before he journeyed, a holy man, up the
mountain of Horeb.

Let us duly reflect on that mystery: the illustrious servant 128
had no strength to climb the steps up to the pinnacle before
that feast was given to him by an angel. We, for our part, ex-
ist in a place deserted of the happiness of glory, in a solitude
apart from all joys; now is the time, O holy Lord, for your
aid, by which we may climb your splendid mountain!

Those who by their deeds teach the words of the Lord 136
are considered as angels to dwellers on earth. Let us ea-
gerly consume the sustenance and the precious nourishment
that is the Lord's teaching; by self-denial let us, through our

on forhæfenesse   her for life,
þæt we þæs muntes mægen   mærþa gestigan
swa se ealda dyde   Elias iu.

    Is to hicganne   hu se halga gewat
145 of þissum wang-stede   wuldres neosian:
hine fyren scryd   feower mærum,
wlangum wicgum,   on weg ferede
on neorxna-wong.   Þær us nergend Crist
gehaten hafað   ham mid blisse,
150 gif we þæt fæsten her   fyrena gelæstað
and þone uplican   æþel secað.

    Nu wæs æt nehstan   þæt us nergend Crist,
halig heofenes weord,   heolp and lærde.
He hine dyppan let   deorum þweale,
155 fulwihtes bæðe,   fyrena bedæled;
and he feowertig daga   firsude mettas,
eac nihta swa feala   nanuht gyltig,
leodum to lare,   þæt hie on lengten sceolan
efen feowertig daga   fæsten hewan.

160   Hine costude þær   Cristes gewinna
on þæm ænete,   eald and fræte,
geseah mærne frean   mannum gelicne
and þa wenan ongann,   wommes gemyndig,
þæt he stræla his   stellan mihte
165 on þam lic-homan;   næs þæs leahtra nan,
ac on hinder gewat   hearmes brytta,
and þær englas hyra   ealdor sohtan.

actions during this life, so fast from acts of sin that we may be able to ascend the glories of that mountain, just as the ancient one, Elijah, did long ago.

One should consider how the holy man left this earth 144
to meet his glory: a fiery chariot with four horses, splendid steeds, bore him away to Paradise. It is there that Christ the savior has promised us a dwelling with joy, if at present we observe a fast from sins and seek after that heavenly homeland.

Next came the period when Christ the savior, the holy 152
guardian of heaven, helped and taught us. He who was free from sins allowed himself to be immersed in a precious cleansing, the font of baptism; and, for forty days and just as many nights, he who bore no guilt at all abstained from foods as a lesson for people that during Lent they should keep the fast for exactly forty days.

Christ's adversary, ancient and perverse, tempted him 160
there in that desert, saw the glorious Lord in the likeness of human beings and, intent on harm, began to hope that he might sink his darts into Christ's body; no sin came of that, but rather the giver of evil departed behind him, and angels sought out their Lord in that place.

Hige, synnig man,   gyf þe susla weard
costian durre,   þonne he Crist dyde,
170   wereda wulder-frean,   womma leasne!
Ne mæg he þæs inne   ahwæt scotian
gif he myrcels næfþ   manes æt egum,
ac he on hinder scriþ,   and þe halig þreat,
englas ærfæste,   æghwær helpað,
175   gif þu dryhtnes her   dædum fylgest.

Hæbbe we nu gemearcod   hu þa mæran iu
feowertig daga   fæsten hewdon;
and we bebeodað   þurh beorn Godes
þæt manna gehwilc   þe ofer moldan wunað
180   ær þam æreste   ures dryhtnes
efen feowertig daga   fæsten hewe
oþ þa nigoþan tid,   and he na bruce
flæsces oþþe fyrna,   þæ læs þe he fah wese.

Sceolan sacerdas   singan mæssan,
185   dæg-hwamlice   dryhten biddan
on þam fæstenne   þæt he freond wese
folce gynd foldan.   And þa fyrna sceolan
þam sacerdan   secgan gehwilce
and þa dymnissa   dædum betan
190   wordes and weorces,   wuldres ealdor
þurh ælmes-dæde   eall gegladian.

Þonne is þearf micel   þeoda mænium
þæt þa sacerdos   sylfe ne gyltan,
ne on leahtrum hiora   ligegen to fæste.
195   Hwa mæg þyngian   þreale hwilcum
wiþ his arwesan,   gyf he him ærur hæfð

Ponder, O sinner, whether the keeper of torments will 168
dare to tempt you, given that he did so to Christ, the glori-
ous Lord of hosts, who was free from sins! He can shoot
nothing into you if he has no target of vice in his sights; in-
stead he will slink back, and a holy troop, faithful angels, will
assist you on every side, if in the present you imitate the
deeds of the Lord.

We have now described how those famous figures long 176
ago kept the fast of forty days; and we command, through
the Son of God, that every single person who dwells on earth
should, for exactly forty days before the resurrection of the
Lord, keep a fast up to the ninth hour, and that he should
not enjoy meat or sins, lest he be condemned.

Priests ought to sing Masses, beseech the Lord daily dur- 184
ing the fast that he would be beneficent to people across
the earth. And all people should confess their sins to those
priests and, by their actions, atone for offenses of word and
deed, and by giving alms they should altogether delight the
Lord of glory.

The multitudes of people therefore have great need that 192
priests, for their part, should not offend or remain too set in
their vices. Who will be able to intercede on behalf of any

bitere onbolgen,   and þæs bote ne deð,
ac þa æbyligþe   ealdere wrohte,
dæg-hwamlice   dædum niwað?

200   Gyf se sacerd hine   sylfne ne cunne
þurh dryhtnes ege   dugeþum healdan,
na þu, folces mann,   fyrna ne gyme
þe gehalgod mann   her gefremme.
Ac þu lare scealt   lustum fremman
205   ryht-hicgennde   þe he to ræde tæchð.
Drince he him þæt drofe;   duge hlutter þe
wæter of wege   —þæt is wuldres lar.

      Ac ic secgan mæg,   sorgum hremig,
hu þa sacerdas   sace niwiað,
210   dæg-hwamlice   dryhten gremiað
and mid æleste   ælcne forlædað
þe him fylian wyle   folces manna.
Sona hie on mergan   mæssan syngað
and forþegide,   þurste gebæded,
215   æfter tæppere   teoþ geond stræta.

      Hwæt, hi leaslice   leogan ongynnað
and þone tæppere   tyhtaþ gelome,
secgaþ þæt he synleas   syllan mote
ostran to æte   and æþele wyn
220   emb morgen-tyd,   þæs þe me þingeð
þæt hund and wulf   healdað þa ilcan
wisan on worulde   and ne wicliað
hwænne hie to mose fon,   mæða bedæled.

servant before his lord if the intercessor himself has already bitterly angered that lord and does not atone for it, but instead, by his actions, renews daily the lord's anger at that past injury?

If the priest is unable to bear himself virtuously out of 200 fear of the Lord, then pay no heed, O layman, to the sins that an ordained person may commit here. Rather you must willingly carry out with righteous intent the teaching that he expounds as counsel. Let him drink the turbid pool; let clear water from the current—that is the doctrine of glory— work good in you.

Yet I can tell, loud in my lamentations, how priests renew 208 the strife, daily anger the Lord and with irreligion lead astray every layperson who desires to follow him. They sing their Masses first thing in the morning, and, consumed and driven by thirst, they roam through the streets, looking for the tavern keeper.

Behold, they falsely take to lying and often urge the tav- 216 ern keeper, tell him that he can, without sinning, supply them oysters to eat and excellent wine at that hour of the morning; in this respect, it seems to me that the dog and wolf practice the same behavior in this world and, lacking moderation, do not hesitate when they may seize a meal.

Hi þonne sittende   sadian aginnað,

225   win seniað,   syllað gelome,

cweðað þæt Godd life   gumena gehwilcum

þæt wines dreng   welhwa mote,

siþþan he mæssan hafað,   meþig þicgan,

etan ostran eac,   and oþerre

230   fisc of flode . . .

Sitting down, they then start to eat their fill, bless the   224
wine, pour it again and again, say that God would concede
to every man that anyone exhausted after having said Mass
might be allowed to take a drink of wine, to eat oysters too,
and others be allowed [to eat] fish from the sea . . .

The Menologium

Crist wæs acennyd,   cyninga wuldor,
on midne winter,   mære þeoden,
ece ælmihtig,   on þy eahteoðan dæg
"hælend" gehaten,   heofon-rices weard.

5   Swa þa sylfan tiid   side herigeas,
folc unmæte,   habbað foreweard gear,
for þy se kalend us   cymeð geþincged
on þam ylcan dæge   us to tune,
forma monað;   hine folc mycel

10 Ianuarius   gerum heton.
And þæs embe fif-niht   þætte fulwiht-tiid
eces drihtnes   to us cymeð,
þæne twelfta dæg   tir-eadige,
hæleð heaðu-rofe,   hatað on Brytene,

15 in foldan her.   Swylce emb feower wucan
þætte Sol-monað   sigeð to tune
butan twam nihtum,   swa hit getealdon geo,
Februarius fær,   frode gesiþas,
ealde æ-gleawe.   And þæs embe ane niht

20 þæt we Marian   mæssan healdað,
cyninges modor,   forþan heo Crist on þam dæge,
bearn wealdendes,   brohte to temple.

The Menologium

Dec. 25 Christ, the glory of kings, was born at midwinter, an illus-
trious prince, eternal and almighty; guardian of heaven,
Jan. 1 he was given the name "savior" on the eighth day thereafter.
Immense hosts, an innumerable company, also observe that   5
same occasion as the New Year, since on that very day the
calends arrive at our dwellings as ordained, the first month;
the vast multitude has called it January, year after year. And   11
five nights later, there comes to us the feast of the eternal
Jan. 6 Lord's baptism, which men brave in battle, blessed with
glory, call Twelfth Night here in the land of Britain. From   15
Feb. 1 then it is likewise four weeks minus two nights that *Sol-
monað* settles among our dwellings, just as wise companions,
ancient scholars of the law, reckoned it long ago, the coming
Feb. 2 of February. And it is one night thereafter that we observe
the Mass of Mary, mother of the king, for on that day she
brought Christ to the temple, the ruler's Son.

Ðænne þæs emb fif-niht   þæt afered byð
winter of wicum,   and se wigend þa
25   æfter seofentynum   swylt þrowade
niht-gerimes,   nergendes þegen,
Mathias mære,   mine gefræge,
þæs þe lencten on tun   geliden hæfde,
werum to wicum.   Swylce eac is wide cuð
30   ymb III and twa   þeodum gewelhwær
his cyme kalend   ceorlum and eorlum—
butan þænne bises   geboden weorðe
feorðan geare;   þænne he furðor cymeð
ufor anre niht   us to tune,
35   hrime gehyrsted   hagol-scurum færð
geond middan-geard   Martius reðe,
Hlyda healic.   Ðænne se halga þæs
emb XI-niht   æþele scynde
Gregorius   in Godes wære,
40   breme in Brytene.   Swylce Benedictus
embe nigon niht þæs   nergend sohte,
heard and hige-strang,   þæne heriað wel
in gewritum wise,   wealdendes þeow,
rincas regolfæste.   Swylce eac rim-cræftige
45   on þa ylcan tiid   em-niht healdað,
forðan wealdend God   worhte æt frymðe
on þy sylfan dæge   sunnan and monan.
    Hwæt, ymb feower-niht   fæder onsende,
þæs þe em-nihte   eorlas healdað,
50   heah-engel his,   se hælo abead
Marian mycle,   þæt heo meotod sceolde
cennan, kyninga betst,   swa hit gecyðed wearð
geond middan-geard;   wæs þæt mære wyrd,
folcum gefræge.   Swylce emb feower and þreo

Feb. 7   Next, five nights later, winter is born away from our dwell-   23
Feb. 24 ings, and it is then seventeen nights after spring has come to
men in their abodes that a warrior, the savior's soldier, re-
nowned Mathias suffered death, as I have heard tell. In the   29
same way, to peoples everywhere, both peasants and nobles,
Mar. 1   the next calends is widely known by its coming three days
later plus two—except when an extra day is ordained in ev-
ery fourth year, in which case it arrives at our dwellings one
night later still—that is, when fierce March, adorned with
frost, journeys over earth, showering hail as it goes, the ex-
Mar. 12 cellent month of *Hlyda*. Then, eleven nights later, Gregory   37
the saint, a noble man celebrated in Britain, departed into
Mar. 21 God's protection. And nine nights after that, Benedict like-
wise sought his savior, a man of toughness and resolve, the
master's servant whom wise men, warriors faithful to their
Rule, praise well in their writings. Moreover, those who   44
skillfully reckon the calendar observe the equinox on that
same feast as well, since in the beginning God the ruler cre-
ated both sun and moon on that very day.

Mar. 25 Four nights after men observe the equinox, behold, the   48
Father sent his archangel who announced to Mary a great
salvation, that she should give birth to the creator, the best
of kings, as had been revealed throughout the earth; that
was a glorious destiny, an event famous among peoples.
Likewise, after a sum of four nights plus three, the savior   54

55   niht-gerimes,   þætte nergend sent
      Aprelis monað,   on þam oftust cymð
      seo mære tiid   mannum to frofre,
      drihtnes ærist;   þænne dream gerist
      wel wide gehwær,   swa se witega sang:
60   "Þis is se dæg   þæne drihten us
      wisfæst worhte,   wera cneorissum,
      eallum eorð-warum   eadigum to blisse."
      Ne magon we þa tide   be getale healdan
      dagena rimes,   ne drihtnes stige
65   on heofenas up,   forþan þe hwearfað aa
      wisra gewyrdum;   ac sceal wintrum frod
      on circule   cræfte findan
      halige dagas.
                      Sculan we hwæðere gyt
      martira gemynd   ma areccan,
70   wrecan wordum forð,   wisse gesingan,
      þæt embe nihgontyne   niht and fifum,
      þæs þe Easter-monað   to us cymeð,
      þæt man reliquias   ræran onginneð,
      halige gehyrste;   þæt is healic dæg,
75   ben-tiid bremu.   Swylce in burh raþe
      embe siex-niht þæs,   smicere on gearwum,
      wudum and wyrtum,   cymeð wlitig scriðan
      Þry-milce on tun,   þearfe bringeð
      Maius micle   geond menigeo gehwær.
80   Swa þi ylcan dæge   æþele geferan,
      Philippus and Iacob,   feorh agefan,
      modige mago-þegnas   for meotudes lufan.
      And þæs embe twa-niht   þætte tæhte God
      Elenan eadigre   æþelust beama,

178

Apr. 1 sends the month of April, during which the glorious feast
of the Lord's resurrection very often occurs as a comfort
for humanity; then joyful celebration is certainly due in ev-
ery place, just as the prophet sang: "This is the day that the
Lord, steadfast in wisdom, created as a source of joy for us,
for generations of men, for all the blessed who dwell on
earth." We cannot keep that occasion by a fixed calendrical   63
date, nor that of the Lord's ascension to the heavens, be-
cause they constantly change according to the ordinances of
learned men; someone wise in years must instead skillfully
calculate the holy days in their cycle.

    We must say more still about the commemoration of the   68
martyrs, proclaim with words and sing with certainty that
Apr. 25 after nineteen nights and five from the coming of *Easter-
monað* to us, an elevation of relics is undertaken, those holy
adornments; that is a notable day, a celebrated time of sup-
May 1 plication. Likewise, six nights later, beautiful in the forest   75
foliage and plants that are its raiment, lovely *Þry-milce* comes
hastening to our abode, May brings great benefit everywhere
among the multitudes. And on the same day those noble   80
companions, Philip and James, valiant, soldiering kinsmen,
gave up their lives for love of the Lord. Two nights thereaf-
May 3 ter, God revealed to blessed Helena the noblest of trees on

85 on þam þrowode   þeoden engla
for manna lufan,   meotud on galgan
be fæder leafe.

        Swylce ymb fyrst wucan
butan anre niht   þætte yldum bringð
sigel-beorhte dagas   sumor to tune,
90 wearme gewyderu.   Þænne wangas hraðe
blostmum blowað,   swylce blis astihð
geond middan-geard   manigra hada
cwicera cynna,   cyninge lof secgað
mænifealdlice,   mærne bremað,
95 ælmihtigne.   Þæs emb eahta and nigon
dogera rimes   þætte drihten nam
in oðer leoht   Agustinus,
bliðne on breostum,   þæs þe he on Brytene her
eað-mode him   eorlas funde
100 to Godes willan,   swa him se gleawa bebead
Gregorius.   Ne hyrde ic guman a fyrn
ænigne ær   æfre bringan
ofer sealtne mere   selran lare,
bisceop bremran.   Nu on Brytene rest
105 on Cant-warum   cyne-stole neah,
mynstre mærum.

           Þænne monað bringð
ymb twa and feower   tiida lange,
ærra Liða   us to tune,
Iunius on geard,   on þam gim astihð
110 on heofenas up   hyhst on geare,
tungla torhtust,   and of tille agrynt,
to sete sigeð.   Wyle syððan leng
grund behealdan   and gangan lator

which the prince of angels suffered for love of humankind,
the creator on the gallows, by his Father's leave.

May 9   Likewise, after the span of a week less one night, summer   87
brings to mortals its bright, sunny days, its warm weather.
Then the meadows promptly blossom with flowers, while
across the earth joy mounts in many orders of living species,
as they in their manifold ways tell forth praises to the king,
celebrate the glorious one, the almighty. It is by a count of   95
May 26   eight plus nine days thereafter that the Lord received Au-
gustine into the next light, he who rejoiced at heart that
here in Britain he had found men obedient to him in accor-
dance with God's will, just as Gregory the wise had com-
manded that he do. Never have I heard before, going back   101
many years, of any man who ever brought over the briny sea
a better doctrine, nor ever have I heard of a more celebrated
bishop. He now rests in Britain, in a famous monastery, near
his throne among the people of Kent.

June 1   Then, two days later plus four, the month of June, *ærra*   106
Liða, brings long days to our dwellings and homes, during
which the jewel that is brightest of stars ascends in the heav-
ens to its highest point in the year, and from that mark de-
scends, sinks to its setting. Henceforth the fairest of lights,   112
of earthly creatures, desires to gaze longer upon the deep

ofer foldan wang   fægerust leohta,
115   woruld-gesceafta.   Þænne wuldres þegn
ymb þreotyne,   þeodnes dyrling,
Iohannes in gear-dagan   wearð acenned,
tyn-nihtum eac;   we þa tiid healdað
on midne sumor   mycles on æþelum.
120   Wide is geweorðod,   swa þæt wel gerist,
haligra tid   geond hæleða bearn,
Petrus and Paulus.   Hwæt, þa apostolas,
þeoden-holde,   þrowedon on Rome
ofer midne sumor,   miccle gewisse,
125   furðor fif-nihtum,   folc-bealo þrealic,
mærne martyrdom;   hæfdon mænige ær
wundra geworhte   geond wær-þeoda,
swylce hi æfter þam   unrim fremedon
swutelra and gesynra   þurh sunu meotudes,
130   ealdor-þegnas.   Þænne ædre cymð
emb twa niht þæs   tidlice us
Iulius monað,   on þam Iacobus
ymb feower-niht   feorh gesealde
ond twentigum,   trum in breostum,
135   frod and fæst-ræd   folca lareow,
Zebedes afera.
                    And þæs symle scriþ
ymb seofon-niht þæs   sumere gebrihted
Weod-monað on tun,   welhwær bringeð
Agustus   yrmen-þeodum
140   hlaf-mæssan dæg.   Swa þæs hærfest cymð
ymbe oðer swylc   butan anre wanan,
wlitig, wæstmum hladen;   wela byð geywed
fægere on foldan.   Þænne forð gewat

and to venture forth later across earth's plain. Next, after
June 24 thirteen nights plus an additional ten, a servant of glory,
John, the Lord's beloved, was born in days long ago; we ob-
serve that feast at midsummer with very great dignity. As it   120
June 29 well deserves, the day of Saints Peter and Paul is honored far
and wide among the children of men. Behold, five days past
midsummer, those apostles loyal to their Lord most cer-
tainly suffered at Rome a horrible public death, a glorious
martyrdom; they had previously performed many wonders
among the peoples, just as they, [Christ's] foremost follow-
ers, would accomplish countless others thereafter, manifest
and visible, through the Son of the creator. Then, two nights   130
July 1 later, there comes to us swiftly, at the opportune time, the
month of July, during which, four nights and twenty later,
July 25 James gave up his life, a man strong at heart, a wise and reso-
lute teacher of peoples, the heir of Zebedee.

And seven nights after that, *Weod-monað,* brightened by   136
Aug. 1 summer, always arrives at our dwellings, August brings to all
peoples everywhere the day of Lammas. After an equal num-
Aug. 7 ber of days minus one, the autumn arrives, lovely and laden
with fruits; its bounty will be beautifully displayed upon the
Aug. 10 earth. Next, three nights after that, faithful to his Lord, the   143

ymb þreo-niht þæs   þeodne getrywe
145 þurh martyrdom,   mære diacon,
Laurentius,   hæfð nu lif wiðþan
mid wuldor-fæder   weorca to leane.
Swylce þæs ymb fif-niht   fægerust mægða,
wifa wuldor,   sohte weroda God
150 for suna sibbe,   sigefæstne ham
on neorxna-wange;   hæfde nergend þa
fægere fostor-lean   fæmnan forgolden
ece to ealdre.   Þænne ealling byð
ymb tyn-niht þæs   tiid geweorðad
155 Bartholomeus   in Brytene her,
wyrd wel-þungen.   Swylce eac wide byð
eorlum geypped   æþelinges deað
ymb feower-niht,   se þe fægere iu
mid wætere oferwearp   wuldres cyne-bearn,
160 wiga weorðlice.   Be him wealdend cwæð
þæt nan mærra man   geond middan-geard
betux wife and were   wurde acenned.
Ond þæs ymbe þreo-niht   geond þeoda feala
þætte Halig-monð,   heleþum geþinged,
165 fereð to folce,   swa hit fore-gleawe,
ealde uþ-witan,   æror fundan,
Septembres fær,   and þy seofoþan dæg
þæt acenned wearð   cwena selost,
drihtnes modor.   Þænne dagena worn
170 ymbe þreotyne   þegn unforcuð,
god-spelles gleaw,   gast onsende
Matheus his   to metod-sceafte,
in ecne gefean.   Þænne ealling cymð
ymb þreo-niht þæs   þeodum wide
175 em-nihtes dæg,   ylda bearnum.

184

illustrious deacon Laurence departed through martyrdom
and now possesses in return, as a reward for his hardships,
life in the presence of the Father of glory. Likewise, five   148
Aug. 15 nights thereafter, the most beautiful of maidens, the glory
of women, sought the God of hosts on the basis of her kin-
ship with his Son, sought a home, secured by victory, in Par-
adise; in return for her nurturing, the savior had then gra-
ciously repaid that woman for all eternity. Then, ten nights   153
Aug. 25 thereafter, the feast of Bartholomew is always honored here
in Britain, an event of distinction. Likewise, four nights
Aug. 29 later, the death of a prince will also be celebrated widely
among men, a warrior who fittingly and worthily sprinkled
with water the regal Son of glory. Concerning him, the ruler   160
said that throughout all the earth no greater person was ever
born to man and woman. And three nights later, across many
Sept. 1 nations, *Halig-monð* makes its way to the people, ordained
for men just as farsighted sages of old predicted it, the com-
ing of September; and on the seventh day thereafter was
Sept. 8 born the best of ladies, the mother of the Lord. Next, after   169
Sept. 21 a sum of thirteen days, Matthew, wise in the gospel, a dis-
ciple of no mean reputation, sent forth his soul to its ap-
pointed destiny, toward everlasting joy. Then, three nights
Sept. 24 later, there comes always to nations far and wide, to the chil-
dren of men, the day of the equinox.

Hwæt, we weorðiað   wide geond eorðan
heah-engles tiid   on hærfeste,
Michaheles,   swa þæt menigo wat,
fif-nihtum ufor   þæs þe folcum byð,
180   eorlum geywed   em-nihtes dæg.
And þæs embe twa-niht   þæt se teoða monð
on folc fereð,   frode geþeahte,
October on tun   us to genihte,
Winter-fylleð,   swa hine wide cigð
185   ig-buende Engle and Seaxe,
weras mid wifum.   Swylce wigena tiid
ymb twentig þæs   twegra healdað
and seofon-nihtum   samod ætgædere
on anne dæg.   We þa æþelingas
190   fyrn gefrunan   þæt hy fore-mære,
Simon and Iudas,   symble wæron,
drihtne dyre;   forþon hi dom hlutan,
eadigne up-weg.   And þæs ofstum bringð
embe feower-niht,   folce genihtsum,
195   Blot-monað on tun,   beornum to wiste,
Nouembris,   niða bearnum
eadignesse,   swa nan oðer na deð
monað maran   miltse drihtnes.
And þy ylcan dæge   ealra we healdað
200   sancta symbel   þara þe sið oððe ær
worhtan in worulde   willan drihtnes.
Syþþan wintres dæg   wide gangeð
on syx-nihtum,   sigel-beortne genimð
hærfest mid herige   hrimes and snawes,
205   forste gefeterad,   be frean hæse,
þæt us wunian ne moton   wangas grene,

Behold, at the harvest, as everyone knows, we honor 176
Sept. 29 widely over earth the feast of the archangel Michael, five
nights after the day of the equinox is manifested to peoples,
revealed to men. And two nights thereafter, by wise counsel, 181
Oct. 1 the tenth month makes its way to the populace, October ar-
rives at our dwellings to bring us abundance — *Winter-fylleð,*
as dwellers on this island, Angles and Saxons, men and
women, widely name that month. They likewise observe, 186
Oct. 28 twenty-seven nights later, the feast of two warriors jointly,
together on a single day. Of those princes we have heard
long ago that the two, Simon and Jude, were always re-
nowned, dear to their Lord; they therefore received glory
as their lot, a blessed ascent. And swiftly November, four 193
Nov. 1 nights later, *Blot-monað,* abundant toward humanity, brings
bounties to our dwellings as sustenance for us mortals, for
the children of men, in such measure that no other month
brings more benevolence from the Lord. And on that same 199
day we observe the feast of all the saints who ever, early or
recently, carried out the will of the Lord in this world.
Nov. 7 Six nights later, far and wide the first day of winter ap- 202
proaches; fettered by frost, at the Lord's command it dis-
patches with its forces of rime and frost the bright, sunny
autumn, so that the green plains, the adornments of earth,

foldan frætuwe.   Þæs ymb feower-niht
þætte Martinus   mære geleorde,
wer womma leas   wealdend sohte,
210 up-engla weard.   Þænne embe eahta-niht
and feowerum   þætte fan Gode
besenctun on sæ-grund   sigefæstne wer,
on brime haran,   þe iu beorna fela
Clementes oft   clypiað to þearfe.
215 And þæs embe seofon-niht,   sige-drihtne leof,
æþele Andreas   up on roderum
his gast ageaf   on Godes wære,
fus on forð-weg.   Þænne folcum bringð
morgen to mannum   monað to tune,
220 Decembris   drihta bearnum,
ærra Iula.   Swylce emb eahta and twelf
niht-gerimes   þætte nergend sylf
þrist-hydigum   Thomase forgeaf
wið earfeðum   ece rice,
225 bealdum beorn-wigan   bletsunga his.
Þænne emb feower-niht   þætte fæder engla
his sunu sende   on þas sidan gesceaft
folcum to frofre.
                    Nu ge findan magon
haligra tiida   þe man healdan sceal,
230 swa bebugeð gebod   geond Bryten-ricu
Sexna kyninges   on þas sylfan tiid.

remain with us no longer. Glorious Martin, a man without   207
Nov. 11 vices, departed four nights after that, sought the ruler, the
guardian of angels above. Next, after eight nights plus four,
Nov. 23 the enemies of God drowned in the gray sea a man steadfast
in victory, plunged him into the ocean depths whom many
men, to their benefit, have long invoked as Clement. Seven   215
Nov. 30 nights later, noble Andrew, being dear to the Lord of victo-
ries and eager to depart, yielded up his soul into God's keep-
ing in the heavens above. The next morning then brings the
Dec. 1 month of December to peoples, *ærra Iula* to humankind
in their dwellings, to the children of men. Likewise, after a   221
Dec. 21 count of eight nights and twelve, the savior himself awarded
bold-minded Thomas an everlasting kingdom in return for
his afflictions, gave his blessing to that daring warrior. It is   226
Dec. 25 then four nights thereafter that the Father of angels sent his
Son into this vast creation as a comfort to its peoples.

Now you are able to discover the saints' feast days that
are to be observed wherever the command of the Saxons'
king extends throughout Britain in this present time.

POEMS ON THE LAST THINGS

Soul and Body

Huru ðæs behofað   hæleða æghwylc
þæt he his sawle sið   sylfa geþence,
hu þæt bið deoplic   þonne se deað cymeð,
asyndreð þa sybbe   þe ær samod wæron,
5   lic ond sawle.   Lang bið syððan
þæt se gast nimeð   æt Gode sylfum
swa wite swa wuldor,   swa him on worulde ær
efne þæt eorð-fæt   ær geworhte.
Sceal se gast cuman   geohðum hremig,
10   symble ymbe seofon-niht   sawle findan
þone lic-homan   þe hie ær lange wæg,
þreo-hund wintra,   butan ær þeod-cyning,
ælmihtig God,   ende worulde
wyrcan wille,   weoruda dryhten.
15   Cleopað þonne swa cearful   cealdan reorde,
spreceð grimlice   se gast to þam duste:
"Hwæt druge ðu dreorega?   To hwan drehtest ðu me,
eorðan fulnes   eal forwisnad,
lames gelicnes?   Lyt ðu gemundest
20   to hwan þinre sawle þing   siðþan wurde,
syððan of lic-homan   læded wære!
Hwæt wite ðu me, weriga?   Hwæt, ðu huru, wyrma gyfl,
lyt geþohtest,   þa ðu lust-gryrum
eallum fulgeodest,   hu ðu on eorðan scealt
25   wyrmum to wiste!   Hwæt, ðu on worulde ær
lyt geþohtest   hu þis is þus lang hider!

192

Soul and Body

It is truly necessary that every man consider for himself his soul's journey, how serious it will be when death comes, separates those kinsmen who were previously united, the body and the soul. Long is the period thereafter when the spirit receives from God himself as much punishment or glory as its earthly vessel wrought for it previously, here in this world. Crying out in grief, the spirit must come, the soul every seventh night unceasingly for three hundred years, to seek out the body that it earlier bore for a long while here— unless the king of nations, almighty God, the Lord of hosts, wills to make an end to this world before then.   9

With a chilling voice, the spirit then calls out thus with anguish, speaks harshly to the dust: "What have you done, O miserable one? Why did you torment me, you wholly corrupt filth of the earth, you likeness of mud? Little did you consider what your soul's future condition would be, once led out of the body! Would you reproach me, you wretch? Lo, you food for worms, when you used to indulge to the full all your horrible desires, little indeed did you consider how you will have to become nourishment for worms in the earth! Lo, in the world you previously gave little thought to how long this condition endures from this time on!   15 ... 22

Hwæt, þe la engel   ufan of roderum
sawle onsende   þurh his sylfes hand,
meotod ælmihtig,   of his mægen-þrymme,
30   ond þe gebohte   blode þy halgan,
ond þu me mid þy heardan   hungre gebunde
ond gehæftnedest   helle witum!
   "Eardode ic þe on innan.   Ne meahte ic ðe of cuman,
flæsce befangen,   ond me fyren-lustas
35   þine geþrungon.   Þæt me þuhte ful oft
þæt hit wære XXX   þusend wintra
to þinum deað-dæge.   A ic uncres gedales onbad
earfoðlice.   Nis nu huru se ende to god!
   "Wære þu þe wiste wlanc   ond wines sæd,
40   þrymful þunedest,   ond ic ofþyrsted wæs
Godes lic-homan,   gastes drynces.
Forðan þu ne hogodest   her on life,
syððan ic ðe on worulde   wunian sceolde,
þæt ðu wære þurh flæsc   ond þurh fyren-lustas
45   strange gestryned   ond gestaðolod þurh me,
ond ic wæs gast on ðe   fram Gode sended.
Næfre ðu me wið swa heardum   helle witum
ne generedest   þurh þinra nieda lust.
Scealt ðu minra gescenta   sceame þrowian
50   on ðam myclan dæge   þonne eall manna cynn
se an-cenneda   ealle gesamnað.
Ne eart ðu þon leofra   nænigum lifigendra
men to gemæccan,   ne meder ne fæder
ne nænigum gesybban,   þonne se swearta hrefen,
55   syððan ic ana of ðe   ut siðode
þurh þæs sylfes hand   þe ic ær onsended wæs.
Ne magon þe nu heonon adon   hyrsta þa readan

Lo, indeed, from heaven above, the angel sent a soul into   27
you through his very own hand, the almighty creator by his
powerful majesty, and purchased you with that holy blood;
and you have shackled me with grievous hunger and impris-
oned me in the torments of hell!

"I used to dwell within you; I could not depart from you,   33
imprisoned in flesh as I was, and your sinful desires op-
pressed me. Very often it seemed to me that it would be
thirty thousand years until your death day. I was always pain-
fully waiting for the two of us to be separated. None too
good, indeed, is the ending now!

"You were flushed with food and sated with wine, you   39
were puffed up with grandeur, and I was thirsting after
God's body, after drink for the spirit. For during life here,
after I was made to dwell within you in this world, you failed
to consider that you were begotten by powerful drives,
through flesh and through sinful desires, and that you were
kept firmly fixed by me, and that I, the soul, was sent into
you by God. Because of your desire for pleasures, you never   47
sheltered me from such dire hell-torments. You will have
to suffer shame for my undoing on that great day when
the only-begotten one [Christ] will gather the entire race of
humanity as a whole. To no one living, not to father or   52
mother or any kinsman, will you be any dearer a compan-
ion than the dark raven, once I have journeyed out of you
unaccompanied, guided by the hand of the very one from
whom I was previously sent. Red-gold ornaments cannot   57

ne gold ne seolfor   ne þinra goda nan,
ne þinre bryde beag   ne þin bold-wela,
60   ne nan þara goda   þe ðu iu ahtest,
ac her sceolon onbidan   ban bereafod,
besliten synum,   ond þe þin sawl sceal
minum unwillum   oft gesecan,
wemman þe mid wordum,   swa ðu worhtest to me.
65   "Eart ðu nu dumb ond deaf,   ne synt þine dreamas awiht.
Sceal ic ðe nihtes swa þeah   nede gesecan,
synnum gesargod,   ond eft sona fram þe
hweorfan on han-cred,   þonne halige men
lifiendum Gode   lof-sang doð,
70   secan þa hamas   þe ðu me her scrife,
ond þa arleasan   eardung-stowe;
ond þe sculon her mold-wyrmas   manige ceowan,
slitan sarlice   swearte wihta,
gifre ond grædige.   Ne synt þine æhta awihte
75   þe ðu her on moldan   mannum eowdest.
Forðan þe wære selre   swiðe mycle
þonne þe wæron ealle   eorðan speda,
(butan þu hie gedælde   dryhtne sylfum!),
þær ðu wurde æt frymðe fugel   oððe fisc on sæ,
80   oððe on eorðan neat   ætes tilode,
feld-gangende   feoh butan snyttro,
oððe on westenne   wildra deora
þæt grimmeste,   þær swa God wolde;
ge þeah þu wære wyrm-cynna   þæt wyrreste,
85   þonne ðu æfre on moldan   man gewurde
oððe æfre fulwihte   onfon sceolde.
"Þonne ðu for unc bæm   andwyrdan scealt
on ðam miclan dæge,   þonne mannum beoð

now bring you from this place, nor can gold nor silver nor any of your goods, nor the ring of your bride nor the wealth of your dwelling, nor any of those goods that you formerly owned; rather here your bones must abide bereft, their sinews shredded, and I, your soul, must often seek you out, against my will, abuse you with words just as you have done me with deeds.

"Now you are speechless and deaf, your joys amount to 65 nothing. I am nevertheless obliged to seek you out at night, wracked with sins, and quickly part from you again at the cock's crow, when the holy offer their hymn of praise to the living God; then I must depart to seek out those dwellings that you have imposed on me here, those merciless abodes; and here many worms of the earth are to chew on you, dark creatures, voracious and greedy, to rend you painfully. Those possessions of yours that you displayed before others here on earth amount to nothing. And so, rather than if you pos- 76 sessed all the earth's wealth (unless you shared it with the Lord himself!), it would have been better for you by far if, from the very beginning, you had been born a bird or a fish in the sea, or foraged your food as a beast on the ground, a grazing herd animal without reason, or the very fiercest of wild animals in a wasteland, if God so willed; indeed, it would have been better had you been the basest of worms than that you ever were born a human being on earth, or ever received baptism.

"You will then have to answer for the two of us on that 87 great day, when to all humanity those wounds will be revealed

wunda onwrigene, þa ðe on worulde ær
90 fyrenfulle men fyrn geworhton.
Ðonne wyle dryhten sylf dæda gehyran
hæleða gehwylces, heofena scippend,
æt ealra manna gehwam muðes reorde
wunda wiðer-lean. Ac hwæt wylt ðu þær
95 on þam dom-dæge dryhtne secgan?
Þonne ne bið nan na to þæs lytel lið on lime aweaxen,
þæt ðu ne scyle for anra gehwylcum onsundrum
riht agildan, þonne reðe bið
dryhten æt þam dome. Ac hwæt do wyt unc
100 þonne he unc hafað geedbyrded oþre siþe?
Sculon wit þonne eft ætsomne siððan brucan
swylcra yrmða, swa ðu unc her ær scrife!"
    Fyrnað þus þæt flæsc-hord, sceall þonne feran onweg,
secan helle-grund, nallæs heofon-dreamas,
105 dædum gedrefed. Ligeð dust þær hit wæs,
ne mæg him ondsware ænige gehatan,
geomrum gaste, geoce oððe frofre.
Bið þæt heafod tohliden, handa toliðode,
geaglas toginene, goman toslitene,
110 sina beoð asocene, swyra becowen,
fingras tohrorene.
Rib reafiað reðe wyrmas;
drincað hloþum hra, heolfres þurstge.
Bið seo tunge totogen on tyn healfa
115 hungregum to frofre; forþan heo ne mæg huxlicum
wordum wrixlian wið þone werian gast.
Gifer hatte se wyrm, þe þa eaglas beoð
nædle scearpran. Se genydde to
ærest eallra on þam eorð-scræfe,

that sinners previously inflicted in the world long ago. Then the Lord himself, the creator of the heavens, will hear the deeds of each and every man, hear in speech from the mouth of every single person his recompense for [Christ's] wounds. But what will *you* say to the Lord there, on the Judgment Day? No member that has grown on a limb [of your 96 body] is so small that you will not then be obliged to give an account for every single one individually, when the Lord is angry in that judgment. But what will the two of us do on our own behalf when he has brought us to life a second time? Then, brought together once more, we will have to experience from that point on such miseries as you have previously ordained for the two us here!"

In this way the soul heaps reproach on its deposit of flesh; 103 then it must journey away, anguished by the body's deeds, seek out the abyss of hell, not at all the joys of heaven. The dust lies where it was; it can offer no answer to the soul, no aid or comfort to the lamenting spirit. The head is split, the hands are in pieces, the jaws gaping, the gums torn, the sinews drawn, the neck gnawed, the fingers decayed. Ferocious 112 worms ravage the ribs; in swarms they gulp down carrion, thirsting for gore. As nourishment for those hungry ones, the tongue is torn into ten pieces; therefore it cannot disgracefully exchange words with the wretched spirit. *Gifer* [Ravenous] is the name of that worm, whose jaws are more piercing than a needle. First of all, he ventures into that 118

120 þæt he þa tungan totyhð   ond þa teð þurhsmyhð
ond þa eagan þurheteð   ufan on þæt heafod
ond to æt-welan   oðrum gerymeð,
wyrmum to wiste,   þonne þæt werie
lic acolod bið   þæt he lange ær
125 werede mid wædum.   Bið þonne wyrma gifel,
æt on eorþan: þæt mæg æghwylcum
men to gemynde,   mod-snotra gehwam!
    Ðonne bið hyhtlicre   þæt sio halige sawl
færeð to ðam flæsce,   frofre bewunden.
130 Bið þæt ærende   eadiglicre
funden on ferhðe.   Mid gefean seceð
lustum þæt lam-fæt   þæt hie ær lange wæg.
Þonne þa gastas   gode word sprecað,
snottre, sigefæste,   ond þus soðlice
135 þone lic-homan   lustum gretaþ:
    "Wine leofesta,   þeah ðe wyrmas gyt
gifre gretaþ,   nu is þin gast cumen,
fægere gefrætewod,   of mines fæder rice,
arum bewunden.   Eala, min dryhten,
140 þær ic þe moste   mid me lædan,
þæt wyt englas   ealle gesawon,
heofona wuldor,   swylc swa ðu me ær her scrife!
Fæstest ðu on foldan   ond gefyldest me
Godes lic-homan,   gastes dryncet.
145 Wære ðu on wædle,   sealdest me wilna geniht.
Forðan ðu ne þearft sceamian,   þonne sceadene beoþ
þa synfullan   ond þa soðfæstan
on þam mæran dæge,   þæs ðu me geafe,
ne ðe hreowan þearf   her on life

grave so that he rends the tongue and penetrates the teeth, and in the head above he eats through the eyes and clears room for other worms to feast and be nourished, once that wretched body has cooled that for a long time previously was clothed in garments. Then it will be nourishment for worms, their food in the earth: that can serve as a reminder to every wise person!

It will then be with greater hope that the holy soul, em- 128 braced with consolation, journeys to its flesh. A message of the happier kind will be discovered in its heart. With joy the soul gladly seeks out the vessel of clay that it previously wore a long while. On that occasion the souls will speak good words, wise and victorious, and sincerely greet the body with good will, in this way:

"Though worms still hungrily assail you, dearest friend, 136 your spirit has now come, beautifully adorned, wreathed with honors, from the kingdom of my Father. Alas, my lord, if only I could guide you with me, so that we two would behold all the angels, the glory of the heavens, just as you previously made provision for me here! You fasted on earth and 143 filled me with God's body, with the drink of the spirit. You were in poverty and gave me abundance of joys. Therefore, when the sinful and the righteous are sorted in two on that glorious day, you need not be ashamed of what you gave me, nor should you feel remorse here in this life for all the many

150   ealles swa mycles   swa ðu me sealdest
on gemot-stede   manna ond engla.
   "Bygdest ðu þe for hæleðum   ond ahofe me
on ecne dream.
Forþan me a langaþ,   leofost manna,
155   on minum hige hearde,   þæs þe ic þe on þyssum
                                hynðum wat
wyrmum to wiste,   ac þæt wolde God,
þæt þu æfre þus laðlic   leger-bed cure.
Wolde ic þe ðonne secgan   þæt ðu ne sorgode,
forðan wyt bioð gegæderode   æt Godes dome.
160   Moton wyt þonne ætsomne   syþþan brucan
swylcra arna   swa ðu unc ær scrife,
ond unc on heofonum   heah-þungene beon.
Ne þurfon wyt beon cearie   æt cyme dryhtnes,
ne þære andsware   yfele habban
165   sorge in hreðre,   ac wyt sylfe magon
æt ðam dome þær   dædum agilpan,
hwylce earnunga   uncre wæron.
Wat ic þæt þu wære   on woruld-rice
geþungen þrymlice   þysses . . ."

things that you will have imparted to me at that gathering place of human beings and angels.

"You made yourself low in men's eyes and raised me up to everlasting joy. Therefore, most beloved, it always grieves me acutely in my thoughts to know that you reside in this degraded condition as food for worms; but God has willed that you should always embrace so loathsome a bed to rest in. I would like to have told you then that you need not sorrow, since we two will be brought together before the judgment of God. Then the two of us will afterward be able to enjoy together such graces as you previously ordained for us, and be utterly perfected in heaven. We will not need to be worried at the Lord's coming and have anxious care at heart concerning our response. Rather the two of us will be able to exult there about our deeds and what merits were ours. I know that, in the kingdom of this world, you were gloriously accomplished at this . . ."

152

160

168

The Soul's Address to the Body
(from the Worcester Fragments)

(Fragment A)

            . . . midden-earde

ond alle þeo isceæfetan   þe him to sculen.

ond mid muchele crefte   þene mon he idihte,

ond him on ileide   lif ond soule.

A5   Softliche he heo isomnede,   ac þær biþ sor idol.

Þet bodeþ þet bearn   þonne hit iboren biþ:

hit greoneþ ond woaneþ   ond mænet þeo weowe,

ond þene seoruhfule siþ   ond þet sori idol—

þet soule schal ond licame   sorliche idælen;

A10   forþon hit cumeþ weopinde   ond woniende iwiteþ.

Deaþ mid his pricke   pineþ þene licame;

he walkeþ ond wendeþ   ond woneþ ofte-siþes.

He sæiþ on his bedde,   "Wo me þet ic libbe,

þet æffre mine lif-dawes   þus longe me ilesteþ!"

A15   For heui is his greoning   ond seohrful is his woaning,

ond al is his siþ   mid seorwe biwunden.

Him deaueþ þa æren,   him dimmeþ þa eiȝen,

him scerpeþ þe neose,   him scrinckeþ þa lippen,

him scorteþ þe tunge,

A20   him trukeþ his iwit,   him teoreþ his miht,

him coldeþ his lime;   liggeþ þe ban stille.

The Soul's Address to the Body
(from the Worcester Fragments)

. . . earth and all the creatures that must return to it; and with great skill he created man and placed in him life and a soul. Gently he mingled them together, but their pain- A5 ful separation is coming. Thus a child prophesies when it is born: it groans and wails and decries that misery, the sorrow- ful journey and the painful separation—that soul and body must sorrowfully part; for weeping a child arrives, and wail- ing it will pass away. With its sting death pains the body; the A11 body tosses and turns and often complains. On its bed it says, "Woe to me that I live, that the days of life endure so long for me!" For grievous is its groaning, and painful is its wailing, and all its course is beset with misery. Its ears A17 grow deaf, its eyes dim, its nose sharpens, its lips shrivel, its tongue retracts, its mind fails, its strength fades, its limbs

Þonne biþ þet soule-hus   seoruhliche bereaued
at also muchele wunne   þe þerinne wunede.
Þus biþ þæs bearnes   bodunge ifulled:
A25   þeo moder greoneþ   ond þet bearn woaneþ.
So biþ þeo burd-tid   mid balewen imenged,
so biþ eft þe feorþ-siþ   mid seoruwen al bewunden.
    Þonne þe licame ond þe sowle   soriliche todæleþ,
þonne biþ þet wræcche lif   iended al mid sori siþ.
A30   Þonne biþ þe feiʒe   iflut to þen flore;
he biþ eastward istreiht,   he biþ sone stif,
he coldeþ also clei;   hit is him ikunde.
Mon hine met mid one ʒerde   ond þa molde seoþþen
ne mot he of þære molde   habben nammore,
A35   þonne þet rihte imet   rihtliche tæcheþ.
Þonne liþ þe clei-clot   colde on þen flore,
ond him sone from fleoþ   þeo he ær freome dude.
Nulleþ heo mid honden   his heafod riht wenden;
heom þuncheþ þet hore honden   swuþe beoþ ifuled,
A40   gif heo hondleþ þene deade,   seoþþen his deaʒes beoþ
                                            agon.
    Sone cumeþ þet wrecche wif,   þe forhoweþ þene
                                   earfeþ-siþ,
forbindeþ þæs dædan muþ   ond his dimme eʒen;
þonne þet wrecche wif   forhoweþ þene earueþ-siþ,
for ufel is þeo wrecche lufe   þonne þeo unblisse cumaþ.
A45   Þonne besihþ þeo soule   sorliche to þen lic-hame . . .

(FRAGMENT B)

". . . woa wrohtest þu me   þeo hwule þet ic wunede inne þe,
for þu were leas ond lutiʒ   ond unriht lufedest;

206

grow chill; the bones lie still. The soul's house will then be painfully bereft of as much joy as ever dwelled within it. Thus the child's prophecy is fulfilled: the mother groans and A24 the child wails. Just as the time of birth is mingled with affliction, so too the time of death is beset with suffering.

When the body and the soul painfully part, miserable life A28 will be utterly ended by that grievous journey. Then the doomed man is placed on the floor; he is laid out facing east, will soon be stiff, grows cold as clay; such is his nature. First he is measured with a stave, and then the earth is measured; from earth he can get no more than what that precise measurement justly determines. The lump of clay then lies cold A36 on the floor, and those to whom he previously showed favor flee from him straightaway. They have no wish to adjust his head properly, using their hands; it seems to them that their hands will be greatly defiled if they touch the dead man, after his days have passed.

Immediately his miserable wife arrives, who curses the A41 dire event, binds up the dead man's mouth and his unseeing eyes; then the miserable wife curses that dire event, for her miserable love is worthless when misfortune comes. Then, sorrowfully, the soul looks to the body . . .

FRAGMENT B

". . . you caused me woe for as long as I dwelled in you, for you were deceitful and cunning, and you loved evil; you

godnesse ond riht   æfre þu onscunedest.

Hwar is nu þeo modinesse,   swo muchel þe þu lufedæst?

B5   Hwar beoþ nu þeo pundes   þurh panewes igædered?

Heo weren monifolde   bi markes itolde.

Hwar beoþ nu þeo gold-fæten   þeo þe guldene comen to
                                       þine honden?

Þin blisse is nu al agon;   min seoruwe is fornon.

Hwar beoþ nu þin wæde   þe þu wel lufedest?

B10   Hwar beoþ þe sibbe   þe seten sori ofer þe,

beden swuþe ȝeorne   þet þe come bote?

Heom þuþte al to longe   þet þu were on liue,

for heo weren grædie   to gripen þine æihte.

Nu heo hi dæleþ heom imong;   heo doþ þe wiþuten.

B15   Ac nu heo beoþ fuse   to bringen þe ut of huse,

bringen þe ut æt þire dure;   of weolen þu ært bedæled.

Hwui noldest þu beþenchen me   þeo hwile ic was innen þe,

ac semdest me mid sunne,   forþon ic seoruhful eam?

Weile, þet ic souhte   so seoruhfulne buc!

B20   "Noldest þu þe makien lufe   wiþ ilærede men,

ȝiven ham of þine gode,   þet heo þe fore beden.

Heo mihten mid salm-songe   þine sunne acwenchen,

mid hore messe   þine misdeden fore biddan;

heo mihten offrian loc   leofliche for þe,

B25   swuþe deor-wurþe lac,   licame Cristes,

þurh þære þu were alesed   from helle-wite;

ond mid his reade blode,   þet he ȝeat on rode.

Þo þu were ifreoed   to farene into heouene,

ac þu fenge to þeowdome   þurh þæs deofles lore.

always scorned goodness and right. Where now is the arrogance that you loved so much? Where now are the pounds that you amassed, penny by penny? They were numerous, tallied in marks. Where now are the golden vessels that B7 came, fashioned from gold, into your hands? Your joy is now entirely gone; my sorrow is in store. Where now are your clothes that you loved well? Where are the kinsmen who sat grieving over you, who prayed very earnestly that healing would come to you? All too long it seemed to them that you B12 kept on living, for they were greedy to grab your possessions. Now they apportion those among themselves; they put you outside. Now, moreover, they are eager to carry you out of the house, to haul you out through your own door; you are deprived of riches. Why did you not want to think about me while I was within you, but rather burdened me with sins, which is why I am filled with sorrow? Alas, that I ever sought out so sorry a carcass!

"You did not want to endear yourself to learned men, to B20 give to them of your wealth so that they would pray on your behalf. With their psalmody they might have extinguished your sins, with their masses might have interceded for your evil acts; they might have beneficently offered sacrifices for your sake, very precious offerings, the body of Christ by which you were freed from the torment of hell; and along with that, his red blood that he shed on the cross. Then you would have been freed to journey into heaven, but, by the devil's teaching, you entered upon slavery.

B30   "Bi þe hit is iseid   —ond soþ hit is—on boken:
    Qui custodit divitias servus est divitiis.
    Þu were þeow   þines weolan;
    noldest þu nouht þærof dælen   for drihtenes willæn,
    ac æfre þu grædiliche   gæderdest þe more.
B35   Luþerliche eart þu forloren   from al þet þu lufedest,
    and ic scal, wræcche soule,   weowe nu driæn.
    Eart þu nu loþ ond unwurþ   alle þine freonden.
    Nu ham þuncheþ alto long   þet þu ham neih list,
    ær þu beo ibrouht   þær þu beon scalt,
B40   on deope sæþe,   on durelease huse.
    Þær wurmes wældeþ   al þet þe wurþest was,
    fulest alre holde   þe þu icwemdest ær
    mid alre þære swetnesse   þeo þu swuþe lufedest.
    Þeo swetnesse is nu al agon,   þet bittere þe biþ fornon;
B45   þet bittere ilæsteþ æffre,   þet swete ne cumeþ þe næffre . . ."

(Fragment C)

    ". . . þuncheþ   þet þu hire bilefdest."
      Ʒet sæiþ þeo sowle   soriliche to þen licame:
    "Ne þearft þu on stirope   stonden mid fotan,
    on nenne gold-fohne bowe,   for þu scalt faren al to howe,
C5   ond þu scalt nu ruglunge   ridæn to þære eorþe,
    utset æt þære dure   (ne þearft þu næffre onʒean cumæn!),
    reowliche riden,   sone beræfed
    at þene eorþliche weole   þe þu iwold ohtest.
    Nu mon mæi seggen bi þe: 'Þes mon is iwiten nu her,

"In books it is said of you—and it is true: *He who keeps* B30
his riches is a slave to riches. You were a slave to your wealth;
you did not wish to dole out any portion of it for the Lord's
sake, but you always greedily gathered more for yourself. In
wickedness you are lost to all that you loved, and I, the mis-
erable soul, must now endure suffering. You are now hateful B37
and despicable to all your friends. Now it seems all too long
to them that you lie nearby before being carried to the place
where you must abide, in a deep pit, a doorless house. There B41
worms will rule over all that was most precious to you; [the
body] that you previously indulged with all the sweetness
that you loved greatly will be the foulest of all carcasses.
Now that sweetness is entirely past, and bitterness is in
store for you; the bitterness will last forever, the sweetness
return to you never . . ."

FRAGMENT C

". . . what you left to it [the soul?] seems."

With sorrow the soul speaks further to the body: "You
need not stand in stirrups with your feet nor mount any
gold-embossed saddle, for you must altogether journey to
agony, and you must now ride backward to earth; once put
out of doors (you need never go back inside!), you must rue-
fully ride, soon bereft of the earthly wealth that you pos-
sessed. It can now be said of you: 'This man is now gone C9

C10   weila, ond his weolæn   beoþ her belæfed;
        nolde he nefre þærof don   his drihtenes wille.'
        Ac æfre þu gæderedest   gærsume on þine feonde;
        nulleþ heo nimen gete   hwo hit biȝete!
        Nafst þu bute weilawei   þet þu weole heuedest.
C15   Al is reowliche þin siþ   efter þin wrecche lif.
            "Þeo men beoþ þe bliþre,   þe arisen ær wiþ þe,
        þet þin muþ is betuned,   þe þu þeo teone ut lettest,
        þe heom sore grulde,   þet ham gros þe aȝan.
        Deaþ hine haueþ bituned   ond þene teone aleid.
C20   Soþ is iseid   on þen salme-bec:
        Os tuum habundavit malitia;
        was on þine muþe   luþernesse ripe.
            "Noldest þu on þine huse   herborwen þeo wrecchen;
        ne mihten heo under þine roue   none reste finden.
C25   Noldest þu næfre helpen   þam orlease wrecchen,
        ac þu sete on þine benche,   underleid mid þine bolstre;
        þu wurpe cneow ofer cneow.   Ne icneowe þu þe sulfen,
        þet þu scoldest mid wurmen   wunien in eorþan.
        Nu þu hauest neowe hus,   inne beþrungen;
C30   lowe beoþ þe hele-wowes,   unheiȝe beoþ þe sid-wowes;
        þin rof liiþ   on þin breoste ful neih.
        Colde is þe ibedded,   cloþes bideled.
        Nulleþ þine hinen   cloþes þe senden,
        for heom þuncheþ al to lut,   þet þu heom bilefdest;
C35   þet þu hefdest onhorded,   heo hit wulleþ heldan.
        Þus is iwitan þin weole;   wendest þet hit þin were!
        Þus ageþ nu þin siþ   efter þin wrecche lif.
        Þe sculen nu waxen   wurmes be siden,
        þeo hungrie feond,   þeo þe freten wulleþ.

hence, alas, and his riches are left behind here; he never wished to accomplish his Lord's will with them.' Rather you always gathered treasures from your enemies; [those treasures] do not care who gets the lot! You have nothing but woe for having possessed wealth. Entirely rueful is your journey after your miserable life.

"People who formerly quarreled with you will be the hap- C16 pier now that your mouth is shut, from which you let fly the insults that sorely aggrieved them, that made them uneasy in your presence. Death has shut that mouth and put aside that insult. Truly is it said in the book of Psalms: *Thy mouth hath abounded with evil;* wickedness was flourishing in your mouth.

"You did not wish to shelter wretches in your house; they C23 could find no rest under your roof. You never wished to help poor wretches, but you sat on your bench, a cushion set beneath you, your legs crossed. You did not know your own self, that you would have to abide with worms in the earth. Now you have a new house, cramped inside; the walls C29 at the ends are low, the walls to either side none too high; your roof lies very close to your chest. Coldly a bed is made for you, stripped of clothes. Your hirelings do not want to give you any clothes, since what you left them seems all too meager to them; they will keep what you had hoarded. Thus C36 your wealth is gone; you fancied that it was yours! Thus your journey now proceeds after your miserable life. Now worms must spring up about you, ravenous enemies who will feed

C40   Heo wulleþ þe frecliche freten,   for heom þin flæsc likeþ.
       Heo wulleþ freten þin fule hold,   þeo hwule heo hit findeþ.
       Þonne hit al biþ agon,   heo wulleþ gnawen þine bon,
       þeo orlease wurmes.   Heo windeþ on þin armes,
       heo brekeþ þine breoste,   ond borieþ þurh ofer al;
C45   heo creopeþ in ond ut: þet hord is hore owen!
       Ond so heo wulleþ waden   wide in þine wombe,
       todelen þine þermes   þeo þe deore weren,
       lifre ond þine lihte   lodliche torenden.
       Ond so scal formelten   mawe ond þin milte,
C50   ond so scal þin . . ."

                    (FRAGMENT D)

       ". . . þu scalt nu . . .   wurmes of þine flæsce;
       þu scalt fostren þine feond   þet þu beo al ifreten.
       Þu scalt nu herborwen   unhol wihte;
       noldest þu ær gode men   for lufe god dælan.
D5   Heo wulleþ wurchen hore hord   on þine heaued-ponne.
       Nulleþ heo bileafen   þine lippen unfreten,
       ac þu scalt grisliche   grennien on men;
       hwo so hit iseiȝe,   he mihte beon offered.
       Reowliche biþ so þin siþ   efter þin wrecche lif.

D10   "Nu me wule swopen þine flor   ond þet flet clensien,
       for hit is heom þe loþre,   þe þu þeron leiȝe.
       Heo wulleþ mid holi-watere   beworpen ec þeo wowes,
       bletsien ham ȝeorne   to burewen ham wiþ þe,
       beren ut þin bed-strau,   beornen hit mid fure.
D15   Þus þu ert nu ilufed,   seoþþen þu me forlure!
       Al hit is reowliche þin siþ   efter þin wrecche lif."

on you. Eagerly will they feed on you, for your flesh delights them. They will feed on your filthy flesh as long as they find C41 it. When that is all gone, those pitiless worms will gnaw on your bones. They will coil about your arms; they penetrate your chest cavity and burrow through it completely; they creep in and out: that treasure is theirs! And so they will C46 make their way widely throughout your belly, rend the guts that were precious to you, fiercely tear to pieces your liver and lungs. And in this way must your stomach and spleen disintegrate, and so must your . . ."

Fragment D

". . . you must now . . . worms from your flesh; you must foster your own enemies, with the result that you are entirely eaten up. You must now shelter foul creatures; previously you did not wish to give goods out of love to those who were good. The worms will make their treasure hoard inside your D5 skull. They will not leave your lips uneaten, but you will have to show to all a frightful grin; whoever sees it might grow afraid. Rueful will be your journey after your miserable life.

"Now someone will want to sweep your floor and wash its D10 surface, as it is the more repellent for your having lain upon it. They also want to sprinkle the walls with holy water, eagerly bless those in order to protect themselves from you; they carry out your bedstraw, burn it with fire. Thus are you loved after you have lost me! Your journey is entirely rueful after your miserable life."

          Ʒet sæiþ þe soule   soriliche to hire licame:
          "Wendest þu, la, erming,   her o to wunienne?
          Nes hit þe nowiht icunde   þet þu icoren hefdest?
D20   Nes hit icunde þe more   þen þine cunne biuoren þe?
          Ne heold ic þine eiʒen opene   þeo hwule ic þe inne was?
          Hwi noldest þu lefen,   þa þu hit iseiʒe,
          hu þine fore-fæderes   ferden biforen þe?
          Nu heo wunieþ on eorþe;   wurmes ham habbeþ todæled,
D25   iscend hore sorhfulle bones   þe þeo sunne wrohten."
              Þa ʒet seiþ þeo soule   soriliche to hire lic-hame:
          "Æfre þu were luþer   þeo hwile þu lif hæfdest.
          Þu were leas ond luti   ond unriht lufedest.
          Mid þine luþere deden   deredest cristene men,
D30   ond mid worde ond mid werke,   so þu wurst mihtest.
          Ic com from Gode   clene to þe isend,
          ac þu hauest unc fordon   mid þine luþere deden.
          Æfre þu were gredi   ond mid gromen þe onfulled;
          unneaþe ic on þe   eni wununge hæfde
D35   for hearde niþe   ond ofer-mete fulle,
          for þin wombe was þin God   ond þin wulder was iscend.
          Forloren þu hauest þeo ece blisse;   binumen þu hauest
                                                                    þe paradis;
          binumen þe is þet holi lond;   þen deofle þu bist isold on
                                                                    hond.
          For noldest þu nefre habben inouh,   buten þu hefdest
                                                                    unifouh.
D40   Nu is þet swete al agon,   þet bittere þe biþ fornon;
          þet bittere ilest þe efre,   þet gode ne cumeþ þe nefre.
          Þus ageþ nu þin siþ   æfter þin wrecce lif.
              "Þu wendest þet þin ende   nefre ne cuman scolde;

With sorrow the soul speaks further to the body: "Alas, D17
poor man, did you think to dwell here forever? Was mortality not wholly innate in you? Was it any more so to you than to your kin before you? Did I not hold your eyes open while I dwelled within you? Since you witnessed it for yourself, D22
why did you not believe how your forefathers departed before you? Now they dwell in earth; worms have reduced them to bits, brought injury to those sorrowful bones that committed sins."

With sorrow the soul then speaks further to its body: "As D26
long as you had life, you were always wicked. You were deceitful and cunning, and you loved evil. You harmed Christians with your wicked actions, with both words and deeds, to the worst degree you could. I arrived pure, sent to you D31
from God, but you have destroyed us both with your wicked actions. You were always greedy and filled with anger; I scarcely had any dwelling place within you on account of your cruel hatred and glutted appetite, for your belly was your God and your glory was disfigured. You have lost ever- D37
lasting happiness; you have deprived yourself of Paradise; from you has that sacred land been withdrawn; you have been sold into the devil's hand. For you never had enough of a thing unless you had it to excess. Now that sweetness is entirely past, and bitterness is in store for you; the bitterness will last forever, the good return to you never. So your journey now proceeds after your miserable life.

"You fancied that your end would never have to come; D43

to longe þolede deaþ þe   þet he nolde nimen þe,

D45   for efre þu arerdest sake   ond unseihte makedest,
ond ic was wiþinnen þe   biclused swuþe fule.
Þu were wed-lowe ond mon-sware   ond were huned inouh,
for þu were mid sunne ifulled   al wiþinne,
for þe deofle lahte his hord   ful neih þine heorte.

D50   Efre þu woldest fullen   al þet was his wille;
ic . . ."

(FRAGMENT E)

". . . noldest þu nefre wurchen drihtenes wille.
. . . iwold ahte."

Þe ȝet seiþ þeo soule   soriliche to hire licame:
"Clene biþ þeo eorþe   ær þu to hire tocume,

E5   ac þu heo afulest   mid þine fule holde;
þet is þet fule hold,   afursed from monnen.
Nu þu bist bihuded   on alre horde fulest,
on deope seaþe,   on durelease huse.
Þu scalt rotien ond brostnian;   þine bon beoþ bedæled

E10   of þære wæde   þe heo weren to iwunede.
Brekeþ liþ from liþe.   Liggeþ þe bon stille
oþ ure drihten eft   of deaþe heo aræreþ,
so he alle men deþ   þonne domes dai cumeþ.
Þonne scalt þu, erming,   up arisen;

E15   imeten þine morþ-deden   þeo þe murie weren,
seoruhful ond sori-mod,   so þin lif wrouhte.

"Nu beoþ þine earen fordutte,   ne dreame ihereþ;
þeo leorneden þeo listen   þa luþere weren,
wowe domes   ond gultes feole.

E20   Oþre beræfedest   rihtes istreones

too long did death endure you, that he did not wish to carry you off, for you were always raising strife and making quarrels, and I was very filthily penned inside you. You were a violator of agreements and breaker of oaths and were hated enough, since you were entirely filled with sin, for the devil had fired his dart very near your heart. You would always carry out all that he willed; I . . ."

Fragment E

". . . you never wished to carry out the Lord's will. . . . had possession."

With sorrow the soul then speaks further to its body: "The earth is pure before you come to it, but you have befouled it with your filthy corpse; that is that filthy corpse, now far removed from living people. Now you are concealed E7 in the foulest of all treasuries, in a deep pit, a doorless house. You must rot and decay; your bones will be deprived of the clothes to which they were accustomed. Limb will sunder E11 from limb. The bones will lie still until our Lord raises them again from death, just he does all people when the Judgment Day comes. At that time, poor man, you must rise up; full of pain and sad at heart, you must confront your deadly actions, which gave you pleasure when committed during your lifetime.

"Now your ears are stopped and hear no joyful sound; E17 they used to take in cunning words that were evil, corrupt judgments and much that was sinful. At the devil's instruc-

þurh þæs deofles lore, þeo þe likede wel,
þe wel tuhte his hearpe ond tuhte þe to him.
Þu iherdest þene dream þe was drihten ful loþ.
He swefede þe mid þen sweiʒe; swote þu sleptest
E25   longe on þine bedde. . . . is þe to chirche.
Ne mostes þu iheren þeo holie dræmes,
þeo bellen rungen, þet unker becnunge wæs;
ne holie lore, þe unker help wære;
ac efre he tuhte þe, þet lut þeo þe iwold ahte.
E30   Ac nu beoþ fordutte þine dream-þurles;
ne ihereþ heo ne more none herunge of þe
ær þeo bemen blowen þe unc becnien sculen
from deaþes dimnesse to drihtenes dome.
Þonne þu scalt iheren þene hearde dom
E35   þe þu on þisse life luþerliche ofeodest."
    Þet ʒet seiþ þe sowle soriliche to hire licame:
"Nu þu bist afursed from alle þine freonden;
nu is þiin muþ forscutted, for deaþ hine haueþ fordutted.
Ne biþ he ne mare undon ær cume þæs heiʒe kinges dom.
E40   Þonne hit biþ isene, so hit on psalme seiþ:
Reddituri sunt de factis propriis rationem;
þonne sculen þeo soule seggen hore deden
wisliche þurh wisdome, for drihten hit wot.
Þonne heo onfoþ hore dom of drihtenes muþe,
E45   also hit is awriten of drihtenes muþe:
Ite maledicti in ignem eternum.
Þonne sculen wit siþien to alre seoruwe mest,
faren mid feondes in þet eche fur,

tion, which pleased you well, you used to rob others of their just earnings; he plucked his harp skillfully and drew you to him. That was the happy noise you used to hear, which was utterly hateful to the Lord. He [the devil] lulled you with that music; sweetly you slept long on your bed. . . . you to church. You cannot hear the holy sounds, the bells when they are rung, which was a signal to us both; nor can you hear the holy teaching that would have been a help to us; instead, the devil was always tugging at you, so that bells and teaching had little power. But now your holes for [hearing] joyful noise are stopped; no longer will they hear any sound for you until those trumpets blow that are to summon us from the darkness of death to the Lord's judgment. Then you will have to hear the harsh judgment that you have wickedly brought on yourself in the present life." E23 E30

With sorrow the soul then speaks further to its body: "Now you are sent far from all your friends; now your mouth is shut tight, for death has stopped it. It will not be opened any more before the judgment of the supreme king arrives. It will then be manifest, as it says in the psalm, that *they shall offer a reckoning for their own deeds;* then the souls must recount their actions prudently and wisely, for the Lord knows all. Then they will receive their judgment from the Lord's mouth, just as it was written down from the Lord's mouth: *Depart from me, you cursed ones, into everlasting fire.* Then the two of us will have to journey to the greatest of all sorrows, depart with demons into the everlasting fire, burn E36 E40

beornen æfre: ende nis þer nefre.

E50 *Et qui bona egerunt ibunt in vitam eternam;*
þonne sculen þeo goden   mid Gode siþian,
echeliche wunien   in alre wuldre mest . . ."

(FRAGMENT F)

". . . me suke to þe:
Os meum aperui et attraxi spiritum;
þu opnedest þin muþ   ond drowe me to þe.
Walawa ond wa is me,   þet ic efre com to þe!

F5 For noldest þu mid þine muþe   bimænen þine neode;
ac efre diȝelliche   þu woldest ham bidernan.
Noldest þu ham siggen   biforen none preosten,
þer sunfulle men   secheþ ham ore,
bimæneþ hore misdeden   ond seoþþen miltse onfoþ,

F10 þurh soþne scrift   siþieþ to Criste,
seggeþ hore sunnen   ond hore soule helpeþ.
Þurh soþe bireousunge   þeo soule reste onfoþ,
ac ne þearf ic nefre resten   þurh þine bireousunge;
ac altogædere ic am forloren   þurh þine luþere deden.

F15 Noldest þu mid muþe   bidden me none miltse.
Nu þu ert adumbed   ond deaþ haueþ þe keiȝe;
mid clutes þu ert forbunden   ond loþ alle freonden
efre ma eft   on to lokienne.
   "Þus is reouliche þin siþ   efter þin wrecche lif,

F20 for þu were biset   þicke mid sunnen,
ond alle heo weren prikiende   so piles on ile.
He biþ þicke mid piles;   ne prikieþ heo hine no wiht,
for al biþ þet softe   iwend to him sulfen,
þet ne mawen his piles   prikien hine sore,

222

there forever: there will be no end to it. *And those who have* E50
done good will depart into everlasting life; then the good are to
journey together with God, dwell forever in the greatest of
all glories . . ."

FRAGMENT F

". . . sucked me to you: *I opened my mouth and drew in breath;*
you opened your mouth and drew me to you. Alas and woe is
me, that ever I came to you! For you never wished to use
your mouth to decry your sins, but rather you always desired
to conceal them in secret. You did not want to speak of them F7
in the presence of any priest, where sinners seek grace for
themselves, lament their wrongful acts and afterward re-
ceive mercy, journey toward Christ by means of genuine
confession, tell their sins and aid their own souls. Through
genuine repentance, souls receive rest; never shall I rest
through your repentance, but I am instead completely lost,
on account of your wicked actions. You did not desire to use F15
your mouth to pray any mercy for me. Now you are struck
dumb, and death holds the key; you are wrapped in rags and
hateful for all of your friends ever to look upon again.

"Thus rueful is your journey after your miserable life, for F19
you were thickly surrounded by sins, and they were all
prickly, like the spines on a hedgehog. That animal is densely
covered with spines; yet they do not prick it at all, since the
soft parts point inward toward its body, so that the spines
cannot painfully prick it, because the sharp part is entirely

F25   for al biþ þet scearpe   him iwend fromward.
        So þu were mid sunne   iset al wiþinne;
        þeo sunfule pikes   prikieþ me ful sore,
        ac al þet softe   was iwend to þe suluen,
        ond efre þet scerpe   scorede me touward;
F30   heo weren iwend   so me wurst was.
        Ic was mid þine prickunge   ipined ful sore,
        ac nu me wulleþ prikien   þeo pikes inne helle,
        pinien me ful sore,   all for þine sunne.
           "Ic was on heihnesse isceapen   ond soule ihoten.
F35   Ic was þe seoueþe isceaft,   so þeo bec seggeþ,
        þe þe almihti God   mildeliche iwrouhte,
        wisliche mid worde;   so hit al iwearþ:
        heouene ond eorþe,   luft ond engles,
        wind ond water,   ond þæs monnes soule.
F40   Þis beoþ þeo seouene   þe ic ær fore seide.
        Þis was makunge   þæs almihties fæder;
        of þissen andweorke   alle þing he iwrouhte,
        and þus hit is iwriten   on holie wisdome:
        'Fiat,' et facta sunt omnia;
F45   he seide 'iwurþe,'   ond alle þing iworþen.
        Þus mid one worde   al hit was iwurþen.
        He iscop þurh þene sune   alle isceafte
        wisliche þurh wisdome,   ond efre he hit wiseþ
        ad imaginem et similitudinem.
F50   Ond ic deore-wurþe   drihtenes onlicnesse . . ."

(FRAGMENT G)

    "... ond ic þe ...   mid loþre lufe,
    ond ic þin wale iwearþ   hu so þu woldest.
    Weila þine fule iwill!   Wo haueþ hit me idon.

pointed outward. In the same way, you were thickset on the F26
inside with sins; the sinful spikes prick me very painfully, but
all the soft part was turned in your direction, and the sharp-
ness was sticking out in my direction; the spines were di-
rected in a way that was worst for me. I was painfully tor-
mented by your pricking, but now the spines are going to
prick me in hell, torment me very painfully, all on account of
your sins.

"I was created in an exalted condition and given the name F34
'soul.' As books recount, I was the seventh creature that al-
mighty God made in his mercy, wisely created through his
word; in this way all came to be: heaven and earth, cloud and
angels, wind and water and the human soul. These are the F40
seven creations that I mentioned before. This was the al-
mighty Father's creative work; out of this material he cre-
ated all other things, and thus it is written in holy wisdom:
Let there be,' and all things were made; he said 'Let there be,'
and all things came to be. Thus with a single word it was all F46
brought into being. Through the Son, as through wisdom,
he wisely fashioned all creation and guides it always *in his
image and likeness.* And I [bore] the precious likeness of the
Lord..."

Fragment G

"... and I ... you with loathsome affection, and I became
your slave according to your wishes. Woe to your filthy de-
sire! It has caused me grief. You filthy maggot food, why

Þu fule maþe-mete,   hwi hauest þu me biswiken?

G5   For þine fule sunne   ic scal nu to helle,

dreiȝen þer wrecche siþ,   all for þine fule lif.

   "Ȝet ic wulle þe ætwiten   mine wea-siþes,

nu ic scal soriliche   siþien from þe.

Nu beoþ þine teþ atruked;   þin tunge is ascorted,

G10   þeo þe facen was   ond þen feonde icwemde.

Mid wowe domes   ond mid gultes feole

oþre birefedest   rihtes istreones,

gæderedest to gærsume,   ac hit is nu all igon

þurh þæs deofles lore,   þe þe licode wel.

G15   Nu liþ þin tunge stille   on ful colde denne.

Nafest þu gaersume þe mo   þe heo was spekinde so,

for heo was faken biforen   ond atterne bihinden;

heo demde feole domes   þe drihten weren loþe.

Iseid hit is on psalme   —ond ful soþe hit is bi hire:

G20   *Lingua tua concinnabat dolos;*

heo ȝeoddede fakenliche   ond þen feonde icwemde.

Heo heou mid hearde worde   ond hunede þa wrecches;

scearp heo was ond kene   ond cwemde þen deofle

mid alle þen sunnen,   so efre was his wille.

G25   A wurþe hire wa   þet heo spekinde was so!

Heo hauef unc þus idemed   to deoppere helle.

   "Nis hit non sellic,   þauh ic segge of boken,

þauh ic soriliche   þet soþe repie,

for ic was ilered   of mine leoue fæder

G30   feire on frumþe,   ær ic toferde.

Ic was Godes douhter,   ac þu amerdest þet foster.

Ic sceolde lif holden   (nouht unleþe he wolde);

sone þu were lifleas,   seoþþen ic þe forleas.

Ic was þin imake,   so þeo bec siggeþ:

have you betrayed me? Because of your filthy sin I must now be off to hell, suffer a miserable fate there on account of your filthy living.

"I will reproach you further for my woeful state, since G7 now I must painfully part from you. Now your teeth are decayed and your tongue draws back, which was false to you and pleased the enemy. With corrupt judgments and much that was sinful you used to rob others of their just earnings, gathered them as treasure; but now, by the devil's teaching, all that pleased you well has passed away. Now your tongue G15 lies quiet in its very cold den. You have none the more treasure for its having spoken so, for it was deceitful in front and poisonous behind; it rendered many judgments that were hateful to the Lord. Concerning the tongue it is said in the G19 psalm—and it is very true: *Thy tongue framed deceits;* it prattled falsely and pleased the enemy. With harsh words it hewed and abused the downcast; it was sharp and piercing and pleased the devil with all its sins, as was ever his desire. May it always have woe for having spoken thus! It has doomed the two of us to the depths of hell.

"It is no wonder, though I recite it from books, though G27 with sorrow I touch upon the truth; for I was suitably taught by my beloved Father in the beginning, before I set out. I G31 was God's daughter, but you ruined that upbringing. I was supposed to sustain life (he did not will any suffering); once I abandoned you, you were immediately lifeless. I was your

G35   *Uxor tua sicut vitis habundans;*
        ic was þe biwedded   wurþliche so win-bowe
        et þen font-stone   þet þu hafest ifuled
        mid þine fule oþes.   Þu hafest þin fulluht forloren.
        Bihinden ond biuoren   feire þu were imerked,
G40   heie on þine heafde   mid þen holie ele;
        þu hauest kine-merke . . .
        Þu scoldest beon on heouene   heih arerd under Gode,
        ȝif þu hit ne forlure   þuruh þæs deofles lore.
        Þine god-fæderes beheten   ær heo þe forleten,
G45   þet þu me scoldest holden   þuruh holie lufe Cristes
        and mid rihtere lawe   leden me to Criste.
        Þu wiþsoke þene deofel   efter drihtenes cwide,
        his modes ond his wrænches   ond his wieles þærto.
        Seoþþen þu hine lufedest   ond forlat drihten,
G50   for þu lufedest þeo lawen   þe drihten weren loþe.
            "Unker team is forloren   þe wit scolden teman.
        So ic was þe betæiht,   þet wit scolden teman;
        þu scoldest beon bearne fæder   ond ic hore moder.
        Wit scolden fostrien bearn   ond bringen heom to Criste.
G55   Þet beoþ þeos bearn,   so so bec mæneþ:
        Filii tui sicut novella olivarum . . ."

spouse, as books say: *Thy wife as a fruitful vine;* like the grape-vine, I was honorably wedded to you at the baptismal font, which you have befouled with your filthy oaths. You have lost your baptism. On the front and back and high on your   G39
head, you were nobly signed with the holy oil; you possess a royal mark . . . You were supposed to be exalted high in heaven, subject to God, if you had not lost that status by the devil's teaching. Before they handed you over, your god-parents promised that you should sustain me through the holy love of Christ and lead me to Christ by righteous living. Echoing the Lord's utterance, you renounced the devil, and   G47
his arrogance and his pomp and his wiles as well. Later on, you loved him and abandoned the Lord, for you loved those laws that were hateful to the Lord.

"The offspring that we were to bear has been lost. I was   G51
entrusted to you so that we should produce offspring; you were to be a father to children and I their mother. We were supposed to rear children and bring them to Christ. The children I mean are these, as books describe: *Thy children as olive plants . . .*"

The Grave

Ðe wes bold gebyld,   er þu iboren were.
Ðe wes molde imynt,   er ðu of moder come.
Ac hit nes no idiht,   ne þeo deopnes imeten;
nes gyt iloced,   hu long hit þe were.
5   Nu me þe bringæð,   þer ðu beon scealt.
Nu me sceæl þe meten   and þa molde seoðða.
Ne bið no þin hus   healice itinbred:
hit bið unheh and lah,   þonne þu list þerinne.
Ðe hele-wages beoð lage,   sid-wages unhege;
10   þe rof bið ibyld   þire broste ful neh.
Swa ðu scealt on molde   wunien ful calde,
dimme and deorcæ.   Þet den fulæt on honde.
Dureleas is þet hus   and dearc hit is wiðinnen.
Ðær þu bist feste bidytt   and dæð hefð þa cæge.
15   Ladlic is þet eorð-hus   and grim inne to wunien.
Ðer þu scealt wunien   and wurmes þe todeleð.
Ðus ðu bist ilegd   and ladæst þine fronden.
Nefst ðu nenne freond,   þe þe wylle faren to,
ðæt efre wule lokien,   hu þet hus þe likie,
20   ðæt æfre undon   ðe wule ða dure
and þe æfter lihten . . .
For sone þu bist ladlic   and lad to iseonne.
For sone bið þin hæfet   faxes bireued;
al bið ðes faxes   feirnes forsceden;
25   næle hit nan mit fingres   feire stracien.

The Grave

A house was built for you before you were born. Earth was
your appointed end before you emerged from your mother.
But it was not prepared, nor its depth measured, nor has yet
been considered what length it should be for you. Now you 5
are brought to the place where you must be. Now someone
must measure you and then the earth. Your house will not
be loftily constructed; it will be low-slung and level when
you lie in it. The walls at the ends are low, those on the sides 9
of little height; the roof is built very close to your chest. In
this way you must remain in the utterly cold earth, dark and
dim. That den grows foul close about you. That house is 13
doorless and dark inside. There you will be securely con-
signed, and death holds the key. Detested is that house of
earth and cruel to abide in. There you must abide, and
worms will dismember you. Thus you will be laid, and thus 17
most repellent to your friends. No friend will you then have
who will want to visit you, who will ever check to see how
that house suits your liking, who will ever undo for you the
door and let light in around you . . . For soon you will be de- 22
tested and loathsome to look upon. For soon your head will
be bereft of hair; gone will be all the loveliness of that hair.
No one will want to stroke it gently with his fingers.

Judgment Day (I)

Ðæt gelimpan sceal   þætte lagu floweð,
flod ofer foldan;   feores bið æt ende
anra gehwylcum.   Oft mæg se þe wile
in his sylfes sefan   soð geþencan.
5   Hafað him geþinged hider   þeoden user
on þam mæstan dæge,   mægen-cyninga hyhst,
wile þonne forbærnan   brego mon-cynnes
lond mid lige.   Nis þæt lytulu spræc
to geheganne!
Hat bið onæled,
10   siþþan fyr nimeð   foldan sceatas,
byrnende lig   beorhte gesceafte;
bið eal þes ginna grund   gleda gefylled,
reþra bronda,   swa nu rixiað
grom-hydge guman,   gylpe strynað,
15   hyra hlaforde   gehlæges tilgað,
oþþæt hy beswicað   synna weardas,
þæt hi mid þy heape   helle secað,
fleogað mid þam feondum.   Him biþ fyr ongean,
droflic wite,   þær næfre dæg scineð
20   leohte of lyfte,   ac a bilocen stondeð,
siþþan þæs gæstes gryre   agiefen weorþeð.
Ufan hit is enge   ond hit is innan hat;
nis þæt betlic bold,   ac þær is brogna hyhst,

Judgment Day (I)

It must come to pass that water will flow, a flood over the earth; it will be the end of life for every single creature. Whoever so wishes can often ponder that truth in his own mind. Our Lord, supreme of mighty kings, has determined to come here on that greatest of days; the prince of humankind will then consume the lands with fire. That will be no trifling exchange of words to hold!

Heat will be stoked, then fire will claim the surfaces of 9 the earth, searing flame grip the bright creation. With glowing coals, furious burning, this whole, vast region will be filled, where cruel-minded men now reign, acquire pomp, vie for means to scorn their Lord—until the wardens of sin have so deceived such people that they seek out hell together with that throng, fly off in the company of those demons. Fire will greet them, wrenching torment where day 18 never shines with light from the sky; rather, once that state of terror is imposed on a soul, the place will remain shut tightly forever. At the top it is narrow, and inside it is hot; that is no splendid building, but the greatest of fears is there;

ne noht hyhtlic ham,   ac þær is helle grund,

25 sarlic siðfæt   þam þe sibbe ful oft
tomældeð mid his muþe.   Ne con he þa mircan gesceaft,
hu hi butan ende   ece stondeð
þam þe þær for his synnum   onsægd weorþeð,
ond þonne a to ealdre   orleg dreogeð.

30 Hwa is þonne þæs ferð-gleaw,   oþþe þæs fela cunne,
þæt æfre mæge heofona   heahþu gereccan,
swa georne þone godes dæl,   swa he gearo stondeð
clænum heortum,   þam þe þisne cwide willað
ondrædan þus deopne?   Sceal se dæg weorþan

35 þæt we forð berað   firena gehwylce,
þeawas ond geþohtas;   þæt bið þearlic gemot,
heardlic here-mægen.   Hat biþ acolod.
Ne biþ þonne on þisse worulde   nymþe wætres sweg
                    . . . fisces eþel.

40 Ne biþ her ban ne blod,   ac sceal bearna gehwylc
mid lice ond mid sawle   leanes fricgan
ealles þæs þe we on eorþan   ær geworhtan
godes oþþe yfles.   Ne mæg nænig gryre mare
geweorþan æfter worulde,   ond se bið wide cuð.

45 Ne tytaþ her tungul,   ac biþ tyr scæcen,
eorþan blædas.
                    Forþon ic a wille
leode læran   þæt hi lof Godes
hergan on heahþu,   hyhtum to wuldre
lifgen on geleafan,   ond a lufan dryhtnes

50 wyrcan in þisse worulde,   ær þon se wlonca dæg
bodige þurh byman   bryne-hatne leg,
egsan ofer-þrym.   Ne bið nænges eorles tir
leng on þissum life,   siþþan leohtes weard

it is no desirable dwelling at all, rather the abyss of hell is there, a painful destiny for anyone who too often rends the bonds of peace by the words of his mouth. He is ignorant of 26 that dark creation, how it endures everlastingly for anyone who is sentenced there for his sins, who will suffer strife forever from that moment on.

Who, then, is so wise, who knows so much that he could 30 ever describe the summits of heaven or readily describe that portion of the good which stands prepared for purified hearts, for those who incline to fear a message as profound as this one? The day must come when we bring forth every one of our crimes, our habitual acts and our thoughts; that will be a dire meeting, a harsh muster. The heat will cool; 37 then there will be nothing in this world except a roar of water . . . the fish's native element. Here will be neither bone nor blood, but every single mortal with body and soul must hear told the reward for all good or evil that we have done before on earth. Throughout this world there can be no greater terror, and it will be known far and wide. Here the stars will not shine, but brightness will pass away, the splendors of the earth.

Therefore I desire always to instruct people so that they 46 offer up praise to God on high, that they live in faith, with their hopes fixed on glory, and that they continually practice love of the Lord in this present world, before that majestic day heralds by a trumpet the raging hot fire, overwhelming terror. Once the guardian of light sends fire over the whole 52 expanse of earth, no man's glory in the present life will exist

ofer ealne foldan fæþm   fyr onsendeð.
55 Lixeð lyftes mægen,   leg onetteð,
blæc byrnende;   blod-gyte weorþeð
mongum gemeldad,   mægen-cyninges þrea.
Beofað eal beorhte gesceaft,   brondas lacað
on þam deopan dæge,   dyneð up-heofon.
60   Þonne weras ond wif   woruld alætað,
eorþan yrmþu,   seoð þonne on ece gewyrht.
Þonne bið gecyþed   hwa in clænnisse
lif alifde.   Him bið lean gearo;
hyht wæs a in heofonum,   siþþan user hælend wæs,
65 middan-geardes meotud,   þurh þa mæstan gesceaft
on ful blacne beam   bunden fæste
cearian clomme.   Crist ealle wat
gode dæde.   No þæs gilpan þearf
synfull sawel,   þæt hyre sie swegl ongean,
70 þonne he gehyrweð ful oft   halge lare,
brigdeð on bysmer.   Ne con he þæs brogan dæl,
yfles ondgiet,   ær hit hine on fealleð.
He þæt þonne onfindeð,   þonne se fær cymeþ,
geond middan-geard   monegum gecyþeð,
75 þæt he bið on þæt wynstre weorud   wyrs gescaden,
þonne he on þa swiþran hond   swican mote,
leahtra alysed.   Lyt þæt geþenceð,
se þe him wines glæd   wilna bruceð,
siteð him symbel-gal,   siþ ne bemurneð,
80 hu him æfter þisse worulde   weorðan mote.
     Wile þonne forgieldan   gæsta dryhten
willum æfter þære wyrde,   wuldres ealdor,
þam þe his synna nu   sare geþenceþ,
mod-bysgunge   micle dreogeð;

any longer. Tempests of air flash, fire hurtles forth, blazing as it burns; bloodshed is charged to many, violence against the king's majesty. The whole bright creation shudders, flames dance, heaven thunders on that awful day.

Then men and women will leave behind the world, the hardships of earth; then they will gaze upon their lasting works. Then it will be revealed who lived his life in a state of purity. A reward will be ready for him; his hope was always heaven, ever since our savior, the creator of the world, in accord with highest providence was bound tightly by a painful fetter to a tree of sheer radiance. Christ knows all good deeds. The sinful soul need not boast that heaven awaits it, since the sinner very often despises holy teaching, brings it into contempt. He does not know his portion in that horror, has no grasp of that misfortune before it falls on him. He will find it out when the calamity comes, when it reveals to many throughout all the world that he will, for the worse, be sorted among the host on the left, when he might have parted toward the right hand, liberated from his sins. The man who enjoys pleasure, cheered with wine, gives little thought to that; he sits flush from banqueting, has no misgivings about his fate, how it may turn out for him beyond this world.

According to each one's destiny, the Lord of souls, the prince of glory, will then reward the desires of any person who now reflects on his sins with sorrow, suffers great remorse in his mind; with acts of beneficence the ruler of

60

68

77

81

85   him þæt þonne geleanað   lifes waldend,
       heofona hyrde,   æfter heonan-siþe
       godum dædum,   þæs þe he swa geomor wearð,
       sarig fore his synnum.   Ne sceal se to sæne beon
       ne þissa larna to læt,   se þe him wile lifgan mid Gode,
90   brucan þæs boldes   þe us beorht fæder
       gearwað togeanes,   gæsta ealdor.
       Þæt is sige-dryhten   þe þone sele frætweð,
       timbreð torhtlice;   to sculon clæne,
       womma lease,   swa se waldend cwæð,
95   ealra cyninga cyning.   Forþon cwicra gehwylc,
       deop-hydigra,   dryhtne hyreð,
       þara þe wile heofona   heahþu gestigan.
          Hwæþre þæt gegongeð,   þeah þe hit sy greote beþeaht,
       lic mid lame,   þæt hit sceal life onfon,
100   feores æfter foldan.   Folc biþ gebonnen,
       Adames bearn   ealle to spræce;
       beoð þonne gegædrad   gæst ond ban-sele,
       gesomnad to þam siþe.   Soþ þæt wile cyþan,
       þonne we us gemittað   on þam mæstan dæge,
105   rincas æt þære rode,   secgað þonne ryhta fela,
       eal swylce under heofonum gewearð   hates ond cealdes,
       godes oþþe yfles;   georne gehyreð
       heofon-cyninga hyhst   hæleþa dæde.
       Næfre mon þæs hlude   horn aþyteð
110   ne byman ablaweþ,   þæt ne sy seo beorhte stefn
       ofer ealne middan-geard   monnum hludre,
       waldendes word.   Wongas beofiað
       for þam ærende   þæt he to us eallum wat.

life, heaven's guardian, will then, after a person journeys hence, reward him for having felt sad and pained on account of his sins. One must not be too lazy, too slow to follow these 88 teachings, if he desires to live with God, to enjoy the dwelling place that the radiant Father, prince of souls, prepares ahead for us. It is the Lord of victories who adorns that hall, 92 constructs it with splendor; the pure, without blemish, are bound to arrive there, just as the ruler said, king of all kings. Therefore every living being, everyone capable of deep reflection, who desires to ascend the heights of heaven, will obey the Lord.

Although one be covered by clay, the body hidden by soil, 98 it will happen nevertheless that it [the body] shall receive life, its vital spirit, after the earthen grave. People will be summoned, all Adam's children, to a council; then the spirit and its bone-hall will be gathered together, united for the journey. The truth will out when we meet on that greatest of 103 days, in the presence of the cross; then we will speak many truths, tell all—hot and cold, good or evil—just as it transpired under heaven; the highest of heavenly kings will eagerly listen to the deeds of men. No one will ever sound a 109 horn or blow a trumpet so loudly that the Lord's resounding voice, the word of the ruler, does not then prove louder to human beings the world over. The plains will tremble at the message that he intends for us all.

Oncweþ nu þisne cwide: cuþ sceal geweorþan
115   þæt ic gewægan ne mæg   wyrd under heofonum,
ac hit þus gelimpan sceal   leoda gehwylcum,
ofer eall beorht gesetu   byrnende lig.
Siþþan æfter þam lige   lif bið gestaþelad,
welan ah in wuldre   se nu wel þenceð.

Now tell forth this account: it must be understood that I   114
am unable to alter destiny under the heavens; rather it must
befall every people in this way, a burning fire over all bright
habitations. Then, after that fire, life will be set on a new
foundation; whoever intends good in the present will pos-
sess riches in glory.

Judgment Day (II)

Hwæt! Ic ana sæt   innan bearwe
mid helme beþeht,   holte tomiddes,
þær þa wæter-burnan   swegdon and urnon
on middan gehæge,   eal swa ic secge.

5   Eac þær wyn-wyrta   weoxon and bleowon
innon þam gemonge   on ænlicum wonge,
and þa wudu-beamas   wagedon and swegdon
þurh winda gryre;   wolcn wæs gehrered
and min earme mod   eal wæs gedrefed.

10   Þa ic færinga   forht and unrot
þas unhyrlican fers   onhefde mid sange,
eall swylce þu cwæde,   synna gemunde,
lifes leahtra   and þa laðan tid,
þæs dimman cyme   deaðes on eorðan.

15   Ic ondræde me eac   dom þone miclan
for man-dædum   minum on eorðan,
and þæt ece ic eac   yrre ondræde me
and synfulra gehwam   æt sylfum Gode,
and hu mihtig frea   eall manna cynn

20   todæleð and todemeð   þurh his dihlan miht.
Ic gemunde eac   mærðe drihtnes
and þara haligra   on heofonan rice,
swylce earm-sceapenra   yfel and witu.
Ic gemunde þis mid me   and ic mearn swiðe,

25   and ic murcnigende cwæð,   mode gedrefed:

Judgment Day (II)

Listen! I was sitting by myself in a grove, surrounded by woods, sheltered by their canopy, where springs murmured and coursed in the middle of the clearing, just as I am describing it. Delightful flowers were springing up, too, and ⁵ blossoming among others on that matchless plain, and the trees swayed and rustled at the terrible onrush of the winds: the clouds were set churning, and my wretched mind grew distressed in every part. Then fearful and joyless, I abruptly ¹⁰ raised in song these dread verses, all exactly as you said, recalling sins, transgressions in life, and the hated hour, the coming of gloomy death upon earth. I fear the great judg- ¹⁵ ment, too, on account of my evil actions on earth; I fear as well, on my own and on every sinner's behalf, the unending wrath of God himself; and I fear how the mighty Lord, by his mysterious power, will divide and pass judgment on the whole human race. I remembered also the gloriousness of ²¹ the Lord and of the saints in the kingdom of heaven, as well as the terrible state and the torments of those in misery. I recalled this to myself, and I lamented greatly; and, with my mind in agitation, I voiced a complaint, saying:

"Nu ic eow, æddran,   ealle bidde
þæt ge wyl-springas   wel ontynan
hate of hleorum,   recene to tearum.
Þænne ic synful slea   swiðe mid fyste,
30   breost mine beate   on gebed-stowe
and minne lic-haman   lecge on eorðan,
and geearnade sar   ealle ic gecige.
Ic bidde eow   benum nu ða
þæt ge ne wandian   wiht for tearum,
35   ac dreorige hleor   dreccað mid wope
and sealtum dropum   sona ofergeotaþ,
and geopeniað man   ecum drihtne.
Ne þær owiht   inne ne belife
on heort-scræfe   heanra gylta,
40   þæt hit ne sy dæg-cuð   þæt þæt dihle wæs,
openum wordum   eall abæred—
breostes and tungan   and flæsces swa some.
Ðis is an hæl   earmre sauwle
and þam sorgiendum   selest hihta,
45   þæt he wunda her   wope gecyðe
uplicum læce,   se ana mæg
aglidene mod   gode gehælan
and ræplingas   recene onbindan.
Ne mid swiðran his   swyþe nele brysan
50   wan-hydige mod   wealdend engla,
ne þone wlacan smocan   waces flæcses
wyle waldend Crist   wætere gedwæscan.
    "Hu ne gesceop þe se scaþa   scearplice bysne
þe mid Criste wæs   cwylmed on rode,
55   hu micel forstent   and hu mære is
seo soðe hreow   synna and gylta?
Se sceaþa wæs on rode   scyldig and manful,

"Now, O channels, I beseech you all that you release your 26
springs fully, hot down my cheeks, quickly forming tears. On
the spot where I pray, a sinful man, I will then strike hard
with my fist, beat my breast, stretch my body upon the
earth, and bewail all the pains that I have merited. With en- 33
treaties I now beseech you not to be sparing with those
tears, but rather disfigure the downcast face by weeping,
drench it at once with salty droplets, and divulge any evil
acts to the eternal Lord. Let no vile sin of any kind go on 38
dwelling there in the cavern of the heart, so that whatever
was undisclosed—whether in the breast, on the tongue, or
in the flesh—might not be made plain as day, entirely di-
vulged in forthright words. The only healing for a wretched 43
soul, the highest of hopes for a remorseful man, is that here
in the present he tearfully disclose his wounds to the heav-
enly physician who alone can, by his beneficence, heal minds
that have fallen away and quickly loose those in bondage.
The ruler of angels will not greatly bruise faltering minds
with his right hand, nor will Christ the ruler extinguish with
water the smoldering wisp of a fragile wick.

"Did the thief who was executed on a cross along with 53
Christ not furnish you a piercing example of how glorious
and how greatly beneficial is genuine remorse for sins and
transgressions? That thief, guilty and evil, was on a cross, 57

mid undædum   eall gesymed;
he drihtene swa þeah,   deaðe gehende,
60   his bena bebead   breost-gehigdum.
He mid lyt wordum   ac geleaffullum
his hæle begeat   and help recene,
and in gefor   þa ænlican geatu
neorxna-wonges   mid nerigende.
65   "Ic acsige þe, la,   earme geþanc,
hwi latast þu swa lange,   þæt þu ðe læce ne cyþst,
oððe hwi swigast þu,   synnigu tunge,
nu þu forgifnesse hæfst   gearugne timan,
nu þe ælmihtig   earum atihtum,
70   heofon-rices weard,   gehyreð mid lustum?
Ac se dæg cymeð   ðonne demeð God
eorðan ymb-hwyrft;   þu ana scealt
gyldan scad wordum   wið scyppend God,
and þam rican frean   riht agyldan.
75   Ic lære þæt þu beo hrædra   mid hreowlicum tearum,
and þæt yrre forfoh   eces deman.
Hwæt ligst þu on horwe   leahtrum afylled,
flæsc, mid synnum?   Hwi ne feormast þu
mid teara gyte   torne synne?
80   Hwi ne bidst þu þe   beþunga and plaster,
lifes læcedomes   æt lifes frean?
Nu þu scealt greotan,   tearas geotan,
þa hwile tima sy   and tid wopes;
nu is halwende   þæt man her wepe
85   and dæd-bote do   drihtne to willan.
Glæd bið se Godes sunu,   gif þu gnorn þrowast
and þe sylfum demst   for synnum on eorðan,
ne heofenes God   henða and gyltas

bearing the full weight of his own wrongful actions; even so, though near death, he commended his prayers to the Lord in the thoughts of his heart. Using words few in number but 61 filled with faith, he swiftly obtained salvation and help, and made his way, accompanying the savior, through the splendid gates of Paradise.

"I ask you, O poor human wit, why you tarry so long, not 65 revealing your condition to the healer, or why you keep quiet now, O sinful tongue, while you have a ready opportunity for forgiveness, and while the almighty guardian of heaven will happily listen to you with attentive ears? But the day will 71 come when God judges the whole span of earth; alone you will have to render in words your reckoning to God the creator and pay your rightful dues to the mighty Lord. I advise 75 you to be quicker with tears of remorse and forestall the wrath of the eternal judge. Why, O flesh, do you wallow in uncleanness, filled with vices, filled with sins? Why do you not wash away those bitter sins with an outpouring of tears? Why do you not beg for salves and plaster, medicine of life 80 from the Lord of life? You should cry, pour forth tears now, while there is time and opportunity for weeping; it is saving here and now for a person to weep and perform penance as the Lord wills. The Son of God will be pleased if you endure 86 sorrow and judge yourself for your sins while on earth; nor will the God of heaven punish anyone more than a single

ofer ænne syþ wrecan wile   ænigum men.
90   Ne scealt þu forhyccan   heaf and wopas
and forgifnesse   gearugne timan.
    "Gemyne eac on mode   hu micel is þæt wite
þe þara earmra byð   for ær-dædum,
oþþe hu egeslice   and hu andrysne
95   heah-þrymme cyningc   her wile deman
anra gehwylcum   be ær-dædum,
oþþe hwylce fore-beacn   feran onginnað
and Cristes cyme   cyþað on eorðan.
Eall eorðe bifað,   eac swa þa duna
100   dreosað and hreosað,
and beorga hliðu   bugað and myltað,
and se egeslica sweg   ungerydre sæ
eall manna mod   miclum gedrefeð.
Eal bið eac up-heofon
105   sweart and gesworcen,   swiðe geþuxsað,
deorc and dim-hiw,   and dwolma sweart.
Þonne stedelease   steorran hreosað,
and seo sunne forswyrcð   sona on morgen,
ne se mona næfð   nanre mihte wiht,
110   þæt he þære nihte   genipu mæge flecgan.
Eac þonne cumað hider   ufon of heofone
deað-beacnigende tacn,   bregað þa earman.
Þonne cumað upplice   eored-heapas,
stiþ-mægen astyred,   styllað embutan
115   eal engla werod,   ecne behlænað,
ðone mæran metod   mihte and þrymme.
Sitt þonne sigel-beorht   swegles brytta
on heah-setle,   helme beweorðod.
We beoð færinga   him beforan brohte,

248

time for insults or transgressions. You must not scorn lamentation and weeping and the ripe time for forgiveness.

"Call to mind as well how great will be the torment of the 92 wretched for their prior acts, or how terrifyingly and how awfully the king will, in his supreme majesty, judge each and every person here according to his prior actions; or call to mind what portents will begin to approach and reveal on earth the coming of Christ. All the earth will tremble and 99 the hills will crumble and collapse; the slopes of mountains will buckle and subside, and the horrible roar of the rough sea will greatly distress the mind of every human being. All 104 the sky above will also become black and dusky, utterly darkened, lightless and dim, and pitch-black confusion. Losing their fixed place, the stars will then plummet, and at morning the sun will quickly darken; nor will the moon have any more power to dispel the blackness of night. Signs portend- 111 ing death will also then approach from heaven, will fill miserable human beings with terror. Then the celestial troops will come, a severe force now rallied; they join formation, the whole host of angels, close ranks powerfully and majestically around the eternal one, the glorious creator. Bright as 117 the sun, the prince of heaven, honored by a crown, will then take his seat on a high throne. In an instant we will be

120 æghwanum cumene   to his ansyne,
þæt gehwylc underfo
dom be his dædum   æt drihtne sylfum.

"Ic bidde, man, þæt þu gemune   hu micel bið se broga
beforan dom-setle   drihtnes þænne;
125 stent hergea mæst   heortleas and earh,
amasod and amarod,   mihtleas, afæred.
Þænne samod becumað   of swegles hleo
eall engla werod,   ecne ymtrymmað.
Þænne bið geban micel   and aboden þider
130 eal Adames cnosl   eorð-buendra
þe on foldan wearð   feded æfre
oððe modar gebær   to manlican,
oþþe þa þe wæron   oððe woldon beon
oþþe towearde   geteald wæron awiht.
135 Ðonne eallum beoð   ealra gesweotolude
digle geþancas   on þære dæg-tide,
eal þæt seo heorte   hearmes geþohte
oððe seo tunge   to teonan geclypede
oþþe mannes hand   manes gefremede
140 on þystrum scræfum   þinga on eorðan.
Eal þæt hwæne sceamode   scylda on worulde,
þæt he ænigum men   ypte oððe cyðde,
þonne bið eallum   open ætsomne,
gelice alyfed   þæt man lange hæl.
145 "Ufenan eall þis   eac byð gefylled
eal uplic lyft   ættrenum lige.
Færð fyr ofer eall,   ne byð þær nan fore-steal,
ne him man na ne mæg   miht forwyrnan.
Eal þæt us þincð æmtig   eah-gemearces
150 under roderes ryne,   readum lige

fetched before him, transported from every corner into his presence, so that each person may receive judgment from the Lord himself according to his deeds.

"I ask that you would remember, O man, how great the 123 terror will then be before the Lord's throne of judgment; the greatest of armies will stand heartless and cowering, amazed and confounded, powerless, afraid. Then, from the vault of heaven, all the hosts of angels arrive together, surround the eternal one. Then there will be a great summons, and to that 127 place will be commanded all the progeny of Adam, of earth dwellers who ever were nurtured on land, or whom any mother ever bore to human likeness, or those who existed, or would have existed, or were ever reckoned at all among future generations. Then the secret thoughts of every per- 135 son will be revealed to all in the course of that day, all hurt that the heart conceived or the tongue called out injuriously, or every evil on earth that human hands committed in dark dens. Every evil action in this world that would have been 141 shameful for someone to reveal or make known to any other person will then be manifest to all at once, and so too what was long hidden will be disclosed.

"Beyond all this, the entire upper air will also be filled 145 with noxious flame. Fire will sweep over everything; nothing will hinder it, nor will anyone manage to fend off its force there. All that seems to us, as far as the eye can see, a void there beneath the expanse of sky will, on that occasion, be

     biŏ emnes mid þy   eal gefylled.

     Đonne fyren lig   blaweŏ and braslaŏ,
     read and reaŏe,   ræsct and efesteŏ,
     hu he synfullum   susle gefremme;
155   ne se wrecenda bryne   wile forbugan
     oŏŏe ænigum þær   are gefremman,
     buton he horwum sy   her afeormad,
     and þonne þider cume   þearle aclænsad.

     "Đonne fela mægŏa,   folca unrim,
160   heora sinnigan breost   swiŏlice beataŏ
     forhte mid fyste   for fyren-lustum.
     Þær beoŏ þearfan   and þeod-cyningas,
     earm and eadig,   ealle beoŏ afæred;
     þær hæfŏ ane lage   earm and se welega,
165   forŏon hi habbaŏ ege   ealle ætsomne.
     Đæt reŏe flod   ræscet fyre
     and biterlice   bærnŏ ŏa earman saula,
     and heora heortan   horxlice wyrmas,
     syn-scyldigra,   ceorfaŏ and slitaŏ.

170   Ne mæg þær æni man   be agnum gewyrhtum
     gedyrstig wesan,   deman gehende,
     ac ealle þurhyrnŏ   oga ætsomne
     breost-gehyda,   and se bitera wop,
     and þær stænt astifad,   stane gelicast,
175   eal arleas heap   yfeles on wenan.

     "Hwæt dest þu, la, flæsc?   Hwæt dreogest þu nu?
     Hwæt miht þu on þa tid   þearfe gewepan?
     Wa þe nu, þu þe þeowast   þissere worulde
     and her glæd leofast   on galnysse,
180   and þe mid stiŏum astyrest   sticelum þæs gælsan!
     Hwi ne forhtas þu   fyrene egsan,

entirely filled with red flame in equal measure. Then flam- 152
ing fire, red and fierce, will sweep and crackle, rush and has-
ten to wreak suffering on sinners; that vengeful burning will
not hold back or show mercy to any man there, unless he
is purged of uncleanness in the present and arrives at that
place then entirely purified.

"Then many a tribe, a countless number of people, will 159
fearfully beat their breasts hard with their fists, on account
of their sinful desires. Beggars and kings of nations alike will
be there, the poor and the prosperous, and all will be terri-
fied; there the poor man and the rich one both face a single
law, since they all face together a single terror. The violent 166
flood crackles with fire and cruelly burns those miserable
souls, and serpents quickly cut and rend the hearts in those
guilty of sin. There before that judge, no one can be confi- 170
dent about his own works, but terror and bitter weeping will
course through the thoughts of all hearts together, and there
the whole dishonorable company will stand rigid, entirely
like stone, in anticipation of their terrible lot.

"Alas, what will you do then, O flesh? What will you en- 176
dure now? What will you achieve by weeping at that time?
Woe to you now who serve this world, who gladly live here
in lust and excite yourself with strong goads of appetite!
Why do you not fear the fiery terror and, for your own sake, 181

and þe sylfum ondræd   swiðlice witu,
ða deoflum geo   drihten geteode,
awyrgedum gastum   weana to leane?

185 Þa oferswiðað   sefan and spræce
manna gehwylces   for micelnysse.
Nænig spræc mæg beon,   spellum areccan
ænegum on eorðan   earmlice witu,
fule stowa   fyres on grunde,

190 þe wæs in grimmum   susle on helle.
Þær synt to sorge   ætsomne gemenged
se þrosma lig   and se þrece gicela,
swiðe hat and ceald   helle tomiddes.
Hwilum þær eagan   ungemetum wepað

195 for þæs ofnes bryne   (eal he is bealuwes full);
hwilum eac þa teþ for miclum cyle   manna þær gryrrað.
Þis atule gewrixl   earm-sceapene men
on worulda woruld   wendað þær inne
betwyx forsworcenum   sweartum nihtum

200 and weallendes pices   wean and þrosme.
Þær nan stefn styreð   butan stearc-heard
wop and wanung,   nawiht elles;
ne bið þær ansyn gesewen   ænigre wihte,
butan þara cwelra   þe cwylmað ða earman.

205 Ne bið þær inne   aht gemeted
butan lig and cyle   and laðlic ful;
hy mid nosan ne magon   naht geswæccan
butan unstences   ormætnesse.
Þær beoð þa wanigendan   welras gefylde

210 lig-spiwelum bryne   laðlices fyres,
and hy wæl-grimme   wyrmas slitað
and heora ban gnagað   brynigum tuxlum.

dread the violent torments that the Lord established long
ago for devils, those accursed spirits, as a reward for their
evils? Those torments exceed in magnitude the thought and   185
speech of every single human being. There can be no words,
no expressing in speech to anyone on earth the wretched
punishments, the foul places at the bottom of the fire that
was in the cruel torments of hell. To inflict pain, smoke-   191
belching flame and binding ice are mingled there, extremely
hot and frigid at the core of hell. There sometimes eyes
weep uncontrollably from the burning in that oven (it is full
of harm); at other times the teeth of those who are there
also grind from the great cold. The unfortunate there expe-   197
rience this horrifying alternation forever and ever, between
black, darkened nights and the agony and thick smoke of
bubbling pitch. No voice sounds there except piercing cries   201
and moans, nothing else; no creature's face is visible there
except those of the tormentors who punish the wretched.
Nothing is found therein except fire and chill and loathsome   205
filth; with their noses, the people there can smell nothing
except the overpowering presence of the stench. Moaning
lips will be filled there with the fire-belching heat of loath-
some flame, and cruel, slaughtering serpents will rend them
and gnaw their bones with burning fangs.

"Ufenon eal þis   bið þæt earme breost
mid bitere care   breged and swenced,
215 for hwi fyrngende flæsc   on þas frecnan tid
hym selfum swa fela   synna geworhte,
þæt hit on cweart-ern   cwylmed wurde,
þær ða atelan synd   ecan witu.

Þær leohtes ne leoht   lytel sperca
220 earmum ænig,   ne þær arfæstnes
ne sib ne hopa   ne swige gegladað
ne þara wependra   worn wihte.
Flyhð frofor aweg;   ne bið þær fultum nan
þæt wið þa biteran þing   gebeorh mæge fremman.

225 Ne bið þær ansyn gemet   ænigre blisse,
ac þær bið angryslic   ege and fyrhtu
and sari mod,   swiðlic grist-bigtung.
Þær bið unrotnes   æghwær wæl-hreow,
adl and yrre   and æmelnes,
230 and þær synnge eac   sauwle on lige
on blindum scræfe   byrnað and yrnað.

    "Þonne deriende   gedwinað heonone
þysse worulde gefean,   gewitað mid ealle;
þonne druncennes   gedwineð mid wistum,
235 and hleahter and plega   hleapað ætsomne,
and wrænnes eac   gewiteð heonone,
and fæst-hafolnes   feor gewiteð,
uncyst onweg   and ælc gælsa
scyldig scyndan   on sceade þonne,
240 and se earma flyhð   uncræftiga slæp,
sleac mid sluman,   slincan on hinder.
Ðonne blindum beseah   biterum ligum

"Beyond all this, the miserable heart will be terrified and 213
stricken with bitter care as to why the offending flesh com-
mitted against it, during this dangerous time, so many sins
that it should therefore be tortured in a prison where there
are horrific, everlasting torments. Not even any small glim-
mer of light shines there for the wretched; neither compas-
sion nor friendship nor hope nor calm cheers that multitude
of weepers. Comfort flees away; no help will be there to pro- 223
vide shelter against those cruel conditions. No semblance
of any happiness will be met there; rather there will be ap-
palling horror and fear and the mind in pain, the violent
gnashing of teeth. Cruel, killing joylessness will be pervasive
there, disease and anger and weariness, and in that dark pit
sinning souls will burn and hurtle about in fire.

"The harmful joys of this world will vanish, depart en- 232
tirely from here; then drunkenness will vanish, together
with food, and laughter and frivolity will bolt away together,
and lust will also depart from here, and stinginess, avarice
will depart far away, and every immoderate appetite will
then guiltily hasten into shadow; and wretched, shallow
sleep will flee, slinking away, listless from exhaustion. Then 242

257

earme on ende   þæt unalyfed is nu;
leofest on life   lað bið þænne,
245   and þæt werige mod   wendað þa gyltas
swiðe mid sorgum   and mid sargunge.
    "Eala, se bið gesælig   and ofer-sælig
and on worulda woruld   wihta gesæligost,
se þe mid gesyntum   swylce cwyldas
250   and witu mæg   wel forbugon,
and samod bliðe   on woruld ealle
his þeodne geþeon,   and þonne mot
habban heofon-rice: þæt is hihta mæst.
Þær niht ne genimð   næfre þeostrum
255   þæs heofenlican   leohtes sciman;
ne cymð þær sorh ne sar   ne geswenced yld,
ne þær ænig geswinc   æfre gelimpeð,
oððe hunger oþþe þurst   oððe heanlic slæp,
ne bið þær fefur ne adl   ne færlic cwyld,
260   nanes liges gebrasl   ne se laðlica cyle.
Nis þær unrotnes   ne þær æmelnys,
ne hryre ne caru   ne hreoh tintrega,
ne bið þær liget   ne laðlic storm,
winter ne þuner-rad   ne wiht cealdes,
265   ne þær hagul-scuras   hearde mid snawe,
ne bið þær wædl ne lyre   ne deaðes gryre
ne yrmð ne agnes   ne ænigu gnornung;
ac þær samod ricxað   sib mid spede,
and arfæstnes   and ece god,
270   wuldor and wurð-mynt,
swylce lof and lif   and leoflic geþwærnes.

whatever is forbidden at present will have finally immersed those wretches in lightless, cruel flames; whatever was dearest to them in life will then be most detested, and sins will roil the weary mind with sorrows and with suffering.

"Ah, how happy, and more than happy, and happiest of creatures forever is he who, through salvation, can well avoid such torments and punishments, and who can, at the same time, prosper joyfully for his Lord through all the present age and be able to possess thereafter the heavenly kingdom: that is the greatest of hopes. There night never overtakes with darkness the beams of heavenly light, and neither sorrow nor pain ever comes there, nor exhausted old age, nor does any hardship ever happen there, not hunger or thirst or shameful torpor; no fever or disease will be there, nor sudden sickness, no crackling of flame or abhorred chill. Neither joylessness nor indolence will be there, neither ruin nor anxiety nor harsh trial; there will be no lightning or abhorred storm, no winter or thunder or any cold at all; no hard hail showers will be there, mixed with snow, nor will poverty or loss or terror of death, no wretchedness or worry or any lamentation; rather peace will reign there, together with prosperity and graciousness and everlasting good, glory and honor, as well as praise and life and pleasant concord.

247

254

261

"Ufenan eal þis   ece drihten
him ealra goda gehwylc   glædlice ðenað,
þær a andweard   ealle weorðaþ
275   and fehþ and geblyssað   fæder ætsomne,
wuldraþ and wel hylt,
fægere frætuað   and freolice lufað
and on heofon-setle   hean geregnað.
His sunu bliðe,   sigores brytta,
280   sylð anra gehwam   ece mede,
heofonlice hyrsta   (þæt is healic gifu!)
gemang þam ænlican   engla werode
and þæra haligra   heapum and þreatum.
Þær hy beoð geþeode   þeodscipum on gemang,
285   betwyx heah-fæderas   and halige witegan,
blissiendum modum,   byrgum tomiddes,
þær þa ærend-racan synd   ælmihtiges Godes,
and betweoh rosena   reade heapas
þær symle scinað.
290   Þær þæra hwittra   hwyrfð mæden-heap,
blostmum behangen,   beorhtost wereda,
þe ealle læt   ænlicu Godes drut,
seo frowe þe us   frean acende,
metod on moldan,   meowle seo clæne.
295   Þæt is Maria,   mædena selast;
heo let þurh þa scenan   scinendan ricu,
gebletsodost ealra,   þæs breman fæder,
betweox fæder and suna,   freolicum werede,
and betwyx þære ecan   uplicum sibbe
300   rice ræd-witan,   rodera weardas.

"Beyond all this, the eternal Lord will gladly provide them 272
with each and every good, where the Father, who is always
present with him, honors them all, receives and gladdens
them, glorifies and preserves them, adorns them beautifully,
loves them unreservedly, and places them on an exalted,
heavenly throne. His gracious Son, the granter of victory, 279
bestows on every one of them an everlasting reward, heav-
enly adornments (that is a sublime gift!) in the midst of the
peerless host of angels and the throngs and companies of
the saints. With minds exulting, they will there be incorpo- 284
rated into those fellowships, among patriarchs and holy
prophets, in the heart of the fortresses where God's messen-
gers are, where they will shine unceasingly among red roses
piled high. There the virginal company of those who are 290
clothed in white goes in procession, the brightest of hosts,
arrayed with blossoms, all of whom God's matchless beloved
leads, that lady and pure young woman who for our sake
bore the Lord, the creator on earth. That is Mary, best of 295
maidens; flanked by fathers and sons in a noble company
and by the everlasting heavenly family, she, being most
blessed of them all, leads through the beautiful, shining
realms of her celebrated Father the powerful counselors and
guardians of the heavens.

"Hwæt mæg beon heardes   her on life,
gif þu wille secgan   soð þæm ðe frineð,
wið þam þu mote   gemang þam werode
eardian unbleoh   on ecnesse,
305   and on upcundra   eadegum setlum
brucan bliðnesse   butan ende forð?"

"If you are willing to tell the truth to anyone who asks, 301 what hardship can there be here in this life, in view of the fact that you are able to dwell forever without stain in that company, and enjoy everlastingly happiness in the blessed habitations of those in heaven?"

Epilogue

A Lament for the English Church
(from the Worcester Fragments)

Sanctus Beda was iboren   her on Breotene mid us,
ond he wisliche   bec awende,
þet þeo englise leoden   þurh weren ilerde.
Ond he þeo cnoten unwreih   þe *Questiuns* hoteþ,
5   þa derne diȝelnesse   þe deor-wurþe is.
Ælfric abbod,   þe we Alquin hoteþ,
he was bocare   ond þe fif bec wende,
Genesis, Exodus, Utronomius,   Numerus, Leuiticus;
þurh þeos weren ilærde   ure leoden on englisc.
10   Þet weren þeos biscopes   þeo bodeden cristendom:
Wilfrid of Ripum,   Iohan of Beoferlai,
Cuþbert of Dunholme,   Oswald of Wireceastre,
Egwin of Heoueshame,   Ældhelm of Malmesburi,
Swiþþun, Æþelwold,   Aidan, Biern of Wincæstre,
15   Paulin of Rofecæstre,   Dunston ond Ælfeih of
Cantoreburi.

Þeos lærden ure   leodan on englisc;
næs deorc heore liht,   ac hit fæire glod.
Nu is þeo leore forleten,   ond þet folc is forloren.

264

Epilogue

A Lament for the English Church
(from the Worcester Fragments)

Saint Bede was born here among us in Britain, and he wisely
translated books through which the English peoples were
instructed. And he untangled the knots that we call *Quaes-*
tiones, the obscure mystery that is precious. Abbot Ælfric, 6
whom we call Alcuin—he was a scholar and translated the
five books: Genesis, Exodus, Deuteronomy, Numbers, Le-
viticus; through these our people were instructed in English.
These were the bishops who preached Christianity: Wilfrid 10
of Ripon, John of Beverly, Cuthbert of Durham, Oswald
of Worcester, Ecgwin of Evesham, Aldhelm of Malmesbury,
Swithun, Æthelwold, Aidan, and Birinus of Winchester,
Paulinus of Rochester, Dunstan and Ælfheah of Canterbury.
These men instructed our people in English; their light was 16
not dim, but it glowed splendidly. Now that teaching is
abandoned, and the people is lost. Now there are others who

Nu beoþ oþre leoden   þeo læreþ ure folc,
20   ond feole of þen lor-þeines losiæþ   ond þet folc forþ mid.
Nu sæiþ ure drihten þus: *Sicut aquila provocat pullos suos
ad volandum   et super eos volitat.*
Þis beoþ Godes word   to worlde asende,
þet we sceolen fæier feþren   festen to him . . .

instruct our people, and many of the teachers perish, and the people along with them. Now our Lord says thus: *As the* [21] *eagle entices her young to fly and hovers over them.* These are the words of God sent into the world, that we should properly set our feathers over them . . .

Appendix A

The Judgment of the Damned
(A Late Old English Sermon
with Embedded Verse)

INTRODUCTION

Just as several poems in this volume illustrate the tendencies of later Old English verse toward "prosaicism" (see above, xi–xii), certain vernacular authors also experimented with the poetic ornamentation of their prose. A number of late Old English sermons contain embedded passages marked by rhythms, alliteration, and, on rare occasions, even the vocabulary of verse. Some of the passages in question are lengthy and conspicuous, others so brief and unobtrusive that modern readers have usually failed to notice them.

It is not clear whether Anglo-Saxon audiences regarded these passages as distinctly poetic or merely as stylistically heightened prose. Latin prose of the period was increasingly using rhyme and rhythm for ornamental effect, but no one then or now would label such passages verse. Whatever its origins, the device of shifting abruptly from prose into something like verse seems to have acquired its own distinctive associations in Old English. It has often been noted, for example, that many of the verse-like passages in vernacular sermons occur in descriptions of Judgment Day, the rewards of heaven, and the pains of hell, as if authors regarded poetic patterning as especially suited to these most urgent and emotive themes. In still other instances, a poetic turn may have resulted from a homilist's direct reliance on Old English verse as a source. Such is the possible relationship, as we have seen, between portions of *Judgment Day (II)* and Napier Homily XXIX, or between the opening of *The Rewards of Piety* and Vercelli Homily XXI and thence Napier Homily XXX.

The Old English prose text with the greatest admixture of verse is a sermon about Judgment Day preserved in different forms in two Vercelli Homilies (nos. II and XXI) and within a composite eleventh-century sermon that also draws from sermons by Archbishop Wulfstan (d. 1023). Editors and critics have long noted the rhythmical and alliterative qualities in the eschatological content that these texts all share. Examining one of the later composite versions of the homily (a mid-eleventh-century copy in Cambridge, Corpus Christi College 201), Eric Stanley has shown that at the core of the sermon stand two long rhythmical passages that, despite their frequent departures from the norms of classical Old English verse, suggest the remains of a now-lost poem (see §§ 8.1–9.2 of the edition below). Stanley titled this partially recoverable poem *The Judgment of the Damned.* Since his study appeared, *The Judgment of the Damned* and the homily around it have become the best-known example of Old English writing from what Stanley termed "the borderland of verse and prose."

To provide an example from that borderland, and to contextualize further the prosaic qualities of certain poems collected in the main part of this volume, I offer here an edition and translation of *The Judgment of the Damned* with its surrounding prose. Those parts of the text that can be construed as poetry are here lineated as verse (following Stanley's edition) and marked off from the prose by indentations. It bears repeating, however, that the medieval copyists of the manuscripts containing this and related sermons did not distinguish prosaic from poetic segments by these or similar conventions of layout. Poetic and nonpoetic texts alike in Old English were normally written out in long lines across the page.

(1) Leofan men: ælmihti God us singallice manað and lærað
þurh his þa halgan bec þæt we soð and riht don her on worlde
on urum life gif we willað heofona rice begitan æfter þisse
worlde and geborgene beon on ðam egeslican dæge þæs mic-
clan domes. Ðæs dæges weorc bið egesful eallum gesceaftum,
swa se apostol cwæð, *in quo omnis creatura congemiscit.*

(2.1) On þam dæge heofon and eorðe cwaciað and heofað
and sæ and ealle þa þe on him sindon. And on ðam dæge
þa hleoðrigendan ligas forglendriað þone blod-gemængedan
middan-eard and þæt man-cyn, þe nu is on idelum gilpe and on
sin-lustum and in ðam woh-gestreonum goldes and seolfres
beswicen, and þæs him naht ne ondrædað ac him orsorh lætað.
(2.2) And on ðam dæge þæt earme man-cyn and þæt synfulle
ofer him silfum heofað and wepað and waniað þæt hi þonne
swiðe forhtigað forðam ðe hig ær nolden heora sinna betan.
(2.3) And on þam dæge on ðam firenan wilme sæ forhwirfeð and
eorðe mid hyre dunum and heofonas mid hire tunglum, and
eal forsingod man-cyn þonne forswelgeð seo firen-lust heora
ærran gewyrhta; and unrihtwise deman and gerefan and ealle þa
woh-geornan world-rican mid heora golde and seolfre and god-
webbum and eallum ungestreonum þonne forwurðað.

(3.1) And on ðam dæge singað þa biman on ðam feower scea-

(1) Beloved: through his holy books, almighty God admonishes and teaches us constantly that during our life in this present world we should practice truthfulness and justice if we want to obtain the kingdom of heaven after this world and be protected on the dreaded day of the great judgment. What is done on that day will be frightful to all creatures, just as the apostle said, [the day] *on which every creature will groan together.*

(2.1) On that day heaven and earth will shake and cry out in grief, and so will the sea and all creatures that are in it. And on that day the roaring flames will devour the blood-soaked earth and the human race too, which at present is deluded in its empty pomp and its sinful desires and its ill-gotten wealth of gold and silver, and which has no fear at all on that account but considers itself to have no cares. (2.2) And on that day the wretched and sinful human race will mourn and weep for itself and lament that they will then feel such terror because they did not want to atone for their sins beforehand. (2.3) And on that day the sea will pass away in the flaming surge, and so will the earth with its mountains and the heavens with their stars, and then the wicked desire of all its previous deeds will swallow up the whole, sinful human race; and corrupt judges and reeves and all the world's powerful who are eager to do wrong will then perish along with their gold and silver and fine clothes and all their ill-gotten gains.

(3.1) And on that day the trumpets will sound at the four cortum middan-eardes. And þonne ealle men arisað of deaðe, and swa hwæt man-cynnes swa eorðe ær forswealh oððe fir for-bærnde and sæ besæncte and wilde deor frætan and fugelas to-bæran—eal þi dæge ariseð. (3.2) On ðam dæge ure drihten cymð mid his þam micclan mægen-þrymme mid þam .ix. endebird-nessum heofon-wara: þæt bið mærlic and wundorlic mægen-þrym! And þonne bið he þam synfullum swiðe wrað æteowed, and þam soðfæstum he bið bliðe gesewen. (3.3) And þonne þa Iudeas magon swutollice geseon þone þe hi ær ahengon and acwealdon. And se soðfæsta dema demeð anra gehwilcum æfter his gewirhtum, swa saw we leorniað on halgum gewritum: *Red-det deus unicuique secundum opera sua,* ðæt is on ure geþeode, "He forgilt þonne anra gehwilcum æfter his agenum gewirhtum."

(4.1) On ðam dæge bið ures drihtenes ansyn, swa we ær sæ-don, reþe and egesful þam synfullum gesewen, and he bið bliðe and milde þam soðfæstum æteowed, þæt is þam þe him to in ðære swiðran healfe þonne beoð gelædde. (4.2) Ða firenfullan witodlice hig beoð þonne on dæg on þare winstran healfe ge-hwirfede, and he þonne rædlice to heom cwið: "Farað ge awir-gedan on þæt ece fir þe wæs deofle gegearwod and his gegængum eallum!"

(5.1) La hwæt, þonne þam firenfullum þinceð þæt nanwiht ne sy

þæs hates   ne þæs cealdes
ne þæs heardes   ne þæs hnesces
ne þæs wraðes   ne þæs wynsumes
ne þæs eaðes   ne þæs earfoðes
ne þæs leofes   ne þæs laðes—

þæt hi þonne mæge fram ures drihtenes lufan ascadan, gif hi þonne þæs gewealdan mihton. (5.2) And þa ungesæligan yrmin-

ners of the earth. And then all people will arise from death, and whatever portion of human-kind the earth has previously swallowed down or fire burned up or ocean drowned or wild beasts eaten or birds carried off—they will all arise on that day. (3.2) On that day our Lord will come with his great majesty, accompanied by the nine orders of heaven's citizens: that will be a splendid and wondrous majesty! And then, to the sinful, he will be revealed as very wrathful, and to the righteous he will appear kind. (3.3) And then the Jews will be able to perceive clearly the one whom they previously hanged and put to death. And the righteous judge will judge every individual in accordance with his deeds, just as we learn in holy writings: *God will reward each one according to his works,* that is in our tongue, "He will then repay every single one in accordance with his own deeds."

(4.1) On that day, as we have stated, our Lord's countenance will appear stern and terrifying to the sinful, and he will be revealed as kind and gentle to the righteous, that is, to those who will then be led toward his right side. (4.2) As for the wicked, surely on that day, then, they will be shunted toward the left side, and then he will say to them: "Depart, you accursed, into the everlasting fire that was prepared for the devil and all his associates!"

(5.1) Lo, to the wicked, then, it seems that there is nothing
so hot or so cold
so hard or so soft,
so angry or so pleasant,
so easy or so difficult,
so cherished or so hated—
nothing that might, on that occasion, cut them off from our Lord's love, if they could then control the outcome. (5.2) And

gas nellað nu þæt geþencan ne his willan wurcan nu hi eaðe magon.

(6) Eala hwæt, þæt is ofer al gemet
    to scamigenne   and to sorgienne
    and on micelre care   to cweðanne
    þæt þa earman synfullan   sculan þonne sare
    aswæman   fram ansene
    ures drihtenes   and ealra haligra
    and from wlite   and fram wuldre
heofona rices, and þanon gewitan in ða ecan tintregu helle wites.

(7) La hwæt, manna mod sindon aþystrode
    and earmlice adisgode   and adwealde
þæt hi æfre sculon læton þæt deað-berende deofol mid un-gemættre costnunge hi to ðam gedwelle, þæt hi swa micle sinne fremman swa hi nu doð, and þæs willan ne wyrcan þe hi of eorðan lame geworhte and mid his gaste geliffæste, and him ece lif begeat.

(8.1) La, hwæt þence we þæt we us ne ondrædað þone towear-dan dæg þæs micclan domes?

    Se is yrmða dæg   and ealra earfoða dæg.

(8.2) On ðam dæge us bið æteowed
    seo geopnung heofona   and engla þrym
    and eal-wihtna rire   and eorðan forwyrd,
    treow-leasra gewinn   and tungla gefeal,
    þunor-rade hlinn   and se þistra storm,
    þara lyfta leoma   and þara liggetta gebrastl,
    þara granigiendran gesceaft   and þara gasta gefeoht,
    þa grymman gesihðe   and þa godcundan miht,
    se hata scur   and hel-wara ream,

yet at present those unhappy wretches do not give it any
thought, nor carry out his will now while they easily can.

(6) Alas, it is, beyond all measure, a thing
to be ashamed of and to grieve over
and to be spoken of in great distress,
that those wretched sinners must then painfully
be confounded before the face
of our Lord and of all the saints,
and before the beauty and the glory

of the kingdom of heaven, and must depart thence into the
punishments of hell's torments.

(7) Lo, the minds of human beings are so darkened
and rendered so miserably foolish and deceived,

that they must continually allow the death-bringing devil to
lead them astray with monstrous temptation so far that they
commit as much sin as they now do, and do not carry out the
will of him who fashioned them from mud of the earth, brought
them to life with his Spirit, and gained for them life everlasting.

(8.1) Lo, what are we thinking, that we are not afraid of that
future day of the great judgment?

That is a day of afflictions and a day of all hardships.

(8.2) On that day will be shown to us
the opening of the heavens, and the host of angels,
the dissolution of all creatures and destruction of the earth,
the strife of unbelievers and the plummeting of the stars,
the crashing of thunderbolts and the dark tempest,
the flashes in the upper air and the crack of lightning,
the destiny of those who groan and the strife of souls,
the horrific sights and the divine powers,
the scalding rain and the uproar of hell's inhabitants,

þara beorga geberst   and þara bimena sang,
se brada bryne ofer eal world   and se bitera dæg,
se miccla cwealm   and þara manna man,
seo sare sorh   and þara sawla gedal,
se sara sið   and se sorhfulla dæg,
þæt brade beala   and se birnenda grund,
þæt bitere wite   and se blodiga stream,
feonda firhto   and se firena ren,
hæþenra granung   and reafera wanung,
heofon-wara ful-mægn   and heora hlafordes þrym,
þæt ongrislice gemot   and seo egesfulle fird,
se reða waldend   and se rihta dom,
ure firena edwit   and þara feonda gestal,
þa blacan andwlitan   and þæt bifigende wered,
se forhta cyrm   and þara folca wop,
þara feonda grimnes
and se hlude heof,
þæt sarige man-cyn   and se synniga heap,
seo granigende neowelnes   and seo forglændrede hell,
þara wyrma ongrype
and þara sorhh-wita mæst,
se niðfulla here
and se teonfulla dæg.

(8.3) On þam dæge us bið eal þillic egsa æteowed. And þa sinful-
lan woldon þonne gewiscan georne gif hi mihton þæt he næfre
acænnede ne wurdon fram fæder ne fram meder, and him þæt
þonne wære leofre þonne eal middan-eard to æhte geseald.

(9.1) La hwæt, we nu ungesælige sind þæt we us bett ne war-

the crumbling of mountains and the sounding of trumpets,
the widespread burning over all the world and the grievous
    day,
the great slaughter and the evil of human beings,
the painful agony and the parting of souls,
the painful journey and the sorrowful day,
the widespread violence and the burning pit,
the harsh torment and the river of blood,
the fright of demons and the fiery rain,
the groaning of pagans and moaning of robbers,
the full strength of heaven's citizens and the majesty of
    their Lord,
the terrifying assembly and the awe-inspiring troop,
the strict ruler and the lawful judgment,
reproach for our crimes and accusation from the demons,
the pallid faces and the trembling troop,
the frightened cry and the weeping of the masses,
the cruelty of the demons
and the loud lament,
the pained human race and the sinful throng,
the groaning abyss and hell consumed with fire,
the striking of the serpents
and the greatest painful torments,
the malicious force
and the day full of hurt.

(8.3) All such terror will be shown to us on that day. And sinners would then eagerly wish that, if they could, they had never been born of a father and mother, and that would then be more precious to them than if all the world were given into their keeping.

(9.1) Lo, we are now unfortunate in that we do not warn our-

niað and þæt we ne ondrædað us þe swiðor þe we dæg-hwamlice
geseoð for urum eagum ure þa nihstan feallan and swiltan.

    (9.2) And þonne sona bið þam lic-haman   laðlic leger
                                            gired,
and in þare cealdan moldan gebrosnoð
and þæt lic þar to fulnesse gewurðeð
and þam wæl-slitendum   wyrmum wurðeð to æte.
Þonne bið sorhlic sar
and earmlic gedal lices and sawle.
(9.3) And gif þonne seo sawle   huru slidan sceal
in ðam ece helle-witu
mid þam werian   and þam awirgedan gaste,
and þar þonne mid deoflum   drohtnoð habban
on morðe and on mane,
on susle and on sare,
on wean and on wyrm-slitum
betweonan deadum and deoflum,
on bryne and on biternesse,
on bealuwe and on bradum lige,
on yrmðum and on earfoðum,
on swilt-cwale   and on sarum sorgum,
in fyrenum bryne   and on fulnesse,
on toða grist-bitum   and on tintregum,
in ang-modnessa   earmra sawla
on cile and on wanunge,
on hungre and on þurste,
on hæte and on earfoðnesse,
on neowlum attre   and on ecere forwirde,
on arleasnesse
and on mistlicum wita cynne,
on muðe and on fædme

selves better and fear the more intensely as we see, day by day,
our neighbors falling and dying before our eyes.

(9.2) And then, for the body, a loathsome grave is readied at
    once,
and it rots in the cold ground,
and there that body turns to corruption
and becomes food for corpse-rending worms.
Then there will be a painful agony
and a miserable parting of body and soul.
(9.3) And [so it will be] if the soul must then indeed descend
into the everlasting torments of hell
with the wretched and accursed spirit,
and there have its existence among devils,
amid murder and evil,
amid torture and pain,
amid woe and rending by serpents,
between the dead and the devils,
in burning and in bitterness
in violence and in widespread flame,
in afflictions and in hardships,
in death and in painful agonies,
in fiery burning and in filth,
amid the grinding of teeth and amid torments,
amid the anxious thoughts of miserable souls
in the cold and in the moaning,
in hunger and in thirst,
in heat and in hardship,
in a poisoned abyss and in everlasting ruin,
in wickedness,
and in various kinds of torture,
in the mouth and in the belly

þæs dead-berendan dracan
se is "deofol" nemned.

(10.1) Eala, leofan men, uton warnian us and georne beorgan
wið þone egsan, and uton geornlice yfeles geswican and þurh
Godes fultum to gode gedon þone dæl þe we don magon. Uton
man and morð æghwar forbugan and ealle fracod-dæda swiðe
ascunian. (10.2) And utan don swa ic lære: utan God lufian in-
weardre heortan eallum mode and eallum mægne and Godes
lage healdan. And uton gecnawan hu læne and hu lyðre þis lif is
on to getruwianne, and hu oft hit wurð raþost forloren and for-
læten þonne hit wære leofost gehealdon. (10.3) Ðeos world is
sorhful and fram dæge to dæge a swa leng swa wirse, forðam þe
heo is on ofstum and hit nealæcð þam ende. And þi heo nære
wurðe þæt hi ænig man lufode ealles to swiðe. Ac lufian we þone
hihstan cyningc and þæt uplice rice, and ondrædan we us symle
þone toweardan dom þe we ealle to sculan.

(11.1) On þam dom ure drihten silf eowað us sona his blodi-
gan sidan and his þirlan handa and þa silfan rode þe he on ahan-
gen wæs, and wile þonne æt us gewitan hu we him þæt geleano-
dan. Wel þam þonne þe Gode ær wel gecwemdan swa swa hi
scoldan. (11.2) Hi þonne siððan eac ece edlean þurh Godes gife
þananforð habbað betweoh englum and heah-englum a to
worlde on heofonan rice, þar næfre leofe ne gedælað ne laðe ne
gemetað, ac ðar halige heapas simle wuniað on wlite and on
wuldre and on winsumnesse. (11.3) Ðar bið mærð and ece blis
mid Gode silfum and mid his halgum in ealra worlda world a
buton ende. Amen.

of the death-bringing dragon
who is called "the devil."

(10.1) Alas, beloved, let us guard and eagerly protect our-
selves against that terror, let us readily leave off doing wrong
and, by God's help, make good that portion we are capable
of doing. Let us everywhere avoid evil and killing, and greatly
shun criminal acts. (10.2) And let us do as I am teaching: from
the depths of our hearts, let us love God with all our mind and
all our strength, and let us uphold God's law. And let us realize
how transitory and worthless this present life is for us to trust
in, and how often it is most quickly lost and left behind when
one would hold on to it most dearly. (10.3) This world is full of
misery and grows worse from day to day the longer it lasts, be-
cause it is hastening onward and the end draws near. And for
that reason it would not be worth anyone's loving it all too
much. Rather let us love the highest king and the celestial king-
dom, and let us always feel dread of the future judgment at
which we must all appear.

(11.1) At that judgment our Lord himself will immediately
show us his bloody sides and his pierced hands and the actual
cross on which he was hung, and then he will find out from us
how we have repaid him for that. At that time it will be well for
those who were well-pleasing to God before, as they ought to
have been. (11.2) Afterward, they will also then possess through
God's grace, from that time forward, an everlasting reward
among the angels and archangels forever in the kingdom of
heaven, where loved ones never part and enemies never meet,
but rather holy companies there abide continually in beauty
and in glory and in delight. (11.3) There will be renown and ev-
erlasting happiness in company with God himself and with his
saints, forever and ever. Amen.

Appendix B

Bilingual Materials from the Divine Office (in Oxford, Bodleian Library, Junius 121)

INTRODUCTION

Three examples of so-called liturgical verse in Old English—*The Gloria patri (I)*, *The Lord's Prayer (III)*, and *The Apostles' Creed*—were copied near one another in the mid-eleventh-century book that is now manuscript Junius 121 in the Bodleian Library, Oxford. There the poems appear as part of a larger group of bilingual prose and verse texts related to the divine office or "liturgy of the hours," the full round of formal prayers and readings that came to be a daily duty for clergy, monks, and nuns. To give modern readers a sense of one context in which Old English "liturgical" poems circulated, and to illustrate once more the cooperation of homiletic prose and verse that was a hallmark of late Anglo-Saxon literature, the relevant portions of the Junius manuscript are included in this appendix. Collectively these materials are often called *The (Old English) Benedictine Office*, a misleading name at best. Monks and secular clergy celebrated slightly different versions of the daily office, and while some features of this compilation in Junius 121 do suggest a monastic or "Benedictine" background, others seem to point to a secular one.[1] In the absence of certainty on this fundamental issue, I drop the term "Benedictine" and refer to the materials simply as the Junius or bilingual *Office*.

The backbone of the compilation is a set of passages in Old English prose justifying the recitation of the daily office and explaining its symbolism (§§ 1–1.4, 2–2.4, 3–3.1, 5–5.3, 6–6.2, 7–7.1, 8–8.3, 9–9.2, 10–10.6, and 11–11.3). Based on a ninth-century Latin treatise, *De clericorum institutione* ("The Instruction of Clerics") by the monk Hrabanus Maurus of Fulda, these prose passages employ a rhythmical style and vocabulary that suggest they were authored or revised by Archbishop Wulfstan of York (d. 1023), the famous homilist and legislator.[2]

Distributed unevenly among the prose passages stand a great many Latin and Old English segments corresponding to parts of the divine office itself. The material is curiously uneven. The compiler has given no liturgical outline for the so-called night office ("Nocturns"), which was the longest, most complex of the services, nor for the most important of the daytime offices, Lauds.[3] Variable amounts of detail are given for the remaining hours: Prime, Terce, Sext, None, Vespers, and Compline. In the actual liturgy, the first four of these, sometimes called "the little hours," shared a very similar form.[4] They began with Psalm 70:1 (Vulgate 69:2), divided into a versicle ("O God, come to my assistance") and response ("O Lord, make haste to help me"), followed by the *Gloria patri* ("Glory be to the Father, and to the Son, and to the Holy Spirit; as it was in the beginning, is now, and ever shall be, forever and ever. Amen"). After this opening, each of the "little hours" had its own Latin hymn, which sometimes varied by day or season. A number of psalms and one or more accompanying antiphons followed, varying over each office and day of the week. After the psalmody, a short reading from scripture, called the *capitulum* ("little chapter"), was recited, followed by the response "Thanks be to God." At some offices there then followed a *responsorium breve* ("short responsory"), then another versicle and response, the *Kyrie*, and the Lord's Prayer. At this point, the secular offices of Terce, Sext, and None ended with a summary prayer (the "collect") and a blessing. The office of Prime continued at length, however, including a long series of individual psalm verses, recited responsorially or silently, known as the *preces* ("prayers") or *capitella de psalmis* ("little chapters from the psalms"). The Apostles' Creed and a *Confiteor* (confession of sin) were inserted among these *preces*. Prime then dovetailed with the community's daily administrative meeting called "Chapter," which involved readings of its own, announcements from the martyrology, prayers, more versicles and responses, and public confessions of faults.

The office of Vespers differed from the "little hours" but involved many of the same components. Its opening versicle and response came from Psalm 141 (Vulgate 140):2; the psalmody then followed immediately, then the short reading (*capitulum*), its following versicle and response, and a hymn. The hymn in turn was followed by the gospel canticle *Magnificat* (Luke 1:46–55) with its proper antiphon. The office concluded in the usual way with the *Kyrie*, Lord's Prayer, *preces* (briefer than at Prime), and a final collect. The last office of the day, Compline, involved still other, minor variations on the day hours.

The preceding sketch does not begin to cover all the variations that so complicated the medieval liturgy of the hours. But the outline may suffice to help modern readers recognize the individual parts in the *Office*, how they are organized, and, above all, how much they omit. At no point does the matter included constitute a full description of any single hour. Even the longest section, for Prime, makes just the briefest reference to the psalmody that was the chief component of the service. The most developed part of the entire text is that covering the *preces* at Prime, which were a relatively minor part of the divine office as a whole. Then again, at later hours, where we expect different *preces*, they are either absent or heavily curtailed. The same is true of other components that recurred throughout the day. An even more striking inconsistency appears in the shifting between languages. Some portions are entirely or mostly in Old English, others alternate Latin with Old English, while still others consist merely of abbreviated cues or tags in Latin, indicating liturgical texts by their incipits (the opening words). The frequent reliance on incipits and the absence of identifying labels for most of the components suggest that any user of the *Office* already had a deep familiarity with the Latin divine office, whether from memory, books, or both.

If its audiences already knew so much, however, what was the point of the Junius *Office* to begin with? Most scholars dismiss out of hand the possibility that the compiler set out to create a full vernacular liturgy of the hours. The preferred view is that the text was conceived for instructional purposes, perhaps to educate secular clergy about their duty to recite the office. It is hard to see, though, what kind of liturgy anyone could have learned to execute from the *Office* alone, with its many gaps and odd proportions. Nor is it clear, if teaching secular clergy to recite the Latin hours was the goal, what purpose was served by substituting long-winded Old English poetic paraphrases for the quite easily remembered Latin *Pater noster*, *Gloria patri*, and Apostles' Creed.

Questions about the nature and purpose of the *Office* become even more complicated in light of the partial overlap between it and texts in other manuscripts. Another eleventh-century book, Cambridge, Corpus Christi College 201, contains a second copy of *The Gloria patri (I)* next to an alternative metrical version of the Lord's Prayer, namely *The Lord's Prayer (II)*. A different part of the same Cambridge manuscript also contains the Wulfstanian prose sections on the allegorical and moral significance of the various hours. The appearance of Old English "liturgical" poems and the prose passages in the same manuscript is certainly arresting, but it must be emphasized that, in Corpus Christi College 201, they do not stand as parts of a larger compilation like the Junius *Office*.

The more intriguing connection between the *Office* and other vernacular writings lies in the compiler's quotation of dozens of individual psalm verses rendered as Old English verse. The largest number of these cluster in the *preces* near the end of Prime (§§ 3.9–10, 12–38, and 40–9), but they also occur elsewhere, translating standard versicles and responses. The compiler rendered none of these anew from the Latin psalm verses quoted alongside the Old English but has instead borrowed from a preexisting Old English verse translation of the psalms, closely related to that in the famous Paris Psalter. The Paris Psalter is a fully bilingual version containing, alongside its Latin text of the Roman psalter, translations into Old English prose of Psalms 1–50 (in the Vulgate numbering), then verse translations of the remaining Psalms 51–150.[5] Where the Junius *Office* quotes from Psalms 51–150 in Old English verse, its text is so close to that of the Paris Psalter as to leave no doubt that a common version underlies both. And since the Junius compiler gives poetic translations of many verses from the *first* fifty psalms (i.e., those for which the Paris Psalter has only prose), the bilingual *Office* bears crucial witness to the existence, at one time, of a complete Old English metrical psalter.

Different readers have drawn different conclusions from the links between the *Office* and items in manuscript 201 of Corpus Christi College, Cambridge, on the one hand, and the Paris Psalter on the other. Like the metrical psalms, the "liturgical" poems and prose passages were probably composed independently of the project that has come down to us as the Junius *Office*.[6] The latter, as we know it, may represent a work in progress or one left unfinished because the compiler's intentions changed midcourse—if, for example, what began as an instructional outline for teaching the secular office came to seem unviable for that purpose, yet salvageable as a framework for bilingual devotions.

As noted above (xix–xx), boundaries between liturgy and private devotion were porous in the earlier Middle Ages, and the Junius *Office* is an excellent illustration of their relationship. Its large amounts of vernacular poetry, both the "liturgical verse" and the metrical psalm quotations, are easier to reconcile with a devotional than with a liturgical or instructional setting. Poetic paraphrases of the Lord's Prayer and other texts were hardly the most efficient way to communicate the content of the Latin originals. In the case of the metrical psalm verses, the Old English and accompanying Latin quotations in the *Office* are not even based on the same versions of the psalter, the Old English depending largely on the Roman version, the Latin on the Gallican. It seems, then, that the poetry in the *Office* was inserted by someone who valued it for the sake of its form *as* verse. Anyone who knew the divine office as well as this compiler did must have recognized that poetry, in the form of psalms, hymns, and canticles, made up the bulk of the Latin liturgical hours. The poetic turn of the Junius *Office* can be understood as an experiment in translating the aesthetic form along with selected content of those hours.

Casting a bilingual text such as this into Modern English translation involves some unavoidable repetition. The Latin quotations and accompanying Old English translations are usually saying almost the same thing, but the differences are numerous and interesting enough to warrant translating both in full. Even more challenging to the present-day translator is the sheer degree of editorial intervention needed to clarify the structure of the *Office* for readers unfamiliar with its liturgical framework. In addition to the brief outline of the various hours provided above, I have inserted into the edition itself many headings to supplement the relatively few and inconsistent ones given in the manuscript. (Editorial insertions of this and similar kinds appear in square brackets.) The frequent biblical quotations in the text are identified in the notes to the translation; there I have also indicated quotations from the Old English metrical psalter, keyed to psalm and verse numbers in Krapp's edition of the Paris Psalter. Latin psalm verses throughout the *Office* are here printed as poetry, each verse being divided as if for responsorial performance.

Space has not permitted the expansion of all textual items for which the manuscript gives only the opening words. I leave unexpanded some obvious or often-repeated components but supply full texts for the hymns in Latin verse. Also expanded are formulaic endings to several of the prayers. The poems *The Gloria patri (I)*, *The Lord's Prayer (III)*, and *The Apostles' Creed* are not repeated here in full but are indicated only by their opening words, followed by cross-references to the complete texts printed earlier in this volume. Ellipses after the opening words of these and other unexpanded incipits indicate that a longer text has been truncated on purpose, not that there is damage to or text accidentally omitted from the manuscript.

Notes

1 For the contradictory evidence, see my notes to the translation at §§ 3.4, 8.6, and 9.6.

2 Ure, *The Benedictine Office*, 30–46, summarizes and extends the argument for Wulfstan's authorship. Most of Ure's attendant claims—such as that Wulfstan was revising material sent to him by Ælfric the homilist—have not won acceptance. Even if Wulfstan wrote or revised the prose sections, he need not have composed other parts of the Junius *Office* or given the whole its present form.

3 Throughout this appendix, I avoid the confusing term "Matins," which in some modern discussions serves as a name for Nocturns, in others for Lauds.

4 The following general descriptions are based on the secular rather than monastic form of the office (but see note 1, above). More detail about the various components may be found in the notes to the translation.

5 Paris, Bibliothèque nationale de France, lat. 8824. The standard editions are O'Neill, *King Alfred's Old English Prose Translation*, and Krapp, ASPR 5:3–150. An edition of the Paris Psalter is in preparation for the Dumbarton Oaks Medieval Library. The same metrical psalter is quoted in *The Menologium*, lines 60–62; see the notes to the translation there.

6 On this point, my view is essentially that of Whitbread, "Poems of the *Benedictine Office*."

[Introduction]

(1) *De officiis diurnalium et nocturnalium horarum.*

(1.1) Godcund þeowdom is gesett on cyriclicum þenungum æfter canoneclican gewunan to nyd-rihte eallum gehadedum mannum. On ælcne timan man sceal God herian and on ælcere stowe georne to Gode clypian. (1.2) Ac þeahhwæðere syndon gesette timan synderlice to ðam anum, þæt gyf hwa for bysgan oftor ne mæge, þæt he huru þæt nyd-riht dæg-hwamlice gefylle eallswa Dauid cwæð: *Septies in die laudem dixi tibi,* þæt is, "Seofon siðon on dæg ic sang ðe, drihten, to lofe and to weorðunge." (1.3) To seldan hit bið, beo hit a seldor on dæg þæt we God herian þonne seofon siðum; ðæt is æne ærest on ærne-morgen, and eft on undern-tide, and on midne dæg, and on non, and on æfen, and on foran-niht, and on uhtan timan. (1.4) Nis æfre æniges mannes mæð þæt he cunne God swa forð geherian swa he wyrðe is. Ac hit is þeah ure ealra þearf þæt we geornlice him þeowian and ðenian þæs ðe we magon and cunnon.

[The Office of Lauds]

(2) *De matutinale officio.*

(2.1) On dæg-red man sceal God herian eallswa Dauid cwæð: *Deus, deus meus, ad te de luce vigilo,* ðæt is, "Min drihten, to þe ic

.

[INTRODUCTION]

(1) *The Liturgical Hours of Day and Night.*

(1.1) Among the services of the church, the divine office has been established according to canonical custom as an obligation on all ordained persons. One should praise God and eagerly call upon him at every time and in every place. (1.2) Nevertheless, certain times are established in particular for that end, so that, should anyone be unable to do so more often because of pressing business, he may at least fulfill the obligation daily, just as David said: *Seven times a day I have given praise to thee,* that is, "Seven times a day have I sung to you, O Lord, in praise and reverence." (1.3) Too seldom it is if we ever praise God less often than seven times in a day, that is once first thing at daybreak, and again in the morning, and at midday, and at the ninth hour, and at evening, and at nightfall, and in the time before dawn. (1.4) It is never in the capacity of any human being to know how to praise God as fully as he deserves. But it is nevertheless the duty of us all that we eagerly serve and attend him to the extent that we are able and know how.

[THE OFFICE OF LAUDS]

(2) *The Morning Office.*

(2.1) At dawn one should praise God just as David said: *O God, my God, to thee do I watch at break of day,* that is, "My Lord, for

wacige of frum-leohte"; and eft he cwæð: *In matutinis, domine, meditabor in te, quia fuisti adiutor meus,* þæt is, "On dæg-red ic smeade ymbe þe, forðam þe ðu wære min fultum." (2.2) Crist is ealles man-cynnes fultum and ealles middan-eardes helpend. On dæg-red hit gewearð þæt ðurh Godes mihte Moyses gelædde þæt Israhelitisce folc of Egipta lande eall unwemme ofer ða readan sæ; and æfter ðam sona seo sylfe sæ besencte and adrencte Godes wiðer-winnan, Pharaonem and eall his gegenge. (2.3) And on dæg-red hit gewearð þæt Crist of deaþe aras and of helle gelædde ealle þa ðe he wolde; and his wiðer-winnan, þæt is deofol sylfne, he besencte and eall his gegenge on helle-susle. (2.4) Þy we sculon on dæg-red God georne herian and him þancian ðære mild-heortnysse þe he on man-cynne þa geworhte þa þa he hit alysde of helle-wite and of deofles gewealde and gerymde þananforð rihtne weg to heofona rice ælcum þara þe his willan gewyrcð her on life. Amen.

[THE OFFICE OF PRIME]

(3) *De prima hora.*

(3.1) On ðære forman dæg-tide, þæt is be sunnon up-gange, we sculon God herian and hine geornlice biddan þæt he þurh his mild-heortnesse mid soðre sunnon lihtincge ure heortan alihte; þæt is, þæt he ðurh his gyfe ure in-geþanc swa alihte þæt us deofol of rihtan wege þurh deriende ðystra belædan ne mæge ne mid syn-grinum to swyðe gehremman.

[Opening versicle and response:]

(3.2) *Deus in adiutorium meum intende, domine ad adiuvandum me festina.*

you do I keep watch from the dawn"; and again he said: *I will meditate on thee in the morning, because thou hast been my helper,* that is, "At dawn I meditated on you, for you were my help." (2.2) Christ is a help to all humankind and a helper to the whole world. It was at dawn that, by God's power, Moses led the people of Israel entirely unharmed through the Red Sea, out of the land of the Egyptians; and immediately thereafter the same sea overwhelmed and drowned God's adversaries, Pharaoh and all his band. (2.3) And it was at dawn that Christ arose from death and led from hell those whom he intended; and he drowned his adversaries, that is the devil himself and all his band, in the torment of hell. (2.4) Therefore we should eagerly praise God at dawn and thank him for the mercy that he showed to humankind when he freed it from the torment of hell and from the devil's control, and, from that time forth, opened a direct way to the kingdom of heaven for everyone who does God's will here in this life. Amen.

[The Office of Prime]

(3) *The First Hour.*

(3.1) At the first hour of the day, that is at the rising of the sun, we should praise God and eagerly pray to him that, through his mercy, he would enlighten our hearts with the light of the true sun; that is, that through his grace he would so enlighten our inner thoughts that the devil is unable to lead us from the straight path by his harmful darkness or hinder us too greatly with the snares of sin.

[Opening versicle and response:]

(3.2) *O God, come to my assistance;*
O Lord, make haste to help me.

Wes, drihten God,   deore fultum;
beheald, drihten, me,   and me hraðe syððan
gefultuma   æt feorh-þearfe.

Gloria . . . [the poem *The Gloria patri (I)*, printed above,
88–92]

Hymnus:

(3.3) *Iam lucis orto sidere*
deum precemur supplices,
[*ut in diurnis actibus*
nos servet a nocentibus.

Linguam refrenans temperet,
ne litis horror insonet;
visum fovendo contegat,
ne vanitates hauriat.

Sint pura cordis intima,
absistat et vecordia;
carnis terat superbiam
potus cibique parcitas,

ut cum dies abscesserit
noctemque sors reduxerit,
mundi per abstinentiam
ipsi canamus gloriam.

Deo patri sit gloria,
eiusque soli filio
cum spiritu paraclyto
et nunc et in perpetuum. Amen.]

Be my cherished help, O Lord God;
look to me, O Lord, and then quickly
aid me in my dire need.

Glory . . . [the poem *The Gloria patri (I),* printed above, 88–92]

Hymn:

(3.3) *Now, at the rising of the daystar,*
let us humbly beseech God
[*that, in our daily actions,*
he would preserve us from the agents of harm.

May he temper and control our tongue
that the din of strife may not resound;
may he cover and nurture our sight
that it may not take in vanities.

May the innermost places of our heart be pure,
and may foolishness depart;
may sparingness in food and drink
curb the insolence of the flesh,

so that, when day departs
and destiny brings on night again,
we may, purified by our abstinence,
sing glory to him.

To God the Father be glory,
and to his only Son,
together with the comforter, the Spirit,
both now and forever. Amen.]

[Psalmody:]

(3.4) *Deus in nomine tuo salvum me fac,*
et in virtute tua libera me.

On þinum þam halgan naman,   gedo me halne, God;
alys me fram laðum   þurh þin leofe mægen.

[*Capitulum:*]

(3.5) *Regi autem seculorum inmortali, invisibili soli deo honor et glo-*
ria in secula seculorum. Amen.
Deo gratias.

[Short responsory:]

(3.6) *Christe Iesu, fili dei vivi cum sancto spiritu: miserere nobis.*
Qui sedes ad dexteram patris: miserere nobis.
Gloria patri . . .
Christe Iesu . . .

[Versicle and response:]

(3.7) *Exurge, domine, adiuva nos,*
et libera nos propter nomen tuum.

Aris, drihten, nu   and us ricene do
fælne fultum,   and us æt feondum ahrede,
forðon we naman þinne   nyde lufiað.

[*Kyrie* and Lord's Prayer:]

(3.8) *Cyrrieleison. Christeleison. Cyrrieleison.*

Pater noster . . . [the poem *The Lord's Prayer (III)*, printed above,
78–81]

[Psalmody:]

(3.4) *Save me, O God, by thy name,*
and free me in thy strength.

    In your holy name, save me, O God;
    free me from enemies through your dear might.

[*Capitulum:*]

(3.5) *Now to the king of ages, immortal, invisible, the only God, be*
    honor and glory forever and ever. Amen.
[Response:] *Thanks be to God.*

[Short responsory:]

(3.6) *Christ Jesus, Son of the living God, together with the Holy*
    Spirit: have mercy on us.
Who sit at the right hand of the Father: have mercy on us.
Glory be to the Father . . .
Christ Jesus . . . [repeating the initial response]

[Versicle and response:]

(3.7) *Arise, O Lord, help us;*
and redeem us for thy name's sake.

    Arise now, O Lord, and quickly provide us
    trustworthy aid, and deliver us from our foes,
    for we zealously love your name.

[*Kyrie* and Lord's Prayer:]

(3.8) *Lord have mercy. Christ have mercy. Lord have mercy.*

Our Father . . . [the poem *The Lord's Prayer (III),* printed above,
    78–81]

[*Preces:*]

(3.9) *Vivet anima mea et laudabit te,*
et iudicia tua adiuvabunt me.

> Leofað sawul min   and ðe lustum hereð,
> and me þine domas   dædum fultumiað.

(3.10) *Erravi sicut ovis que perierat;*
require servum tuum, domine, quia mandata tua non sum oblitus.

> Ic gedwelede swa   þæt dysige sceap,
> þæt ðe forwurðan   wolde huru;
> la, sec þinne esne   elne, drihten,
> forðon ic ðinra beboda ne forgeat   beorhtra æfre.

[Apostles' Creed:]

(3.11) *Credo in deum* . . . [the poem *The Apostles' Creed,* printed
above, 82–87]

[*Preces* (continued):]

(3.12) *Et ego ad te, domine, clamavi,*
et mane oratio mea perveniet te.

> Ic me to ðe,   ece drihten,
> mid mod-gehygde   mægne clypode,
> and min gebed   morgena gehwylce
> fore sylfne ðe   soðfæst becume.

(3.13) *Verba mea auribus percipe, domine;*
intellege clamorem meum.

> Word þu min onfoh,   wuldres ealdor,
> and mid earum gehyr,   ece drihten.

(3.14) *Intende voci orationis mee,*
rex meus et deus meus.

[*Preces:*]

(3.9) *My soul shall live and shall praise thee;*
and thy judgments shall help me.

My soul shall live and shall praise you willingly,
and with works your judgments will come to my aid.

(3.10) *I have gone astray like a sheep that is lost:*
seek thy servant, Lord, for I have not forgotten thy commandments.

I have strayed like the senseless sheep
that has willed indeed to be lost to you;
lo, seek with zeal after your servant, O Lord,
for I have never forgotten your splendid commands.

[Apostles' Creed:]

(3.11) *I believe in God* . . . [the poem *The Apostles' Creed,* printed
above, 82–87]

[*Preces* (continued):]

(3.12) *But I, O Lord, have cried to thee,*
and in the morning my prayer shall reach thee.

To you, eternal Lord,
have I strongly cried out with my thoughts,
and may my prayer arrive, righteous
before your presence, every morning.

(3.13) *Give ear, O Lord, to my words;*
understand my cry.

O ruler of glory, receive my words
and listen with your ears, O eternal Lord.

(3.14) *Hearken to the voice of my prayer,*
O my king and my God.

Ongyt mine clypunga   cuðum gereorde,
beheald min gebed   holdum mode;
þu eart min cyning   and eac ece God.
(3.15) *Quoniam ad te orabo, domine;*
mane exaudies vocem meam.

Forðon ic to ðe,   ece drihten,
soðum gebidde,   and ðu symble gehyr
morgena gehwylce   mine stefne.
(3.16) *Mane adstabo tibi et videbo,*
quoniam non deus volens iniquitatem tu es.

Ic þe æt stande   ær on morgen
and ðe sylfne geseo;   forðon ic to soðe wat
þæt ðu unriht ne wilt   ænig, drihten.
(3.17) *Vias tuas, domine, notas fac michi,*
et semitas tuas edoce me.

Do me wegas þine   wise, drihten,
and me ðinra stiga   stapas eac gelær.
(3.18) *Dirige me in veritate tua, et doce me,*
quia tu es deus salutaris meus,
et te sustinui tota die.

Gerece me on ræde   and me ricene gelær,
þæt ic on þinre soðfæstnysse   simble lyfige.
(3.19) *Reminiscere miserationum tuarum, domine,*
et misericordie tue que a secula sunt.

Wes ðu gemyndig   miltsa þinra,
þe ðu, drihten, dydest   syððan dagas wæron,
and ðu wislice   þas woruld gesettest.
(3.20) *Delicta iuventutis mee et ignorantias meas ne memineris,*
    domine,
secundum magnam misericordiam tuam memor esto mei, deus.

Recognize my cries by their familiar voice,
look upon my prayer with a gracious mind;
you are my king and eternal God as well.

(3.15) *For to thee will I pray, O Lord;*
in the morning thou wilt hear my voice.

For to you, eternal Lord,
will I sincerely pray; listen always
to my voice, every morning.

(3.16) *In the morning I will stand before thee, and will see,*
because thou art not a God that willest iniquity.

Early in the morning I stand before you
and behold you; therefore do I know it to be true
that you, O Lord, do not will anything unjust.

(3.17) *Show, O Lord, thy ways to me,*
and teach me thy paths.

Make your ways certain to me, O Lord,
and also teach me the steps of your paths.

(3.18) *Direct me in thy truth, and teach me;*
for thou art God my savior,
and on thee have I waited all the day long.

Guide me in your counsel, and teach me swiftly,
that I may live always in your righteousness.

(3.19) *Remember, O Lord, thy works of compassion,*
and thy mercies that are from the beginning of the world.

Recall those mercies of yours
that you performed, O Lord, since days began
and you wisely established this world.

(3.20) *The sins of my youth and my ignorances do not remember,*
    O Lord;
according to thy mercy remember thou me, O God.

Ne gemynega þu me   minra fyrena
gramra to georne,   þe ic geong dyde
and me uncuðe   æghwær wæron;
for ðinre þære myclan   mild-heortnysse
weorð gemyndig min,   mihtig drihten.

(3.21) *Iudica, domine, nocentes me;*
expugna inpugnantes me.

Dem, drihten, nu   þa me deredon ær,
afeoht swylce   þa me fuhtan to.

(3.22) *Adprehende arma et scutum,*
et exsurge in adiutorium michi.

Gegrip gar and scyld,   and me georne gestand
on fultume   wið feonda gryre.

(3.23) *Effunde frameam et conclude adversus eos qui me persecuntur;*
dic anime mee: salus tua ego sum.

Heald me here-wæpnum   wið unholdum,
and wige beluc   wraðum feondum
þe min ehtend   ealle syndon;
sæge þonne syððan   sawle minre
þæt ðu hire on hæle   hold gestode.

(3.24) *Repleatur os meum laude tua, ut possim cantare gloriam tuam,*
tota die magnificentiam tuam.

Sy min muð and min mod   mægne gefylled,
þæt ic þin lof mæge   lustum singan
and wuldor ðin   wide mærsian
and ðe ealne dæg   æghwær herian.

Do not too readily recall to me
my hostile crimes that I committed as a youth
and were unnoticed everywhere about me;
for the sake of your great mercy,
remember me, O mighty Lord.

(3.21) *Judge thou, O Lord, them that wrong me;*
overthrow them that fight against me.

Now judge, O Lord, those who previously harmed me,
and fight those who fought against me.

(3.22) *Take hold of arms and shield,*
and rise up to help me.

Grasp spear and shield, and stand firm before me
as a help against the terror of enemies.

(3.23) *Bring out the sword, and shut up the way against them that*
persecute me;
say to my soul: "I am thy salvation."

With your weapons preserve me from the hostile,
and with battle prowess protect me from cruel enemies
who are all my persecutors;
then afterwards say to my soul
that you faithfully stood firm for the sake of its salvation.

(3.24) *Let my mouth be filled with praise, that I may sing thy glory,*
thy greatness all the day long.

Let my mouth and my mind be greatly filled,
that I may willingly sing your praise
and widely celebrate your glory
and extol you in every place, the whole day long.

(3.25) *Averte faciem tuam a peccatis meis,*
et omnes iniquitates meas dele.

> Awend þine ansyne   a fram minum
> fræcnum fyrenum,   and nu forð heonon
> eall min unriht adwæsc   æghwær symle.

(3.26) *Cor mundum crea in me, deus,*
et spiritum rectum innova in visceribus meis.

> Syle me, halig God,   heortan clæne,
> and rihtne gast,   God, geniwa
> on minre gehigde   huru, min drihten.

(3.27) *Ne proicias me a facie tua,*
et spiritum sanctum tuum ne auferas a me.

> Ne awyrp þu me,   wuldres ealdor,
> fram ðinre ansyne   æfre to feore,
> ne huru on weg aber   þone halgan gast,
> þæt he me færinga   fremde wyrðe.

(3.28) *Redde michi letitiam salutaris tui,*
et spiritu principali confirma me.

> Syle me þinre hælu   holde blisse,
> and me ealdorlice   æþele gaste
> on ðinne willan getryme,   weroda drihten.

(3.29) *Eripe me, domine, ab homine malo,*
a viro iniquo libera me.

> Genere me wið niþe   on naman þinum,
> fram yfelum men,   ece drihten.

(3.30) *Eripe me de inimicis meis, deus meus,*
et ab insurgentibus in me libera me.

> Ahrede me, halig God,   hefiges niðes
> feonda minra,   þe me feohtað to;
> alys me fram laðum   þe me lungre
> onrisan willað,   nymþe þu me ræd gife.

(3.25) *Turn away thy face from my sins,*
and blot out my iniquities.

Turn your face from my sins always,
from my terrible crimes, and from this time forward
snuff out all my wickedness always and everywhere.

(3.26) *Create a clean heart in me, O God,*
and renew a right spirit within my innermost parts.

Grant me, O holy God, a pure heart,
and renew, O God, a just spirit
within my mind, O my Lord.

(3.27) *Cast me not away from thy face,*
and take not thy Holy Spirit from me.

O ruler of glory, cast me not away
from your face forever,
nor indeed take away the Holy Spirit,
so that it suddenly grows estranged from me.

(3.28) *Restore unto me the joy of my salvation,*
and strengthen me with a perfect spirit.

Grant me the cherished joy of your salvation,
and strongly fortify me with a noble spirit
in your will, O Lord of hosts.

(3.29) *Deliver me, O Lord, from the evil man;*
rescue me from the unjust man.

Rescue me, in your name, from hatred,
from the evil man, O eternal Lord.

(3.30) *Deliver me from my enemies, O my God,*
and defend me from them that rise up against me.

Save me, O holy God, from the grievous hatred
of my enemies who attack me;
free me from those hostile ones, who desire swiftly
to rise up against me, unless you provide me help.

(3.31) *Eripe me de operantibus iniquitatem,*
et de viris sanguinum salva me.

 Genere me fram niðe naht-fremmendra
 þe her unrihtes ealle wyrceað,
 and me wið blod-hreowes weres bealuwe gehæle.

(3.32) *Sic psalmum dicam nomini tuo, deus, in seculum seculi,*
ut reddam vota mea de die in diem.

 Swa ic naman þinum neode singe,
 þæt ic min gehat her agylde
 of dæge on dæg, swa hit gedefe wese.

(3.33) *Exaudi nos, deus salutaris noster,*
spes omnium finium terre et in mari longe.

 Gehyr us, hælend God, þu eart hiht ealra
 þe on ðisse eorðan utan syndon
 oððe feor on sæ foldum wuniað.

(3.34) *Benedic anima mea domino,*
et omnia interiora mea nomen sanctum eius.

 Bletsa, mine sawle, bliðe drihten,
 and eall min inneran his þone ecan naman.

(3.35) *Benedic anima mea domino,*
et noli oblivisci omnes retributiones eius.

 Bletsige, mine sawle, bealde drihten,
 ne wilt ðu ofergeotul æfre weorðan
 ealra goda þe he ðe ær dyde.

(3.36) *Qui propitiatur omnibus iniquitatibus tuis,*
qui sanat omnes languores tuos.

 He þinum man-dædum miltsade eallum
 and ðine adle ealle gehælde.

(3.37) *Qui redemit de interitu vitam tuam,*
qui sanat in bonis desiderium tuum.

(3.31) *Deliver me from them that work iniquity,*
and save me from bloody men.

    Rescue me from the hatred of evildoers
    who here commit all manner of wickedness,
    and save me from the bloodthirsty man's violence.

(3.32) *So will I sing a psalm to thy name forever and ever,*
that I may pay my vows from day to day.

    So will I zealously sing to your name,
    that I may repay my promises here
    from day to day, as may be fitting.

(3.33) *Hear us, O God our savior,*
who art the hope of all the ends of the earth, and in the sea far off.

    Hear us, O savior God, who are the hope of all
    who exist in the outer regions of this earth,
    or who dwell in lands far over the sea.

(3.34) *Bless the Lord, O my soul,*
and let all that is within me bless his holy name.

    Happily bless the Lord, O my soul,
    and all that is inside me bless his eternal name.

(3.35) *Bless the Lord, O my soul,*
and never forget all he hath done for thee.

    Boldly bless the Lord, O my soul,
    and desire never to forget
    all the good things that he has previously done for you.

(3.36) *Who forgiveth all thy iniquities,*
who healeth all thy diseases.

    He has shown mercy for all your wrongful deeds
    and has healed all your infirmities.

(3.37) *Who redeemeth thy life from destruction,*
who satisfieth thy desire with good things.

Se alysde þin lif   leof of forwyrde,
fylde þinne willan   fægere mid gode.
(3.38) *Qui coronat te in miseratione et misericordia,*
renovabitur sicut aquile iuventus tua.

He ðe gesigefæste   soðre mildse
and ðe mild-heorte   mode getrymede;
eart ðu edniwe   earne gelicost
on geoguðe nu   gleaw geworden.

[Confession of sin:]

(3.39) *Confiteor domino deo celi . . .*

[*Preces* (continued):]

(3.40) *Converte nos, deus salutaris noster,*
et averte iram tuam a nobis.

Gehweorf us hraðe,   hælend drihten,
and ðin yrre fram us   eac oncyrre.
(3.41) *Dignare, domine, die isto*
sine peccato nos custodire
(3.42) [*Miserere nostri domine, miserere nostri.*]

Mildsa us nu ða,   mihtig drihten,
mildsa us.
(3.43) *Fiat misericordia tua, domine, super nos,*
quemadmodum speravimus in te.

Wese þin mild-heortnys,   mihtig drihten,
wel ofer us,   swa we wenað on ðe.
(3.44) *Domine, salvum fac regem,*
et exaudi nos in die qua invocaverimus te.

Do, drihten, cyng   dædum halne,
and us eac gehyr   holdum mode,
swylce we ðe daga,   drihten, cigen.

He has redeemed your precious life from destruction,
graciously fulfilled your desires with good.
(3.38) *Who crowneth thee with mercy and compassion;*
thy youth shall be renewed like the eagle's.
In true mercy he has crowned you victorious,
and he has compassionately fortified your mind;
like the eagle, you will be renewed,
made keen in youth even now.

[Confession of sin:]

(3.39) *I confess to the Lord God of heaven . . .*

[*Preces* (continued):]

(3.40) *Convert us, O God our savior,*
and turn off thy anger from us.
Turn us swiftly, O saving Lord,
and divert your anger from us as well.
(3.41) *Deign this day, O Lord,*
to preserve us without sin.
(3.42) [*Have mercy on us, O Lord, have mercy on us.*]
Have mercy on us now, O mighty Lord,
have mercy on us.
(3.43) *Let thy mercy, O Lord, be upon us,*
as we have hoped in thee.
Let your mercy, O mighty Lord,
rest well over us, as we hope in you.
(3.44) *O Lord, save the king,*
and hear us in the day that we shall call upon thee.
Save the king, O Lord, by your works,
and also hear us with a favorable mind,
on whatever day we cry to you, O Lord.

(3.45) *Salvum fac populum tuum, domine, et benedic hereditati tue;*
et rege illos et extolle illos usque in aeternum.

> Hal do þin folc,   halig drihten,
> and ðin yrfe eac   eal gebletsa;
> rece þu heo swylce   and on riht ahefe,
> þæt hi on worulde   wynnum lifigen.

(3.46) *Fiat pax in virtute tua,*
et abundantia in turribus tuis.

> Sy ðe on ðinum mægne sib   mæst and fyrmest,
> and on þinum torrum   wese tidum genihtsum.

(3.47) *Domine, exaudi orationem meam,*
et clamor meus ad te perveniat.

> Þu min gebed,   mære drihten,
> gehyr, heofones weard,   and gehlyde min
> to ðe becume,   þeoda reccend.

(3.48) *Miserere mei, deus,*
secundum magnam misericordiam tuam.

> Mildsa me, mihtig drihten,   swa ðu manegum dydest,
> æfter ðinre þære mycelan   mild-heortnysse.

(3.49) *Domine deus virtutum, converte nos,*
et ostende faciem tuam et salvi erimus.

> Gehweorf us, mægna God,   and us milde æteow
> þinne andwlitan;   ealle we beoð hale.

[THE CHAPTER MEETING]

[Response to the martyrology reading:]

(4.1) *Pretiosa est in conspectu domini*
mors sanctorum eius.

(3.45) *Save, O Lord, thy people, and bless thy inheritance,*
and rule them and exalt them forever.

    Save your people, O holy Lord,
       and also bless all your inheritance;
       guide them as well, and exalt them justly,
       that they may live among joys forever.

(3.46) *Let peace be in thy strength,*
and abundance in thy towers.

    May peace, foremost and greatest, be in your strength,
       and may it be abundant in your towers at the due times.

(3.47) *Hear, O Lord, my prayer,*
and let my cry come to thee.

    O glorious Lord, hear my prayer,
       and let my cry, O guardian of heaven,
       come to you, ruler of nations.

(3.48) *Have mercy on me, O God,*
according to thy great mercy.

    Have mercy on me, mighty Lord, as you have to many,
       according to your great compassion.

(3.49) *O Lord God of hosts, convert us,*
and show thy face, and we shall be saved.

    Turn us, O God of powers, and kindly show us
       your countenance; we will all be saved.

[THE CHAPTER MEETING]

[Response to the martyrology reading:]

(4.1) *Precious in the sight of the Lord*
is the death of his saints.

[Collect:]

(4.2) *Sancta dei genetrix, virgo Maria, et omnes sancti dei intercedant pro nobis peccatoribus ad dominum deum nostrum ut mereamur ab eo adiuvari et salvari, qui vivit et regnat deus per [omnia saecula saeculorum. Amen.]*

[Versicle and response:]

(4.3) *Deus in adiutorium meum intende;*
domine ad adiuvandum me festina.

    Wes, drihten God,   deore fultum;
      beheald, drihten, me,   and me hraðe syððan
    gefultuma   æt feorh-þearfe.
Gloria patri . . .

[*Kyrie* and Lord's Prayer:]

(4.4) *Kyrrieleison* . . .
Pater noster . . . et ne nos inducas . . .

[Versicles and responses:]

(4.5) *Respice in servos tuos et in opera tua, domine,*
et dirige filios eorum.

    Geseoh þine scealcas   swæsum eagum
    and on þin agen weorc,   ece drihten,
    and heora bearn gerece   bliðum mode.
(4.6) *Et sit splendor domini dei nostri super nos,*
et opera manuum nostrarum dirige super nos,
et opus manuum nostrarum dirige.

[Collect:]

(4.2) *May the virgin Mary, holy mother of God, and all God's saints intercede for us sinners to the Lord our God, that we may deserve to be helped and saved by him who lives and reigns, God throughout [all ages. Amen.]*

[Versicle and response:]

(4.3) *O God, come to my assistance;*
O Lord, make haste to help me.
　　Be my cherished help, O Lord God;
　　look to me, O Lord, and then quickly
　　aid me in my dire need.
Glory be to the Father . . .

[*Kyrie* and Lord's Prayer:]

(4.4) *Lord have mercy . . .*
Our Father . . . and lead us not . . .

[Versicles and responses:]

(4.5) *Look upon thy servants and upon their works,*
and direct their children.
　　With kindly eyes look upon your servants
　　and on your own works, eternal Lord,
　　and guide their children with a joyful mind.
(4.6) *And let the brightness of the Lord our God be upon us;*
and direct thou the works of our hands over us,
yea, the work of our hands do thou direct.

Wese us beorhtnys ofer   bliðan drihtnes,
ures þæs godan Godes   georne ofer ealle;
gerece ure hand-geweorc   heah ofer usic.
Gloria patri . . .

[Collect:]

(4.7) *Oremus: Dirigere et sanctificare ac regere digneris, domine deus rex, creator celi et terre, hodie quaesumus, cotidie corda et corpora nostra, actus quoque et sermones nostros, in lege tua et in preceptis mandatorum tuorum, ut hic et ubique per te semper salvi et liberi esse mereamur, salvator mundi, qui cum patre et spiritu sancto vivis et regnas deus per omnia secula seculorum. Amen.*

[Final versicle, response, and blessing:]

(4.8) *Adiutorium nostrum in nomine domini,*
qui fecit celum et terram.
Benedicite . . .
Deus dei filius nos benedicere dignetur.

[THE OFFICE OF TERCE]

(5) *De officio tertie hore.*

(5.1) On undern we sculon God herian forðam on undern-timan Crist wæs ðurh þara Iudea dom to deaðe fordemed and toweard þære rode gelæd, þe he syððan on þrowode for ealles middan-eardes alysednysse. (5.2) And eft æfter his æriste on Pentecostenes dæg com se halga gast on undern-timan ofer ða

Let the brightness of the joyous Lord be over us,
the brightness of our good God readily over all;
direct the works of our hands high above us.
Glory be to the Father . . .

[Collect:]

(4.7) Let us pray: Lord God, king, creator of heaven and earth: we be-
seech you today that you would deign every day to guide, sanctify, and
govern in your law and in the teachings of your commandments our
hearts and our bodies, our actions and our words; that here and ev-
erywhere we may deserve to be saved and set free by you, O savior of
the world, who live and reign together with the Father and the Holy
Spirit, God throughout all ages. Amen.

[Final versicle, response, and blessing:]

(4.8) Our help is in the name of the Lord
who made heaven and earth.
Pronounce the blessing . . .
May God the Son of God deign to bless us.

[THE OFFICE OF TERCE]

(5) The Office of the Third Hour.

(5.1) At midmorning we should praise God because at the
hour of midmorning Christ was condemned to death by judg-
ment of the Jews and was led to the cross on which he would
suffer thereafter for the redemption of all the world. (5.2) And
likewise, after his resurrection, on the day of Pentecost, at mid-
morning the Holy Spirit came upon the apostles where they

apostolas þær hi ætgædere gesamnode wæron, and hi ealle sona gefyllede wurdon swa swyðe mid Godes gyfe þæt hi ealra gereorda getingnesse hæfdon, and heora lar wearð geond ealne middan-eard syððan gecyðed and gedæled þeodum to helpe. (5.3) Undern is dæges ðridde tid; þonne is eac rihtlic þæt we to þære þriddan tide þa halgan ðrynnesse geornlice herian.

[Opening versicle and response:]

(5.4) *Deus in adiutorium meum intende* . . .
Gloria patri . . .

Hymnus:

(5.5) *Nunc sancte nobis spiritus,*
[*unus patris cum filio,*
dignare promptus ingeri
nostro refusus pectori.

Os, lingua, mens, sensus, vigor
confessionem personet;
flamescat igne caritas,
accendat ardor proximos.

Presta, pater piissime
patrique compar unice
cum spiritu paraclito
et nunc et in perpetuum. Amen.]

[Psalmody:]

(5.6) *Psalmus.*

were gathered together, and at once they were all filled so mightily with the grace of God that they possessed fluency in all languages, and throughout all the world their teaching became known and was spread as a help to the nations. (5.3) Midmorning is the third hour of the day; it is therefore also appropriate that at the third hour we eagerly praise the holy Trinity.

[Opening versicle and response:]

(5.4) *O God, come to my assistance . . .*
Glory be to the Father . . .

Hymn:

(5.5) *Now, O Holy Spirit,*
[*the one Spirit of the Father with the Son,*
condescend to be planted willingly within us,
infused within our hearts.

Let mouth, tongue, mind, perception, and strength
sound forth their confession;
let charity blaze up aflame,
its heat kindle those around it.

Grant this, O most merciful Father,
and you, the Father's sole equal,
together with the comforter, the Spirit,
both now and forever. Amen.]

[Psalmody:]

(5.6) *Psalm.*

Capitulum:

(5.7) *Gratia vobis et pax a deo patre nostro et domino Iesu Christo.*
Deo gratias.

[Versicle and response:]

(5.8) *Adiutor meus . . .*

[*Kyrie* and Lord's Prayer:]

(5.9) *Kyrrieleison. Christeleison. Cyrrieleison.*
Pater noster . . .

[*Preces:*]

(5.10) *Ego dixi: domine miserere mei;*
sana animam meam quia peccavi tibi.
   Ic nu mægene cweðe,   "Miltsa me, drihten,
   hæl mine sawle,   forðon me hreoweð nu
   þæt ic firene on ðe   fremede geneahhige."
(5.11) *Convertere, domine, aliquantulum,*
et deprecabilis esto super servos tuos.
   Gehweorf us hwæt-hwygu,   halig drihten;
   wes ðinum scealcum   wel eað-bene.
(5.12) *Mitte eis, domine, auxilium . . .*
Domine exaudi . . .
Dominus vobiscum . . .

Collecta:

(5.13) *Domine deus qui hora tertia diei ad crucis poenam pro mundi*
salute ductus es, te suppliciter deprecamur ut de preteritis malis nostris

Capitulum:

(5.7) *Grace be to you and peace from God our Father and from the Lord Jesus Christ.*
[Response:] *Thanks be to God.*

[Versicle and response:]

(5.8) *Be thou my helper . . .*

[*Kyrie* and Lord's Prayer:]

(5.9) *Lord have mercy. Christ have mercy. Lord have mercy.*
Our Father . . .

[*Preces:*]

(5.10) *I said: "O Lord, be thou merciful to me;*
heal my soul, for I have sinned against thee."
I now say with strength, "Have mercy on me, O Lord,
heal my soul, because I now regret
that I committed sins against you often."
(5.11) *Return, O Lord, a little,*
and be entreated in favor of thy servants.
Turn to us a little, O holy Lord;
be most pliant toward your servants' prayers.
(5.12) *Send them help, O Lord . . .*
Hear, O Lord . . .
The Lord be with you . . .

Collect:

(5.13) *Lord God, who for the salvation of the world were led to the punishment of the cross at the third hour of the day, we humbly pray*

semper aput te inveniamus veniam et de futuris iugiter habeamus cus-
todiam, qui cum patre [vivis et regnas in unitate spiritus sancti deus
per omnia saecula saeculorum. Amen.]

[THE OFFICE OF SEXT]

(6) *De officio sexte hore.*

(6.1) On midne dæg we sculon God herian forðam to mid-
des dæges Crist wæs on rode aðened and us ealle ða þurh his
ðrowunge mid his deor-wyrðan blode gebohte of deofles an-
wealde and of ecan deaðe. (6.2) And ðy we sculon on ðone ti-
man to Criste beon georne clypigende and hine herigende þæt
we mid þam geswytelian þæt we gemyndige beon þære myclan
mild-heortnysse þe he on man-cynne geworhte þa ða he let
hine sylfne syllan to cwale for man-cynnes ðearfe.

[Opening versicle and response:]

(6.3) *Deus in adiutorium meum intende . . .*
Gloria patri . . .

Hymnus:

(6.4) *Rector potens, verax [deus,*
qui temperas rerum vices,
splendore mane instruis
et ignibus meridiem:

extingue flammas litium,
aufer calorem noxium,
confer salutem corporum
veramque pacem cordium.

that from you we would always find pardon for our past wrongs and receive protection continually against future ones; you who with the Father [lives and reigns, in the unity of the Holy Spirit, God throughout all ages. Amen.]

[THE OFFICE OF SEXT]

(6) *The Office of the Sixth Hour.*

(6.1) At midday we should praise God because at the middle of the day Christ was stretched out on the cross and then, through his passion, redeemed us all by his precious blood from the devil's power and from everlasting death. (6.2) And therefore at that hour we should be eagerly calling out to Christ and praising him, that we may demonstrate thereby that we remember the great compassion that he showed to humankind when he allowed himself to be handed over to death for humanity's need.

[Opening versicle and response:]

(6.3) *O God, come to my assistance . . .*
Glory be to the Father . . .

Hymn:

(6.4) *O mighty ruler, true [God,*
who control the changes in all things,
you clothe the morning with splendor
and the midday with scorching flame:

quench the fires of strife,
dispel the damaging heat;
deliver health for our bodies
and true peace for our hearts.

Presta, pater piissime
patrique compar unice
cum spiritu paraclito
et nunc et in perpetuum. Amen.]

Capitulum:

(6.5) *Omnia autem probate, quod bonum est tenete; ab omni specie*
  mala abstinete uos.
Deo gratias.

[Versicle and response:]

(6.6) *Dominus regit me . . .*

[Kyrie:]

(6.7) *Cyrrieleison. Christeleison. Kyrrieleison.*

Collecta:

(6.8) *Domine Iesu Christe qui sexta hora pro nobis in cruce ascendisti*
et Adam de inferno eruisti eumque in paradyso restituisti, te quaesu-
mus ut ab omnibus peccatis nostris eripere nos iubeas et in operibus tuis
sanctis semper custodias, Iesu Christe, qui cum [patre vivis et regnas in
unitate spiritus sancti deus per omnia saecula saeculorum. Amen.]

[THE OFFICE OF NONE]

(7) *Ad nonam.*

(7.1) On non-timan we sculon God herian forðam on þone
timan Crist gebæd for ðam þe him deredon and syððan his gast

Grant this, O most merciful Father,
and you, the Father's sole equal,
together with the comforter, the Spirit,
both now and forever. Amen.]

Capitulum:

(6.5) *But prove all things; hold fast that which is good; from all ap-*
pearance of evil refrain yourselves.
[Response:] *Thanks be to God.*

[Versicle and response:]

(6.6) *The Lord ruleth me . . .*

[*Kyrie:*]

(6.7) *Lord have mercy. Christ have mercy. Lord have mercy.*

Collect:

(6.8) *Lord Jesus Christ, who at the sixth hour mounted the cross on*
our behalf and rescued Adam from hell and restored him to Paradise;
we beseech you that you would bid us all be rescued from our sins and
would preserve us in your holy works, O Jesus Christ; who with [*the*
Father lives and reigns, in the unity of the Holy Spirit, God through-
out all ages. Amen.]

[THE OFFICE OF NONE]

(7) *At None.*

(7.1) At the ninth hour we should praise God because at that
hour Christ prayed for those who harmed him, and after that

asende; and on ðone timan sculon geleaffulle men hi georne ge-
biddan and gemunan þæt wundor þæt ða geworden wearð þa
se sylfa for man-cyn deað geþolode þe eallum man-cynne lifes
geuðe.

[Opening versicle and response:]

(7.2) *Deus in adiutorium meum intende . . .*
Gloria patri . . .

Hymnus:

(7.3) *Rerum deus, tenax uigor*
[*inmotus in te permanet,*
lucis diurnae tempora
successibus determinans:

largire clarum vespere,
quo vita nusquam decidat,
sed praemium mortis sacrae
perennis instet gloria.

Presta, pater piissime
patrique compar unice
cum spiritu paraclito
et nunc et in perpetuum. Amen.]

Capitulum:

(7.4) *Alter alterius honera portate et sic adimplebitis legem Christi.*
Deo gratias.

he sent forth his spirit; and at that hour all believers should eagerly pray and remember the wondrous thing that occurred when the same one who bestowed life on the whole human race suffered death for humanity's sake.

[Opening versicle and response:]

(7.2) *O God, come to my assistance . . .*
Glory be to the Father . . .

Hymn:

(7.3) *O God of all things, a constant [strength*
abides immovable within you,
imposing measure on the hours
of daylight, one following another:

grant us a bright evening
in which life may never fail,
but rather let glory everlasting approach,
the recompense for a holy death.

Grant this, O most merciful Father,
and you, the Father's sole equal,
together with the comforter, the Spirit,
both now and forever. Amen.]

Capitulum:

(7.4) *Bear ye one another's burdens, and so you shall fulfill the law of*
    Christ.
[Response:] *Thanks be to God.*

[Versicle and response:]

(7.5) *Ab occultis meis munda me, domine . . .*

[*Kyrie:*]

(7.6) *Kyrrieleison. Christeleison. Kyrrieleison.*

Collecta:

(7.7) *Domine Iesu Christe qui hora nona in crucis patibulo confitentem latronem intra menia paradysi transire iussisti, tibi suppliciter confitentes peccata nostra deprecamur deleas et post obitum nostrum paradisi nobis gaudia introire concedas, salvator mundi, qui cum patre* [*vivis et regnas in unitate spiritus sancti deus per omnia saecula saeculorum. Amen.*]

[THE OFFICE OF VESPERS]

(8) *Ad vesperum.*

(8.1) On æfen we sculon God herian; on ðone timan man offrode on þære ealdan æ and mid recels-reocan on ðam temple þæt weofod geornne weorðode Gode to lofe. (8.2) And on æfen-timan ure drihten offrode æt his æfen-gereorde and dælde his discipulum þurh halig geryne hlaf and win for his sylfes lichaman and for his agen blod. And on æfen-timan hit wæs þæt Ioseph Cristes lic-haman of rode alinode. (8.3) Þonne we agen myccle þearfe þæt we swylc gemunan and Gode þancian and on þone timan ure gebedu urum drihtne georne offrian, ealswa Dauid cwæð:

(7.5) *From my secret [sins] cleanse me, O Lord . . .*

[*Kyrie:*]

(7.6) *Lord have mercy. Christ have mercy. Lord have mercy.*

Collect:

(7.7) *Lord Jesus Christ, who on the gibbet of a cross did command at the ninth hour that the confessing thief should pass within the walls of Paradise; humbly confessing to you our own sins, we pray that you would blot them out and grant us entry after our death into the joys of Paradise, O savior of the world, who with the Father [lives and reigns, in the unity of the Holy Spirit, God throughout all ages. Amen.]*

[THE OFFICE OF VESPERS]

(8) *At Evening.*

(8.1) At evening we should praise God; in the old law, sacrifice was offered at that hour and the altar in the Temple was eagerly reverenced with incense as an act of praise to God. (8.2) And at the evening hour our Lord offered a sacrifice at his supper and, through the holy sacrament, distributed to his disciples bread and wine for his own body and his own blood. (8.3) And it was at the evening hour that Joseph took Christ's body down from the cross. We therefore ought to have great need that we remember such things and give thanks to God and eagerly make an offering of our prayers to the Lord at that hour, just as David said:

[Opening versicle and response:]

(8.4) *Dirigatur, domine, ad te oratio mea,*
sicut incensum in conspectu tuo.

    Sy on ðinre gesihðe   mines sylfes gebed
    full ricene gereht,   swa recels bið,
    þonne hit gifre   gleda bærnað.
Gloria patri . . .

[*Capitulum:*]

(8.5) *Gratia domini nostri Iesu Christi et caritas dei et communicatio*
    sancti spiritus sit semper cum omnibus nobis.
Deo gratias.

[Versicle and response:]

(8.6) *V: Adiutorium nostrum in nomine domini,*
R: qui fecit celum et terram.

[Hymn:]

(8.7) *O lux, beata trinitas,*
[*et principalis unitas,*
iam sol recedit igneus;
infunde lumen cordibus.

Te mane laudent carmina,
te deprecemur vesperi;
te nostra supplex gloria
per cuncta laudet secula.

Deo patri sit gloria,
eiusque soli filio

[Opening versicle and response:]

(8.4) *Let my prayer, O Lord, be directed*
as incense in thy sight.
 Into your sight let my prayer be
 very swiftly directed, just as incense is,
 when devouring coals burn it up.
Glory be to the Father . . .

[*Capitulum:*]

(8.5) *The grace of our Lord Jesus Christ, and the charity of God, and*
the communication of the Holy Spirit be with all of us always.
[Response:] *Thanks be to God.*

[Versicle and response:]

(8.6) *V: Our help is in the name of the Lord,*
R: who made heaven and earth.

[Hymn:]

(8.7) *O light, O blessed Trinity*
[and foremost unity,
already the fiery sun is withdrawing;
pour forth your light into our hearts.

Let our songs praise you in the morning,
let us beseech you in the evening;
let our humble "Gloria"
render you praise through all ages.

To God the Father be glory,
and to his only Son,

331

cum spiritu paraclyto
et nunc et in perpetuum. Amen.]

[Versicle and response:]

(8.8) *V: Dirigatur, domine, ad te oratio mea . . .*

[Antiphon and *Magnificat:*]

(8.9) *(Evangelio:) Misericordia dei et sanctum nomen eius super ti-*
  mentes eum.
  (Psalmus:) Magnificat . . .

[*Kyrie* and Lord's Prayer:]

(8.10) *Kirrieleison. Christeleison. Kyrrieleison.*
Pater noster . . . et ne nos inducas in temptationem . . .

[*Preces:*]

(8.11) *Ego dixi: domine . . .*

Collecta:

(8.12) *Oremus: Vespere et mane et meridie maiestatem tuam suppli-*
citer exoramus, ut expulsis de cordibus nostris peccatorum tenebris ad
veram lucem que Christus est nos facias pervenire; per [*eundem domi-*
num nostrum Iesum Christum filium tuum, qui tecum vivit et regnat
in unitate spiritus sancti deus per omnia saecula saeculorum. Amen.]

[THE OFFICE OF COMPLINE]

(9) *Ad completorium.*

 (9.1) On foran-niht we sculon God herian ær we to bedde
gan and gemunan þæt Crist on byrgene neah foran-nihte bebyr-

together with the comforter, the Spirit,
both now and forever. Amen.]

[Versicle and response:]

(8.8) *V: Let my prayer, O Lord, be directed to you . . .*

[Antiphon and *Magnificat:*]

(8.9) *(At the gospel [canticle]:) The mercy of God and his holy name*
    are upon those who fear him.
(Psalm:) My soul doth magnify . . .

[*Kyrie* and Lord's Prayer:]

(8.10) *Lord have mercy. Christ have mercy. Lord have mercy.*
Our Father . . . and lead us not into temptation . . .

[*Preces:*]

(8.11) *I said, "O Lord . . ."*

Collect:

(8.12) *Let us pray: At evening, morning, and midday we humbly im-*
plore your majesty that, driving out the darkness of sins from our
hearts, you would have us led to the true light, which is Christ; through
[*the same, our Lord Jesus Christ, your Son, who lives and reigns with*
you and the Holy Spirit, God throughout all ages. Amen.]

[THE OFFICE OF COMPLINE]

(9) *Compline.*

   (9.1) In the early part of the night we should praise God be-
fore we go to bed, and should remember that it was approach-

ged wearð and ðær his lic-haman on gereste swa lange swa his willa wæs. (9.2) Þonne age we þæs micle þearfe þæt we þæt geþencan and us sylfe on ðone timan Gode betæcan ær we to bedde gan and hine biddan þæt he us gedefre reste geunne and wið deofles costnunga gescylde swa his wylla sy.

[Opening versicles and responses:]

(9.3) *Converte nos, deus . . .*
Deus in adiutorium meum . . .

Hymnus:

(9.4) *Te lucis ante terminum,*
[*rerum creator, poscimus,*
ut solita clementia
sis presul ad custodiam.

Procul recedant somnia
et noctium fantasmata,
hostemque nostrum comprime,
ne polluantur corpora.

Presta, pater omnipotens,
per Iesum Christum dominum,
qui tecum in perpetuum
regnat cum sancto spiritu. Amen.]

[Second hymn:]

Christe, qui lux es et dies,
[*noctis tenebras detegis*

ing early night when Christ was buried in the tomb, and there his body rested for as long as was his will. (9.2) Therefore we ought to have great need that we ponder that and commend ourselves to God at that hour before we go to bed, and pray to him that he would grant us fitting rest and shield us, as his will may be, against the devil's temptations.

[Opening versicles and responses:]

(9.3) *Convert us, O God . . .*
O God, come to my assistance . . .

Hymn:

(9.4) *Before the end of day*
[*we ask of you, O creator of all*
that, with your customary mercy,
you would take charge of our safekeeping.

Let dreams depart far off
and the illusions of night,
and restrain our enemy,
that our bodies may not be defiled.

Grant this, O most merciful Father,
and you, the Father's sole equal,
together with the comforter, the Spirit,
both now and forever. Amen.]

[Second hymn:]

O Christ, who are light and day,
[*you roll back the darkness of night,*

lucisque lumen crederis
lumen beatum predicans:

precamur, sancte domine,
defende nos in hac nocte.
Sit nobis in te requies;
quietam noctem tribue,

ne gravis somnus irruat
nec hostis nos subripiat
nec caro illi consentiens
nos tibi reos statuat.

Oculi somnum capiant,
cor ad te semper vigilet.
Dextera tua protegat
famulos qui te diligunt.

Defensor noster, aspice,
insidiantes reprime;
guberna tuos famulos,
quos sanguine mercatus es.

Memento nostri, domine,
in gravi isto corpore;
qui es defensor animae
adesto nobis, domine.

Deo patri sit gloria,
eiusque soli filio
cum spiritu paraclyto
et nunc et in perpetuum. Amen.]

and you are believed to be light from light,
proclaiming a blessed radiance:

we pray, O holy Lord,
defend us in this night.
Let our rest be in you;
grant us a peaceful night,

so that heavy sleep does not overtake us
or the enemy steal upon us,
or the flesh, by assenting to him,
make us guilty in your sight.

Let our eyes have their slumber,
but let our hearts keep watch for you always.
Let your right arm protect
those servants who love you.

Look to us, O our defender,
hold at bay those who scheme against us;
direct your servants
whom you have bought with blood.

Remember us, O Lord,
while we are in this encumbering body;
as you are the defender of our souls,
be present with us, O Lord.

To God the Father be glory,
and to his only Son,
together with the comforter, the Spirit,
both now and forever. Amen.]

[*Capitulum:*]

(9.5) *Tu in nobis es, domine, et nomen sanctum tuum invocatum est super nos; ne derelinquas nos, domine deus noster.*
Deo gratias.

[Versicle and response:]

(9.6) *Custodi nos, domine, ut pupillam oculi . . .*

[*Kyrie,* Lord's Prayer, and Apostles' Creed:]

(9.7) *Kyrrieleison. Christeleison. Kyrieleison.*
Pater noster . . .
Credo in deum patrem . . .

[Blessing, versicle, and response:]

(9.8) *Benedicamus patrem . . .*
Benedictus es, domine . . .
Benedicat et custodiat nos omnipotens deus. Amen.
Dignare, domine, nocte ista . . .

[Collect:]

(9.9) *Oremus: Visita, domine, habitationem istam et omnes insidias inimici ab ea longe repelle. Angeli tui nos in ea pace custodiant et benedictio tua sit super nos semper; per* [*Christum dominum nostrum. Amen.*]

[Final dialogue and blessing:]

(9.10) *Dominus vobiscum . . .*
Benedicamus domino . . .

[*Capitulum:*]

(9.5) *But thou, O Lord, art among us, and thy name is called upon by us; forsake us not, O Lord our God.*
[Response:] *Thanks be to God.*

[Versicle and response:]

(9.6) *Keep us, O Lord, as the apple of thine eye . . .*

[*Kyrie,* Lord's Prayer, and Apostles' Creed:]

(9.7) *Lord have mercy. Christ have mercy. Lord have mercy.*
Our Father . . .
I believe in God the Father . . .

[Blessing, versicle, and response:]

(9.8) *Let us bless the Father . . .*
Blessed are you, O Lord . . .
May almighty God bless and keep us. Amen.
Deign this night, O Lord . . .

[Collect:]

(9.9) *Let us pray: O Lord, visit this dwelling and drive far away from it all the traps of the devil. Let your angels guard us in peace, and let your blessing be upon us always; through* [*our Lord Jesus Christ. Amen.*]

[Final dialogue and blessing:]

(9.10) *The Lord be with you . . .*
Let us bless the Lord . . .

Benedictio dei patris omnipotentis et filii et spiritus sancti maneat semper nobiscum. Amen.

[THE OFFICE OF NOCTURNS]

(10) *De nocturnali caelebratione.*

(10.1) On uhtan we sculon God herian ealswa Dauid cwæð, *Media nocte surgebam ad confitendum tibi super iudicia iustitie tue,* ðæt is, "To middre nihte ic aras and andette drihtenes doma rihtwisnesse." (10.2) Crist sylf bead þæt we georne wacian sceoldan. He cwæð, *Vigilate ergo quia nescitis quando veniet dominus,* ðæt bið, "Waciað georne forðam þe ge nyton hwænne eower drihten cymð." (10.3) And eft he cwæð, *Beati servi illi quos cum venerit dominus,* þæt is, "Eadige beoð þa men þe se hlaford wacigende gemet þonne he tocymð"; þæt is, ure drihten þonne he to dome cymð þonne he wile witan hwa wacigende beo on godum dædum. (10.4) Us is mycel ðearf þæt we geornlice wacian and wære beon, forðam nele deað na cyðan hwænne he cuman wyle þe ma þe þeof, ac he cymð þonne man læst wenð. Þonne bið se swyðe gesælig se ðe bið þonne wacigende. (10.5) Se bið wacigende se ðe a smeaþ ymbe Godes willan and ymbe his agene þearfe and on ðam geendað, and se bið sleac and slæpende se ðe fullgæð eallum his lyðrum lustum ðurh deofles lare and on ðam geendað. (10.6) And þonne age we mycle þearfe þæt we geornlice wacian and a wære beon wið deofles costnunga, and þæt we georne to Gode clypian and to him geearnian þæt he us gefylste ðurh his mild-heortnysse þæt we on

*May the blessing of God the Father almighty and of the Son and of the
Holy Spirit abide with us always. Amen.*

(10) *The Celebration of the Night Office.*

(10.1) In the part of night before dawn we should praise God
just as David said: *I rose at midnight to give praise to thee, for the
judgments of thy justification,* that is, "At midnight I arose and
confessed the righteousness of the Lord's judgments." (10.2)
Christ himself commanded that we should keep watch eagerly.
He said, *Watch ye therefore, for you know not when the lord of
the house cometh,* that is, "Keep watch eagerly, because you do
not know when your Lord is coming." (10.3) And again he said,
*Blessed are those servants whom the lord when he cometh [shall find
watching],* that is, "Blessed will be those whom the lord finds
keeping watch when he arrives"; that is, our Lord, when he
comes to render judgment, intends to know who is keeping the
watch by good deeds. (10.4) We have great need that we eagerly
keep watch and remain on guard, for death will not announce
when he wishes to come any more than will a thief, but rather it
will come when one least expects. The person who is keeping
watch at that time will then be very fortunate. (10.5) He keeps
watch who is constantly thinking about the will of God and
about his own needs and meets his end while in that condition;
he is lazy and sleepy who, at the devil's instruction, indulges
all his base desires and meets his end while in that condition.
(10.6) And therefore we ought to have great need that we ea-
gerly keep watch and remain on guard against the devil's temp-
tations, and that we readily cry out to God and earn from him
that he would assist through his mercy, so that at the end of our

urum ende-timan swa wacigende beon on godum dædum þæt
we syððan a us gerestan magan and motan on ecere reste.

[Epilogue]

(11.1) Leofan men, nu ic hæbbe be suman dæle ahrepod be ðam
dæg-hwamlican tidan-þenungan ðe man to nyd-rihte don sceall.
Þonne is mycel þearf þæt man understande þæt man toeacan
þam oft and unseldan sceall God herian and to Gode clypian
for manegum neodan eallswa se apostol cwæð, *Sine intermissione
orate*, þæt is, "Beoð a symble eow gebiddende to Gode georne."
(11.2) And eft se apostol cwæð, *Sive enim manducatis sive bibitis
sive aliud quid facitis, omnia in gloriam dei facite*, þæt is, "Gyf ge
etan, oððon drincan, oððon elles-hwæt wyrcean, don þæt ge
don, doð eall Gode þanciende and herigende." (11.3) Beo þæt
ðinga þæt hit beo þæt se man to note wyrcean wylle, bidde he
God fultumes, aa him spewð þe bet, eallswa Dauid cwæð, *Adiu-
tor meus esto domine*, þæt is, "Min drihten, beo min fultum, and
ne forlæt ðu me." (11.4) And eft he cwæð, *Adiutorium nostrum
in nomine domini, qui fecit celum et terram*, þæt is, "Ure fultum is
God þe gesceop and geworhte heofonas and eorðan and ealle
gesceafta." God us gefultumige to ure ðearfe swa his wylla sy.
Amen.

lives we may be so watchful in good works that we can and may thereafter rest in an everlasting rest.

[EPILOGUE]

(11.1) Beloved, I have now in some measure touched upon the daily liturgical hours that ought to be performed as an obligation. It is very necessary to understand, then, that in addition to these offices one ought to praise God often and frequently, and call upon him for many needs, just as the apostle said: *Pray without ceasing,* that is, "Be always praying eagerly to God." (11.2) And again the apostle said, *Therefore, whether you eat or drink, or whatever else you do, do all to the glory of God,* that is, "If you eat or drink or do anything else, whatever thing you do, do it all while thanking and praising God." (11.3) Whatever it may be that one intends to do in discharging his duty, let him pray to God for help, and it will always turn out the better for him, just as David said: *Be thou my helper, O Lord,* that is, "My Lord, be my help, and do not abandon me." (11.4) And again he said, *Our help is in the name of the Lord who made heaven and earth,* that is, "God is our help, who fashioned and made the heavens and the earth and all creatures." May God help us in our need, as it may be his will. Amen.

Note on the Texts

Although I have consulted facsimiles of the manuscripts to check a number of specific readings, the Old English texts and apparatus in this book have been established mainly from previous editions. In keeping with one aim of the Dumbarton Oaks Medieval Library, the purpose of this volume is not to compete with scholarly editions already available but to provide serviceable texts and translations that, it is hoped, will bring some lesser-known works before a wider public. Where existing editions have required substantial updating, I have again depended primarily on others' published textual criticism and resisted the urge to offer new conjectures unless strongly justified.

Since this book relies on scattered primary and secondary materials, and since the challenges of editing vary from poem to poem, a brief headnote precedes the textual notes to each item. The headnotes indicate the manuscripts in which the poems survive, identify the edition that serves as the basis for my text, and briefly outline any unusual editorial difficulties. The reader may assume that, unless otherwise stated, not only the text but the emendations and apparatus for each poem are essentially those of the base edition(s) identified here.

The matter following each headnote may have the look

of a critical apparatus but is not intended as such. The limited purpose of these notes is to provide two kinds of information. First, they indicate where an edition departs from the original manuscript. Most scribal corrections and alterations are reported, whereas purely orthographic and minor morphological variants are usually not. Significant variants (for texts in multiple copies or versions) and modern editorial conjectures are reported selectively, usually to support an emendation or point out an interesting alternative. Second, the notes mark any substantial departures of my own from the adopted base editions. "Substantial" changes do not include minor adjustments of capitalization, paragraphing, and format, which have all been made silently. They do, however, include emendations proposed by others or by me. Changes to the punctuation of the base edition are noted only if they significantly affect the meaning of the text, and then they are discussed not here but in the Notes to the Translations.

Abbreviations

ASPR = The Anglo-Saxon Poetic Records: A Collective Edition. New York, 1931–1953. (See individual editions by Krapp and Dobbie in the Bibliography, below.)

DOE = *Dictionary of Old English: A–G* (Online). Ed. Antonette diPaolo Healey. Toronto, 2007.

Notes to the Texts

The Panther

Manuscript: Exeter, Cathedral Library, 3501, fols. 95v–96v.

This edition: Adapted from Krapp and Dobbie, ASPR 3:169–71, with additional paragraph breaks. I have also consulted the helpful edition by Squires, *Old English Physiologus,* 37–40 (text) and 47–68 (commentary); as well as Muir, *Exeter Anthology* 1:266–69 (text) and 2:581–84 (commentary).

4 world: worl   12 dun-scrafum: a *altered from* u   13 bearn: beard   14 cyþað: cyþan   15 æghwam: æthwam   20 secgað: a *altered from* e   21 guman: um *written over an erasure*   33 ængum: ægnum   34 sægde: sæde *with* g *inserted between* æ *and* d   38 þeod-wiga: þeoð wiga   39 ge-biesgad: ge biesgað   41 gewelgad: gewelgað   43 wynsumast: y *altered from* i   48 frætwum: frætwa   56 eað-mede: eaðmedum *with* um *marked for deletion and* e *written above by a different hand*   59 grund: d *altered from* ð   68 sceata: scea tan   71 ungnyðe: ungnyde

The Whale

Manuscript: Exeter, Cathedral Library, 3501, fols. 96v–97v.

This edition: Adapted from Krapp and Dobbie, ASPR 3:171–74, with additional paragraph breaks. I have also consulted Squires, *Old English Physiologus,* 41–44 (text) and 69–96 (commentary); and Muir, *Exeter Anthology* 1:270–73 (text) and 2:585–88 (commentary).

6 þam: a *is an unfinished* æ   15 sælað: setlað; *see the notes to the translation*   18 streame: *final* e *altered from* a   28 nowe: noþe; *see the notes to the translation*   38 þonne: on *written over an erasure*   40 hricge: hringe; *see the notes to the translation*   48 bisenceð: bisen ceð *with* en *written over an erasure*   58 gewiteð: ge witað   64 bisceawað: ð *altered from* d   70 ofer: *fol-*

347

lowed by an erased letter   ferhð-gereaht: ferhtgereaht   83 dryhtne: dryht-
ene *with the first* e *marked for deletion*

THE PARTRIDGE

Manuscript: Exeter, Cathedral Library, 3501, fols. 97v–98r (but see below).

This edition: Adapted from Krapp and Dobbie, ASPR 3:174. I have also
consulted Squires, *Old English Physiologus,* 46 (text) and 97–101 (com-
mentary); and Muir, *Exeter Anthology* 1:274–75 (text) and 2:581 and 589–91
(commentary), although Muir treats this material as fragments from two
distinct poems (see below).

This item is incomplete, owing to loss of a leaf from the manuscript.
Line 2a of the printed text contains the final words from the bottom of fol.
97v in the Exeter Book. Most readers have assumed that those lines began
another *Physiologus* poem that formed a triptych with *The Panther* and *The
Whale* (see the Introduction). Whether the text on the other side of the
lacuna (i.e., beginning at the top of the next surviving folio, 98r) is from
the same or a different poem is a matter of disagreement. In his recent
edition of the Exeter Book, Muir breaks with the older view of these two
fragments as the two ends of a single poem. Accepting arguments by Con-
ner ("Exeter Book Codex," 234), Muir regards lines 1–2a, from the bottom
of fol. 97v, as all that remain of the bird poem (which he still calls *The Par-
tridge*). Conner and Muir view the lines after the lacuna (i.e., from line 3b in
the edition printed here) as the conclusion to a different poem altogether,
which they rename *Homiletic Fragment (III)*. There is thus no present con-
sensus about this part of the Exeter Book. For the purposes of presenting
the material here, I follow the traditional interpretation of the two frag-
ments as parts of a single poem. At least, the arguments favoring that idea,
and favoring the identification of the bird in line 1 as a partridge, have not,
in my view, been convincingly overturned (see the notes to the transla-
tion).

6 hell-firena: *altered from* hellfira

THE PHOENIX

Manuscript: Exeter, Cathedral Library, 3501, fols. 55v–65v.

This edition: Adapted from Krapp and Dobbie, ASPR 3:94–113, with additional paragraph breaks. I have also consulted Muir, *Exeter Anthology* 1:164–87 (text) and 2:468–85 (commentary); and especially Blake, *The Phoenix*. Specifically, I have adopted Blake's punctuation over that of Krapp and Dobbie for lines 56, 72, 154 (I put a full stop for Blake's semicolon), 267, and 322.

2 londa: a *altered from* e   10 spedig: *one letter erased after this word*   15 fnæst: fnæft *with* n *written over an erasure*   64 flod-wylmum: fold wylmum   71 gehongne: gehongene *with second* e *marked for deletion*   72 waniað: wuniað   103 sidne: siðne   108 swegl-condelle: swel condelle *with* g *later inserted after the first* e   110 baða: *the second* a *altered from* e   115 holm-þræce: holm wræce   124 togeanes: to heanes   126 hremig: remig   133 wynsumra: winsumra *with* y *written above* i   137 swegh-leoþres: sweg leoþres   143 onbrygdeð: *final* ð *altered from* d   148 bigengan: bigenga   154 grene: rene   155 wyn: *not in the manuscript; supplied by Krapp and Dobbie, following earlier editors*   156 side: d *altered from* ð   157 no men: nomen *with* e *altered from* a   171 holt-wuda: a *altered from* u   173 heofun-hrofe: heofum hrofe   197 gehwæs: gewæs *with* h *written above, now partially obscured by wear*   199 swetest: swetes *left unamended by Krapp and Dobbie and Blake, but the latter regards as if* swetest   206 stencum: *an erasure follows*   211 geondwliteð: liteð *written over an erasure, possibly by a different scribe*   217 heoro-dreorges: heore dreorges   225 ligþræce: lig þræce *with* lig *written over an erasure, possibly by a different scribe*   229 sweþrað: eþ *and* ð *are written over erasures*   234 scylle: *second* l *written over an erasure*   240 weorþeð: *second* e *altered from* a   241 eal: al *written over an erasure*   243 wæstmas: wæsmas   248 gefean: ge feon   251 ead-wela: ead welan   264 eft: ft *written over an erasure*   288 segn: þegn; *Blake and Muir argue to retain the manuscript reading*   294 wrixled: wrixleð   303 gold-fate: ol *written over an erasure*   306 brogden: bregden   324 somniað: somnað   325 eastan: *part of an unfinished letter* (s?) *between* e *and* a   327 sceawiaþ: þ *altered from* n   330 fægran: *thus the manuscript, adopted by Blake and Muir; Krapp and Dobbie emend to* fægerran   332 gewritum: gewritu   333 marm-stane: mearm stane *with the first* e *marked for deletion and* r *partly erased*   336 gehwone: gehwore   342 wafiað: wefiað   365 þeceð: eceð *written over an erasure*   371 fylle: fille *with* y *written above* i   377 mon-cynnes: *the scribe began to write* monn-   382 æfter: f *written over an erasure*   386 wuldre: worulde   393 geascad: d *altered from* ð

396 sceata: sceates   407 Wurdon: wordon *with* v *written above the first* o
421 togeanes: to heanes   425 wordum: weordum   443 wel: we   477
heortan: eortan   477 geleafan: *Muir perceives an alteration from* geleasun
488 sendeð: sendað   491 læded: lædaþ   495 gefremmaþ: þ *altered from*
n   507 gifre: g *over an erasure*   511 astelleð: astellað   512 ban gegædrað:
bange. gædrað *with the period written over an erasure*   513 lifes: liges
519 hweorfað: o *altered from* a   531 hit: t *written over an erasure of one letter*
(perhaps s)   559 agan: *one letter erased after the first* a   584 siþiaþ: *final* þ
corrected from n   586 ead-welum: um *possibly altered from* an   588 weo-
redum: *the second* e *is written over an erasure*   599 bliþan: bliþam
601 symle: l *altered from* b   606 glengeð: *first* e *altered from* i   612 ne
weþel: newe þel *with a* þ *erased after* newe   613 hearda: hearde   624 geon-
gra: a *altered from* u *and followed by one erased letter*   625 strengðu:
strenðu   635 singað: singad   648 onwæcneð: on wæcned   650 helpe:
elpe   651 lif: *part of* f *is written over an erasure*   652 swa: *traces of one letter
erased between* s *and* w   fiþru: fiþrum *with* m *erased*   659 wynsumne: *sec-
ond* n *altered from* u   667 auctor: actor *with* u *written above* ac *and an inser-
tion mark below*   670 motun: motum   672 lisse: se *is written over an era-
sure*   673 *almae*: alma   674 *mitem*: mittem

The Lord's Prayer (I)

Manuscript: Exeter, Cathedral Library, 3501, fol. 122r.
   This edition: Adapted from Krapp and Dobbie, ASPR 3:223–24. I have
also consulted Muir, *Exeter Anthology* 1:349 (text) and 2:688–89 (com-
mentary).

   1 halig: . . . g; *the opening initial plus approximately ten letters before part of* g
have been lost to fire damage; Muir reconstructs halig *but indicates room for
roughly five letters preceding that*   2 geweorðad: ge weordad   10 freodom:
freo don

The Lord's Prayer (II)

Manuscript: Cambridge, Corpus Christi College 201, pp. 167–69.
   This edition: Adapted from Dobbie, ASPR 6:70–74. I have also con-
sulted Ure, *Benedictine Office,* 103–6 (text) and 128–31 (commentary).

17 ræcað: ræcð   34 sibbe and lufe: sib and lufu; *see the notes to the transla-tion*   35 beorhtnysse: beorhtnys; *see the notes to the translation*   47 sinre: þinre   48 æþele: æþela   73 ælcre gecynde: ælcege cynd   96 arisað: ariseð   98 gebrosnodon: gebrosnodon eft   106 bið: beoð   112 alyseð: alysað   113 forgifað: gifað   122 gifnesse: gifnes

THE LORD'S PRAYER (III)

Manuscript: Oxford, Bodleian Library, Junius 121, fol. 45r–v.
This edition: Adapted from Dobbie, ASPR 6:77–78.

32 þencað: þenceð   44 þu: *added above the line*

THE APOSTLES' CREED

Manuscript: Oxford, Bodleian Library, Junius 121, fols. 46r–47r
This edition: Adapted from Dobbie, ASPR 6:78–80. I have also con-sulted Ure, *Benedictine Office*, 87–89 (text) and 124–25 (commentary).

9 þu ða menegu: ða þu manega   15 sanctan: Scā   38 recene: recen 67 þær: ær *with capital thorn omitted*   dælest: dældest

THE GLORIA PATRI (I)

Manuscripts: Oxford, Bodleian Library, Junius 121, fols. 43v–44v (siglum J); Cambridge, Corpus Christi College 201, pp. 169–70 (siglum C).
This edition: Adapted from the edition by Dobbie, ASPR 6:74–77, based on J. The apparatus reports only substantial variants from C; omitted are most differences of spelling or word division. I have also consulted Ure, *Benedictine Office*, 83–85 (text) and 122–24 (commentary).

1 *Gloria:* Gloria patri *J;* ła *C*   geopenod: geopnod *C*   6 wuldre: wo-rulde *J;* world *C*   8 eall: ealle *C*   10 feorh-hyrde: feorh hyrda *C*   15 hige-frofer: hige frofre *J C*   and halig gast: *omitted in C*   18 worulde: worlde *C* frofer: frofre *J C*   20 gewrohtest: geworhtest *C*   24 mænego: manega *C*   25 gewrohtest: geworhtest *C*   26 and on þone: *omitted in C* 29 gemærsodest: þu mærsodest *C*   32 halige: haligne *J C*   33 drihtnes: drihtenes *C*   35 And nu and symble: and nu symle *C*   37 heo: hig *C* 38 woruld: world *C*   standeþ: standað *C*   40 heriað: heriað heriað *C* 46 worulda woruld: worlda world *C*   48 heah-þrymnesse halige gastas *C;*

heah þrynnesse haliges gastes *J; see the notes to the translation* 52 Haligdomas: halig domas *J;* haligdomes *C* heofones: heofonas *C J* 53 word *C; omitted in J* 54 syndon: synd *C* 61 oruð and sawul: orð and sawle *C*

The Gloria patri (II)

Manuscript: London, British Library, Cotton Titus D. xxvii, fol. 56r–v.
This edition: Adapted from Dobbie, ASPR 6:94.

The Kentish Hymn

Manuscript: London, British Library, Cotton Vespasian D. vi, fols. 68v–69v.
This edition: Adapted from Dobbie, ASPR 6:87–88, with different paragraph breaks. I have also consulted Keefer, *Liturgical Verse,* 119–29.

5 ænglum: ænlum 6 gehwilcum: gewilcum *with* h *added above the line* goodes: godes *with a second* o *added above* 8 bile-wit: bilewitne 10 weorðlican: *omitted but then added above the line by the original scribe* 11 ðinra: ðara 15 cynincg: cynicg *with a second* n *added above between* i *and* c 17 angla: anla *with* g *added above* 23 ðu: ðy 25 follc: foll *with* c *added above* 26 Israela: isla *with* rae *added above by the original scribe* 28 ðrowunga: ðrowuga *with* n *added above* ðiostra: ðriostre; *Dobbie does not emend* 31 gemyndig: *see the notes to the translation* 34 sceppend: scepped *with* n *added above* 37 ana: *omitted but then added above the line by the original scribe* 39 nergende: nergend 42 heah-cyninc: heahcynic *with* n *added above between* i *and* c

Cædmon's Hymn

This edition: On the two versions of this poem, see the notes to the translation. The present edition is adapted from Dobbie, ASPR 6:105, which takes as a base manuscript Cambridge, University Library, Kk. 5.16, fol. 128v (siglum M), and reports variants from Saint Petersburg, Russian National Library, Lat. Q.v.I.18 (L); Dijon, Bibliothèque municipale 574 (D); and Paris, Bibliothèque nationale de France, lat. 5237 (P). The most complete critical edition of the poem is now O'Donnell, *Cædmon's Hymn,* esp. 205–30, to which the reader is referred for minute collations. The apparatus that follows here is selective, its principal aim being to report lexical variants or such errors as might have seemed like plausible significant variants to a medieval reader. I therefore omit most orthographic and minor inflectional differences, as well as numerous botched readings produced by the uncomprehending scribes of D and P.

1 Nu: Nu pue *D P corrupting* Nu we   hefaen-ricaes: hefunrincaes *P* 3 uuldur-fadur: fadur *P*   5 ærist: uerst *with* a *written above* u *D;* raerist *P* aelda: ældu *L;* eordu *D P*   6 heben: efen *D P*   til: to *L D P*   scepen: sceppend *L D P*   9 foldu: fold^v *M;* foldu *L;* on foldu *D;* ol foldu *P*

GODRIC'S HYMN

This edition: The so-called *Hymn* of Saint Godric of Finchale is transmitted in various forms in at least ten manuscripts (not counting additional versions in Latin translation). Reconstructing its twelfth-century language and meter nevertheless involves a good deal of speculation. What I print is essentially the reconstruction arrived at by Zupitza, "Cantus beati Godrici," 423, along with his apparatus of variants. Zupitza's lines 1–4 are based mainly on Oxford, Bodleian Library, Laud misc. 413, fol. 39v (siglum A); lines 5–8 mainly on London, British Library, Royal 5.F.vii, fol. 85r (siglum F). The eight other witnesses to the *Hymn* in English are, with their sigla assigned by Zupitza: London, British Library, Harley 153 (B); Cambridge, University Library, Mm. iv. 28 (C); London, British Library, Harley 322 (D); Oxford, Bodleian Library, Douce 207 (G); London, British Library, Cotton Otho. B.v (H); Cambridge, Corpus Christi College 26 (I); London, British Library, Cotton Nero D.v (K); and London, British Library, Harley 1620 (L).

Manuscripts A B C D are copies or reworkings of the *Libellus de vita et miraculis S. Godrici* by Reginald of Durham, in which the story of Godric's reception of the hymn is chap. 110 (Stephenson, 118–19). Manuscript F is Geoffrey of Durham's rewriting of the same. In the remaining witnesses, Reginald's account has been absorbed into chronicles by Roger of Wendover (manuscripts G H) and Matthew Paris (I K L).

1 Sainte: Seinte *B D G H I K L;* Sancte *C*   uirgine: clane uirgine *G I K L;*
clene uirgine *H*   2 Iesu: iesus *D*   Cristes: crist *G*   3 onfo: vn fo *B;* on
fong *D*   scild: schild *D F;* child *B;* sciso *G*   help: *omitted in I K L*   Go-
dric: Godrich *I K L;* godrich *D H;* gorich *G*   4 onfang: on fong *D*   heh-
lic: hehliche *B;* hehtlic *C;* eȝhtlech *A;* heȝilich *F;* hegliche *D;* heali *G H;*
hæali *I;* hali *K;* halali *L*   wið: widh *G I K L;* þidh *H;* þið *F*   in: ine *D;* i *C*
ric: rich *H I K L;* rych *D;* riche *A F G;* Riche *C*   5–8 *omitted in A B C D*
5 Sainte: Seinte *G H I K L*   Cristes: XPistes *F;* crestes *H*   bur: bour *G*
6 maidenes: meidenes *H I L;* medenes *K;* maidenus *G*   clenhad: clenhed
G; cleuad *L*   flur: flour *G H*   7 dilie: deliuere *G*   mine: min *F*   sinne:
sennen *G H I K L*   rixe: rix *F;* regne *G*   in: i *H I K L*   min: mi *G*   8 bring:
brig *G*   winne: wunne *H;* pinine *I K L;* blisse *G*   wið: widh *H I K L;* wit
G   self: þi self *G;* þe selfd *F*

A Prayer

Manuscripts: London, British Library, Cotton Julius A. ii, fols. 136r–37r
(siglum J); and (for lines 1–15b) London, Lambeth Palace 427, fol. 183v (sig-
lum L).

This edition: Adapted from Dobbie, ASPR 6:94–96, which is based on
manuscript J. For lines 1–15b, the apparatus reports variants from L, ex-
cluding minor differences of spelling. For more detail concerning differ-
ences between the two copies, the reader may consult Keefer, *Liturgical
Verse,* 162–74.

5 hy: heo *L*   ealdor: al dor *L*   6 forðan: for þon *L*   læca: læc a *with one
letter erased after* c *L*   9 Gemilsa: gemilda *L*   þynum: þyne *J;* þinum *L*   11
þe *L;* þeo *J*   12 deofle: deoflon *J;* deoflū *L*   14 he ða *J; omitted in L*
15 bute: butan *L*   yfeles: yfles *L*   geswyce: ge swice *L (the L copy ends here)*
42 lifiende: lifiend *J*   51 Ðyn: *the first letter not visible because of damage to
the manuscript J*   73 lænan: hlænan *J*

Resignation (A)

Manuscript: Exeter, Cathedral Library, 3501, fols. 117v–18v.

This edition: Adapted from Krapp and Dobbie, ASPR 3:215–17, with ad-
ditional paragraph breaks. I have also consulted the edition and notes by
Anderson, *Two Literary Riddles,* 200–209; and those by Muir, who retitles

the poem "Contrition A" (*Exeter Anthology* 1:336–38 and 2:670–73); and the separate edition by Malmberg, *Resignation.*

This poem was long considered to be of a piece with the verses that continue at the top of fol. 119r in the Exeter Book. Critics occasionally noted, however, that the poem printed here as *Resignation (A)* differs in language, style, and ideas from the lines that followed on the next folio in the manuscript. Only in 1976 did a detailed study (Bliss and Frantzen, "Integrity of *Resignation*") make the case that what had been viewed as a single poem was in fact two. Bliss and Frantzen argue that, between present-day fols. 118 and 119 of the manuscript, a leaf has been lost that contained the end of the first poem, now called *Resignation (A),* and the beginning of a second, now called *Resignation (B).* Most studies subsequently have accepted the Bliss-Frantzen argument, but not all (see, e.g., Klinck, "*Resignation*").

In dividing up the Old English poetic corpus for the Dumbarton Oaks Medieval Library, the series editors have decided to include *Resignation (A)* among the Christian devotional poems in the present volume. *Resignation (B)* will appear in a later volume dedicated to elegiac, sapiential, and other types of short poem.

4 þe: *not in the manuscript* 57 sculon: scul *with two additional letters burned away* 68 meorda: meor da *with one letter erased between* r *and* d

ALMSGIVING

Manuscript: Exeter, Cathedral Library, 3501, fols. 121v–22r.

This edition: Adapted from Krapp and Dobbie, ASPR 3:223. I have also consulted Muir, *Exeter Anthology* 1:347 (text) and 2:684–85 (commentary).

HOMILETIC FRAGMENT (I)

Manuscript: Vercelli, Biblioteca Capitolare, CXVIII, fol. 104r–v.

This edition: Adapted from Krapp, ASPR 2:59–60, with some adjustment of paragraph breaks.

5 swa: swa swa 23 stinge: *not in the manuscript; supplied by most editors* 43 bot: *not in the manuscript; supplied by Krapp*

Homiletic Fragment (II)

Manuscript: Exeter, Cathedral Library, 3501, fol. 122r–v.

This edition: Adapted from Krapp and Dobbie, ASPR 3:224, with an added paragraph break. I have also consulted Muir, *Exeter Anthology* 1:350–51 (text) and 2:690 (commentary).

9 fulwiht: fulwihte   13 bedygled: . . . edygled   15 Siþþan: siþ . . . an

Aldhelm

Manuscript: Cambridge, Corpus Christi College 326, pp. 5–6. There the poem is copied between the Latin table of contents and preface to Aldhelm's prose treatise on virginity *(De virginitate)*.

This edition: Adapted from Dobbie, ASPR 6:97–98; see the notes to the translation for other sources consulted.

4 æþele: æþel   Angol-Sexna: angel sexna *with* o *written above the first* e   12 sceal: seal   13 ealneg: *the final* g *is mostly erased*   16 *dinamis:* dinams; *Dobbie accepts the manuscript reading*   17 *the text seems to break off incomplete, but see the notes to the translation*

Thureth

Manuscript: London, British Library, Cotton Claudius A. iii, fol. 31v.

This edition: Adapted from Dobbie, ASPR 6:93. I have also benefited greatly from the recent reedition, translation, and study by Clunies Ross and Edwards, "Thureth," 360.

The Rewards of Piety

Manuscript: Cambridge, Corpus Christi College 201, pp. 165–67.

This edition: Adapted from Dobbie, ASPR 6:67–70, where this material was edited as two separate poems, *An Exhortation to Christian Living* and *A Summons to Prayer* (lines 1–82 and 83–114, respectively, of the text printed here). There is no gap or physical loss of text, but *Þænne* at line 83 of the printed edition begins with a large colored capital in the manuscript, and the form of the verses that follow, as they mix Latin and Old English, differs strikingly from what comes before. In 1989 Fred Robinson published a new analysis of the two items as a single work, renamed by him *The Rewards of Piety*. The present edition is based on Dobbie's texts, with some additional paragraph breaks and other corrections, but adopting Robinson's title and presentation of the material as a single work.

This poem was used as a source by the author of an anonymous sermon now known as Vercelli Homily XXI (Scragg, *Vercelli Homilies,* 351–62), which was (including its quotation of the poem) revised into Napier Homily XXX (Napier, *Wulfstan,* 143–52). The relationship of *The Rewards of Piety* to these prose works was first discussed by Whitbread (see especially "Two Notes," 193–98; and "'Wulfstan' Homilies," 348–56). But some of Whitbread's views have been corrected by Scragg, "Napier's 'Wulfstan' Homily," 209–10. The most recent and far-reaching analysis of the poem's relations to other Old English texts (especially those nearby in the manuscript) is Zacher, "Rewards of Poetry."

13 bringað: b *altered from* þ   21 byrden: byr dæn *with the first half of* æ *marked for deletion*   34 gelyfð: belyfð *with* b *marked for deletion and* g *written above*   47 forhæfdnessum: forhæfnessum *with* d *added above between* f *and* n   54 fremman: frēm n *with* a *added below by a different hand*   58 ongyte: y *written over an erasure*   66 *Dobbie makes* embe þæt *the beginning of a new, incomplete line; I follow Robinson by moving* embe þæt *to the end of the preceding b-verse*   79 gebindan: binde *with* ge *added above*   83 sedens: sedentem   84 *see the notes to the translation*   85 þinre: þine   95 *clementem deum:* clemens deus   98 þa: þe   bodade: boda   101 *roga:* rogo   102 bidde: *omitted then added above the line by the original scribe*   friclo: fricolo *with the first* o *marked for deletion*   103 *sanctos:* sancti   104 *beatos et iustos:* beatus et iustus   106 *regenti:* regentem   110 þe: he   *lucem:* luce   112 restað: restat

INSTRUCTIONS FOR CHRISTIANS

Manuscript: Cambridge, University Library, Ii.1.33, fols. 224v–27v.

This edition: There is no satisfactory edition yet of this interesting poem, on which a great deal of work remains to be done by textual critics, historical linguists, and source hunters. The sole surviving copy is late, from the second half of the twelfth century, and its language is at times closer to early Middle than to Old English. The meter likewise poses difficulties; scholars disagree whether certain of its perceived defects are corruptions or were present in the poet's original. The present edition and translation are provisional at best, their aim being to consolidate some of the more plausible suggestions offered about the text during the past fifty years. I have adopted as a basis the edition and lineation by Rosier ("'Instructions for Christians,'" 1–18). Into his text, however, are incorporated numerous corrections offered later by Rosier himself ("Addenda to 'Instructions for Christians'"), as well as by Robinson ("Notes and Emendations," 360–62), and Torkar ("Textkritische Anmerkungen"). At a few points I have also benefited from Youngs's dissertation ("'Instructions for Christians'"). The sole manuscript copy of the poem has received numerous medieval corrections and glosses, many of them in a hand different from that of the original scribe. For an account of these alterations, the reader is referred to the notes accompanying Rosier's edition and to Youngs's dissertation. The textual notes that follow here omit scribal glosses as well as scribal corrections of a purely orthographic or otherwise nonsubstantive kind.

3 ðe: *added in the margin, possibly by a different hand*   13 is: *incompletely erased*   14 hreowe: *altered to* hreowsie *by a different hand*   misdæda: *Torkar suggests the emendation* womdæda *(cf. line 51) to restore alliteration*   33 weles: *added above the line, perhaps by the original scribe*   34 oht: *altered to* noht   36 locest: locst *with* e *added above*   43 æfre: æfre *with initial* n *added above*   44 behatest: behastest *with* s *after* a *erased*   46 wyrrest: *altered to* wyrrs   getreowa: *altered to* getreowþa *by a different hand*   47 scyle: scylen   48 his: is   54 ðe: ðe he   55 gehwylce: gewylce *with* h *added above*   56 weriað: *not in the manuscript; supplied by Rosier*   be: he   64 hwæthwugo: *marked for deletion in the manuscript, with* cræftes *written above by a different hand*   69 gold: god; *see notes to the translation for lines 69–75*   70 ungelice: gelice; *see notes to the translation for lines 69–75*   79 bearne: *altered from* bearna; *Rosier suggests* bearnum *but does not emend*   82 weorlda: *the scribe began to write* weoru   mycelne: mycele *with* n *added above by the original scribe*   85 gelæredon: gelærdon *with* e *added above by the original scribe*   96 gifeð: gifð; *Rosier emends for the sake of meter*   105 best: heft; *emended*

by Rosier 106 gehwilces: gehwlces *with* i *scratched above* 120 heah-gestreon: heahgestron *with* e *added between* r *and* o *by the original scribe* 121 mycelne: mycele *with* n *added above by the original scribe* 124 ge-hwylce: gehylce *with* w *added above by the original scribe* 153 drihten Godd: *Torkar notes that emending to* weroda Godd *would restore alliteration to the line* 154 monige: *altered to* mænige; *see the notes to the translation* 156 wordum cwæð: word on cwæð *with* on *at line end; Rosier prints* word oncwæð, *but see Torkar, 168–70* 163 sið: siðgeare; *see the note to the transla-tion for this line* 167 gehygd: *not in the manuscript; supplied by Rosier* 169 gecyrre: cyrre *with* ge *added above, possibly by a different hand* 172 æt his forð-siðe: forman siðe *altered by a different hand to* forðsiðe, *with* æt *and* his *being marginal additions* 176 Godes: s *erased* 185 gif him ne licað: *Rosier notes that emending to* gif ne licað him *would restore alliteration to the line* 189 madm-ceoste: c *written over erased* s 196 scyle: syle *with* c *added above by the original scribe* 197 unrihtwise: unrihtwis *with final* e *added above, possibly by a different hand* 201 þæt he: þæt þæt he; *see the notes to the translation for lines 201–6* 202 sece: secan 204 wille: wolde ær: þær; *for both emendations, see the notes to the translation for lines 201–6* 212 sinum: þi-num; *emended by Rosier* 213 þeawa: þeaum; *see the notes to the translation* 216 forceorran: foceorran *with* r *added above between* o *and* c *by the original scribe* 221 gearowe: gearo þe; *emended by Robinson* 224 þonne: þone 226 heah-cræftiga: heahcræftig; *Rosier suggests* heahcræftiga *but does not emend* 229 wera: *altered to* wara, *possibly by the original scribe* æghwilcum: men *is written above, intended either as a gloss or an insertion* 234 dwæsta: *Rosier emends to* dwæsca, *but see Torkar, 171–72* 239 þe ne: þonne 242 ymben ænigne: *Rosier prints* ymbe nænige, *but see Torkar, 173–74* eorð-buendra: *over* -buendra *a different hand has added* -lic þincg 244 æighwyl-cum: æigþwylcum 251 habben: habbe

SEASONS FOR FASTING

Manuscripts: The text of this poem is best preserved in a sixteenth-century transcription, now London, British Library, Additional 43703, fols. 257r–60v (siglum L), made by Laurence Nowell from an Anglo-Saxon orig-inal largely destroyed by fire in 1731 (London, British Library, Cotton Otho B. ix). Independent transcriptions of small parts of the poem were made by Whelock in the seventeenth century and Wanley in the eighteenth

NOTES TO THE TEXTS

(Grant, "Note on 'The Seasons for Fasting,'" 302–3). The form of the poem is remarkable, having been composed in regular stanzas of eight lines. One apparent exception to that pattern probably indicates corruptions in the text (see the notes to the translation).

This edition: Adapted from ASPR 6:98–104, but Dobbie's edition there invited many subsequent suggestions for improvement, chiefly from Sisam (*Studies,* 45–60). I have also benefited from the edition and notes by Holthausen ("Ein altenglisches Gedicht"); studies by Leslie ("Textual Notes"), Grant ("Note on 'The Seasons for Fasting'"), and Schabram ("Zur Interpretation der 18. Strophe"); and editions, translations, and commentaries in two unpublished dissertations, namely Greeson, "Observance Poems," 179–95 and 213–56, and Hilton, "Edition and Study" 46–80.

5 þurh: þurh þurh *L* 8 sceolde: sceold *L* 12 weorc: weorce *L* 14 sigora: sigona *L* 16 gewyrpan: ḡ wyrþan *L; see the notes to the translation* 20 þrealic: þreoring *L* 30 worulde: woruld *L* 35 þone hyht gehateð *Sisam;* þone hyht and gehateð *L Dobbie; see the notes to the translation* 38 womme: wōmo *L* 40 him dogera *Sisam;* him do geara *L;* him geara *Dobbie* 44 her *Holthausen; omitted L* 47 We: Þe *L* 48 wucan: wircan *L* 50 nemneð: nemnað *L* 51 dihte: dyh te *with* i *written above* y *L* 57 gelesu: ḡ lu se *with* lu se *struck through and* lesen *then written L; see the notes to the translation* 58 þære: þær *L* cumeð: cumað *L* 70 side *Holthausen; omitted L* 71 fæsten: fæste *L* gelæstan: ḡ læsten *L* 72 þære: þær *L* 80 seofoþa: feoroþa *L* 82 gerynum: ḡ rinū *with* i *marked for deletion and* y *written above L* 84 butan: butan butan *repeated across a page break L* 85 þicgan: þingan *L Dobbie* 86 demeð þeodlic *Sisam;* þeodlic demeð *L Dobbie* 88 Bryttan oððe Francan *Sisam;* brytt franca *across a line break L; see the notes to the translation* 90 iu: in *L* 92 sylfe: sylf *L* 93 rices: rice *L* 98 geond: ḡeond *L* filiað: fihað *L* 99 gedemde: ḡdēda *L* 109 anbat: anbate *L* 111 gesealde: ḡ scealde *L* 115 orþancum: on þancū *L* 118 leoran: leora *L* 124 se gestrangud: ge se strangud *L* 129 þegen: hegen *L* 136 eorþ-bugendum: eorþ burgendū *L* 140 fæstan: sæstan *L* 143 dyde: dyda *L* 155 bæðe: bað *L* 156 firsude mettas: firude metta *L* 165 lic-homan: lichoman an *L* 168 Hige synnig man *Sisam;* higesynnig man *Dobbie* 172 myrcels: myrcelrs *L* 173 þreat *Holthausen; omitted L* 177 feowertig: þ feowertig *L* 179 ofer moldan *Sisam;* for moldan *L Dobbie* 183 wese: were *L* 189 dymnissa: dȳnisca *L*

360

193 sylfe: sylfne *L*   199 dæg-hwamlice: dæg ghamlice *L*   200 sylfne: sylne *L*   202 na þu *Sisam;* nu þa *L Dobbie*   ne: ni *L*   203 gehalgod: ḡ halgode *L*   204 fremman: frēnan *L*   205 ræde: rædi *L*   206–7 *see the notes to the translation*   207 lar: lare *L Dobbie; Greeson prints* lar *but does not record as an emendation*   211 æleste: *see the notes to the translation*   220 þæs: þæ *L*   me þingeð: þingað me *marked for transposition L*   222 wicliað *Holthausen;* wigliað *L Dobbie; see the notes to the translation for lines 222–23*   223 hwæne: hwænne *L*   225 win seniað *L Sisam;* sinne semað *Dobbie*   226 cweðað þæt Godd life *Sisam;* cwedað godd life *L; see the notes to the translation for lines 226–28*   227 welhwa: wel wel hwa *L*   229 oþerre *Sisam;* oþerne *L Dobbie*

THE MENOLOGIUM

Manuscript: London, British Library, Cotton Tiberius B. i, fols. 112r–14v.

This edition: Adapted from Dobbie, ASPR 6:49–55, with additional paragraph breaks. Not much textual criticism has been published on this difficult poem, but I have benefited from detailed discussions in Greeson's commentary ("Observance Poems," 256–87); and in Karasawa's articles "Note on the Old English Poem *Menologium* 3b" and "Problems in the Editions of the *Menologium.*"

15 emb: *one letter (e?) erased after* b   25 swylt: swylc *with* c *in a later hand, over an erasure*   65 þe: he   71 and fifum: *not in the manuscript; a conjecture adopted by Dobbie*   76 embe siex niht þæs: *not in the manuscript; a conjecture adopted by Dobbie*   78 Þry-milce: þrymlice   91 blis: bliss *with the second* s *added by a later hand*   96 dogera: o *altered to* a *by a later hand*   101 a fyrn: awyrn   107 feower: þreo   114 leohta: lohta *with* e *added above by a later hand*   134 ond: on   138 welhwær: wel hwæt   151 on: *not in the manuscript; supplied by Dobbie*   156 wyrd: wyrð   188 seofon: fif   206 moton: mot   213 fela: felda   215 leof: lof   229 tiida: tiid

SOUL AND BODY

Manuscripts: Vercelli, Biblioteca Capitolare, CXVIII, fols. 101v–3v (siglum V); with variants from Exeter, Cathedral Library, 3501, fols. 98r–100r (siglum E).

This edition: Two versions of this poem survive. *Soul and Body (I),* in the tenth-century Vercelli Book, consists of a long address by the damned soul to its decaying body (lines 1–127 of my edition), followed by the beginning of an address by a redeemed soul to its body (lines 128–69 of my edition); the text breaks off abruptly where a leaf has been lost from the manuscript. The second version, *Soul and Body (II)*, survives in the tenth-century Exeter Book and consists only of the damned soul's address, very similar but not identical to the corresponding portion of *Soul and Body (I)*. The relationship between the two versions is still debated, but I favor the view that both derive independently from an earlier text that consisted of only the damned soul's address and that the speech by the saved soul in *Soul and Body (I)* is likely the work of a different poet (see Orton, "Disunity"; Moffat, "Scribal Revision").

While critical scholarship has usually treated the two versions apart, Moffat's recent edition (*Old English* Soul and Body) has revived the precedent for printing a conflated text, and that is the course I follow here. I adopt as a base Krapp's edition of *Soul and Body (I)* at ASPR 2:54–59, but I incorporate substantial material—including entire lines at 83–84, 100, and 113—from *Soul and Body (II)*, as edited by Krapp and Dobbie at ASPR 3:174–78. Significant differences between the two, excluding spelling variants, are reported in the notes below, where the siglum V signals readings from the Vercelli *Soul and Body (I)*, and E readings from the Exeter *Soul and Body (II)*. Where the lineations of the two versions differ, the line numbers of E are given parenthetically alongside its variants.

While relying greatly on Moffat's recent reeditions, translations, and commentaries for both versions (*Old English* Soul and Body), I have also consulted Grein's conflated edition of 1857 ("Reden der Seelen an den Leichnam," 198–204), as well as the translation of *Soul and Body (I)* by Shippey (*Poems of Wisdom and Learning*, 104–11), the editions and commentaries for both versions by Ricciardi ("Grave-Bound Body," 142–84), and the edition and commentary for *Soul and Body (II)* by Muir (*Exeter Anthology* 1:276–80 and 2:592–96).

2 sið *E;* sið sið *V* geþence *V;* bewitige *E*   4 þe *V;* þa þe *E*   7 on *V;* in *E* 12b–14b buton ær *through* weoruda dryhten *V;* butan ær wyrce ece dryhten, / ælmihtig God, ende worlde *E (13–14)*   16 se *V; omitted E* 17 druge: druh *V;* drugu *E; the emendation is Sisam's (Studies, 34)*   18 for-

wisnad *V;* forweornast *E*   19 gemundest *V;* geþohtes *E*   20 þing *V;* sið *E*   21 syððan of *V;* siþþan heo of *E*   22a ðu *E;* ðuðu *V*   23b–27a þa ðu lust-gryrum *through* þe la engel *V;* hu þis is long hider, / and þe þurh engel *E* *(23b–24a)*   24 eallum fulgeodest: *Krapp prints* eallum *as the last word of line 23b and emends to* ful geeodest *in 24; lines 23b–26a are omitted in E*   30 þe *V;* þe þa *E (27)*   31 mid *V; omitted E (28)*   33 on *V;* in *E (30)*   Ne meahte ic ðe of cuman *V;* No ic þe of meahte *E (30)*   36 hit *V; omitted E (33)*   wære *E (33):* wær *V*   37 A *V;* Hwæt *E (34)*   38 huru *V; omitted E (35)*   god *E (35);* goð *V*   40 ic *E (37); omitted V*   42 Forðan þu ne hogodest *V;* Þær þu þonne hogode *E (39)*   43 syððan *V;* þenden *E (40)*   on *V;* in *E (40)*   45 gestryned *V;* gestyred *E (42)*   me *V;* mec *E (42)*   47 wið: mid *V; omitted E (44)*   swa heardum *V;* swa heardra *E (44)*   witum *V;* wita *E (44)*   48 ne generedest *V;* ned gearwode *E (45)*   nieda: meda *V;* neoda *E (45)*   49 Scealt ðu *V;* Scealt þu nu hwæþre *E (46)*   gescenta *E (46);* gesynta *V*   50 eall *V; omitted E (47)*   51 an-cenneda: acenneda *V;* ancenda *E (48)*   gesamnað *V;* gegædrað *E (48)*   52 ðu *V;* þu nu *E (49)*   54 gesybban *V;* gesibbra *E (51)*   þonne *E (51);* þonn *with final* e *added later V*   57 magon *E (54);* mæg *V*   þa *E (54);* þy *V*   59a–60b   ne þinre *through* iu ahtest *V; omitted E*   59 bold-wela: gold wela *V;* abidan *E (56)*   61 onbidan *V;* abidan *E (56)*   62 synum *V;* seonwum *E (57)*   sceal *E (57);* sceal ⁊ *with the tironian abbreviation partially rubbed out V*   63 unwillum: unwillu *V;* unwillan *E (58)*   64 þe *V; omitted E (59)*   65 nu *V; omitted E (60)*   synt *V;* sindan *E (60)*   66 swa þeah *V;* seþeah *E (61)*   69 lifiendum Gode *V; transposed E (64)*   70 her *V;* ær *E (65)*   72 her *V; omitted E (67)*   73 slitan sarlice *V;* seonowum beslitan *E (68)*   wihta *V;* wihte *E (68)*   74 æhta awihte *V;* geahþe wiht *E (69)*   75 þe *V;* þa *E (70)*   77 speda *V;* spede *E (72)*   79 frymðe *V;* frumsceafte *E (74)*   80 on *V; omitted E (75)*   82 oððe *V;* ge *E (77)*   wildra deora *E (77);* wild deora *V*   83a–84b grimmeste *through* þæt wyrreste *E (78–9);* wyrreste, þær swa God wolde, / ge þeah ðu wære wyrma cynna / þæt grimmeste, þær swa God wolde *V (83a–85b)*   87 bæm *V;* bu *E (82)*   88 mannum *V;* eallum mannum *E (83)*   89 wunda *V;* wunde *E (84)*   on *V;* in *E (84)*   92 hæleða *through* scippend *V; omitted E*   93 gehwam *E (87);* gehwæs *V*   94 wunda: wunde *V E (93); see the notes to the translation*   95 þam *V; omitted E (89)*   96 nan na *V;* nænig *E (90)*   aweaxen *V;* geweaxen *E (90)*   97 anra gehwylcum onsundrum *V;* æghwylc anra onsundran *E (91)*   99 þam *V; omitted E (93)*   100 þonne he *through* oþre siþe *E (94); omitted V*   102   her *V; omitted E (96)*   103   onweg: on weg *with a w erased before* o *V;* on weg *E (97)*   105   Ligeð *E (105);* liget *V*   107   geomrum gaste *V; transposed E (102)*   110   sina *V;* seonwe *E (105)*   111   fingras tohrorene *V; omitted E*   113   drincað *through* þurstge *E (107); omitted V*   114   Bið seo tunge totogen *E (108);* beoð hira tungan totogenne *V (113)*   115   heo ne mæg *E (109);* hie ne magon *V (114)*   huxlicum *V;* horsclice *E (109)*   116   wrixlian *V;* wrixlan *E (110)*   117   þe þa eaglas *V;* þam þa geaflas *E (111)*   118   genydde to: genydde to me *V;* geneþeð to *E (112)*   120   þæt *V; omitted E (114)*   teð *V;* toþas *E (114)*   121–22   *these two lines are transposed in E (115–16)*   123   þæt *V;* bið þæt *E (117)*   124   bið *V; omitted E (118; cf. 117)* he *E (118); omitted V*   125   wyrma *V;* wyrmes *E (119)*   126   æt *E (120); omitted V*   127   gemynde *through* gehwam *V;* gemyndum modsnottera *E (121)*   133   sprecað: sprecat *V*   136   þeah ðe: ah ðæ *V*   139   arum: earum *V*   152   ahofe me: ahofeme me *with the first* me *erased V*   160   syþþan: syþan *V; see the notes to the translation*   161   swylcra arna swa ðu unc ær scrife: *not in the manuscript; see the notes to the translation for 160–61*   165   hreðre: reðre *V*

THE SOUL'S ADDRESS TO THE BODY

Manuscript: Worcester, Cathedral Library, F. 174, fols. 63v–66v.

This edition: Adapted from Buchholz, *Fragmente der Reden der Seele,* 1–10, but for many improvements to Buchholz's text and lineation I am indebted to Moffat's edition and notes in *Soul's Address to the Body,* as well as to the text and notes by Ricciardi ("Grave-Bound Body," 192–281). I have not been able to see the more recent dissertation by Johansen ("'Worcester Fragments'"), but his article "Cohesion of the Worcester Fragments," 161, has provided a better reading for Fragment G, line 49.

The so-called Worcester Fragments pose extreme challenges to editors and translators. The top and bottom of each manuscript page have been cut away, resulting in significant loss of text. Even where the letter forms are preserved, moreover, they can be difficult to read. For the most detailed account of the manuscript and of past editors' attempts to emend the text or reconstruct damaged portions, the reader is referred to Moffat's critical edition.

For the present volume, it has been necessary to adopt a greatly simplified approach both to establishing the text and to reporting editorial interventions. The reader may assume that, unless otherwise noted, the text printed and translated here is Buchholz's and incorporates his emendations and suppletions of missing letters or words. The following apparatus gives manuscript readings (identified by the siglum W), in which missing letters of any extent are indicated by ellipses (. . .). The notes indicate conjectures by other editors only where I have adopted their readings over Buchholz's. The notation "Moffat +" signals a conjecture that Moffat joins one or more other editors in adopting against Buchholz's text.

Fragment A

1 midden-earde: middenearde *Moffat+;* . . . enearde *W Buchholz;* 3 crefte þene: cre . . . ne *W* 4 isomnede: isom . . . *W* 7 greoneþ ond woaneþ: . . . eþ *W;* woaneþ *Moffat* 9 ond licame: . . . ame *W* 11 Deaþ: . . . eaþ *W* 12 oftesiþes: . . . iþes *W* 14 longe: . . . ge *W* 16 al is: al . . . *W* 17 dimmeþ þa: dimmeþe *W* 19 þe: . . . *W* 21 lime: . . . *W;* liche *Moffat;* muþ *Buchholz* 23 at also: . . . lso *W* 24 bodunge: . . . unge *W* 26 burdtid: . . . rdtid *W* 28 todæleþ: to . . . eþ *W* 30 feiȝe *Moffat+;* . . . ȝe *W Buchholz* 32 coldeþ *Moffat+;* . . . deþ *W Buchholz* 33 molde: mol . . . *W* 35 rihtliche: . . . tliche *W* 37 fleoþ: . . . *W* 38 wenden: wen . . . *W* 40 þene deade: þe . . . eade *W* agon *Moffat;* igon *Buchholz* 41 forhoweþ: . . . oweþ *W* 43 þonne *Moffat+;* . . . ne *W;* Ec *Buchholz* wrecche: riche *W* 44 þonne *Moffat+;* . . . nne *W;* inne *Buchholz* 45 lic-hame: lich . . . *W*

Fragment B

1 woa wrohtest: *only the bottoms of these letters are visible in W;* woa wrohtest *is Moffat's reconstruction; Buchholz and two others have conjectured* Hwui noldest beþenchen 2 unriht: u . . . riht *W* 4 þeo modinesse: þe . . . dinesse *W* 5 panewes *Moffat+;* . . . newes *W Buchholz* 7 nu: . . . *W* 8 nu: . . . *W* 9 þu: þ . . . *W* 10 þe sibbe þe seten *Moffat+;* þe seten *W Buchholz* 11 þet: . . . *W* 13 weren: . . . ren *W* 14 heo: . . . *W* 15 bringen: b . . . gen *W* 17 þu beþenchen: þ . . . þenchen *W* 18 forþon: fo . . . *W* 20 þu þe makien: þ . . . kien *W* 21 fore: fo . . . *W* 23 hore: . . . re *W* 24 leofliche: leofli . . . *W* 26 alesed: alese . . . *W* 28 were: we . . . *W*

29 deofles: de . . . *W*   31 *servus:* ser . . . *W*   33 dælen: d . . . *W*   35 Luþerliche: lu . . . liche *W*   36 soule weowe: soul . . . we *W*   38 þuncheþ: . . . cheþ *W*   39 beon: be . . . *W*   41 al þet þe wurþest: al . . . wurþest *W*   42 fulest alre holde *Hall;* fuweles quale holde *W;* fuweles qualeholde *Buchholz*   43 þære *Moffat+;* . . . *W;* kunde *Buchholz*   44 bittere: b . . . *W*   45 næffre: . . . *W*

Fragment C

1 þuncheþ: . . . heþ *W*   þet þu hire bilefdest: *the tops of the letters are missing; this reconstruction is Moffat's*   3 þearft: . . . rft *W*   4 scalt: . . . t *W*   6 utset: ut . . . t *W*7 sone: . . . e *W*   8 at: ac *W*   9 seggen: . . . gen *W*   11 nolde: . . . de *W*   12 gærsume on: gær . . . n *W*   14 weilawei: . . . lawei *W*   15 lif: . . . *W*   17 þe þu: . . . *W*   19 Deaþ: . . . þ *W*   20 salme-bec: salme . . . c *W*   22 ripe: rife *Moffat;* ri . . . e *W*   23 Noldest: . . . dest *W*   24 þine: . . . e *W*   25 wrecchen: wrec . . . n *W*   27 cneow: . . . ow *W*   28 wunien: . . . nien *W*   30 þe hele-wowes: . . . helewewes *W*   31 neih: . . . h *W*   33 senden: sen . . . *W*   35 onhorded heo *Moffat;* onhor . . . eo *W;* onhorded *Buchholz*   37 ageþ *Moffat;* . . . *W;* is *Buchholz*   39 þeo: . . . *W*   40 heom: . . . *W*   41 findeþ: fin . . . *W*   43 wurmes: wur . . . *W*   45 heo creopeþ *Moffat;* . . . reopeþ *W;* heo reoweþ *Buchholz*   46 þine wombe: þi . . . be *W*   48 lodliche: lod . . . *W*

Fragment D

1 þu scalt nu *Moffat+; no reconstruction in Buchholz*   wurmes: . . . mes *W*   3 þu: . . . *W*   4 god dælan: go . . . lan *W*   6 nulleþ: n . . . *W*   7 grennien on al: grennien o . . . *W;* grennien on men *Moffat, whose notes also consider* grennien on al; grinnien ond gristbitien *Buchholz*   9 efter þin: efte . . . *W*   11 heom þe *Moffat;* h . . . *W;* ham *Buchholz*   12 holi-watere: holiwatere *Moffat;* holi watere *Buchholz*   wowes *Moffat+;* w . . . *W;* wæde *Buchholz*   13 bletsien: blecsian *W*   14 beornen: b . . . *W*   16 reowliche: re . . . *W*   18 Wendest: . . . dest *W*   19 icoren: icore . . . *W*   21 þine eiȝen: þin . . . *W*   23 þine fore-fæderes: þinef . . . *with* ford *written above W;* þin forefæderes *Buchholz;* þine fordfæderes *Moffat*   25 iscend hore: isc . . . *W*

26 lic-hame: l . . . *W*   28 lufedest: lufede . . . *W*   29 Mid þine: . . . *W*
30 mihtest: mihte . . . *W*   31 Ic com: . . . *W*   33 Æfre: . . . *W*   34 hæfde:
hæ . . . *W*   36 was: . . . *W*   38 binumen: bi . . . men *W*   39 nefre habben:
nefr . . . ben *W*   40 biþ: bi . . . *W*   42 þin siþ: þ . . . *W*   44 longe þolede:
long . . . lede *W*   45 makedest: . . . *W*   47 were: . . . *W*   49 lahte his
hord: l . . . ord *W Buchholz;* leide his hord *Moffat* +

Fragment E

1 noldest: . . . est *W*   wille: . . . *W*   2 iwold: . . . ld *W*   4 eorþe ær: eor
. . . *W*   6 fule hold: fu . . . d *W*   8 deope: . . . *W*   10 of þære: . . . ære *W*
11 stille: stil . . . *W*   12 oþ *Moffat;* . . . *W;* Ac *Buchholz*   13 cumeþ: . . . eþ *W*
15 weren: . . . n *W*   17 ne dreame *Moffat;* . . . me *W;* heo none herunge ne
Buchholz   19 feole: . . . *W*   22 wel: . . . *W*   23 þe *Ricciardi;* he *W Buchholz*
drihten ful: drih . . . ul *W*   27 þet unker: . . . nker *W*   29 þet lut þeo *Mof-*
fat; . . . eo *W;* to him ne heo *Buchholz*   32 sculen: scu . . . *W*   33 from: . . .
rom *W*   34 hearde: . . . rde *W*   36 soriliche: . . . iche *W*   38 nu: . . . *W*
40 so hit *Moffat* +; . . . t *W;* so he hit *Buchholz*   42 soule: . . . ule *W*
44 Þonne: . . . ne *W*   45 drihtenes: . . . tenes *W*   47 siþien: si . . . *W*
49 æfre: . . . fre *W*   51 sculen: . . . n *W*   52 wuldre mest: wuld . . . *W*

Fragment F

2 *spiritum:* sp̄m *with the top of* s *and the suspension mark cut away Moffat;*
ipsum *Buchholz*   3 þu opnedest þin muþ: þu . . . *W;* þu . . . dest þin muþ
Moffat +; þu opnedest þin bon *Buchholz*   5 noldest þu: nold . . . *W*
6 woldest ham: wold . . . *W*   8 sunfulle: . . . le *W*   9 miltse onfoþ: milts
. . . foþ *W*   11 hore soule: hor . . . *W*   13 þearf ic: þe . . . *W*   14 forloren
þurh: forlor . . . *W*   15 miltse: milts . . . *W*   17 forbunden: forb . . . den *W*
19 reouliche þin: reoulic . . . *W*   20 sunnen *Moffat;* sunne . . . *W;* sunne
Buchholz   21 heo *Moffat;* . . . *W;* sunnen *Buchholz*   22 heo hine: he . . . *W*
24 piles prikien: pil . . . kien *W*   26 were: we . . . *W*   28 al þet: . . . *W*
29 touward: touwar . . . *W*   30 for: . . . *W*   31 ipined ful: ipin . . . *W*
33 sore all: so . . . *W*   sunne *Moffat;* synne *Buchholz*   35 seoueþe: se . . . *W*
37 wisliche: wisli . . . *W*   39 water ond: wate . . . *W;* water and *Moffat;* wa-

ter *Buchholz* 41 makunge: ma . . . *W* 43 þus: þ . . . *W* 45 iwurþe ond: iwu . . . *W* 47 þurh þene *Moffat;* þurh . . . þene *W;* þurh hit þene *Buchholz* 49 *ad imaginem:* . . . maginem *W* 50 onlicnesse: onlicn . . . *W*

Fragment G

1 þe . . . : þe . . . æ . . . e *W Moffat;* þe imæne *Buchholz* 2 þu woldest: . . . dest *W* 4 maþe-mete: maþe . . . te *W* 5 to helle *Moffat+;* . . . e *W;* inne helle *Buchholz* 7 ætwiten mine *Moffat+;* ætwi . . . ne *W;* ætwiten þe *Buchholz* 9 atruked þin *Moffat+;* atru . . . *W;* atrukied þin *Buchholz* 10 icwemde *Moffat;* icweme *W Buchholz* 11 domes: . . . *W* 13 gærsume: . . . me *W* 15 tunge: . . . e *W* 16 so: . . . *W* 17 for *Moffat;* . . . *W; no word supplied by Buchholz* 18 weren: . . . *W* 20 dolos: . . . *W* 21 ʒeoddede: ʒeo . . . de *W* 22 hunede *Moffat+;* . . . de *W;* chidde *Buchholz* 24 sunnen so: sun . . . *W* 26 unc þus idemed *Moffat;* unc . . . ed *W;* unc demed *Buchholz* 28 soriliche *Moffat;* . . . e *W;* wræcche soule *Buchholz* 30 ic toferde *Moffat;* . . . ferde *W;* ic forferde *Buchholz* 32 nouht unleþe: . . . nleþe *W* 34 so þeo: . . . *W* 36 so win-bowe: . . . *W;* so win-bowe *Moffat;* in wedde *Buchholz; see the note to the translation for this line* 38 fulluht: ful . . . *W* 40 mid þen: . . . en *W* 42 heih arerd *Moffat;* heih . . . *W;* heihmod *Buchholz* 44 beheten: . . . en *W* 46 mid rihtere: . . . ihtere *W* 47 cwide: cwi . . . *W* 48 his modes: . . . modes *W* 49 forlat *Johansen;* for . . . inne *W Moffat;* forlunne *Buchholz* 51 is forloren: . . . loren *W* 53 scoldest: . . . st *W* 54 bringen heom to: bring . . . o *W* 56 *novella olivarum*: nouell . . . *W;* nouella oliuarum [. . .] *Moffat;* nouellae oliarum in circuitu mensae suae *Buchholz*

The Grave

Manuscript: Oxford, Bodleian Library, Bodley 343, fol. 174r.

This edition: Adapted from Buchholz, *Fragmente der Reden der Seele,* 11; I have also consulted the text and notes by Ricciardi, "Grave-Bound Body," 185–91.

1 gebyld: gebyld *written a second time, then erased* 7 hus: hus hus *with second* hus *erased* 15 eorð-hus: *after this word the scribe wrote then erased and*

dæð hefð *(cf. line 14)*   19   hu: hu þe *I adopt Ricciardi's emendation*
23–25 *the final three verses have been added by a later thirteenth-century hand*

JUDGMENT DAY (I)

Manuscript: Exeter, Cathedral Library, 3501, fols. 115v–17v.

This edition: Adapted from Krapp and Dobbie, ASPR 3:212–15. I have also consulted the more recent edition by Muir, *Exeter Anthology* 1:331–35 (text) and 2:668–69 (commentary).

9 onæled: onhæled   14 gylpe: l *altered from an unidentifiable letter*
19 næfre: r *is written over an erasure*   23 bold: blod   28 onsægd: g *is writ-ten over an erasure*   29 dreogeð: eð *is written over an erasure*   30 ferð-gleaw: forð gleaw   31 heofona: *second* o *altered from* a   42 geworhtan: ge weorhtan *with second* e *marked for deletion*   51 byman: y *altered from* i
52 bið: ið *is written over an erasure*   nænges: *followed by an erased let-ter*   62 clænnisse: ni *are written over an erased letter*   64 hælend: hæ len-des *with* lendes *beginning a new line*   70 ful: fol   74 monegum: mon-gegum   75 gescaden: gesceaden *with second* e *marked for deletion*   88 sceal: e *is written over an erasure*   95 gehwylc: gewylc   99 lic: l *altered from* i
103 cyþan: cyþam   104 hyhst: hst *are written over an erasure*   hæleþa: hæle *at line end,* la *beginning the next line*

JUDGMENT DAY (II)

Manuscript: Cambridge, Corpus Christi College 201, pp. 161–65.

This edition: Adapted from Dobbie, ASPR 6:58–67. I have inserted ad-ditional paragraph breaks and incorporated some suggestions from the most recent edition and commentary by Caie, "*Judgement Day II.*" Unusual for an Old English poem, this one has a sort of title in the manuscript. Be-fore the opening verse, the scribe has written in capitals: *Incipit versus Bede presbiteri de die iudicii: Inter florigeras fecundi cespites* [sic] *herbas flamine vento-rum resonantibus undique ramis* ("Here begin the verses by Bede the priest concerning the day of judgment: *Inter florigeras*" etc. [the remaining Latin simply quotes the first two lines of the poem *De die iudicii*]). Likewise, at the end of the poem, the scribe inserts: *Her endað þeos boc þe hatte* Inter flo-rigeras, *þæt is on englisc "Betwyx blowende" þe to Godes rice farað and hu þa þrowiaþ þe to helle faraþ* ("Here ends this book that is called *Inter florigeras,* that is, in English, 'Between the blossoming,' who go to the kingdom of God, and how those who go to hell will suffer").

As noted in the Introduction, this poem supplied a substantial amount of material for a composite eleventh-century homily, now Homily XXIX as printed in Napier, *Wulfstan,* 134–43. On the relation of *Judgment Day (II)* and perhaps the adjacent poem in the manuscript, *The Rewards of Piety,* to the anonymous homilies, see Whitbread, "'Wulfstan' Homilies" 348–56. For the most detailed study of the relationship between the poem and homily, now see Ogawa, *Language and Style,* 110–23.

13 laðan: langan; *see the notes to the translation* 23 yfel: yfes 28 of: os 45 wope: wopa 47 aglidene mod: Aglidene gyltas. mod god; *see the notes to the translation* 50 wan-hydige mod: wan hydig gemod; *see the notes to the translation* 51 flæcses: flæsces 63 and in: 7 n *with* i *added above the line before* n 66 cyþst: cysth 94 hu egeslice: hit egeslic 101 hliðu: hlida 109 nanre: *first two letters altered from* m 112 tacn: *not in the manuscript; see the notes to the translation* 125 hergea mæst: he *followed by an erasure of five or six letters; the restoration comes from Napier Homily XXIX* 127 swegles: sweges 129 Þænne: æne 130 eorð-buendra: eorbuen-dra 131 feded: fedend 140 scræfum: scræfe *with* e *marked for deletion and* ū *written above* 149 Eal: Eeal 152 blaweð: blawað 154 gefremme: gefremede 155 wrecenda: wreceda *with* n *added above* bryne: brynæ *with the* a *of the ligature marked for deletion* 157 afeormad: d *altered from* n 170 be agnum: bearnū 174 astifad: astifed *with* e *marked for deletion and* a *written above* 178 nu þu þe: þe *not in the manuscript, supplied by Dobbie* þeowast: þeowest *with second* e *marked for deletion and* a *written above* þissere worulde: *not in the manuscript; see the notes to the transla-tion* 187 areccan: areccen *with second* e *marked for deletion and* a *written above* 189 fule: *see notes to the translation* 197 earm-sceapene: earm sceape 200 þrosme: þrosmes 201 stefn: stef ne 208 unstences: un stence 209 wanigendan: wani gendran *with* r *marked for deletion* 215 fyrngende: fyrgende 222 wependra: wera 226 ac þær: þæt *(abbre-viated)* 227 grist-bigtung: grisgbigtung 229 adl: eald 230 synnge: synne 233 gewitað: gegitað *with the second* g *marked for deletion and* w *writ-ten above* 239 scyndan: scyndum *with* u *marked for deletion and* a *written*

above þonne: þone   244 leofest: leofes   248 wihta: wiht na   250 witu: witū   252 þonne: þone *with additional* n *written above the line*   253 heofonrice: hofonrice *with* e *added above the line between* h *and* o   254 genimð: genipð þeostrum: þeostra   265 snawe: swa se   267 ænigu: nænigu   271 geþwærnes: ge hwærnes *with* þ *inserted after* h *by a later hand*   275 geblyssað: geblysað   277 lufað: lifað   278 geregnað: gerinnað   283 þreatum: þreapū   288 rosena: rosene   290 þæra: þære *with* e *marked for deletion and* a *written above*   291 beorhtost: beortost   298 suna: sunu; *see the notes to the translation*

Epilogue: A Lament for the English Church

Manuscript: Worcester, Cathedral Library, F. 174, fol. 63r.

This edition: Adapted from Hall, *Selections from Early Middle English* 1:1 (text) and 2:225–28 (commentary). I have also consulted Dickins and Wilson, *Early Middle English Texts,* 1–2 (text) and 151–52 (commentary). For the lineation of the text as verse, I have adopted many suggestions from the more recent study by Brehe ("Reassembling the First Worcester Fragment," esp. 530–31). I retain the traditional distinction between this poem and the remaining matter preserved among the Worcester Fragments, namely *The Soul's Address to the Body* (see the text and notes in this volume). It has been suggested, however, that the present *Lament for the English Church* (also called "The First Worcester Fragment," "St. Bede's Lament," and various other titles) originally served as a prologue to the soul-and-body material; for this view, see most recently Johansen, "Cohesion of the Worcester Fragments." At many places in the manuscript, letters are missing or illegible (see the notes to the text for *The Soul's Address to the Body,* above). Those missing or damaged letters, of whatever extent, are indicated by ellipses (. . .) below.

1 Sanctus: anctus   2 bec: *not in the manuscript; Dickins-Wilson and Brehe supply* bec; *Hall suggests* writen   3 englise: englisc *Hall*   4 cnoten: c . . . ten   5 deor-wurþe: de . . . wurþe   7 fif: *not in the manuscript; supplied by all editors*   9 þurh: þu . . .   10 biscopes þeo: biscop . . .   11 Ripum: Sipum   12 Cuþbert: Cuþb . . .   15 Paulin: . . . lin   Dunston ond Ælfeih: s. Dunston ond s. Ælfeih   16 lærden: læ . . .   17 nu is: *not in the manuscript*   18 læreþ: lær . . .   20 ure: *not in the manuscript*   21 eos volitat:

e... 24 feþren: feþ...; *see the notes to the translation*   festen to him: *not in the manuscript*

APPENDIX A

Manuscripts: Cambridge, Corpus Christi College 201, pp. 78–80 (siglum C). Closely related versions of this eleventh-century composite homily are also found in London, British Library, Cotton Cleopatra B. xiii, fols. 2r–7v (siglum N); Oxford, Bodleian Library, Hatton 114, fols. 1r–4v (siglum H); and, with an altogether different ending for the piece, Cambridge, Corpus Christi College 419, pp. 182–204 (siglum B). The homily has been edited from N, collated with the three other manuscripts, by Napier, *Wulfstan,* 182–90 (his Homily XL); and more recently by Scragg, *Vercelli Homilies,* 53–65 (rectos), from B and H (Scragg's sigla N and O). The material common to all these versions of the composite homily appears in the earlier Vercelli Homily II (siglum V₁), a large portion of which was also incorporated into a different Vercelli Homily (no. XXI, siglum V₂), which happens to contain still more embedded verse from different sources. The ties among all these versions pose extremely complex questions that cannot be entered into here; readers seeking more detail should consult Scragg, *Vercelli Homilies,* 48–49, Wright, "More Old English Poetry," 250–51, and now the detailed discussion by Ogawa, *Language and Style,* 65–79 and 88–102.

This edition: Adapted from Stanley, "*Judgement of the Damned,*" 360–68, and following his lineation of the verse passages. I have expanded tironian *et* as Old English *and,* inserted paragraph breaks, and added section numbers. In the following apparatus, variants from the several related anonymous homilies are not reported unless they furnish an emendation of C or provide a very plausible alternative. More complete apparatus are available in Napier, *Wulfstan,* 182–90, and Scragg, *Vercelli Homilies,* 53–63 (rectos).

2.1 woh-gestreonum *B H N;* woh-gestreones *C*   3.1 sceatum *B H N;* sceattum *V₁;* sceaftum *C*   3.2 endebirdnessum: *corr. from* endebirdnesse *C*   4.1 him to in: hig in to *C;* him to *B H;* to *N*   4.2 deofle *N;* deoflum *B C H*   5.1 þonne þam *B H N;* þon þam *with possible erasure over the* n   6 scamigenne: smeagenne *B H;* smeagende *N*   8.2 eal-wihtna: eall-wihtna *V₁ V₂;* hell-wihta *B,* hel-wihta *H N; see the notes to the translation*   þistra storm:

þystra storm *V₁ V₂;* þeostra þrosm *B H N*   8.3 gewiscan: *corr. from* geswican *C*   9.2 leger *V₁ V₂ C;* leger-bed *B H N*   9.3 fyrenum bryne *B H N;* syrenum bryne *C*   10.3 nære wurðe: nære wyrðe *H;* wære wurðe *C*   lufode: ne lufode *with* ne *inserted above by a different hand C*   rice *H N; omitted C*

Appendix B

Manuscripts: Oxford, Bodleian Library, Junius 121, fols. 42r–55v (siglum J). The prose sections and one of the poems *(The Gloria patri (I))* are also found in Cambridge, Corpus Christi College 201 (siglum C), pp. 112–14 and 167–60, respectively.

This edition: Adapted from Ure, *Benedictine Office,* 81–102. I have inserted section numbers, additional paragraph breaks, and countless small changes of formatting and punctuation. A very extensive apparatus would be necessary to report all variant readings for those parts of the text with multiple manuscript witnesses, namely the prose passages and the metrical psalm verses. (The poems *The Gloria patri (I), The Lord's Prayer (III),* and *The Apostles' Creed* have their full apparatus elsewhere in this volume.) Ure's edition gives a detailed account of these variants, and the overwhelming majority of them are not substantial, having usually to do with minor differences of spelling or small additions, omissions, and transpositions of words that do not affect the overall sense. For instance, the Latin titles to the prose passages differ in J and C, and the two manuscripts also often differ slightly in the amount of Latin they quote as incipits, or in the way they truncate those quotations (such as *et cetera* against *et reliqua*). Sometimes the prose passages in C introduce Old English translations of Latin with *þæt is on englisc* where J has only *þæt is.* For the purposes of the present edition, it has not seemed worthwhile to report such differences as these, for which interested readers may simply consult Ure's apparatus. The main purpose of the notes below, then, is simply to report where the printed text departs from J or has adopted a reading from corresponding parts of C or *The Paris Psalter* (= P) over that of J, or where a few substantial variants in C or P seem worthy of note.

For the Latin texts of the hymns (at §§ 3.3, 5.5, 6.4, 7.3, 8.7, 9.4), I have based the editions on those in Milfull, *Hymns,* with various adjustments of spelling and punctuation. For the terminations of the prayers (at §§ 4.2,

5.13, 6.8, 7.7, 8.12, 9.9), I have simply used the standard modern formulas of the Roman liturgy. There is no way to be certain that these were precisely the ones intended by the compiler, but they are probably not too far off.

1 et: *omitted J* 1.4 cunnon: *C adds* Amen 2.1 fultum: fultum æt neode *C* 3.3 *Iam:* am *J* 3.6 *fili:* filii *J* 3.10 þæt ðe: þætte *P* 3.14 *Intende:* ntende *J* 3.16 ætstande: ætstande *J* 3.17 stapas: stapa *J* 3.23 *frameam:* framea *J* 3.26 min: mi *J* 3.28 ðinne: ðinre *J* 3.29 niþe: *corrected from* in þe *J* 3.30 lungre *P;* luge *J* 3.31 *viris:* uiri *J* 3.32 þæt ic *P;* ic *omitted J* 3.37 Se: He *P* 3.39 *Confiteor: first letter erased J* 3.41 *peccato:* peccata *J* 3.42 *Miserere nostri, domine, miserere nostri: omitted J; see notes to the translation.* 3.44 drihten cyng: drihten god *with* cyng *written above the second word in a different hand J* 3.45 yrfe: yrre *J* wynnum: synnum *J* 3.47 heofones *P;* heofonas *J* 4.2 *vivit et regnat:* uiuis et regnas *J* 4.3 drihten me: me drihten *J* 4.5 Geseoh þine: Beseoh on þine *P* 4.6 *sit:* si *J Gloria:* loria *J* 5 *tertie:* iii^{tio} *J* 5.2 gereorda: *corrected from* gereorde *J* 6.4 *Hymnus:* ymnus *J* 6.5 *Capitulum:* capitula *J* 7 *Ad nonam:* Ad ix *J* 7.3 *Hymnus:* ymnus *J* 7.6 *Kyrrieleison (2nd):* Kyrrie *with no abbreviation mark J* 8.2 þurh halig: þurh alig *J* of rode: *one letter erased before* rode *(correction from* offrode?*) J* 8.6 *The abbreviations V(ersiculum) and R(esponsum) are reversed.* 9 completorium: completorio *J* 9.5 *before the capitulum, an abbreviation that might be expanded* in noctem *(thus Ure) or* in nocturnam? 9.7 *Kyrrieleison. Christeleison. Kyrieleison:* yrrieleison risteleison yrieleison *J* 9.9 *per [Christum etc.]:* per eundem *J* 10.1 and andette drihtenes doma rihtwisnesse *C;* et cetera *J* 11.1 to Gode georne *C; omitted J* 11.2 *aliud quid:* aliquid qui *J* 11.4 God þe gesceop: drihtenes naman gelang þe gescop *C* gesceafta: *C ends here, adding* Amen

Notes to the Translations

The following notes are keyed to line or section numbers in the Old English texts. As a help to the reader, comments here usually begin by quoting a portion of the lines under discussion. Quotations for that purpose may employ ellipses to save space; such ellipses should not be confused with ones used elsewhere in the book to indicate actual gaps in the texts. For other remarks on the translations generally, see the Introduction, xxxv–xxxvi.

The Panther

I have consulted translations by Gordon, *Anglo-Saxon Poetry,* 252–53, and Bradley, *Anglo-Saxon Poetry,* 352–55.

20b–30a "Just as men with sainted souls recount that Joseph's tunic" etc. (*Swa hæleð secgað, / gæst-halge guman, þætte Iosephes tunece* etc.): Cf. Genesis 37:3. The coat of many colors is a minor detail in the biblical source (see also Genesis 37:23 and 31–33) and is only briefly alluded to in one of the Latin versions (Y) of the *Physiologus* (see Squires, *Old English Physiologus,* 21 and 102).

69–74 "Thus did the wise man, Saint Paul, say" etc. (*Swa se snottra gecwæð sanctus Paulus* etc.): Though introduced as if a quotation, the lines that follow do not closely translate any verses from the Pauline epistles. To judge from the Y-Recension of the Latin *Physiologus,* the poet may have encountered at this point in his

375

source a combination of Ephesians 3:10 and Galatians 5:22–23, introduced by the tag *Sicut apostolus Paulus dixit* (Squires, *Old English Physiologus,* 102–3, though her commentary at 68 suggests that Ephesians 2:7–9 is the intended echo). The evidence of these Latin analogues apart, the poet may also be recalling 1 Corinthians 12:1–31.

The Whale

I have consulted translations by Gordon, *Anglo-Saxon Poetry,* 254–55, and Bradley, *Anglo-Saxon Poetry,* 355–57.

7b   "*Fastitocalon*": A corruption of Greek ἀσπιδοχελώνη "tortoise shell (?)" or perhaps, by folk-etymology, "poisonous tortoise." As Squires observes (*Old English Physiologus,* 71), it seems probable that the word was etymologically opaque to the Old English poet and was simply taken on faith from a version of the Latin *Physiologus.*

13a   "tether" *(gehydað):* The meaning of the Old English is disputed. My translation follows the current consensus that this verb is related to the noun *hȳd* ("hide, skin"). Some early editors plausibly suggested emending to *gehȳðað* ("they harbor").

15a   "tie" *(sælað):* For *setlað* in the manuscript, I accept the emendation first proposed by Cook and adopted by both Squires and Muir. The manuscript reading does, however, yield acceptable sense ("they bring their vessels to rest") and is retained by Krapp and Dobbie. The emendation, on the other hand, works nicely with the kenning *sæ-mearas* ("sea horses") [= ships] in the same half-line; cf. *yð-mearas* ("horses of the waves") at line 49a.

28a   "with that vessel" *(mid þa nowe):* The manuscript has *mid þa noþe.* Because a rare noun *nōþ* does occur once in the sense "boldness, audacity," Krapp and Dobbie take the present form as adverbial instrumental "boldly," a view that Muir seems to endorse (*Exeter Anthology* 2:586). Other suggested definitions include "catch, booty?" (Grein and Köhler, *Sprachschatz der angelsächsischen Dichter,* 509, s.v. *nōð,* sense 2), which suits the context but has no substantial basis. I follow Squires, who emends to *nowe* ("ship, ocean vessel"), a reading proposed by Meritt (*Fact and Lore,* 29–30; see Squires's commentary in *Old English Physiologus,* 80–81).

37a "with those oath breakers" *(æt þam wær-logan):* Other possible translations include "from" instead of "with" (cf. *DOE,* s.v. *æt,* Prep. and Adv., sense I.D.4); and "oath breaker" (singular).

40b–41a "fixed securely to his back" *(on his hricge biþ/fæste gefeged):* The manuscript has *on his hringe* etc., literally "on his ring." All recent editors defend the manuscript by noting that *hring* may refer to a link of chain or, figuratively, to a "circle" or limit of jurisdiction (Squires, *Old English Physiologus,* 4; Muir, *Exeter Anthology* 2:587). Even so, I adopt the emendation *hricge,* first proposed by Cosijn ("Anglosaxonica IV," 127), since "back" is obviously suitable in context. The chief objection—that the devil, not the whale, is being described at this point—can be answered by the corresponding image in line 73 where sinners "cling to" the devil *(him on cleofiað).*

49a "horses of the waves" *(yð-mearas):* I.e., ships (cf. *sæ-mearas* at line 15a, above). This type of compact, riddling metaphor, known as a kenning, was a traditional feature of Old English poetry.

50a "water traveler" *(wæter-þisa):* Literally, something that moves quickly or forcefully through the water. This and related compounds in *-þisa* more commonly refer to ships.

70a "in violation of the soul's due" *(ofer ferhð-gereaht):* The meaning of the Old English phrase is debated; my translation follows the interpretation suggested by Krapp and Dobbie in ASPR 3:316–17, and by the *DOE,* s.v. *ferhþ-geriht.*

82b Although there is no physical damage to the manuscript at this point, a break in the sense and alliteration suggests loss of at least one and a half lines.

THE PARTRIDGE

1b "concerning a certain bird" *(bi sumum fugle):* The identification of the "certain bird" as a partridge is a reasonable inference but nothing more. In the Latin and Greek sources, the partridge usurps other birds' nests and attempts to raise others' young as its own; the hatchlings, however, sensing instinctively that the partridge is not a true parent, abandon it and seek out their real parents as soon as they can fly. The *Physiologus* allegorizes the partridge as the devil and the hatchlings as Christians who, recognizing the devil's false claims, abandon him and seek out God, their true parent. The theory that this poem concerned a partridge requires that the now missing folio after 97v developed an allegory more or less in the vein just described, then concluded (where the text resumes on fol. 98r, or lines 3–16 of the edition) with a biblical exhortation that Christians return to God as his true children (see notes for lines 4–11, below). Of course, this theory depends on the assumption that verses at the bottom of fol. 97v and the top of 98r preserve opening and closing fragments of a single poem—a view now rejected by Conner and Muir (see the notes to the text). In light of those doubts, other scholars have also reopened the question of whether the "certain bird" is a partridge at all (Drout, "'The Partridge' is a Phoenix;" but cf. the rebuttal by Pakis, "Defense of 'The Partridge'").

4–11   "the word that the Lord of glory has spoken" etc. (*þæt word þe gecwæð wuldres ealdor* etc.): Though presented as if a direct quotation, the following lines have no single biblical source. Some of the identified echoes include Isaiah 55:7, Ezekiel 33:12, and 2 Corinthians 6:18, but the ideas of God's merciful "turning" toward human beings and counting them as his children and "brethren" to one another could have come from many places in the scriptures. For a full analysis of the biblical echoes and their suitability as a conclusion to the allegory of the partridge, see Biggs, "Eschatological Conclusion."

THE PHOENIX

My debts to the commentary in Blake, *The Phoenix*, are extensive. Among the many available translations of this poem, I have consulted Gordon, *Anglo-Saxon Poetry*, 239–51, and Bradley, *Anglo-Saxon Poetry*, 284–301. On the legends of the phoenix and the relation of this poem to Lactantius's *De ave phoenice* and other sources, see the Introduction.

3b–4   "inaccessible to many" etc. (*Nis . . . mongum gefere* etc.): The detail may be taken at face value or as an example of the kind of understatement that is frequent in Old English verse. On the latter reading, the poet means that the place is accessible to *no* human beings. Compare lines 491–92, below, where "many from the race of men" (*monge . . . fyra cynnes*) must mean *all* human beings who have ever lived.

9a   "that isolated land" (*þæt ig-lond*): Literally "island," but later (lines 28–32) the poet clarifies that this earthly Paradise is a kind of plateau higher than the tallest mountains on earth. It is unclear whether the poet envisions the place as literally surrounded by water at all times, and not just during the great flood of Genesis (see lines 41b–46). Some pre-Christian traditions did imagine the earthly Paradise as an island or group of islands.

12   "the celebration of singing voices, a door to the heavenly kingdom" (*hleoþra wyn, heofon-rices duru*): The image of Paradise as a doorway to heaven comes from the Latin source (*De ave phoenice* 2). The poet's yoking of that image to the joyful sound of voices strikes most readers as odd. If a textual corruption is not responsible for the awkward apposition, I would incline to follow Blake's suggestion (*The Phoenix,* 65) that the voices are those of angels (cf. lines 615–37).

35a   "splendid yields" (*beorhte blede*): The Old English noun *bled* (sometimes spelled *blæd*) may refer to "fruit" in the strict sense of edible, seed-bearing produce, but it may also refer to harvested food more generally, as well as to inedible things that plants yield (leaves, foliage, twigs, shoots, blades); see *DOE,* s.v. *blēd, blǣd.* Throughout the poem, I also translate the word as "fruit(s)" or "leaves, foliage" as context seems to warrant, but the determination is sometimes hard to make, as in lines 38, 71, 194 (in the compound *wudu-bleda*), 207, 402, and 466.

41b–46   "When a surge of water" etc. (*Swa iu wætres þrym* etc.): I.e., the great flood described in Genesis 7–8. For the height of the flood waters, see Genesis 7: 18–20.

72b–80a   While the general sense is clear, editors have punctuated and emended these lines in many different ways. My treatment, beginning a new sentence at 72b but not at 74a, follows Blake instead of Krapp and Dobbie.

137b   "nor the swan's feather" *(ne swanes feðre):* At this point the Latin source refers only to a commonplace idea that swans *sing* a beautiful song as they die *(De ave phoenice* 49). The belief that swans in flight produced beautiful music with their feathers is more unusual, but it does inform one of the Old English riddles (Krapp and Dobbie's *Riddle* 7, at ASPR 3:184–85).

166b   "the land of the Syrians" *(Syr-wara lond):* The poet has omitted or altered other details of the phoenix's itinerary in the Latin source, but the reference to Syria is retained. As pointed out by Hill ("*Syrwarena lond*"), a medieval reader would probably have understood by "Syria" a large region of the Near East that included the Holy Land and Jerusalem, the site of Jesus's resurrection.

173b–74   "people on earth call it a phoenix tree, after the name of the bird" *(þone hatað men/fenix on foldan, of þæs fugles noman):* I.e., Greek φοῖνιξ "date palm." As Blake notes *(The Phoenix,* 71), the claim that the tree is named after the bird, and not vice versa, is rare in phoenix lore and comes directly from the Latin source *(De ave phoenice* 70).

179b–81   "nothing at all harmful can injure it by acts of malice" etc. *(ne mæg him bitres wiht/scyldum sceððan* etc.): Blake punctuates this as a new sentence and agrees with other critics who assert that the thing which cannot be harmed here (i.e., the antecedent of *him*) is the bird, not the tree. But the Latin source, *De ave phoenice,* lines 71–72, was probably understood as referring to the tree at this point: *in quam* [sc. *palmam*] *nulla nocens animans prorepere possit,/lubricus aut serpens aut avis ulla rapax* ("into which [palm tree] no harmful creature can creep, neither the slippery snake nor any greedy bird").

194a   "pleasant spices" *(wyrta wynsume):* At its first appearance in the poem (line 172), Old English *wyrt* means "root," but in the present line and hereafter the noun always refers to the fragrant roots, shoots, leaves, or herbs that the phoenix gathers for building its nest (cf. lines 196, 213, 265, 273, 430, 465, 474, 529, and 653;

cf. also the participle *gewyrtad* in 543). For this sense, no single word in Modern English is an entirely adequate translation; I have settled on "spice(s)" or "fragrant plant(s)" in most instances.

240b   "its roasted flesh" *(bræd):* My translation follows the *DOE,* s.v. *bræde, bræd,* sense 2, in taking *bræd* as related to the noun that literally means "cooked meat." Another possibility raised by Griffith ("Old English *bræd"*) is to take the form here as a perfect passive participle of the verb *brædan* "to spread, grow"; thus he translates lines 240b–41, "Then he is grown all anew, born again" etc. Lindström ("*The Phoenix"*) proposes emending to *blæd* in the sense "breath, animating spirit."

242b–57a   "rather in the way that . . ." etc. *(sumes onlice* etc.): The elaborate agricultural metaphor that follows is a good example of the poet's expansive tendencies; the Latin *(De ave phoenice* 100) merely says that the phoenix's ashy remains are *seminis instar* ("in the form of a seed"). The Christian symbolism depends on verses such as John 12:24 and 1 Corinthians 15:36–38. Blake's commentary (*The Phoenix,* 74) offers selected patristic analogues.

260b   "sweet dew" *(mele-deawes):* Literally "honeydew," a "sweet sticky substance found on the leaves and stems of trees and plants, held to be excreted by aphides: formerly imagined to be in origin akin to dew" (from the *Oxford English Dictionary* online; there see also *mildew,* n., sense 1).

285a   "adding ash to ashes" *(ascan to eacan):* Literally, "as an increase to ash"; see *DOE,* s.v. *ēaca,* senses 1.a–b. Blake, Muir, and others regard *to eacan* as adverbial and construe the phrase as a continuation of *ban gebringeð* in line 283a, hence translating "brings the bones . . . and the ashes in addition."

287a   "in that isolated land" *(on þam ea-londe):* As at line 9, the translation here again hedges the question of whether the poet imagines Paradise to be a literal island.

308b   "the crest above" *(se scyld ufan):* I follow Blake's interpretation, but the meaning of the Old English term *scyld* in the present context is uncertain.

355b–60   "Only God, the almighty king, knows what the bird's sex is" etc.

(*God ana wat,/cyning ælmihtig, hu his gecynde bið* etc.): Readers of the Old English poem are hardly prepared for this strange comment. The transition is less abrupt in the Latin source, where the pertinent lines are the climax of that poem in which the phoenix is praised as an emblem of virginal procreation, a special sign of God's favor (*De ave phoenice* 161–70). The Anglo-Saxon version obscures the point by awkwardly dividing the corresponding Old English lines into two separate sections (as lines 355b–60 and 374b–80). As a result, the initial remark about the phoenix's sex is logically stranded; I have punctuated it as a parenthetical.

376 "the inheritor, in turn, of an ancient heirloom" (*eft yrfe-weard ealdre lafe*): I.e., the remains of the burned phoenix itself. The Old English word *laf* literally means "remnant, what is left behind, relic." Cf. lines 267b–74a, especially at 273a, where the remains are also called *wæl-reaf* ("spoils of battle").

393–417a These lines briefly recount from Genesis 2–3 the fall of Adam and Eve and their loss of Paradise.

397a "*neorxna-wong*": This is a widely attested Old English translation of *paradisus* ("paradise"). The second element of the compound is usually understood to be *wang* ("plain, field, place, land"). There is much debate but no consensus about the etymology of the strange-looking first constituent, *neorx(e)na-*. For a summary of views, see Brown, "Neorxnawang."

407b "busy teeth" (*toþas idge*): A notorious crux. For want of a better solution I follow the interpretation in Blake's commentary (*The Phoenix*, 80). For further discussion and yet another possible fix, see Bammesberger, "Old English *Phoenix*, l. 407b."

420b–21 "until the king of glory . . . by his coming forth to meet the saints" (*oþþæt wuldor-cyning/þurh his hider-cyme halgum togeanes*): I.e., until Christ's harrowing of hell, which was believed to have taken place between the crucifixion and resurrection. The "saints" mentioned are presumably the patriarchs, prophets, and other righteous who had died before Christ's resurrection and therefore could not enter heaven until Christ rescued them from hell.

450b   "in the time of danger" *(on þa frecnan tid):* I.e., at Judgment Day;
        see Blake, *The Phoenix,* 81, whose interpretation I follow. Krapp
        and Dobbie emend to *on þas frecnan tid* ("at this perilous time"),
        i.e., in the present life.

506b   "red gold": The phrase *æpplede gold* occurs only three times in
        surviving Old English poems (never in prose). Its precise mean-
        ing is unknown. Some scholars take it as a color term, "red,
        ruddy" (a quality that Anglo-Saxons often associated with gold),
        while others infer the meaning "spherical" or "round." The as-
        sumption in either case is that the adjective is related to the
        noun *æppel* ("apple, sphere").

548b–69 "Listen to the prophecy of Job's verses" etc. *(Gehyrað wite-
        dom / Iobes gieddinga* etc.): What follows is an elaborated para-
        phrase of Job 29:18: "I shall die in my nest, and as a palm tree
        shall multiply my days." While the verse does not actually men-
        tion the legendary bird, the link was possible because of the ref-
        erence to the palm, the Greek name for which, *phoenix,* was fa-
        miliar to the poet (see lines 171–74, with the note to 173b–74).
        Medieval commentaries on this particular verse from Job, how-
        ever, do not often relate the palm tree to the bird; see Blake, *The
        Phoenix,* 21; Pulsiano, "*The Phoenix*" 5–6.

587   "the righteous sun" *(seo soþfæste sunne):* From Malachi 4:2, widely
        interpreted as an epithet for Christ, the "Sun of Righteous-
        ness."

598b–601 "the work of every inhabitant shines brightly like the sun" etc.
        (Weorc anra gehwæs beorhte bliceð . . . sunnan gelice): Cf. Ecclesiasti-
        cus 17:16.

622–24 "'Peace and wisdom be yours, O true God'" etc. ("*Sib si þe, soð
        God, ond snyttru-cræft*" etc.): Cf. Apocalypse 7:11–12.

625–29 "'Great, boundless'" etc. ("*Micel, unmæte*" etc.): Cf. Apocalypse
        4:8, although the paraphrase in the following lines is perhaps
        closer to the Old Testament source of that verse, namely Isaiah
        6:3, or to the adaptation of the latter in the Mass-chant known
        as the *Sanctus.*

667–77 The macaronic verses that conclude the poem are unusually well
        executed, since the b-verses occasionally satisfy demands of

both vernacular alliterative and Latin quantitative meter; see Milfull, "Formen und Inhalte," 481–84.

The Lord's Prayer (I)

7a–8a   "our lasting bread" *(hlaf userne . . . þone singalan):* The Latin text of the prayer asks only for "our daily bread" *(panem nostrum quotidianum);* the Old English adjective *singalan* conveys the sense "continuing, enduring" but perhaps also "perpetual, everlasting." If the latter is meant, the poet may be recalling John 6:49–52 and 55–59.

The Lord's Prayer (II)

7   The line is metrically deficient, but there is no gap in sense; cf. line 78.

15–19   "'Holy, holy are you'" etc. (*"Halig eart þu, halig"* etc.): These lines render very loosely the fixed chant from the Mass known as the *Sanctus:* "Holy, holy, holy Lord God of hosts, heaven and earth are full of your glory; Hosanna in the highest! Blessed is he who comes in the name of the Lord; Hosanna in the highest!" Drawn from two passages of scripture, Isaiah 6:3 and Matthew 21:9, the *Sanctus* has been part of the Christian Eucharistic liturgy since the later fourth century.

22b–23a   "in many tongues, seventy-two in number" *(manegum gereordum, / twa and hund-seofontig):* The belief that all the world's languages totaled seventy-two was an old and enduring commonplace, the symbolic appeal of that number being reinforced by the total of seventy-two disciples sent out by Christ (see Luke 10:1–20) and of seventy-two books in the Bible. The topos of seventy-two peoples and seventy-two languages appears widely in Old English writings, including works attributed to King Alfred (d. 899), sermons by Ælfric of Eynsham (d. ca. 1010) and other homilists, the prose *Solomon and Saturn* dialogue, and other texts. See Sauer, "Die 72 Völker und Sprachen."

26–29   "they honor your works" etc. (*Þa wurþiað þin weorc* etc.): Perhaps compare Psalm 66 (Vulgate 65):1–8, inviting "all the earth" and the "gentiles" to join in praising God. For the poet's remark that non-Christians could naturally (*þurh gecynd,* line 27) attain to knowledge of God, cf. Romans 1:19–20.

34–35   "where we will encounter peace and love together, brightness for our eyes and all delight" (*þar we sibbe and lufe samod gemetað, / eagena beorhtnysse and ealle mirhðe):* The manuscript has nominatives *sib and lufu . . . beorhtnys,* all emended by Dobbie to yield accusative objects for *we . . . gemetað.* It is tempting to adopt the more economical solution, proposed in Ure's edition, of emending *þar we* to *þar þe,* making the following nouns the subjects of *gemetað.* In that case, translate "where peace and love come together" etc., perhaps intending to echo Psalm 85:10 (Vulgate 84:11).

35a   "brightness for our eyes" (*eagena beorhtnysse):* Perhaps cf. Job 11:17–19, which links the ideas of brightness and consoling safety.

66b   "exalted emperor" (*heah casere):* In surviving Old English texts, the loanword *casere* ("emperor," from Latin *caesar*) is only rarely applied to God; in addition to the present instance, see *The Phoenix,* line 634b.

78   A half-line of text may have dropped out here, though there is no gap in sense; cf. line 7.

91–92   "and commend our souls into your own hand" (*and þe betæcan . . . sawle ure on þines silfes hand):* Cf. Christ's dying words on the cross at Luke 23:46, quoting Psalm 31:5 (Vulgate 30:6).

110   "while our powers were greatest" (*þa hwile þe ure mihta mæste wæron):* I.e., the powers to choose and act belong only to the living; after death, the body and soul can only passively suffer the consequences of those choices.

132–33a   "In one of your hands you might easily hold the entire world" (*Þu miht on anre hand eaðe befealdan / ealne middan-eard):* Here by "world" may be meant the whole cosmos; cf. Isaiah 40:12.

134–37   "*Amen.* / May it be as you" etc. (*Amen. Sy swa þu* etc.): The optative expression *sy swa* ("may it be so") and variations thereon appear frequently as literal translations of Hebrew "Amen"; see

Keefer, "In Closing," 211–21, and cf. line 57 of *The Gloria patri (I)*, and lines 46–47 of *The Lord's Prayer (III)*.

THE LORD'S PRAYER (III)

I have consulted the translation by Bradley, *Anglo-Saxon Poetry*, 539–41.

20b–23   "our bread . . . that is Christ the pure, the Lord God" *(hlaf urne . . . þæt is se clæna Crist, drihten God):* Cf. John 6:41.

46–47   *"Amen:* So let it be" *(Amen: Weorðe þæt):* The poet is aware of the literal meaning of the Hebrew "Amen"; see *The Lord's Prayer (II)*, lines 134–37, and the note to the translation there.

THE APOSTLES' CREED

I have consulted Bradley's translation in *Anglo-Saxon Poetry*, 541–43.

8–9   "you both made the depths of the sea and know the number of the brilliant stars" *(ðu gar-secges grundas geworhtest, / and þu ða menegu canst mærra tungla):* Cf. Proverbs 8:27–29; Psalm 147 (Vulgate 146):4.

10–26   "*And in Jesus Christ, his only Son, our Lord*" etc. *(Et in Iesum Christum filium eius unicum, dominum nostrum* etc.): The following section (lines 11–26) expansively paraphrases not only the Latin clause given from the Apostles' Creed but the two that follow in the source: "who was conceived by the Holy Spirit, [and] born of the Virgin Mary."

17b–18   "conceived you, her own Father, as a child within her breast" *(and ðe fæder sylfne / under breost-cofan bearn acende):* Discussions of Christ's incarnation often invoked the paradox that the creature gave birth to her own creator, the daughter to her Father-maker. As I take it, *sylfne* is simply emphatic and so does not imply any unorthodox view that Mary gave birth to "the Father himself," i.e., the first person of the Trinity. Reference to the breast or chest cavity *(breost-cofa)* as the seat of conception is unusual and may simply be a poetic metonymy for "womb;" see *DOE*, s.v. *brēost-cofa*, sense 2.

27–35   "*Who suffered under Pontius Pilate*" etc. (*Passus sub Pontio Pilato* etc.): The following lines also paraphrase the continuation in the Latin source: "was crucified, died, and was buried. He descended into hell."

28   "Pilate the Pontian" (*se Pontisca Pilatus*): In Old English writings, the first element of the name Pontius Pilate is routinely treated as an attributive adjective—"Pontian" or "Pontic," i.e., pertaining to the region of Pontus on the Black Sea—rather than as, correctly, the name of a Roman *gens*. This confusion is found in some Christian Latin sources, too, such as Martin of Braga's *De correctione rusticorum*.

32b   "Joseph buried him" (*Iosep byrigde*): Joseph of Arimathea is not mentioned in the texts of the Apostles' or Nicene Creeds, but his role was well known, being prominent in all four gospels (Matthew 27:57–60; Mark 15:42–46; Luke 23:50–53; John 19:38–42) as well as in apocrypha such as the Gospel of Nichodemus.

36–44   "*On the third day he rose from the dead*" etc. (*Tertia die resurrexit a mortuis* etc.): The following lines also paraphrase the continuation in the Latin source: "he ascended to the heavens and sits at the right hand of God the Father almighty; from there he will come to judge the living and the dead."

40a   "secret teachings" (*runum*): While there were traditions attributing to the resurrected Christ secret teachings meant only for the initiate, by the plural of *run* the poet probably just means "(religious) mysteries," including Jesus's revelation of the typological and prophetic significances of Old Testament scriptures (see Luke 24:25).

42–44   "He said that he would leave no one behind" etc. (*cwæð þæt he nolde nænne forlætan* etc.): Not in the Apostles' Creed or any other profession of faith; perhaps the poet has in mind John 14:2–3 and/or John 6:39.

56a   "with a united mind" (*þurh ænne geþanc*): The phrase evokes the literal meaning of *catholicam* ("universal").

64–67   "And I believe in the resurrection . . . *And in life everlasting,* / where you will bestow life without end on all" (*And ic þone ærest . . . getreowe . . . Et vitam eternam, / þær ðu ece lif eallum dælest*): Whereas the other Latin lines inserted into the poem remain grammatically separate from the surrounding Old English, here syntactic constructions cross and incorporate the dividing Latin phrase *Et vitam ęternam*. The result invites comparison with the examples of macaronic Old English-Latin verse at the conclusion of *The Rewards of Piety* and *The Phoenix*.

THE GLORIA PATRI (I)

15   "an exalted comforter of hearts and a holy spirit" *(heah hige-frofer and halig gast)*: Grammatically these noun phrases seem to refer back to "Son" *(sunu)* in 12b, the second person of the Trinity. The titles "comforter" and "Holy Spirit," however, traditionally belong to the third person in the Trinity. There is a sense, though, in which the poet could refer to the resurrected and ascended Christ as "a holy spirit." Perhaps that general meaning and the more technical, Trinitarian one *("the* Holy Spirit") are intended simultaneously.

40   "All holy choirs" *(Ealle . . . halige dreamas)*: I.e., the heavenly choirs of angels and saints.

46a   "forever and ever" *(on worulda woruld)*: The Old English is a close translation of the Latin *in saecula saeculorum* ("in ages of ages," *saeculum* = "*this* world, *this* present age"). Early modern translators of the phrase sometimes rendered it "world without end."

48   "sanctified spirits of the supreme majesty *(heah-prymnesse halige gastas)*:" Alternatively, translate "sublime forces, holy spirits." As indicated in the notes to the text, I prefer the reading of C at this line. The text of J *(heah prymnesse haliges gastes)* "the high Trinity of the Holy Spirit," makes little sense, though elsewhere Old English poets did pun on the similarity of *prymnes* ("majesty, glory") and *prines* ("Trinity"); see Frank, "Late Old English *Prymnys* 'Trinity.'"

THE GLORIA PATRI (II)

2a   "to the Father [be glory] on earth" *(fæder on foldan)*: I construe and punctuate *on foldan* ("on earth") as indicating where the act of offering glory should occur. Alternatively, translate *fæder* as vocative ("O Father").

THE KENTISH HYMN

As noted in the Introduction, this short poem consists chiefly of a free paraphrase of the liturgical hymn *Gloria in excelsis deo* ("Glory to God in the highest"), itself an early Christian elaboration of the angelic chorus at Christ's birth (Luke 2:14). Possible brief echoes of other sources, including the hymn *Te deum* and various creeds, are discussed by Keefer, *Liturgical Verse*, 119–22.

1–6   "let us glorify the Lord of hosts" etc. (*Wuton wuldrian weorada dryhten* etc.): Cf. the words of the principal source, the *Gloria in excelsis deo*: "Glory to God in the highest, and on earth peace to men of good will."

7–14   "we praise you and we bless you" etc. (*We ðe heriað halgum stefnum* etc.): Cf. the *Gloria in excelsis deo*: "We praise you, we bless you, we worship you, we glorify you because of your great glory."

15–21   "you are the king of kings" etc. (*Ðu eart cyninga cyningc* etc.): Cf. the *Gloria in excelsis deo*: "Lord God, heavenly king, God the Father almighty; Lord Jesus Christ, only begotten Son."

22–28   "You are . . . the holy lamb" etc. (*Ðu eart . . . ðæt halige lamb* etc.): Cf. the *Gloria in excelsis deo*: "Lord God, lamb of God, you who take away the sins of the world: have mercy on us."

29–35   "you sit on a lofty throne" etc. (*ðu on hæah-setle . . . sitest* etc.): Cf. the *Gloria in excelsis deo*: "you who sit at the right hand of God the Father, receive our prayer."

31b   "mindful of souls" (*gasta gemyndig*): The precise meaning of the phrase is uncertain. As I have translated, it is implicitly concessive: i.e., although Christ has ascended to heaven, he remains mindful of souls on earth. Compare the frequent use of Old English *gemyndig* in glosses and translations of Psalm 8:4 (Vulgate 8:5), "What is man, that thou [God] art mindful (*gemyndig*, Latin *memor*) of him?" Alternatively, emend *gemyndig* in line 31 to *gymend* ("governor, ruler") and interpret *gasta* as referring to the spirits of the angels and saints already in heaven.

36–43   "Truly, you are holy always" etc. (*Ðu eart soðlice simle halig* etc.):

Cf. the *Gloria in excelsis deo:* "For you alone are the holy one, you alone are the Lord, you alone are the most high, Jesus Christ, with the Holy Spirit in the glory of God the Father.

Cædmon's Hymn

Unlike most Old English poems, this one survives in multiple copies, and those bear witness to transmission of the text in two versions, Northumbrian and West Saxon. To most modern readers, the substantive difference between the two will seem slight indeed—just one word (see the note to line 5b, below). But to scholars of Old English poetry such minor differences are important, as they suggest how reciters or copyists of texts may have played a role in altering received material; see O'Keeffe, *Visible Song,* 23–46.

5b   "for the children of men" *(aelda barnum):* The text in this half-line distinguishes the two surviving versions of *Cædmon's Hymn* from each other. The Northumbrian version of the poem, printed here, has *aelda barnum* and is believed to be older than the version that is better attested in West Saxon, which reads "for the children of earth" *(eorðan bearnum).* Note, however, that manuscripts D and P, linguistically allied with the Northumbrian version, also record forms of *eorðan,* more typical of the West-Saxon line of transmission. *Cædmon's Hymn* regularly circulated in the margins of Latin copies of Bede's *Ecclesiastical History,* next to Bede's account of Cædmon (see the Introduction). When an Old English abridged version of Bede's work was made in early tenth-century Mercia, the Old English poem was incorporated directly into the main text.

Godric's Hymn

See the Introduction as well as the notes to the text.

A Prayer

21a   "O light from light!" *(Æla, leohtes leoht!):* Perhaps an echo of the Nicene Creed, in which Christ is called *lumen de lumine* "light from light."

58–60   "of all gods you are the great one, powerful and benevolent, and the eternal king of all creatures" (*þu eart se miccla and se mægen-stranga / and se ead-moda ealra goda / and se ece kyning ealra gesceafta):* Cf. Psalm 95 (Vulgate 94):3.

RESIGNATION (A)

I have consulted the translations by Bradley, *Anglo-Saxon Poetry,* 386–89, and Anderson, *Two Literary Riddles,* 200–209.

1–2a   "May almighty God keep me, may the holy Lord help me!" (*Age mec se ælmihta God, / helpe min se halga dryhten!):* The first line is evidently short, but past editors have not assumed any loss of text. This opening may echo one of the widely used formulas at the beginning of many hours in the divine office, "O God, make speed to save me, O Lord make haste to help me" (Psalm 69:2 in the Roman version of the Vulgate psalter; cf. Psalm 70:1 in the Hebrew and modern English versions).

15b   "the great thief" (*Regn-þeof):* I.e., the devil. This rare compound occurs only once elsewhere, in the poem *Exodus,* at line 539.

36b–37a   "Behold, you have granted me much . . . here" (*Hwæt, þu me her fela / . . . forgeafe):* Considering the defective alliteration of line 37, some editors detect loss of at least a word, possibly a whole verse or more, between lines 36b and 37a, though there is not necessarily any gap in sense.

47a   "given over to malice" (*æfestum eaden).* Different translations of this half-line have been proposed, depending on varied interpretations of *æfestum* as from *æfest* ("malice") or *æfæst* ("pious, righteous"). Likewise *eaden* is a rare word with the sense "granted, accorded," though elsewhere it appears in contexts unambiguously positive, unlike here. My translation follows that suggested by the *DOE,* s.v. *ēaden.*

63a   "anxiously preoccupied" (*hædre gehogode):* The meaning of the phrase is disputed. As O'Donnell points out ("*Hædre* and *hædre gehogode*"), although an adverb *hædre* ("oppressively, anxiously") appears in older dictionaries, the evidence supporting it is weak. O'Donnell argues that the phrase is *hædre gehogode* ("brightly intended").

66a   "on occasion": The Old English *feam siþum* literally means "on a few occasions," which in the present context is probably understatement for "I am *always* fearful" etc.

70   "with..." *(mid...)*: The word *mid* is the last one on fol. 118v, after which a leaf has been lost. The text that continues at the top of fol. 119r probably belongs to a different poem; see the explanation in the note to the text.

ALMSGIVING

I have consulted translations by Bradley, *Anglo-Saxon Poetry,* 395–96, and Anderson, *Two Literary Riddles,* 225.

5–9   "Just he might... with water" etc. (*Efne swa he mid wætre* etc.): Cf. Ecclesiasticus 3:33.

HOMILETIC FRAGMENT (I)

At several points I have found useful the partial translations and discussion by Randle, "The 'Homiletics' of the Vercelli Book Poems."

8–15a   "the prophet" *(se witiga)*: I.e., King David, credited with authorship of the biblical psalms. The lines that follow (9–15a) paraphrase Psalm 28 (Vulgate 27):3.

18b–30   "They are a peculiar sort" etc. (*Ænlice beoð* etc.): The extended simile may depend on patristic commentaries on Psalm 118 (Vulgate 117):12.

30b   "secret wounds" *(dyrne wunde)*: I.e., either the wicked themselves have been "wounded" through succumbing to temptation, or they nurture in their hearts the "wounds" that they intend to inflict on others through slander; perhaps both meanings are intended.

32b   "the ancient one" *(se ealda)*: I.e., the ancient foe, the devil.

HOMILETIC FRAGMENT (II)

Most modern commentators assume that this is an excerpt from a longer poem that does not survive in full. I have consulted the translation in Anderson, *Two Literary Riddles,* 231–33.

8–11a   "There is one faith" etc. (*An is geleafa* etc.): Cf. Ephesians 4:5–6.

14a   "unformed matter": Here the Old English word is actually "trees" *(treowum)*. Charles D. Wright suggests to me that this puzzling reference reflects the poet's awareness of Latin *silva* or Greek ὕλη, literally "tree(s), forest," as a cosmological term for the primal material of creation.

17–19   Significant portions of lines 17b and 19 are damaged beyond recovery in the manuscript. They perhaps involved an allusion to Mary's virginal conception of Christ through the agency of the Holy Spirit.

Aldhelm

This poem poses extraordinary difficulties, especially in lines 6a–13a. Its many Grecisms appear to have been lifted from a glossary by someone who did not know or care how to inflect them in their new syntactic environment. Other problems arise from apparent corruptions of the transmitted text and from its incomplete ending (but see the note to line 17, below). In addition to the translations and discussions by Dobbie in ASPR 6:194; Robinson, *"Rewards of Piety,"* 184–85; and Whitbread, "Old English Poem *Aldhelm,"* I have consulted translations by Wrenn, *Study of Old English Literature,* 58–59; Orchard, *Poetic Art of Aldhelm,* 282; and Abram, "Aldhelm and the Two Cultures," 1381. My rendering departs substantially from all these at several places.

3a   "Aldhelm" *(Ealdelm):* Aldhelm (d. 710 or 711), abbot of Malmesbury and, from ca. 705, bishop of Sherborne. In the later Anglo-Saxon period he was renowned especially as the author of a difficult Latin prose treatise on virginity *(De virginitate)* and of a long Latin poem based on the same (see the following note).

    "a glorious poet" *(æþele sceop):* Aldhelm also wrote a poetic version of his treatise on virginity, and it is probably that to which our poet refers. According to a post-Conquest tradition preserved by William of Malmesbury, however, Aldhelm also enjoyed a high reputation as an Old English poet and used that skill to evangelize his countrymen.

6a   *"the toil and the burden" (ponus et pondus):* From this point through 13a, it is far from clear what the poet intended to say. Dobbie

(ASPR 6:194) takes *ponus* as πόνος ("labor, toil") and regards both it and *pondus* as nominatives, hence in apposition to *Biblos* (line 5b). On this reading, the book is referring to itself as a "labor, work of toil" and as a "weight, hefty thing" (cf. Robinson's "an opus and an authority"). I follow Wrenn and Whitbread, however, in taking *ponus et pondus* as accusative objects of *secgan* in 8a (if not of some verb in an intervening line that has been lost—perhaps after line 5). The incorrect inflection of *ponus* is no objection, given the poet's failures elsewhere on that score (e.g., *boethia,* line 14).

7   "the lamentation of that young man, sorrowful *at present*" *(geonges geanoðe geomres iamiamque):* Detailed arguments for my interpretation of this deeply problematic line will have to wait for a future occasion. In brief, I hesitantly follow the majority of translators who (1) take *geanoðe* as a form of a rare noun meaning "lamentation" (on the evidence of Gothic *gaunōþu,* "mourning") and (2) take *geonges* as a substantive "young man," modified by *geomres* ("sad"). Who this young man is, however, and why he should be "sad" and lamenting, are questions left open by all the translations that I have consulted. Whitbread argues that the personified book is describing the anguished toil of its unnamed scribe. I suggest instead that the poet is alluding to Aldhelm as he describes himself in the epilogue to the prose *De virginitate,* where he laments the administrative burdens that keep him from a life of ascetic contemplation (see the note to line 6a, "*the toil and the burden*").

9–10a   "*lowliness . . . more often a constant help to him, hardship in his native country" (euthenia oftor on fylste, / æne on eðle):* Again, the problems in these lines cannot be fully analyzed here. The form *euthenia* seems at first glance one of the more straightforward Grecisms in the text, transliterating εὐθηνία ("provision, plenty, abundance"), and so most translators have taken it. Likewise *æne* in line 10a is usually interpreted as αἴνη ("praise, fame"). Despite the near consensus as to the meaning of these forms, no reading has sought to explain what this "abundance" refers to, or why a figure who possesses that and "fame" should be introduced as "sad" (7) and as one who suffers slander (if that is the gist of lines

10b–11a; q.v.). My translation supposes that the poet or his glossarial source has confused the meaning of *euthenia* with that of some similar-looking word, such as ἐυωνία ("cheapness, lowliness," Latin *vilitas*), or εὔθυναι ("correction, chastisement"). Similarly, for *æne* instead of αἴνη ("praise, fame") accepted by nearly all translators, I propose ἀνία ("grief, sorrow, distress, trouble"). On this reading, the poet is expressing a conventional monastic view that humiliation and hardship, however painful, refined the ascetic Aldhelm.

10b   "and the fact as well that he is" *(ec ðon ðe se is):* This half-line is very suspect in itself, the more so since a page-break divides *ðe* and *se.* Several translators have wished for a reading *him* instead of *se.*

12b–13a   *"the self-mastery, the toil that he sustains" (labor quem tenet, / encratea):* The reference to "toil" *(labor)* could refer to the writing of the *De virginitate,* but, in combination with *encratea* (ἐγκράτεια, "self-control, continence"), the reference is again probably to Aldhelm's inferred exercise of monastic discipline generally and chastity in particular. The form *encratea* could be nominative (hence in apposition with *labor* in 12b) or ablative (thus translate: "the labor that he sustains by means of self-control").

15b   *"in this lesser world" (micro in cosmo):* The Grecism *microcosmos* occurs with the same pedantic tmesis (as *micro in cosmo*) early in Aldhelm's preface to the prose *De virginitate* (Lapidge and Herren, *Aldhelm: The Prose Works,* 60).

17   The text stops midsentence after line 17, but there is no gap or physical loss from the manuscript. It seems either the poem was incomplete in its exemplar or the scribe decided not to finish copying it. Robinson ("*Rewards of Piety*," 185–86) raises the possibility that the poem is not incomplete but that its final sentence was meant to dovetail syntactically with the opening of the Latin preface that immediately follows in the manuscript.

THURETII

I have consulted the translation and commentary by Clunies Ross and Edwards, "Thureth," 360.

1a   "pontifical:" A literal translation of *halgung-boc,* a compound that occurs nowhere else in Old English, would be "blessing book" or "consecration book." A "pontifical" was a book containing texts for those religious ceremonies that required a bishop's presence rather than that of an ordinary priest. Pontificals were often combined with another type of bishop's book called a "benedictional" (containing special blessings recited by the bishop before communion at Mass). The manuscript that now preserves the poem *Thureth* contains portions of what were originally three different service books, all of them containing matter from pontificals, and one containing part of a benedictional. The leaves that preserve the poem, which is copied in an early eleventh-century hand, belong to the earliest of the three pontificals (now called "Claudius Pontifical (I)"), probably the book that is personified as the first-person speaker of *Thureth.* Claudius Pontifical (I) may have belonged for a time to the famous Anglo-Saxon preacher and lawmaker Archbishop Wulfstan of York (d. 1023); see Jones, "Wulfstan's Liturgical Interests," 334–46.

2   "covered me with ornaments" *(me . . . frætewum belegde):* At the time the poem was written, the pontifical manuscript to which it refers evidently had a valuable binding adorned with precious metals and perhaps jewels.

3a   "Thureth" *(Þureð):* I.e., the name of the patron, thought to be the same person as the "Thored" who appears in a legal document (a grant of land to Christ Church Cathedral, Canterbury) that is now bound in the same manuscript as the poem. For further discussion of Thureth's identity, see ASPR 6:xc, and the study by Clunies Ross and Edwards, "Thureth," 360. Thored probably would have commissioned the precious binding only, not the copying of the manuscript, the contents of which would have been chosen by the bishop.

6a   "he" *(he):* Alternatively, take the antecedent of the pronoun as God (the one "who created light itself" in line 4); see Clunies Ross and Edwards, "Thureth," 360–61, who translate "He [= Thureth] is mindful of all the mighty works / which He [= God] is able to bring about on earth."

8–9   "for his willingness in remembering to designate many treasures for an offering to his creator" *(þæs þe he on gemynde madma manega/wyle gemearcian metode to lace):* I take *manega* as a late form or miscopying of *monige* and construe it as the object of *gemearcian*. Clunies Ross and Edwards (360) construe the two lines very differently: "because, mindful of many treasures, he wishes to designate (me) as an offering to the Lord."

THE REWARDS OF PIETY

I have consulted translations by Robinson, *"Rewards of Piety,"* 189–93, and Zacher, "Rewards of Poetry," 102–4.

2a   "prosperous" *(blowende):* The adjective literally means "flowering, blossoming." Critics who read this poem as part of a deliberately constructed series in the manuscript (Cambridge, Corpus Christi College 201; see above, xxxiii–xxxiv) note that the poem *Judgment Day (II),* which there immediately precedes *The Rewards of Piety,* opens with a reference to a "blossoming" natural setting (see that poem, as well as the accompanying notes to the text).

12   This is the first of a number of short lines that, while incomplete so far as length and alliteration go, show no discernible gap in sense. I follow Dobbie and Robinson in assuming that no text has been lost; likewise at lines 39 and 46.

17–18   "maintain . . . a fear of the creator" etc. *(hafa metodes ege* etc.): Cf. Psalm 111 (Vulgate 110):10; also Proverbs 1:7 and 9:10.

29b   "intently": The Old English word *ealninga* is regarded by the *DOE* as a variant spelling of the adverb *ealnunga* ("altogether, entirely, wholly, utterly"), and the *DOE* editors recommend a contextual translation "earnestly" in the present instance. Another possibility would be to associate the word with *ealning,* another adverb that can mean "all the time, continually, ever" (see *DOE,* s.v., sense 2).

33b   "That will be an offering to the Lord" *(Þæt bið drihtnes lac):* I take "That" to refer both to the total reliance on God mentioned in lines 29–31a and to the quiet exercise of charity mentioned in line 32. Perhaps cf. Isaiah 1:11–17, although the idea recurs throughout the Old Testament; cf. Psalm 51:16–17 (Vulgate 50:18–19); Hosea 6:6.

57a "gray-haired warrior" *(har hilde-rinc):* In an otherwise prosaic composition, this half-line preserves a conspicuous echo of traditional heroic and sapiential poetry (see the Introduction). It is also possible, however, that the force of such formulas has grown so weak in late Old English religious verse that the author means nothing more here than "old man."

84 Whereas the short lines can be defended in the Old English text (see note to line 12, above), the seeming absence of balancing Latin b-verses here and again in line 85 likely does indicate some problem. Fulk and Cain (*History of Old English Literature,* 254 n. 37) propose that no substance has been lost, but that rather line 84b was something like *animae tuae,* which a scribe accidentally translated into Old English *saule þinre* as he copied.

94–95 Defective alliterations raise the possibility of missing or corrupt text. When the regular alliteration resumes at line 96, the poet seems to be talking not about God himself (cf. line 96) but about the angel Gabriel's role in the Annunciation to Mary.

Instructions for Christians

6 "no one will fail to notice those four when he meets them" *(he ne missað na ða he gemetað):* Following Youngs ("'Instructions for Christians,'" 114), I assume that the subject "he," which lacks an antecedent, is introducing a gnomic statement about a righteous everyman, and that *ne missað* is understatement (i.e., he will take great care to observe the following four behaviors).

11a "means in this world": This is a contextual translation of *woruld-þinga* (literally "things in/of the world"), an Old English term otherwise usually negative, being set in opposition to spiritual or heavenly things; cf. Robinson's translation of the present instance as "secular things" ("Notes and Emendations," 361).

21–23 "To no one are sufferings in this world" etc. *(Ne synd þa prowunga* etc.): Cf. Romans 8:18.

63–92   The poem's concerns with wealth could imply a lay audience, which makes the emphasis on learning and teaching in this section all the more remarkable. For the possible relevance of the latter themes to lay "wisdom," see Upchurch, "Pastoral Care and Political Gain," 69–76.

66   "to those who burn with love" (*þæm ðe wællað lufæ on wisdome*). Youngs ("'Instructions for Christians,'" 117) translates *wællað* as "desires," presuming derivation from *willan*. I translate as if from *weallan* ("be hot, seethe, boil"), a verb associated with passionate love elsewhere in Old English.

69–74   "Concealed skill" etc. (*Se forholena cræft* etc.): Cf. Ecclesiasticus 20:31–32: "Wisdom that is hid, and treasure that is not seen: what profit is there in them both? Better is he that hideth his folly, than the man that hideth his wisdom." Comparison with the biblical source, identified by Torkar ("Textkritische Anmerkungen," 176–77), suggests that some text has dropped out after line 70a and that the original reading of 69b may have been "gold" (Old English *gold*), not "good" (Old English *god*) as in the manuscript. Emending *gelice* ("alike") to *ungelice* ("unlike") would likewise bring the sense of the lines closer to the biblical maxim. Even so, Rosier and Youngs do not emend either word. Rosier does allow some loss of text after line 70a, which he nevertheless ends with a full stop; Youngs accepts the reading "good" and assumes that no text is missing.

87–88   "Learning humbles every king" etc. (*Heo geeadmodað eghwylcne kyng* etc.): As Torkar notes ("Textkritische Anmerkungen," 170), the ideas here may echo Proverbs 11:2: "Where pride is, there also shall be reproach: but where humility is, there also is wisdom."

92b   "sets the handmaid free" (*þeowne gefreolsað*)*:* Perhaps cf. Judith 16:28. Some medieval exegetes allegorized the freeing of Judith's handmaid, mentioned in that biblical verse, as the liberation of carnally minded persons through Christian teaching, exhortation, and correction; see, for example, Hrabanus Maurus, *Expositio in librum Iudith* (PL 109:590C).

106–9a   "Everyone's priest is called a *sacerdos*" etc. (*Is se mæsse-preost monna gehwilces/sacerd gehaten* etc.): Robinson ("Notes and Emendations," 361–62) points out that these lines refer to a commonplace medieval etymology of *sacerdos* as derived from *sacer* ("sacred") plus *do* ("I give"), loosely equivalent to the phrase *clæne sellan* at line 109a.

113   "A 'monk' is so called because of community" *(Þæt is for gemænan þæt we munuc nemniað):* Like the poet's remarks on *sacerdos* (lines 106–9), the present line involves an etymology, this time of "monk" *(munuc).* The point is somewhat confused, however, since that term was more often etymologized as "one who lives alone," i.e., an ascetic solitary. Either the poet actually has in mind the etymology of another term for monk, namely "cenobite" (Latin *coenobita,* "one who shares in a communal life"), or he is recalling alternative etymologies of *monachus* as "one who lives in unity, oneness, with others." See Leclercq, *Études sur le vocabulaire monastique,* 8–9 and 22–26.

117–23   "Though, after the model of David, I have composed" etc. *(þeah ic . . . æfter Dauiðe dihtum sette* etc.): As I translate the text, it refers not to specific teachings attributed to David but to the precedent of setting moral admonition in verse (i.e., the biblical book of Psalms). The sense of the entire passage is: Although I have, using this form of poetic address, singled out the wealthy for admonishment, my listeners should not conclude that riches in themselves impede salvation (lines 117–23); rather they do so only if the wealthy turn prideful on account of their riches (124–30).

154a   "claim" *(monige):* Despite its alteration to *mænige* in the manuscript (which Rosier's edition accepts), the original reading *monige* (from *monian,* "claim, demand of a person what is due") is preferable, as noted by Torkar, "Textkritische Anmerkungen," 166.

157–62   "'Travel now through all the realm of earth'" etc. *("Far nu ymbe æll eorðan rices"* etc.): Cf. Jeremiah 5:1.

163b   "too late" *(to sið):* The manuscript has "to siðgeare," which Rosier (20) takes as "eager for travel," hence "impatient." He notes such a word is not recorded elsewhere in Old English and that it does not appear in the dictionaries. Youngs ("'Instructions for Christians,'" 108, note to her line 181) observes, however, that *-geare* has apparently been added by a later hand and that all the other adjectives in lines 163–64 refer to laziness or sluggishness; hence the original *sið* ("late") fits the context better.

188–89   "That is not a beggar's hand" etc. (*Nis þæt þearfan hand* etc.): Variations on the maxim *Manus pauperis gazophylacium est Christi* ("A pauper's hand is the treasury of Christ")—i.e., to place alms in a pauper's hand is to store up treasure for oneself in heaven—occur in popular sermons by early Christian Latin authors such as Peter Chrysologus and Caesarius of Arles. The saying is repeated by numerous medieval writers.

196–99   "'Even though I myself declare'" etc. (*"Þeah ic sylfe cweðe"* etc.): A paraphrase of Ezekiel 33:14–16. The poet has evidently erred in attributing the citation to Isaiah, although some verses in that book (e.g., 22:14 and 55:7) offer similar ideas.

201–6   These lines are hardly translatable as copied in the manuscript, and previous scholarship offers few useful suggestions. I follow Youngs ("'Instructions for Christians,'" 110) by ignoring Rosier's full stop at the end of 203 and deleting one *þæt* from the manuscript's *þæt þæt* at the beginning of line 201. But Youngs's further deletion of one entire *þæt he wolde* in 204, as alleged dittography, is not helpful. On the other hand, emending the first *wolde* in 204 to a present subjunctive *wille* and the adverb *þær* to *ær* produces a line that is not only coherent but follows a favorite rhetorical device of this poet, i.e., to contrast earlier and later conditions in the life of an individual; cf. lines 51–54, 91, 101–3, 153–54, 179–80, 221–23, 231–34, 235–40.

213b   "by steps of moral character" (*mid þeawa stepum*). Youngs ("'Instructions for Christians,'" 123) translates both instances of "stepum" as the same word, *stæp* ("step, pace"), though this would perhaps require emendation of *þeawum* to *þeawa* (genitive plural). The emendation is unnecessary if the second instance of "stepum" were taken as an adjective *steap* in its sense "lofty, high, exalted," but that word appears to have been used only of actual, physical height; I find no unambiguous instance of its transfer to moral qualities. I therefore accept Youngs's translation but emend to *þeawa*.

229–34   "Wisdom is a light" etc. (*Wisdom is leoht* etc.): The commonplace association of lights or lamps with wisdom needs no specific source, but in medieval exegesis the link appears most frequently with reference to the Parable of the Wise and Foolish Virgins with their lamps (Matthew 25:1–13). Closer in some respects to the poet's image is the parallel found in a sermon by Caesarius of Arles (Homily 12, at *PL* 67:1074A: "and, for its lamp extinguished by pride, let the soul strive to obtain the oil of humility and love, while there is time to gather and purchase it"). References to a *lucerna* being extinguished by pride or the "wind" of pride also occur repeatedly in works by Augustine of Hippo.

234b   "snuffed . . . out" (*dwæsta*): Rosier emended the manuscript reading *dwæsta* to *dwæsca* (3rd singular present subjunctive). But Torkar argues persuasively for the manuscript reading as a late form of *dwæscdon* ("Textkritische Anmerkungen," 171–72).

238–40   "nor, indeed . . . in old age" etc. (*ne huru on ylde* etc.): These lines are obscure. My emendation of 239b is based on a rhetorical pattern favored by the poet elsewhere ("He will not be able to do X who has not previously done Y"); see the note to lines 201–6, above. Rosier does not emend but translates, "nor indeed shall he ever become well served in old age than (?lest) he wished before to serve very well according to his measure." For want of a better suggestion I follow Rosier's explanation of 240a *on his tale mette* as related to *tælmet* ("measure"). Also awkward is *tale* [= *tela?*] *wel,* taken by Rosier and Youngs as "very well."

257–62   "there are altogether three victorious paths" etc. (*sige-fæste weogas syndon ealle þreo* etc.): Cf. 1 Corinthians 13:13.

Seasons for Fasting

I have benefited from consulting Greeson, "Observance Poems," 179–96; Hilton, "Edition and Study," 61–69; the several studies mentioned already in the notes to the text, above; and Richards, "Old Wine in a New Bottle."

16b   "mend" *(gewyrpan):* The emendation (for manuscript *gewyrþan*) and suggested translation "amend" are Dobbie's; Sisam (*Studies,* 53) argues for keeping the manuscript reading, which he would translate "leave be, leave alone."

23a   The half-line is metrically deficient, but context suggests that not more than a word or two has dropped out.

29b   "in token to their beloved [Lord]" *(leofum to tacne):* The word "Lord" is not in the Old English, and the half-line might be translated a number of different ways.

30b   "free from blemishes . . ." *(womma bedæled . . .):* Sisam (*Studies,* 47) suggests that after line 30 as many as two lines have dropped out, the content of which might have smoothed the transition between lines 30 and 31 as they now stand. The stanza concluded by line 30 is also exceptional for containing six rather than the usual eight lines, another clue that text has been lost.

35a   "he promises the same hope" *(þone hyht gehateð):* Dobbie, trying to preserve the manuscript's *þone hyht and gehateð,* argues that the form *hyht* represents a verb *hyhteþ,* though it must then take the somewhat unusual sense "hopes *for someone*" or "causes hope." Sisam's suggestion (*Studies,* 53–54) to delete *and* and take *hyht* as a noun, modified by *þone,* is not without its own problems but yields a less strained reading.

43b–45a   "the dates . . . written down" *(þa mearce . . . gebrefde):* Richards ("Old Wine in a New Bottle," 351–52) suggests that the Old English terms used here were borrowed from the technical vocabulary of the medieval computus (the science of reckoning time).

48b   The Old English involves alliteration of *wucan* ("week") with a vowel not only here but again in lines 58, 67, and 72, suggesting a late West-Saxon pronunciation of the noun as if *ucan;* see Sisam, *Studies,* 51–52.

57b   "as it includes the readings" *(þe gelesu hafað):* The manuscript has *gelu se* altered to *gelesen;* Dobbie prints *þe gelesen hafað* and considers the line hopelessly corrupt, as does Sisam (*Studies,* 54); Leslie ("Textual Notes," 556) discusses two other solutions, neither persuasive. With Hilton ("Edition and Study," 29 and 75), I relate the corruption to *geles* ("reading, study"). Hilton (30 and 63) would translate the half-line as "those who have learning" (mod-

403

ifying *leodum* in 56b), whereas I suggest that the relative clause modifies *lofe* closer by in line 57a, and that plural *gelesu* (or *gelese*) bears its more literal sense "readings." On this interpretation, the half-line clarifies the one before it: the summer Ember Days also include the most conspicuous liturgical feature of the occasion, the reading of twelve lessons on the Saturday.

73b   "mysteries": See *DOE*, s.v. *dyrne* (noun), where it is also allowed that *deornum* in the present instance could be an adjective ("secret, mysterious") modifying "words and deeds" in 74a. Sisam (*Studies*, 54) suggests an emendation to *deorum* (adjective) in the sense "noble" or "of great worth."

88a   "Bretons or Franks" (*Bryttan oððe Francan,* for the manuscript's *brytt franca* across a line break): I adopt the conjecture proposed by Sisam (*Studies*, 51–52). Dobbie and Greeson emend to *bryttan Franca* ("princes of the Franks"), but Sisam's *oððe* has respectable authority (Grant, "Note on 'The Seasons for Fasting,'" 304). The reference to competing foreign customs suggests a memory of the earlier tenth century, when Breton refugees, fleeing Viking attacks, were welcomed by King Æthelstan. In lines 87–90, the poet seems to regard the continental practice of placing spring and summer Ember Fasts in the first week of March and second week of June, respectively, as a mimicry of Old Testament custom, now superseded by the "Gregorian" decree, observed among the English, that would place those fasts in the first week of Lent and in the week following Pentecost Sunday. On the widespread belief in Gregory's influence on this custom, see the note to lines 93b–94.

93b–94   "the keeper . . . Gregory, pope over men" (*Romana rices hyrde,/ Gregoriæ, gumena papa):* I.e., Gregory I (or "the Great"), pope from 590–604. Various texts surviving from Anglo-Saxon England suggest a wide acceptance of the belief that Gregory had indeed sanctioned the arrangement of the Ember Days current there. On the Anglo-Saxons' particular devotion to Gregory for other reasons too, see the notes to the translation of *The Menologium*, at lines 39–40a.

103–10   The association of Moses's forty-day fast (cf. Exodus 34:28) with the Christian institution of Lent is commonplace in patristic and medieval sources.

112b   "enveloped in flame" (*bæle behlæned*): Cf. Exodus 19:18.

120–27 On Elijah's food in the wilderness and ascent of Horeb, see 1 Kings (Vulgate 3 Kings) 19:4–8.

136–37 Cf. Malachi 2:7: "For the lips of the priest shall keep knowledge, and they shall seek the law at his mouth; because he is the angel of the Lord of hosts." My translation of this section follows the interpretation by Schabram ("Zur Interpretation der 18. Strophe," 301–6).

140   "fast from acts of sin" (*fæstan . . . firene dædum*): Cf. line 150. This figurative expression meaning "to give up/cease from sinning" is probably based on a Latin one, *ieiunare a peccatis,* that was commonplace in patristic and medieval discussions of fasting.

144–48a "how the holy man left" etc. (*hu se halga gewat* etc.): Cf. 2 Kings (Vulgate 4 Kings) 2:11–12.

160–67 This account of Jesus's temptation follows Matthew 4:1–11 more closely than the parallel version at Luke 4:1–13.

164   "that he might sink his darts" (*þæt he stræla his stellan mihte*): Cf. Ephesians 6:16.

166a   "departed behind" (*on hinder gewat*): Cf. Matthew 4:10.

182a   "up to the ninth hour" (*oþ þa nigoþan tid*): I.e., roughly 3:00 PM. On the rules for fasting at issue here and, implicitly, in the criticism of wayward clergy at the end of the poem (lines 208–30), see Frank, "Old English *æræt.*"

183a   "meat or sins" (*flæsces oþþe fyrna*): The clever zeugma underscores the idea that fasting involves abstinence from sin as well as from foods; cf. line 140 and the note to the translation there. Greeson ("Observance Poems," 243) attempts to revive Holthausen's emendation to *flæsces oþþe fisca* ("meat or fishes").

206–7   "Let him drink" etc. (*Drince he* etc.): Dobbie drastically emended 206b to *oððe þæt dæghluttre.* The manuscript reading is well defended by Sisam (*Studies,* 56–57) and Schabram ("*Seasons for Fasting* 206f."). The latter (at 225–26) demonstrates that the poet took the image from Ezekiel 34:18–19, probably via an exegesis by Gregory the Great in his treatise the *Pastoral Care*, bk. 1, chap. 2.

211a   "with irreligion" *(mid æleste):* Dobbie emended to *æfeste* "with malice," but Sisam (*Studies*, 57) and Greeson ("Observance Poems," 250) persuasively argue for the manuscript reading *æleste*, even though the word is attested nowhere else. The word is now recognized by the *DOE*, s.v. *ǣ-lyste* "neglect of (religious) law."

222b–23a   "do not hesitate when they may seize a meal" *(ne wicliað / hwænne hie to mose fon):* For a verb, the manuscript has *wigliað* ("divine, foresee"), which Dobbie defends in this context (though he then corrects *hwænne* to *hwæne*, "whom"). Sisam (*Studies*, 58) emends to *bewitiað* ("care for, heed"). Holthausen ("Ein altenglisches Gedicht," 199 and 201), and Greeson and Hilton after him, emend to *wicliað*, from a rare verb *wiclian* ("to hesitate, waver").

226–28   "say that God would allow to every man" etc. *(cweðað þæt Godd life gumena gehwilcum* etc.): The manuscript has *cweðað godd life;* the emendation *cweðað* is widely accepted, but the rest has never been adequately explained. I adopt Sisam's emendation and interpretation (*Studies*, 58), though it too is not entirely satisfactory. More recent scholarship has struggled to rescue the manuscript reading. Hence Greeson translates "they propose for a good life [*goddlife*] for everyone that each . . . person be allowed" etc. ("Observance Poems," 195). Hilton ("Edition and Study," 69) and Richards ("Old Wine in a New Bottle," 361) take the manuscript's *godd life* for a toast ("Good life!"). Holthausen emends to a substantive adjective *godlice*, "the fine (fellows)," sarcastic in the context ("Ein altenglisches Gedicht," 199).

The Menologium

Early modern antiquaries gave this poem its obscure title. In English, "menologium" (or "menologion" or "menology") has always been a rare term and applied to texts as varied as calendars of church feasts, commemorative lists of the dead, and (in Eastern Orthodoxy) books containing saint's legends in calendrical sequence. As discussed in the Introduction, the generic backgrounds of this Old English poem seem to lie in versified ecclesiastical calendars in medieval Latin and Old Irish.

When translating this technical poem, one is tempted to suppress its many repetitions (such as frequent connectives "And then . . ." and "After that, . . ."), not to mention the poet's tiresome habit of expressing numbers periphrastically, such as "X-number of days later, plus/minus Y-number." For the most part, however, I have retained these features in the translation since they were probably not incidental to what the poet regarded as his achievement in versifying such technical matter. Even so, it is not hard to understand why few translations of this poem have been published. I have consulted the rather free rendering into Modern English verse by Malone, "Old English Calendar Poem"; but more helpful is Greeson's dissertation, "Observance Poems," 196–212 (text) and 256–87 (commentary).

One of the more interesting features of this poem is its preservation of the Old English names for the various months, which agree, except in one instance (March), with those given and explained by Bede in *De temporum ratione* ("On the Reckoning of Time"), chap. 15, which I quote at the appropriate points below from Wallis's translation (but omitting her square brackets). Note that the Old English names for January (*Geola,* here spelled *Iula*) and July *(Liða)* are not actually given but are implicit in the names for December and June, viz. "the earlier *Iula*" and "the earlier *Liða.*" Readers desiring more background on the medieval liturgical calendar or particular saints and their feasts may consult Harper, *Forms and Orders of Western Liturgy,* 45–57; Farmer, *Oxford Dictionary of Saints;* and Cross and Livingstone, *Oxford Dictionary of the Christian Church.*

3b   "on the eighth day thereafter" *(on þy eahteoðan dæg):* I.e., eight days counted *inclusively* separate the feast of Jesus's nativity (Christmas, December 25) from that of his naming and circumcision (January 1). This is the only count that the poet reckons in this way (which would be the normal manner of numbering days in Latin). All the counts that follow will be *exclusive* of the starting term. Karasawa ("Note on the Old English Poem *Menologium* 3b") explains the apparent exception in line 3b as a

reflex of the widespread Latin liturgical designation for the
Feast of the Circumcision as the "Octave" of Christmas (i.e., the
eighth day [inclusive] after Christmas).

4a   "was given the name 'savior'" *("hælend" gehaten):* The poet alludes
to a widely known etymology of the name Jesus as "the Lord is
salvation." Old English *hælend* literally means "healing" or "sav-
ing."

7a   "the calends" *(se kalend):* Latin *kalendae* was the common term
for the first day of a month. Already among certain classical
Latin poets, however, the meaning of *kalendae* was extended to
include the month as a whole. It is in the latter sense that the
Menologium poet seems to use the term in the present line and
again in 31.

11b–12a   "the feast of the eternal Lord's baptism" *(fulwiht-tiid / eces driht-
nes):* Commonplace patristic and medieval traditions associated
the feast of Epiphany (January 6) not only with the adoration of
the Magi (Matthew 2:1–12) but also with two events from the
gospel accounts of Christ's later life, namely his baptism in the
Jordan by John the Baptist (Matthew 3:13–17, Mark 1:9–11, Luke
3:21–22), and the performance of his first public miracle at the
wedding feast in Cana (John 2:1–11).

16a   *Sol-monað* (February); "Solmonath can be called 'month of cakes,'
which they [the pagan Anglo-Saxons] offered to their gods in
that month" (Wallis, *Bede: The Reckoning of Time,* 54).

20   The "Mass of Mary" *(Marian mæssan),* or feast of the Purifi-
cation, on February 2 would later be known in the English-
speaking world as Candlemas. The poet will include the other
major Marian feasts at the appropriate points: the Annunciation
(March 25) at lines 48–54, the Assumption (August 15) at 148–53,
and the Nativity of Mary (September 8) at 167–69.

37a   *Hlyda* (March); Bede gives a different name, *Hreð-monað,* "named
for their goddess Hretha, to whom they sacrificed at this time"
(Wallis, *Bede: The Reckoning of Time,* 54).

39–40a   Saint Gregory I (or "the Great"), pope from 590 until his death
in 604, was especially honored by the Anglo-Saxons for the part
he played in their conversion to Christianity; see the note to
lines 97b–106a.

40b–44a Saint Benedict of Nursia (d. ca. 550) was widely venerated as one of the founders of western monasticism. The famous *Rule* attributed to him accounts for the poet's colorful description of monks as "warriors faithful to their Rule" (*rincas regolfæste,* line 44).

46–47 "since in the beginning God the ruler created both sun and moon" etc. *(forðan wealdend God worhte æt frymðe . . . sunnan and monan):* Some medieval authorities identified the fourth day of creation, when God fashioned the sun and the moon (Genesis 1:14–19), with the date of the vernal equinox (March 21); Bede discusses this and alternative opinions in his *Reckoning of Time,* chap. 6 (Wallis, 24).

60–62 "'This is the day'" etc. ("*Þis is se dæg*" etc.): Cf. Psalm 118 (Vulgate 117):24. The poet quotes from a preexisting Old English verse translation of the psalms, most fully preserved in the Paris Psalter. The latter, however, has *eorð-tudrum* ("offspring of earth") in place of *eorð-warum* ("inhabitants of earth") in our quotation. On the currency of the Old English metrical psalms in other late Anglo-Saxon contexts, see the introduction to Appendix B.

63–65 "We cannot keep that occasion by a fixed calendrical date" etc. (*Ne magon we þa tide be getale healdan / dagena rimes* etc.): These lines refer to the fact that Easter Sunday, the most important day in the Christian calendar, does not fall on a fixed date but varies from one year to the next. In the seventh-century Anglo-Saxon church, the proper method for calculating the date of Easter was a matter of contention between Irish and Roman missionaries.

68b–74 The occasion here described was known as "the Greater Rogation" (April 25), a day observed by fasting, ceremonial processions, litanic prayers, and preaching on penitential themes. Saints' relics, usually housed in precious containers, formed the focal point of the processions. It is to such relics that the poet refers in lines 73–74a.

72a *Easter-monað* (April); "Eosturmonath has a name which is now translated 'Paschal month,' and which was once called after a goddess of theirs named Eostre, in whose honour feasts were celebrated" (Wallis, *Bede: The Reckoning of Time,* 54).

78a   *Þry-milce* (May); "Thrimilchi was so called because in that month the cattle were milked three times a day; such, at one time, was the fertility of Britain or Germany, from whence the English nation came to Britain" (Wallis, *Bede: The Reckoning of Time,* 54).

83–87a   The claimed discovery of the True Cross by Saint Helena (d. ca. 330), mother of the emperor Constantine, came to be commemorated in the medieval west on May 3. A lengthy Old English poem, *Elene,* surviving in the tenth-century compilation known as the Vercelli Book, narrates in detail the dramatic events of Helena's search for the cross on which Christ was crucified.

97b–106a Saint Augustine, sent as a missionary to the Anglo-Saxons by Pope Gregory the Great (see 100b–101a), became the first archbishop of Canterbury, which office he held until his death, some time between 604 and 609.

106a   "in a famous monastery" *(mynstre mærum):* I.e., Saint Augustine's Abbey, the burial site of many early archbishops of Canterbury.

106b–9a "the month of June" etc.: Past editors disagree how to construe these lines, in which the subjects and direct objects are not clearly distinguishable and the syntax of *tiida lange* (107b) is uncertain. My translation follows the gist of Greeson's; he provides a good discussion of the problems in "Observance Poems," 270–71.

108a   *ærra Liða* (June); "Litha means 'gentle' or 'navigable,' because in both these months [i.e., June and July] the calm breezes are gentle, and they were wont to sail upon the smooth sea" (Wallis, *Bede: The Reckoning of Time,* 54).

116b   "the Lord's beloved" *(þeodnes dyrling):* The reference in 115b–119 is to the feast of the birth of Saint John the Baptist (June 24). On the basis of *dyrling* ("beloved, favorite"), Greeson suggests that the poet has confusedly bestowed on John the Baptist an epithet belonging to John the Evangelist, who was commonly identified as "the beloved disciple" mentioned in John 13:23, 19:26, 20:2, 21:7, and 21:20 ("Observance Poems," 272–73). But Old English *dyrling* was a term applied to various apostles and saints; see the *DOE,* s.v. *dyrling,* sense 1.a.i.

138a *Weod-monað* (August); "Weodmonath means 'month of tares,' for they are very plentiful then" (Wallis, *Bede: The Reckoning of Time,* 54).

140a "the day of Lammas" *(hlaf-mæssan dæg):* This name for August 1 refers to a medieval English custom of offering in church a loaf made from the first harvest.

146a Saint Laurence, an early Christian deacon, was famously martyred in 258 by being grilled alive.

151a "in Paradise" *(on neorxna-wange):* The Old English word refers here to the heavenly Paradise, but elsewhere it can also name earthly paradises; see the note to the translation of *The Phoenix,* line 394.

157b–60a "the death of a prince" etc. *(æþelinges deað* etc.): Although the poet does not directly name this saint, clues in the following description, as well as the given date, make plain that Saint John the Baptist is meant. His martyrdom by beheading was commemorated on August 29.

160b–62 "Concerning him the ruler said" etc. *(Be him wealdend cwæð* etc.): Cf. Matthew 11:11.

164a *Halig-monð* (September); "Halegmonath means 'month of sacred rites'" (Wallis, *Bede: The Reckoning of Time,* 54).

184a *Winter-fylleð* (October); "They called the month in which the winter season began 'Winterfilleth,' a name made up from 'winter' and 'full Moon,' because winter began on the full Moon of that month" (Wallis, *Bede: The Reckoning of Time,* 54).

195a *Blot-monað* (November); "Blodmonath is 'month of immolations,' for then the cattle which were to be slaughtered were consecrated to their gods. Good Jesu, thanks be to thee, who hast turned us away from these vanities and given us grace to offer to thee the sacrifice of praise" (Wallis, *Bede: The Reckoning of Time,* 54).

208a Saint Martin of Tours (d. 397).

214a Saint Clement of Rome, an early pope, martyred ca. 100. My translation attempts to capture the poet's learned reference to "Clement" as both a proper noun and an adjective (Latin *clemens,* "merciful, kind").

221a *ærra Iula* (December); "The months of Giuli [i.e., December and

January] derive their name from the day when the Sun turns back and begins to increase, because one of these months precedes this day, and the other follows" (Wallis, *Bede: The Reckoning of Time*, 54).

SOUL AND BODY

I have consulted Moffat's translations and commentary in *Old English* Soul and Body, as well the translation of *Soul and Body (I)* by Shippey (*Poems of Wisdom and Learning*, 104–11), and the editions and commentaries for both versions by Ricciardi ("Grave-Bound Body," 142–84).

9–11a   "the spirit must come, the soul every seventh night unceasingly for three hundred years, to seek out the body" *(Sceal se gast cuman . . . symble ymbe seofon niht sawle findan/þone lic-homan):* The notion that damned souls might enjoy periodic release from their torments has roots in ancient Jewish and Christian lore. Its currency in the early medieval west owes much to the popularity of the apocryphal text known as the *Visio Pauli* or *The Apocalypse of St. Paul.* One particular tradition about the "soul's respite" that eventually emerged was that this release occurred every Sunday, an idea perhaps reflected in the Old English poet's reference to "every seventh night"; see also lines 62–63, 66–71, and 103–4, below. Moffat (*Old English* Soul and Body, 32–33) provides further background on this apocryphal detail and its analogues in other Old English texts.

23b   "horrible desires" *(lust-gryrum):* The meaning of the compound is uncertain. My translation is close to Shippey's "terrible pleasures" (*Poems of Wisdom and Learning,* 105); alternatively, emend to *lust-grynum* ("snares of desire"), as in Grein's edition ("Reden der Seelen an den Leichnam," 199).

27–29a   "from heaven above, the angel sent a soul into you through his very own hand, the almighty creator" etc. (*þe la engel ufan of roderum/sawle onsende þurh his sylfes hand,/meotod ælmihtig* etc.): The grammar in these lines of the Vercelli *Soul and Body (I)* indicates that "the angel" and "the almighty creator" refer to the same being, namely Christ as God the creator. By contrast, the Exeter *Soul and Body (II)*, lines 24–26, says that "the almighty creator sent a soul into you through an angel" etc. As Moffat notes (*Old English* Soul and Body, 68–69), the latter, less orthodox form might be explained as tinkering by a copyist unfamiliar with exegetical traditions that interpreted some Old Testament references to "the angel of the Lord" as the preincarnate Christ; the strengths and weaknesses of this solution are well reviewed by Ricciardi, "Grave-Bound Body," 160–64.

40b–41 "thirsting after God's body, after drink for the spirit" *(ofþyrsted wæs / Godes lic-homan, gastes drynces):* I.e., the bread and wine of communion at Mass; see also lines 143b–44, below.

42–46 "For during life here . . . you failed to consider" etc. (*Forðan þu ne hogodest her on life* etc.): The meaning of these lines is not entirely plain. The alternative version in the Exeter *Soul and Body (II)* differs significantly (see the notes to the text). Moffat argues that lines 42–48 may be a single sentence, wherein 42–46 are a long clause subordinate to 47–48 (*Old English* Soul and Body, 70–72).

44–45a "that you were begotten by powerful drives, through flesh and through sinful desires" *(þæt ðu wære þurh flæsc ond þurh fyren-lustas / strange gestryned):* My interpretation of these lines follows Shippey's (*Poems of Wisdom and Learning,* 107); i.e., the soul suggests that the body was conceived in corruption, because sexual procreation has been tainted with concupiscence, whereas the soul has its origin in heaven.

49a "undoing" *(gescenta):* Soul and Body (I) in the Vercelli manuscript reads *gesynta* ("health, salvation"). I follow earlier editors and translators in supposing that the Exeter *Soul and Body (II)*, line 46, preserves the better reading, *gescenta,* a rare noun related to the verb *gescendan* ("to confuse, overthrow").

62a "sinews" *(synum):* The manuscript's *besliten synum* could mean "torn by sins." But, as Moffat's commentary points out, both context and the corresponding form *seonwum* at *Soul and Body (II),* line 57, make "sinews" the better choice (*Old English* Soul and Body, 74).

93–94a "in speech from the mouth of every single person his recompense for [Christ's] wounds" (*æt ealra manna gehwam muðes reorde / wunda wiðer-lean*): These lines are a crux; solutions are surveyed by Ricciardi, "Grave-Bound Body," 173–74; and Moffat, *The Old English* Soul and Body, 77–78. The form *wiðerlean* has been interpreted as a noun "repayment," or an infinitive verb "recriminate, blame." I take it as the noun and emend *wunde* (recorded in both manuscripts) to *wunda*. For the idea that all people must divulge their works on Judgment Day to find out whether their good deeds have sufficiently "repaid" Christ for suffering on the cross, compare *The Judgment of the Damned* (Appendix A), § 11.1. Less plausibly, emend *wunde* in Soul and Body 94a to *punda* "(monetary) pounds, talents," since scribes occasionally confused the letter p with the Anglo-Saxon form of *w* (the runic character p or *wynn*). The resulting line, translated "a repayment of talents," would allude to Christ's Parable of the Talents/Pounds (Matthew 25:14–30; Luke 19:12–26), an allegory of the Last Judgment suited to the present context. The version of the parable in Luke 19 (at verse 22: "Out of thy own mouth I judge thee, thou wicked servant") is possibly echoed in the wording of the Old English poem at line 93: "by speech from the mouth of every single person" will sinners condemn themselves.

111 "the fingers decayed" (*fingras tohrorene*): The line is short but there is no obvious gap in sense; there is nothing corresponding to this line in the Exeter *Soul and Body* (II). Grein posited as a lost b-verse *fet toclofene* ("the feet split apart").

112–27 "Ferocious worms ravage the ribs" etc. (*Rib reafiað reðe wyrmas* etc.): Thompson (*Dying and Death,* 138–43) notes the important polysemy of Old English *wyrmas,* here "maggots, worms" but with obvious overtones of aggressive, punishing serpents, which feature in both Christian and pagan representations of hell.

114–16 "the tongue is . . .; therefore it cannot" etc. (*Bið seo tunge. . . ; forþan heo ne mæg* etc.): Inexplicably, the Vercelli *Soul and Body (I)* shifts to a plural subject here: *beoð hira tungan totogenne. . . ; forþan hie ne magon* etc. ("their tongues will be torn. . . ; therefore they will not be able" etc.). Following several previous editors, I adopt the singular forms from the Exeter *Soul and Body (II)*, lines 108–10. Moffat provides a useful discussion of the passage in his commentary (*Old English* Soul and Body, 79).

133–35   "the souls will speak . . . and sincerely greet the body" (*þa gastas . . . sprecað . . . ond þus soðlice þone lic-homan . . . gretaþ*): The shift from a singular soul (line 128) to the plural "spirits" and accompanying plural verbs, then back to the singular "body" (*þone lic-homan,* 135), is awkward and hints at some corruption in the text.

153   "to everlasting joy" (*on ecne dream*): I take this as the beginning of a new line, as do Shippey (*Poems of Wisdom and Learning,* 110) and Moffat (*Old English* Soul and Body, 63). Although the result appears to be an incomplete verse, there is no evident gap in sense, nor have past editors posited any significant loss. In his edition, Krapp makes *on ecne dream* conclude the preceding b-verse (152 in my lineation).

161   "such graces as you previously ordained for us" (*swylcra arna swa ðu unc ær scrife*): This line does not appear in the manuscript but is a conjectural restoration proposed long ago by Grein ("Reden der Seelen an den Leichnam," 204, apparatus) and revived by Shippey (*Poems of Wisdom and Learning,* 110 and 140). The restored lines 160–61 thus deliberately echo the damned soul's words earlier, at 101–2. Alternatively, print ellipses after 160 to indicate at least one missing line of text.

169   The poem ends abruptly in mid-line; a leaf has gone missing from the Vercelli Book between present-day fols. 103 and 104.

THE SOUL'S ADDRESS TO THE BODY

A6–10   "Thus a child prophesies" etc. (*Þet bodeþ þet bearn* etc.): The belief that human suffering and mortality are symbolically heralded by newborns' cries was an early Christian and medieval commonplace, influenced by Wisdom 7:1–6.

A17–21   "Its ears grow deaf" etc. (*Him deaueþ þa æren* etc.): Such lists of the signs of death (or merely of old age) appear in many medieval texts; see Robbins, "Signs of Death."

A30b   "placed on the floor" (*iflut to þen flore*): This and the following lines have suggested to some scholars a custom, known from other sources, of placing the body of a dying or recently dead person upon a haircloth spread on the floor, with ashes poured on it in the shape of a cross (Ricciardi, "Grave-Bound Body," 220).

A33–35 Cf. *The Grave,* line 6.

B20a "You did not want to endear yourself to learned men" *(Noldest þu þe makien lufe; MS noldest þ . . . kien lufe):* Despite attempts at reconstruction, the syntax of the line remains unclear. Moffat prefers *Noldest þu makien lufe* and inclines to view *lufe* as an error for *lofe* ("praise") but does not emend *(Soul's Address to the Body,* 65). Other editors have suggested *lokien lufe,* "look to, take heed of love" (?). The line may be corrupt in addition to being lacunose.

B31 "He who keeps his riches is a slave" etc. *(Qui custodit divitias servus est divitiis):* The paradox that wealth enslaves echoes a number of biblical verses (cf. Proverbs 11:28; Ecclesiasticus 5:9 and 12; Matthew 6:24), not to mention certain Greek and Roman moralists. The Latin quoted by the poet at B30 is not directly from the Bible but is closest to a passage from Saint Jerome's commentary on Matthew (at 6:24): *Qui enim divitiarum servus est, divitias custodit ut servus* ("For he who is a slave to riches guards those riches as a slave would"). Jerome's statement was repeated and adapted by numerous medieval authors.

B37–40 Cf. *The Grave,* lines 17–18, 22, 5, 13, and 16.

C5 "you must now ride backward to earth" *(þu scalt nu ruglunge ridæn to þære eorþe):* Being forced to ride facing backward on a horse was evidently a ritual form of humiliation; see Mellinkoff, "Riding Backwards." This poet's striking adaptation of the motif—imposing the shame on a corpse "riding" to its grave—is apparently original.

C21 "Thy mouth hath abounded with evil" *(Os tuum habundavit malitia):* Psalm 50 (Vulgate 49):19.

C29–32 Cf. *The Grave,* lines 7–11.

C38–D7 An unusually graphic development of "the feast of the worms" motif is a symptom shared by the present *Soul's Address* and the earlier Old English *Soul and Body* (Ricciardi, "Grave-Bound Body," 240–41): compare fragment C, lines 38–39, with *Soul and Body* 112–13, C40 with *Soul and Body* 72–74a, C41–42 with *Soul and Body* 61–62a, C44 with *Soul and Body* 112, D6–7 with *Soul and Body* 108–9 and 120–21.

D19b   "mortality": The half-line in question, *þet þu icoren hefdest,* literally means "what you had chosen," but the object of the choice is unexpressed. I translate as if the poet is echoing an Old English idiomatic use of the verb "to choose" in euphemisms for death, such as "to choose another light" or "to choose the earth" (see *DOE,* s.v. *cēosan,* sense 1.a.i); cf. *Soul and Body* 157b, above. Ricciardi takes this and the following lines as statements and argues that the referent of *þet þu icoren hefdest* is the body's worldly and shortsighted way of living generally ("Grave-Bound Body," 248). Moffat also treats the two lines as statements but draws no definite conclusion as to their meaning (*Soul's Address to the Body,* 96).

D36   "your belly was your God and your glory was disfigured" *(for þin wombe was þin God ond þin wulder was iscend):* Cf. Philippians 3:19.

E22–25   "he plucked his harp skillfully and drew you to him" etc. *(þe wel tuhte his hearpe ond tuhte þe to him* etc.): A similar image of the devil as a harpist occurs in Homily X of the tenth-century Vercelli Book (Scragg, *Vercelli Homilies,* 200). The present lines in *The Soul's Address,* however, develop the theme by contrasting the devil's harp with church bells (cf. E26–29, developing a commonplace medieval allegory of church bells as the "voices" of Christian teaching and preaching). Ignoring the bells, the sinful body will finally be roused, too late, by the music of the trumpets on Judgment Day (cf. E32–33).

E30   "holes for [hearing] joyful noise" *(dream-purles):* I.e., the ears. This rare compound is difficult to render into Modern English except by periphrasis. The meaning is nevertheless clear both from context and from the two constituents, *dream* ("joyful noise"), and *þyrel* ("hole, aperture"); cf. Old English *nos-þyrel* ("nostril"), *eag-þyrel* ("eye-opening," i.e., "window").

E41   *"they shall offer a reckoning for their own deeds"* (*Reddituri sunt de factis propriis rationem):* The Latin quoted is in fact not from any biblical psalm but from an ancient Christian profession of faith called the Athanasian Creed.

E44b–45 The awkward repetition of the phrase "from the Lord's mouth" (*of drihtenes muþe*) in so short a space suggests a copyist's error. Perhaps in the first instance (line 44) the reference was to sinners' being condemned by the words out of their *own* mouths; cf. *Soul and Body* 93.

E46   *"Depart from me, you cursed ones, into everlasting fire"* (*Ite maledicti in ignem eternum):* Matthew 25:41.

E50   *"And those who have done good will depart into everlasting life"* (*Et qui bona egerunt ibunt in vitam eternam):* From the so-called Athanasian Creed; cf. E41.

F2   *"I opened my mouth and drew in breath"* (*Os meum aperui et attraxi spiritum):* Psalm 119 (Vulgate 118):131.

F20–33 "for you were thickly surrounded by sins, and they were all prickly, like the spines on a hedgehog" etc. (*for þu were biset picke mid sunnen, / ond alle heo weren prikiende so piles on ile* etc.): Medieval exegetical works, homilies, encyclopedias, bestiaries, and other didactic sources do develop moral allegories about the hedgehog, but the emphasis is usually on the animal's defensive strategy of curling into a ball, not on its spiny coat. No source has, to my knowledge, been identified for the simile as deployed here.

F35–40 "I was the seventh creature" etc. (*Ic was þe seoueþe isceaft* etc.): This particular scheme of *seven* elements—heavens (= fire?), earth, cloud (or air), angels, wind, water, and the human soul—as the material (*andweorke*, F42) of all things does not, to my knowledge, occur elsewhere. There are distant analogues, at least, in the enumerations of three or four primal elements (sometimes including angels and the soul) offered by various early Genesis commentaries of supposedly Irish origins. I am grateful to Charles D. Wright for elucidation of this passage.

F44   *"'Let there be,' and all things were made"* (*'Fiat,' et facta sunt omnia):*

The Latin line is not a direct quotation but echoes language repeated throughout the creation account in Genesis 1.

F49   *"in his image and likeness" (ad imaginem et similitudinem):* Cf. Genesis 1:26. The notion that creation "in God's image" referred to the endowment of human beings with an immortal, rational soul was a commonplace.

G20   *"Thy tongue framed deceits" (Lingua tua concinnabat dolos):* Psalm 50 (Vulgate 49):19.

G35   *"Thy wife as a fruitful vine" (Uxor tua sicut vitis habundans):* Psalm 128 (Vulgate 127):3. See the following note.

G36   "like the grapevine" *(so win-bowe):* The entire phrase has been lost from the manuscript. While Buchholz's reconstruction *to wedde* ("in pledge") is acceptable, I prefer Moffat's conjecture "like the grape-vine" (*Soul's Address to the Body,* 107–8), which more closely approximates *vitis* ("vine") in the Latin psalm verse just quoted in G35.

G37–48   "at the baptismal font" etc. *(et pen font-stone* etc.): This passage develops a series of linked allusions to precise moments in the medieval baptismal ritual. Before baptism, the child was anointed with oil on its chest and back (G39); after baptism followed an anointing on the top of the head (G40). The accompanying prayers in the ritual, not to mention various medieval sermons and commentaries, drew attention to parallels between baptismal anointings and those of kings at their coronations (G41). The godparents made a series of vows on behalf of the child (G44), including renunciations of the devil and his pride and vainglory (G47–48).

G51–56   The metaphor of marriage between body and soul, introduced at G34–36, is now skillfully transformed into a metaphor of parentage. The focus of this development is a quotation in G56 of Psalm 128 (Vulgate 127):3. Moffat's commentary on this passage notes that the "children" of soul and body referred to in these lines are probably to be understood as an allegorical representation of a Christian's good works.

G56   *"Thy children as olive plants . . ." (Filii tui sicut novella olivarum . . .):*

Psalm 128 (Vulgate 127):3. The text breaks off in mid-line; no more of it is known to survive.

THE GRAVE

7–10   "Your house will not be" etc. (*Ne bið no þin hus* etc.): These lines closely resemble *The Soul's Address to the Body*, C29–32. Compare also *The Grave*, lines 17–18, 22, 5, 13, and 16, with *The Soul's Address to the Body*, lines B37–40.

21   "and let light in around you" (*and þe æfter lihten*): The line is short and probably incomplete, making the translation uncertain.

23–25:   These lines were not originally part of the poem; see the notes to the text.

JUDGMENT DAY (I)

I have consulted translations by Mackie, *Exeter Book, Part II*, 157–63; Shippey, *Poems of Wisdom and Learning*, 121–25; and Anderson, *Two Literary Riddles*, 191–99.

1b–2a   "water will flow, a flood over the earth" (*lagu floweð, / flod ofer foldan*): The destructive element at the end times is more normally identified as fire, not water. (God had in fact promised never to send another general flood; see Genesis 9:13–15.) Scripture itself compares the ultimate fire with the earlier destruction of the world by the great flood in Genesis (see Matthew 24:37–39; 2 Peter 3:6), but that is clearly an analogy only. Fire is described as *like* a flood in another Old English account of Judgment Day, namely in the poem *Christ (III)*, lines 984–88 (Krapp and Dobbie, ASPR 3:30); see also *Judgment Day (II)*, lines 166–67, below. But the present poet clearly envisions a watery flood preceding the final conflagration (and perhaps also following it; cf. lines 38–39). Caie (*Judgment Day Theme*, 99–101) suggests some other possible influences, including eschatological references to floods in Old Irish and Old Norse sources. Anlezark (*Water and Fire*) explores in depth the frequently apocalyptic resonances of floods in Old English literature.

20b   "the place will remain shut tightly forever" *(a bilocen stondeð):* No
      subject for this clause is expressed in the Old English. I suggest
      it is "the place," implicit in the subordinating conjunction *þær* in
      line 19 and anticipating the antecedent of the pronoun "it" *(hit)*
      in lines 22ff. But some other translators take the subject as
      "light" (from *leohte,* line 20) that is being "shut *out*" of hell.
      According to the *DOE,* s.v. *be-lūcan,* the verb by itself normally
      means "to shut" (intransitive) or "to shut in, confine"; where it
      means "shut out," it is always accompanied by a clarifying ad-
      verb or preposition.

51a   "by a trumpet" *(þurh byman):* Here and at lines 109–12a, the
      sounding of a trumpet reflects another biblical motif (e.g., Mat-
      thew 24:31; 1 Corinthians 15:52).

56a   "blazing as it burns" *(blæc byrnende):* I take the Old English adjec-
      tive as a form of *blāc* ("bright, shining" or "flashing"), but it might
      also be from *blæc* ("pale" or "dark"), since the fires of Judgment
      Day were often associated with the fires of hell, and the latter
      were believed to emit no light.

58a   "shudders" *(Beofað):* The poet refers to one or possibly two
      earthquakes, another biblical detail (cf. Matthew 24:7; Apoca-
      lypse 6:12, 8:5, etc.) repeated confusingly in the poem; see also
      line 112b.

67a   "by a painful fetter" *(cearian clomme):* It is unclear whether this is
      merely a poetic periphrasis for Christ's being nailed to the cross
      or if the poet imagined Christ as literally bound or chained. Old
      English writings often use terms for bondage in their stock de-
      scriptions of devils and the damned in hell. Mention of bonds at
      the crucifixion may intend to symbolize Christ's substitutionary
      endurance of hell's torments.

75–76 "that he will, for the worse, be sorted among the host on the
      left" etc. *(þæt he bið on þæt wynstre weorud wyrs gescaden* etc.): Cf.
      Matthew 25:32–34 and 41.

105a "in the presence of the cross" *(æt þære rode):* The detail that an
      imposing cross will loom over those assembled at Judgment Day
      is not biblical but does occur in other Old English sources, e.g.,
      Vercelli Homily 2, lines 12–13 (Scragg, *Vercelli Homilies,* 55); the

poem *Christ (III)*, lines 1083–88 (Krapp and Dobbie, ASPR 3:33); and the poetic sermon on the Last Judgment printed in Appendix A, § 11.1.

JUDGMENT DAY (II)

I have consulted the translation by Bradley, *Anglo-Saxon Poetry*, 528–35, and the translation and commentary in Caie, "*Judgment Day II.*" The Latin source, the poem *De die iudicii* attributed to Bede, is here quoted from the edition by Fraipont (*Versus Bedae*, 439–44).

1–25   Like the Latin source, the Old English poem begins with the speaker's description of a *locus amoenus*. The Old English version departs from the Latin, however, by elaborating several details. The description of the brook and flowering plants (lines 3–6), for example, is not in the Latin and recalls evocations of Paradise in other Old English poems. Likewise, where the source describes the rustling leaves as part of a pastoral allusion, the Old English version has the wind's more forceful disturbance of the trees serve as a transition to the speaker's troubled thoughts. Caie provides a detailed discussion of these and other changes to the Latin source; see his "*Judgement Day II*," 58–64.

12   "all exactly as you said, recalling sins" etc. (*eall swylce þu cwæde, synna gemunde* etc): Some ingenious explanations have been proposed for this abrupt turn to an unidentified "you" (see Caie, *Judgment Day Theme*, 131 n. 2). The most plausible, however, is that the Old English poet has mistranslated his Latin source or been misled by a false reading in it. Lines 12–13 of the Old English render *De die iudicii* 6–7 (Fraipont, *Versus Bedae*, 439): *utpote commemorans scelerum commissa meorum, / et maculas vitae, mortisque inamabile tempus* ("in as much as I [was] recalling the transgressions of my sins, the blemishes on my life, and the detested occasion of death"). Either the translator's copy read *commemoras* (hence, "in as much as *you* recall," etc.), or the word was written *commemorās* but the translator failed to notice the nasal abbreviation above the *a*.

13b   "the hated hour" (*þa laðan tid*): The scribe wrote *lan*, which a different hand has altered to *langan* in the manuscript. The Old English original probably had *laðan* ("hated, loathed"), rightly translating *inamabile* ("unlovable, detested") in the Latin source (see the note to line 12, above).

45–46a   "disclose his wounds to the heavenly physician" (*wunda . . . gecyðe/uplicum læce*): The image of sin as a wound or sickness that must be disclosed to Christ, the divine physician, in order to be healed is a patristic commonplace widely invoked by medieval texts, especially those of the penitential tradition.

47   "by his beneficence, heal minds that have fallen away" (*aglidene mod gode gehælan*): The line as copied in the manuscript is corrupt (*Aglidene gyltas. mod god gehælan*). I follow Dobbie's solution in the ASPR text, but many other improvements have been suggested.

50a   "faltering" (*wan-hydige*): The line is corrupt but most editors agree in restoring an adjective *wan-hydige*, elsewhere meaning "foolish, lacking thought or sense." In the present context, however, *wan-hydige mod* clearly renders *quassatos . . . animos* ("crushed . . . minds") in the Latin source, *De die iudicii* 25. See the following note for the biblical source.

51b   "of a fragile wick:" The manuscript has *waces flæsces* ("of the weak flesh"), but most editors assume *flæsces* stands for an original form *flæcses* or *fleacses* ("flax"), with the contextual meaning "flaxen (wick)," derived ultimately from Isaiah 42:3 via the poem, *De die iudicii* 26 (*lini tepidos . . . fumos*). See Caie, "*Judgement Day II*," 37–38.

53–64   The example of the thief on the cross alludes to Luke 23:32–33 and 39–43.

100   This is the first of several short lines in the poem; see also 104, 121, 270, and 289. At none of these, however, is there any gap in sense. See also the note to line 196.

112a   "signs" (*tacn*): The Old English word is not in the manuscript but can be confidently supplied on the basis of the Latin source, *De die iudicii* 56 (*signa*) as well as the corresponding passage in the related prose homily (*tacne*).

114b   "join formation": I consider Old English *styllan* here to mean

423

something like "take position"; but the verb can also mean "jump, leap," in which case *styllað embutan* means "they leap [into position] about" Christ, here depicted as both military commander and judge.

166   "The violent flood crackles with fire" *(Ðæt reðe flod ræscet fyre)*: Cf. *Judgment Day (I)*, lines 1b–2a, above, and the accompanying note to the translation there.

178b   "this world:" Not in the manuscript, this b-verse *(þissere worulde)* is supplied from the parallel passage in the homiletic version, Napier Homily XXIX.

189a   "foul" *(fule):* Dobbie plausibly emends to *fulle* ("full"); if that is correct, translate "places full of fire at the bottom," etc.

196   The first half of this line is uncharacteristically long, leading Caie to print *hwilum eac þa teþ* as a separate half-line without a corresponding b-verse. On the poet's apparent tolerance of such short lines, see the note to line 100, above.

215–17   "why the offending flesh committed against it, during this dangerous time, so many sins that it should therefore be tortured in a prison" *(for hwi fyrngende flæsc on þas frecnan tid / hym selfum swa fela synna geworhte, / þæt hit on cweart-ern cwylmed wurde):* The antecedents of *hym selfum* and *hit* are not certain, but I assume that both refer to "flesh" *(flæsc,* line 215), an interpretation supported by the Latin source, *De die iudicii* 106–8.

242–43   "Then whatever is forbidden … in lightless, cruel flames" *(Ðonne blindum beseah … þæt unalyfed is nu):* The syntax of these lines admits various interpretations; my translation follows that suggested by the *DOE,* s.v. *be-sēon²*.

298–300   "flanked by fathers and sons" etc. *(betweox fæder and suna* etc.): The Old English lines involve several difficulties and have been variously interpreted. I adopt Whitbread's emendation ("Text-Notes," 532) of *sunu* to plural *suna* and understand these "fathers and sons" (line 298) as Mary's spiritual kindred in the family of all saints, whereas the "Father" of line 297b is the first person of the Trinity. This is more or less the interpretation of Caie, "Judgement Day II," 103 and 127–28, and one that accords well with the text of the Latin source at this point *(De die iudicii* 149–

50). Even so, some syntactic problems in the passage remain un-
resolved, and a very different interpretation is offered by Hill,
"Kingdom of the Father."

Epilogue: A Lament for the English Church

I have consulted the translations by Brehe, "Reassembling the First
Worcester Fragment," 530–31, and Donoghue, "Tremulous Hand," 81–82.

1–3   "Saint Bede was born . . ." etc. (*Sanctus Beda was iboren* etc.): The
Venerable Bede (d. 735) was the greatest scholar of the early
Anglo-Saxon church. Despite the poet's claim that he trans-
lated many works into English, only one short vernacular poem,
called *Bede's Death Song,* is plausibly attributed to Bede (but see
above, xxxviii n. 13).

4b   "*Quaestiones*" (*Questiuns*): Many patristic and medieval works of
biblical exegesis took the form (and sometimes the title) of
quaestiones, i.e., questions and answers about difficult points of
literal or allegorical interpretation of the scriptures. It is not
certain whether the poet here alludes to some authentic work
by Bede or to another work mistakenly attributed to him.

6–9   "Abbot Ælfric, whom we call Alcuin" etc. (*Ælfric abbod, þe we
Alquin hoteþ* etc.): Ælfric of Eynsham (d. ca. 1010) translated
portions of Genesis but probably not the parts of other Old Tes-
tament books included in the Old English *Heptateuch* (contain-
ing translations or paraphrases of Genesis, Exodus, Leviticus,
Numbers, Deuteronomy, Joshua, and Judges). So far as anyone
knows, Ælfric never called himself "Alcuin." The latter name be-
longs to a famous earlier scholar, Alcuin of York and Tours, who
died on the continent in 804. Alcuin wrote many works, one of
which, known as the *Questions on Genesis (Quaestiones in Genesim),*
was translated by Ælfric into Old English. It is possible that
such a link has simply confused the poet or the sources on
which he is relying. Or, as Brehe suggests, Ælfric, whose works
were known and appreciated at eleventh- and twelfth-century
Worcester, may have actually received there the complimentary

nickname "Alcuin" ("Reassembling the First Worcester Fragment," 531).

8   The order of the books given here is incorrect, and the poet or scribe has garbled the name "Deuteronomy." Brehe corrects the former but not the latter error ("Reassembling the First Worcester Fragment," 530–31).

11–15   This list of saints is arranged not chronologically but geographically according to the resting places of their relics, starting in the north and proceeding roughly counterclockwise through the west midlands, the southwest, and ending with Canterbury in the southeast (Brehe, "Reassembling the First Worcester Fragment," 532). Despite their grouping by region, most of the figures named here received wide veneration as saints in late Anglo-Saxon England. They are:

Wilfrid of Ripon, archbishop of York (664–678)
John of Beverly, archbishop of York (706–721)
Cuthbert of Durham, bishop of Lindisfarne (685–687)
Oswald, bishop of Worcester (961–992) and archbishop of York (971–992)
Ecgwin of Evesham, bishop of Worcester (ca. 693–717)
Aldhelm of Malmesbury, bishop of Sherborne (ca. 705–709)
Swithun, bishop of Winchester (ca. 852–ca.865)
Æthelwold, bishop of Winchester (963–984)
Aidan (see note to line 14b, below)
Birinus, bishop of Dorchester (634–ca. 650)
Paulinus, archbishop of York (625–633), then bishop of Rochester (633–644)
Dunstan, archbishop of Canterbury (959–988)
Ælfheah, archbishop of Canterbury (1006–1012)

The poet's assertion (line 16) that all these figures instructed the people in their own language (i.e., Old English) may derive from popular traditions or from claims made by these saints' biographers. But such claims were conventional in the *vitae* of medieval confessor-saints. On the place of the vernacular in the late Anglo-Saxon church, see the Introduction, ix–xi and xix.

14b   "Aidan . . . of Winchester" *(Aidan . . . Wincæstre):* The other bishop-saints named in this line—Swithun, Æthelwold, and Birinus—are all correctly linked to Winchester. (Although Birinus, as first bishop of the West Saxons, had his see at Dorchester, his cult was later closely associated with Winchester.) The inclusion here of Aidan, presumably the early bishop-saint of Lindisfarne (635–651), appears to disrupt the geographical organization of the list, but it is not necessarily an error. Veneration of Saint Aidan was revived in Wessex in the tenth century, after his relics were supposedly translated to Glastonbury (Brehe, "Reassembling the First Worcester Fragment," 532–33). The possibility does remain, however, that Saint Aidan of Lindisfarne has been confused with some other "Aidan" or similarly named saint.

17a   "their light was not dark" *(næs deorc heore liht):* Cf. Matthew 6:23.

20–21   *"As the eagle entices her young"* etc. (*Sicut aquila provocat pullos suos* etc.): Cf. Deuteronomy 32:11.

24b   "feathers" *(feþren):* Only the first three letters *feþ* are visible in the manuscript, leading most editors and translators to perceive an early form of the noun *feþren,* "feathers" (proposed by Donoghue, "Tremulous Hand," 82) makes better sense in view of the Latin just quoted in line 21.

APPENDIX A

At many points my translation is indebted to Stanley's, printed alongside his edition of the sermon. The notes below do not comment on details of the homilist's eschatological teachings that have already been discussed in the Introduction and in notes to the poems concerning Judgment Day.

1   "on which every creature" etc. (*in quo omnis creatura* etc.): Cf. Romans 8:22.

3.3   "God will reward" etc. (*Reddet deus* etc.): Cf. 2 Timothy 4:14.

4.2   "Depart, you accursed" etc. (*Farað ge awirgedan* etc.): Cf. Matthew 25:41.

5.1   "there is nothing . . . cut them off from our Lord's love" *(nan-*

wiht ne sy . . . fram ures drihtenes lufan ascadan): In the present context a bitterly ironic echo of Romans 8:38–39.

8.2   "the opening wide of the heavens . . . the dissolution of all creatures and destruction of the earth" *(seo geopnung heofona . . . eal-wihtna rire and eorðan forwyrd):* Perhaps cf. Isaiah 64:1–2: "O that thou wouldst rend the heavens, and wouldst come down: the mountains would melt away at thy presence. They would melt as at the burning of fire, that thy name might be made known to thy enemies: that the nations might tremble at thy presence."

"of all creatures" *(eal-wihtna):* Stanley ("Judgement of the Damned," 364 and 378) suggests emending *eal-wihtna* ("all creatures") to *el-wihtna* ("alien creatures"), referring to the damned. Other versions of the homily offer the reading *hell-wihta* ("creatures from hell").

"the crumbling of mountains" *(þara beorga geberst):* Stanley ("Judgement of the Damned," 365) translates "the bursting open of the grave-mounds."

11.1   "the actual cross" *(þa silfan rode):* See the note to the translation of *Judgment Day (I),* line 105a, above.

Appendix B

The following notes can supply only some of the information that the *Office* assumes its readers will already possess. For further information about the liturgical framework, see, in addition to the introduction to this appendix, the very accessible overview by Harper, *Forms and Orders of Western Liturgy,* 73–108, and the more advanced discussions in Tolhurst's *Introduction to the English Monastic Breviaries.* In translating the inserted Latin hymns, I have consulted Milfull's *Hymns of the Anglo-Saxon Church.*

1.1   "all ordained persons" *(eallum gehadedum mannum):* "Ordained" is a technical term applied to bishops, priests, deacons, and lower clergy, all of whom underwent sacramental rites of "ordination."

It is not entirely clear, however, whether the opening of the Junius *Office* refers only to secular clergy or means to include monastics as well. In late Old English usage, monks are also referred to as "ordained" (*gehadode*), whether in the sacramental sense (because more and more monks in the period were also ordained priests, deacons, etc.), or in a more general sense, based on the perception that all monastics entered their own separate "order" when they took their vows.

1.2   "*Seven times a day*" etc. (*Septies in die* etc.): Psalm 119 (Vulgate 118):164.

2.1   "*O God, my God*" etc. (*Deus, deus meus* etc.): Psalm 63:1 (Vulgate 62:2).

       "*I will meditate*" etc. (*In matutinis* etc.): Psalm 63:6–7 (Vulgate 62:7–8).

3.2   "*O God, come to my assistance*" etc. (*Deus in adiutorium meum* etc.): Psalm 70:1 (Vulgate 69:2). For the Old English verses, cf. Paris Psalter 69:1.

3.3   This hymn was sung invariably at Prime. The Latin text is adapted from Milfull, *Hymns*, 127–28.

3.4   "*Save me, O God*" etc. (*Deus in nomine tuo* etc.): Psalm 54:1 (Vulgate 53:3). For the Old English verses, cf. Paris Psalter 53:1. No function for this psalm quotation is specified in the manuscript, but I accept the view of Houghton ("The *Old English Benedictine Office* and its Audience"), who infers that the placement of *Deus in nomine tuo* between the hymn and *capitulum* suggests an incipit for the regular psalmody of Prime in its secular rather than monastic form. Psalm 54 (Vulgate 53) is the expected beginning of the psalm series for secular Prime on weekdays; it would then have been followed by Psalm 119 (Vulgate 118):1–16, and 119 (Vulgate 118):17–32. Throughout the *Office*, the quoted Latin psalm verses tend to follow the Gallican version of the psalter while the Old English translates the Roman. But here at § 3.4 both the Latin and the Old English reflect the Roman reading *libera me* ("free me") against the Gallican *iudica me* ("judge me").

3.5   "*Now to the king*" etc. (*Regi autem* etc.): 1 Timothy 1:17.

3.6   Modeled on the longer and more complex chanted responsories at Nocturns, the "brief response" *(responsorium breve)* appears in both secular and monastic usages. In liturgical performance, the present instance would have involved a full repetition of the first line *(Christe ... miserere nobis)* before the second, then a full repetition after the *Gloria patri*.

3.7   *"Arise, O Lord"* etc. *(Exurge, domine* etc.): Psalm 44 (Vulgate 43):26.

3.9–49   This long series of psalm verses corresponds essentially to what are known as the *preces* ("prayers") or *capitella de psalmis* ("little chapters from the psalms") normally recited at this point in the office of Prime. The precise form and use of the *preces* varied considerably in the earlier Middle Ages. It is nevertheless clear that their structure and content here in the *Office* (where they include the Apostles' Creed and *Confiteor*) accord generally with the so-called "Gallican *capitella*" inventoried by Tolhurst, *Introduction to the English Monastic Breviaries*, 30–36.

3.9   *"My soul shall live"* etc. *(Vivet anima mea* etc.): Psalm 119 (Vulgate 118):175. For the Old English verses, cf. Paris Psalter 118:175.

3.10   *"I have gone astray"* etc. *(Erravi sicut ovis* etc.): Psalm 119 (Vulgate 118):176. For the Old English verses, cf. Paris Psalter 118:176.

3.12   *"But I, O Lord"* etc. *(Et ego ad te* etc.): Psalm 88:13 (Vulgate 87:14). For the Old English verses, cf. Paris Psalter 87:13.

3.13   *"Give ear, O Lord"* etc. *(Verba mea* etc.): Psalm 5:1 (Vulgate 5:2).

3.14   *"Hearken to the voice"* etc. *(Intende voci* etc.): Psalm 5:2 (Vulgate 5:3).

3.15   *"For to thee will I pray"* etc. *(Quoniam ad te orabo* etc.): Psalm 5:3 (Vulgate 5:4).

3.16   *"In the morning I will stand"* etc. *(Mane adstabo* etc.): Psalm 5:4 (Vulgate 5:5).

3.17   *"Show, O Lord, thy ways"* etc. *(Vias tuas, domine* etc.): Psalm 25 (Vulgate 24):4.

3.18   *"Direct me in thy truth"* etc. *(Dirige me in veritate tua* etc.): Psalm 25 (Vulgate 24):5.

3.19   *"Remember, O Lord"* etc. *(Reminiscere* etc.): Psalm 25 (Vulgate 24):6.

3.20   "*The sins of my youth*" etc. (*Delicta iuventutis* etc.): Psalm 25 (Vulgate 24):7.

3.21   "*Judge thou, O Lord*" etc. (*Iudica, domine* etc.): Psalm 35 (Vulgate 34):1.

3.22   "*Take hold of arms*" etc. (*Adprehende arma* etc.): Psalm 35 (Vulgate 34):2.

3.23   "*Bring out the sword*" etc. (*Effunde frameam* etc.): Psalm 35 (Vulgate 34):2.

3.24   "*Let my mouth be filled*" etc. (*Repleatur os meum* etc.): Psalm 71 (Vulgate 70):8. For the Old English verses, cf. Paris Psalter 70:7.

3.25   "*Turn away thy face*" etc. (*Averte faciem tuam* etc.): Psalm 51:9 (Vulgate 50:11).

3.26   "*Create a clean heart*" etc. (*Cor mundum crea* etc.): Psalm 51:10 (Vulgate 50:12).

3.27   "*Cast me not away*" etc. (*Ne proicias me* etc.): Psalm 51:11 (Vulgate 50:13).

3.28   "*Restore unto me*" etc. (*Redde michi* etc.): Psalm 51:12 (Vulgate 50:14).

3.29   "*Deliver me, domine*" etc. (*Eripe me, O Lord* etc.): Psalm 140:1 (Vulgate 139:2). For the Old English verses, cf. Paris Psalter 139:2.

3.30   "*Deliver me from my enemies*" etc. (*Eripe me de inimicis meis* etc.): Psalm 59:1 (Vulgate 58:2). For the Old English verses, cf. Paris Psalter 58:1.

3.31   "*Deliver me from them that work*" etc. (*Eripe me de operantibus* etc.): Psalm 59:2 (Vulgate 58:3). For the Old English verses, cf. Paris Psalter 58:2.

3.32   "*So will I sing a psalm*" etc. (*Sic psalmum dicam* etc.): Psalm 61:8 (Vulgate 60:9). For the Old English verses, cf. Paris Psalter 60:6.

3.33   "*Hear us, O God*" etc. (*Exaudi nos, deus* etc.): Psalm 65:5 (Vulgate 64:6). For the Old English verses, cf. Paris Psalter 64:6.

3.34   "*Bless the Lord, O my soul*" etc. (*Benedic anima mea domino* etc.): Psalm 103 (Vulgate 102):1. For the Old English verses, cf. Paris Psalter 102:1.

3.35   "*Bless the Lord, O my soul*" etc. (*Benedic anima mea domino* etc.):

Psalm 103 (Vulgate 102):2. For the Old English verses, cf. Paris Psalter 102:2.

3.36   *"Who forgiveth"* etc. (*Qui propitiatur* etc.): Psalm 103 (Vulgate 102):3. For the Old English verses, cf. Paris Psalter 102:3.

3.37–38   *"Who redeemeth . . . who satisfieth"* etc. and *"Who crowneth . . . shall be renewed"* etc. (*Qui redemit . . . sanat* etc. and *Qui coronat . . . renovabitur* etc.): Cf. Psalm 103 (Vulgate 102):4–5, and, for the Old English verses, Paris Psalter 102:4–5. In both Latin and Old English, the wording of these verses follows the Roman psalter. The usual Gallican version swaps the latter halves of each verse, thus: *Qui redemit . . . qui coronat* etc. (102:4) and *Qui replet . . . renovabitur* etc. (102:5). In § 3.37, the reading *sanat* ("satisfieth" in the Douay-Rheims version) is not a common reading in either version but has probably been repeated by accident from Psalm 103 (Vulgate 102):3, just quoted at § 3.36.

3.39   A formulaic confession of sin is indicated, probably followed by the response-prayer *Misereatur* etc. Which form of confession was intended here is unclear; the incipit, *Confiteor Domino Deo celi,* is not the one that would become standard in the Roman rite (*Confiteor deo omnipotenti . . .*). Our formula does however resemble a briefer one that occurs, with variations, in some later medieval English books associated with the Sarum rite: *Confiteor deo celi, beate Marie, omnibus sanctis eius, et vobis: peccavi nimis in cogitatione, locutione, et opere, mea culpa. Precor sanctam Mariam, omnes sanctos dei, et vos orare pro me. Amen* ("I confess to the God of heaven, to blessed Mary, to all his saints, and to you: I have sinned exceedingly in thought, word, and deed by my own fault. I ask saint Mary, all God's saints, and you to pray for me. Amen").

3.40   *"Convert us, O God"* etc. (*Converte nos, deus* etc.): Psalm 85:4 (Vulgate 84:5). For the Old English verses, cf. Paris Psalter 84:4.

3.41   Unlike most of the surrounding verses, this item does not come from the psalms, which may explain why it has no following translation into Old English poetry. The Latin verse nevertheless appeared routinely in the "Gallican" form of the *preces;* see Tolhurst, *Introduction to the English Monastic Breviaries,* 34.

3.42   "*Have mercy on us*" etc. (*Miserere nostri* etc.): Psalm 123 (Vulgate 122):3. The Latin portion is omitted from the manuscript. Ure is probably right to assume an omission of the Latin by a simple copying error, since the Old English poetic translation does follow (*Benedictine Office*, 126). For the Old English, cf. Paris Psalter 122:4.

3.43   "*Let thy mercy*" etc. (*Fiat misericordia* etc.): Psalm 33 (Vulgate 32):22.

3.44   "*O Lord, save the king*" etc. (*Domine, salvum fac regem* etc.): Psalm 20:9 (Vulgate 19:10).

3.45   "*Save, O Lord, thy people*" etc. (*Salvum fac populum tuum* etc.): Psalm 28 (Vulgate 27):9.

3.46   "*Let peace*" etc. (*Fiat pax* etc.): Psalm 122 (Vulgate 121):7. For the Old English verses, cf. Paris Psalter 121:7.

3.47   "*Hear, O Lord, my prayer*" etc. (*Domine, exaudi orationem meam* etc.): Psalm 102:1 (Vulgate 101:2). For the Old English verses, cf. Paris Psalter 101:1.

3.48   "*Have mercy on me*" etc. (*Miserere mei* etc.): Psalm 51:1 (Vulgate 50:3). For the Old English verses, cf. Paris Psalter 50:1.

3.49   "*O Lord God of hosts*" etc. (*Domine deus virtutum* etc.): Psalm 80:19 (Vulgate 79:20). For the Old English verses, cf. Paris Psalter 79:18.

4.1–8   Depending on the season, the office of Prime could lead directly into Chapter, a daily business meeting for members of a religious community. The Junius *Office* gives no direct notice that Prime has ended, but we infer thus since the components at § 4.1–8 (plus many more) would normally have figured in the daily Chapter office. For more detailed descriptions of Chapter in some late Anglo-Saxon monastic and secular communities, see Symons, *Regularis concordia*, 17–18; and Langefeld, *Enlarged Rule of Chrodegang*, 367–68.

4.1   "*Precious in the sight*" etc. (*Pretiosa est in conspectu* etc.): Psalm 116 (Vulgate 115):15

4.3   "*O God, come to my assistance*" etc. (*Deus in adiutorium meum* etc.): Psalm 70:1 (Vulgate 69:2). For the Old English verses, cf. Paris Psalter 69:1.

4.4   Here and at the rest of the hours, the *Pater noster*, when mentioned, seems to refer to the simple Latin prayer and not a repetition of the Old English poetic paraphrase. The same is true for the Apostles' Creed *(Credo in deum),* recited again at § 9.7.

4.5   "*Look down*" etc. (*Respice* etc.): Psalm 90 (Vulgate 89):16. For the Old English verses, cf. Paris Psalter 89:18.

4.6   "*And let the brightness*" etc. (*Et sit splendor* etc.): Psalm 90 (Vulgate 89):17. For the Old English verses, cf. Paris Psalter 89:18

4.8   "*Our help*" etc. (*Adiutorium nostrum* etc.): Psalm 124 (Vulgate 123):8. "Pronounce the blessing" etc. (*Benedicite* etc.): Comparative evidence suggests that *Benedicite* here functioned as a versicle, to which a response was simply *Deus* ("God"). The grammar and hence the correct translation of this versicle and response are disputed.

5.4   "*O God, come to my assistance*" *(Deus in adiutorium meum intende):* Psalm 70:1 (Vulgate 69:2). For the Old English verses, cf. Paris Psalter 69:1.

5.5   This hymn was sung at Terce every day through much of the year, excepting Lent and Pentecost. The Latin text is adapted from Milfull, *Hymns*, 129–30.

5.6   This is one of only two references in the entire *Office* to the expected regular psalmody, but no precise incipits are given. For the other instance, which has no identifying label in the manuscript, see § 3.4.

5.7   "*Grace be to you*" etc. (*Gratia vobis* etc.): Colossians 1:3.

5.8   "*Be thou my helper*" *(Adiutor meus):* Psalm 27 (Vulgate 26):9.

5.10–12   The few verses quoted here look like a greatly reduced version of *preces* for the end of Terce, but it is impossible to know if these were all the compiler intended or if they were meant as cues for some fuller series, such as that documented by Tolhurst, *Introduction to the English Monastic Breviaries*, 40–41.

5.10   "*I said 'O Lord'*" etc. (*Ego dixi: domine* etc.): Psalm 41:4 (Vulgate 40:5).

5.11   "*Return, O Lord*" etc. (*Convertere, domine* etc.): Psalm 90:15 (Vulgate 89:13). For the Old English verses, cf. Paris Psalter 89:15.

Both the Latin quotation and the Old English version reflect the reading *aliquantulum* ("a little") of the Roman psalter against the Gallican variant *usquequo* ("how long").

5.12   *"Send them help, O Lord" (Mitte eis, domine, auxilium):* Cf. Psalm 20 (Vulgate 19):2.

"*Hear, O Lord*" *(Domine exaudi):* Psalm 102:1 (Vulgate 101:2).

"*The Lord be with you*" *(Dominus vobiscum):* Both here and later at § 9.10, the *preces* end with a common ritual dialogue. In full, it would be: V. *Dominus vobiscum* / R. *Et cum spiritu tuo* / V. *Oremus* ("The Lord be with you / And with your spirit / Let us pray"). The final collect for the hour follows immediately.

6.3   "*O God, come to my assistance*" *(Deus in adiutorium meum intende):* Psalm 70:1 (Vulgate 69:2). For the Old English verses, cf. Paris Psalter 69:1.

6.4   This hymn was sung at Sext every day through much of the year, excepting Lent and Pentecost. The Latin text is adapted from Milfull, *Hymns*, 131.

6.5   "*But prove all things*" etc. (*Omnia autem probate* etc.): 1 Thessalonians 5:21–22.

6.6   "*The Lord ruleth me*" *(Dominus regit me):* Psalm 23 (Vulgate 22):1.

7.2   "*O God, come to my assistance*" *(Deus in adiutorium meum intende):* Psalm 70:1 (Vulgate 69:2). For the Old English verses, cf. Paris Psalter 69:1.

7.3   This hymn was sung at None every day through much of the year, excepting Lent and Pentecost. The Latin text is adapted from Milfull, *Hymns*, 132.

7.4   "*Bear ye one another's burdens*" etc. (*Alter alterius honera portate* etc.): Galatians 6:2.

7.5   "*From my secret [sins]*" etc. (*Ab occultis meis* etc.): Psalm 19:12 (Vulgate 18:13).

8.4   "*Let my prayer, O Lord*" etc. (*Dirigatur, domine, ad te oratio mea* etc.): Psalm 141 (Vulgate 140):2. For the Old English verses, cf. Paris Psalter 140:2.

8.5   "*The grace of our Lord*" etc. (*Gratia domini nostri* etc.): 2 Corinthians 13:13.

8.6   *"Our help"* etc. (*Adiutorium nostrum* etc.): Psalm 124 (Vulgate 123):8. This and § 8.8 are the only parts of the *Office* in which the copyist has attempted to indicate responsorial structure by inserting the cues *V(ersiculum)* and *R(esponsum)* before the parts of the verse. These abbreviated signs, however, are reversed in the manuscript at § 8.6, from which Billett concludes that the item is not a versicle and response but a *responsorium breve.* If correct, his interpretation is significant, since the presence of a short responsory at this point would point to the monastic rather than secular office (Billett, "Divine Office," 435).

8.7   Some of the surviving Anglo-Saxon hymnals associate this hymn with first Vespers of Sunday (i.e., the Vespers office on Saturday evening). The Latin text is adapted from Milfull, *Hymns,* 109.

8.8   *"Let my prayer, O Lord"* etc. (*Dirigatur, domine, ad te oratio mea*): Psalm 141 (Vulgate 140):2. For the Old English verses, cf. Paris Psalter 140:2.

8.9   *"(At the gospel [canticle])" (Evangelio):* Medieval service books may refer to the *Magnificat* (Luke 1:46–55) at Vespers and the *Benedictus* (Luke 1:68–79) at Lauds as "the gospel [canticle(s)]." Thus, here the *Office* identifies the antiphon to accompany the *Magnificat* by the label *(In) evangelio* "[the antiphon] for the gospel [canticle]." The antiphon quoted is based on Luke 1:49–50.
       "(Psalm:) My soul doth magnify" ((Psalmus:) Magnificat): The abbreviation *P.* before the incipit in the manuscript probably stands for "Psalm." Sung daily at Vespers, the *Magnificat* is drawn from Luke 1:46–55, not from the book of Psalms. The tag *P(salmus)* here may only intend to indicate that the following text is performed with a proper antiphon, in the manner of psalmody.

8.11   *"I said, 'O Lord'" (Ego dixi: domine):* Psalm 41:4 (Vulgate 40:5). Here the psalm verse suggests the start of another series of *preces,* the length and composition of which cannot be determined. For the evidence available from other sources, see Tolhurst, *Introduction to the English Monastic Breviaries,* 40–41.

9.3   *"Convert us, O God" (Converte nos, deus):* Psalm 85:4 (Vulgate 84:5).

"O God, come to my assistance" (Deus in adiutorium meum): Psalm 70:1 (Vulgate 69:2).

9.4 Unlike at all the other hours, the compiler here gives incipits of two distinct hymns for Compline, *Te lucis ante terminum* and *Christe qui lux es.* The assignment of these two hymns varied in late Anglo-Saxon secular and monastic service books; see Milfull, *Hymns,* 133–36.

9.5 *"But thou, O Lord, art among us"* etc. *(Tu in nobis es, domine* etc.): Cf. Jeremiah 14:9.

9.6 *"Keep us, O Lord"* etc. *(Custodi nos, domine* etc.): Cf. Psalm 17 (Vulgate 16):8. After this versicle and response, and before the following *Kyrie* (see § 9.7), the canticle *Nunc dimittis* (a.k.a. the Song of Simeon, from Luke 2:29–32) would normally follow in the secular divine office. The absence of the *Nunc dimittis* at this point in the Junius *Office* may indicate that the compiler of the text was accustomed to the monastic (Benedictine) form of the liturgical hours (Billett, "Divine Office," 435).

9.7 *"I believe in God the Father" (Credo in deum patrem):* The Apostles' Creed; see the note above to § 4.4.

9.8 The first two incipits in this series are taken from the end of another office canticle, the *Benedicite.* Their expanded form might be *Benedicamus patrem et filium cum sancto spiritu; laudemus et superexaltemus eum in saecula. Benedictus es in firmamento caeli, et laudabilis et gloriosus in saecula* ("Let us bless the Father and Son, with the Holy Spirit; let us praise and exalt him forever. Blessed are you in the firmament of heaven, and [you are] worthy of praise and glorious forever"). After the blessing formula, the prayer *Dignare, domine, nocte ista* adapts to this time of day the versicle and response recited earlier at Prime (see § 3.41).

9.10 *"The Lord be with you"* etc. *(Dominus vobiscum* etc.): For this dialogue, see the note above to § 5.12. The following formula *Benedicamus domino* was answered by the response *Deo gratias* ("Thanks be to God").

10.1 *"I rose at midnight"* etc. *(Media nocte surgebam* etc.): Psalm 119 (Vulgate 118):62.

10.2 *"Watch ye therefore"* etc. *(Vigilate ergo* etc.): Mark 13:35.

10.3   *"Blessed are those servants"* etc. (*Beati servi illi* etc.): Luke 12:37.

11.1   *"Pray without ceasing"* (*Sine intermissione orate):* 1 Thessalonians 5:17.

11.2   *"Therefore, whether you eat or drink"* etc. (*Sive enim manducatis sive bibitis* etc.): 1 Corinthians 10:31.

11.3   *"Be thou my helper"* etc. (*Adiutor meus esto* etc.): Psalm 27 (Vulgate 26):9.

11.4   *"Our help"* etc. (*Adiutorium nostrum* etc.): Psalm 124 (Vulgate 123):8.

Bibliography

This is by no means a complete bibliography but rather includes only primary and secondary works cited in the introductions, texts, translations, and notes. For systematic coverage of bibliography, readers should consult Stanley B. Greenfield and Fred C. Robinson, *A Bibliography of Publications on Old English Literature to the End of 1972* (Toronto, 1980), as well as the annual bibliographies in the *Old English Newsletter* and in the journal *Anglo-Saxon England.*

EDITIONS AND TRANSLATIONS OF PRIMARY SOURCES

Allen, Michael J. B., and Daniel G. Calder, trans. *Sources and Analogues of Old English Poetry: The Major Latin Sources in Translation.* Cambridge, 1976.

Anderson, James E., ed. and trans. *Two Literary Riddles in the Exeter Book: Riddle 1 and The Easter Riddle.* Norman, Okla., 1986.

Anlezark, Daniel, ed. and trans. *Old Testament Narratives.* Dumbarton Oaks Medieval Library [DOML 7]. Cambridge, Mass., 2011.

Blake, N. F., ed. *The Phoenix.* Manchester, 1964. Revised reprint for Exeter Medieval Texts and Studies, Exeter, 1990.

Bradley, S. A. J., trans. *Anglo-Saxon Poetry.* London. 1982. Revised reprint, London, 1995.

Buchholz, Richard, ed. *Die Fragmente der Reden der Seele an den Leichnam in zwei Handschriften zu Worcester und Oxford.* Erlanger Beiträge zur englischen Philologie 6. Erlangen, 1890.

Caie, Graham D., ed. and trans. *The Old English Poem "Judgement Day II."* Anglo-Saxon Texts 2. Cambridge, 2000.

Clunies Ross, Margaret, and Craig Edwards, eds. and trans. "Thureth: A

Neglected Old English Poem and Its Place in Anglo-Saxon Scholarship." *Notes and Queries* 246, new series 48 (2001): 359–70.

Colgrave, Bertram, and R. A. B. Mynors, eds. and trans. *Bede's Ecclesiastical History.* Oxford, 1969.

Curley, Michael J. *Physiologus.* Austin, Tex., 1979. Revised reprint, Chicago, 2009.

Dickins, Bruce, and R. M. Wilson, eds. *Early Middle English Texts.* Cambridge, 1951.

Dobbie, Elliott Van Kirk, ed. *The Anglo-Saxon Minor Poems.* ASPR 6. New York, 1942.

Fraipont, J., ed. *Versus Bedae presbyteri de die iudicii.* In *Bedae venerabilis opera, pars IV: Opera rhythmica,* ed. J. Fraipont, 439–44. Corpus Christianorum, Series Latina 122. Turnhout, 1955.

Gordon, R. K., trans. *Anglo-Saxon Poetry.* Revised reprint, London, 1954.

Greeson, Hoyt St. Clair, ed. and trans. "Two Old English Observance Poems: *Seasons for Fasting* and *The Menologium*—An Edition." Unpublished PhD diss., University of Oregon, 1970.

Grein, C. W. M., ed. "Reden der Seelen an den Leichnam." In *Bibliothek der angelsächsischen Poesie,* ed. C. W. M. Grein, 1:198–204. 1st ed. Göttingen, 1857.

Haines, Dorothy, ed. and trans. *Sunday Observance and the Sunday Letter in Anglo-Saxon England.* Anglo-Saxon Texts 8. Cambridge, 2010.

Hall, Joseph, ed. *Selections from Early Middle English, 1130–1250.* 2 vols. Oxford, 1920.

Hilton, Chadwick Buford, Jr., ed. and trans. "An Edition and Study of the Old English *Seasons for Fasting.*" Unpublished PhD diss., University of Tennessee, 1984.

Holthausen, Ferdinand, ed. "Ein altenglisches Gedicht über die Fastenzeiten." *Anglia* 71 (1953): 191–201.

Johansen, Jan Geir, ed. "'The Worcester fragments' (Worcester Cathedral Ms. F.174, ff.63r–66v): An Edition, with Diplomatic Transcription, Notes and Glossary." Unpublished PhD diss., University of Sheffield, 1985.

Keefer, Sarah Larratt, ed. *Old English Liturgical Verse: A Student Edition.* Peterborough, Ontario, 2010.

Krapp, George Philip, ed. *The Paris Psalter and the Meters of Boethius.* ASPR 5. New York, 1932.

———. *The Vercelli Book.* ASPR 2. New York, 1932.

Krapp, George Philip, and Elliott Van Kirk Dobbie, eds. *The Exeter Book.* ASPR 3. New York, 1936.

Langefeld, Brigitte, ed. and trans. *The Old English Versions of the Enlarged Rule of Chrodegang, edited together with the Latin Text and an English Translation.* Texte und Untersuchungen zur englischen Philologie 26. Frankfurt am Main, 2003.

Lapidge, Michael, and Michael Herren, trans. *Aldhelm: The Prose Works.* Cambridge, 1979.

Mackie, W. S., ed. and trans. *The Exeter Book, Part II: Poems IX–XXXII.* Early English Text Society, Original Series 194. London, 1934.

Malmberg, Lars, ed. *Resignation.* Durham and St. Andrews Medieval Texts 2. Durham, 1979.

Malone, Kemp, trans. "The Old English Calendar Poem." In *Studies in Language, Literature, and Culture of the Middle Ages and Later,* ed. E. Bagby Atwood and Archibald A. Hill, 193–99. Austin, Tex., 1969.

McClure, Judith, and Roger Collins, eds. and trans. *Bede: The Ecclesiastical History of the English People; The Greater Chronicle; Bede's Letter to Egbert.* Oxford, 1994.

Milfull, Inge B., ed. and trans. *The Hymns of the Anglo-Saxon Church: A Study and Edition of the "Durham Hymnal."* Cambridge Studies in Anglo-Saxon England 17. Cambridge, 1996.

Moffat, Douglas, ed. and trans. *The Old English* Soul and Body. Cambridge, 1990.

———, ed. *The Soul's Address to the Body: The Worcester Fragments.* Medieval Texts and Studies 1. Lansing, Mich., 1987.

Muir, Bernard J., ed. *The Exeter Anthology of Old English Poetry: An Edition of Exeter Dean and Chapter MS 3501.* 2 vols. Revised second edition. Exeter, 2000.

Napier, A., ed. *Wulfstan: Sammlung der ihm zugeschriebenen Homilien nebst Untersuchungen über ihre Echtheit.* 1883. Reprinted with a bibliographical supplement by Klaus Ostheer, Dublin, 1967.

O'Donnell, Daniel Paul, ed. *Cædmon's Hymn: A Multi-Media Study, Edition and Archive.* Cambridge, 2005.

O'Neill, Patrick P., ed. *King Alfred's Old English Prose Translation of the First Fifty Psalms.* Medieval Academy Books 104. Cambridge, Mass., 2001.

Ricciardi, Gail Dana Dauterman, ed. "The Grave-Bound Body and Soul: A Collective Edition of Four Related Poems from *The Vercelli* and *Exeter Books,* Bodley and Worcester Manuscripts." Unpublished PhD diss., University of Pennsylvania, 1976.

Robinson, Fred C. "*The Rewards of Piety:* Two Old English Poems in their Manuscript Context." In *Hermeneutics and Medieval Culture,* ed. P. J. Gallacher and Helen Damico, 193–200. Albany, N.Y., 1989. Reprinted in his *The Editing of Old English,* 180–95, Oxford, 1994.

Rosier, James L., ed. "'Instructions for Christians': A Poem in Old English." *Anglia* 82 (1964): 4–22.

Scragg, D. G., ed. *The Vercelli Homilies and Related Texts.* Early English Text Society, Original Series 300. Oxford, 1992.

Shippey, T. A., ed. and trans. *Poems of Wisdom and Learning in Old English.* Cambridge, 1976.

Squires, Ann, ed. *The Old English Physiologus.* Durham Medieval Texts 5. Durham, 1988.

Stanley, Eric Gerald. "*The Judgement of the Damned,* from Corpus Christi College Cambridge 201 and Other Manuscripts, and the Definition of Old English Verse." In *Learning and Literature in Anglo-Saxon England: Studies Presented to Peter Clemoes on the Occasion of his Sixty-Fifth Birthday,* ed. Michael Lapidge and Helmut Gneuss, 363–91. Cambridge, 1985.

Stephenson, Joseph, ed. *Libellus de vita et miraculis S. Godrici, heremitae de Finchale, auctore Reginaldo monacho Dunelmense.* Publications of the Surtees Society 20. London, 1847.

Symons, Thomas, ed. and trans. *Regularis concordia Anglicae nationis monachorum sanctimonialiumque: The Monastic Agreement of the Monks and Nuns of the English Nation.* London, 1953.

Thorpe, Benjamin, ed. and trans. *The Homilies of the Anglo-Saxon Church, the First Part, Containing the* Sermones catholici *or Homilies of Ælfric, in the Original Anglo-Saxon, with an English Version.* 2 vols. London, 1844–1846.

Ure, James M., ed. *The Benedictine Office: An Old English Text.* Edinburgh University Publications in Language and Literature 11. Edinburgh, 1957.

Wallis, Faith, trans. *Bede: The Reckoning of Time.* Translated Texts for Historians 29. Liverpool, 1999.

Youngs, Susan Grinna, ed. and trans. "A New Edition of 'Instructions for Christians': CUL Ii. 1. 33." Unpublished PhD diss., University of Wisconsin, Madison, 1995.

Zupitza, Julius. "Cantus beati Godrici." *Englische Studien* 11 (1888): 401–32.

Secondary Works

Abram, Christopher. "Aldhelm and the Two Cultures of Anglo-Saxon Poetry." *Literature Compass* 4/5 (2007): 1354–77.

Anlezark, Daniel. *Water and Fire: The Myth of the Flood in Anglo-Saxon England.* Manchester, 2006.

Bammesberger, Alfred. "The Old English *Phoenix*, l. 407b: *topas idge.*" *Neuphilologische Mitteilungen* 101 (2000): 45–49.

Biggs, Frederick M. "The Eschatological Conclusion of the Old English *Physiologus.*" *Medium Ævum* 58 (1989): 286–97.

Billett, Jesse D. "The Divine Office and the Secular Clergy in Later Anglo-Saxon England." In *England and the Continent in the Tenth Century,* ed. David Rollason, Conrad Leyser, and Hannah Williams, 429–71. Studies in the Early Middle Ages 37. Turnhout, 2010.

Bliss, Alan, and Allen J. Frantzen. "The Integrity of *Resignation.*" *Review of English Studies,* new series 27 (1976): 385–402.

Bredehoft, Thomas A. *Early English Metre.* Toronto Old English Series 15. Toronto, 2005.

Brehe, S. K. "Reassembling the *First Worcester Fragment.*" *Speculum* 65 (1990): 521–36.

Brown, Alan K. "Neorxnawang." *Neuphilologische Mitteilungen* 74 (1973): 610–23.

Caie, Graham D. *The Judgment Day Theme in Old English Poetry.* Publications of the Department of English, University of Copenhagen, 2. Copenhagen, 1976.

———. "Text and Context in Editing Old English: The Case of the Poetry in Cambridge, Corpus Christi College 201." In *The Editing of Old English,* ed. D. G. Scragg and Paul E. Szarmach, 155–62. Cambridge, 1994.

Conner, Patrick. "The Structure of the Exeter Book Codex (Cathedral Library, MS. 3501)." *Scriptorium* 40 (1986): 233–42.

Cosijn, P. J. "Anglosaxonica IV." *Beiträge zur Geschichte der deutschen Sprache und Literatur* 23 (1898): 104–30.

Cross, F. L., and E. A. Livingstone, eds. *The Oxford Dictionary of the Christian Church.* 3rd rev. ed. Oxford, 2005.

Donoghue, Daniel. "The Tremulous Hand and Flying Eaglets." *English Language Notes* 44 (2006): 81–86.

Drout, Michael D. C. "'The Partridge' is a Phoenix: Revising the Exeter Book *Physiologus.*" *Neophilologus* 91 (2007): 487–503.

Farmer, David Hugh, ed. *The Oxford Dictionary of Saints.* 5th ed. Oxford, 2003.

Forbes, Helen Foxhall. "*Diuiduntur in quattuor:* The Interim and Judgement in Anglo-Saxon England." *Journal of Theological Studies* 61 (2010): 659–84.

Förster, Max. "Zur Liturgik der angelsächsischen Kirche." *Anglia* 66 (1942): 1–51.

Frank, Roberta. "Late Old English *Þrymnys* 'Trinity': Scribal Nod or Word Waiting to be Born?" In *Old English and New: Studies in Language and Linguistics in Honor of Frederic G. Cassidy,* ed. Joan H. Hall, Nick Doane, and Dick Ringler, 97–110. New York, 1992.

———. "Old English *æræt*—'too much' or 'too soon'?" In *Words, Texts and Manuscripts: Studies in Anglo-Saxon Culture Presented to Helmut Gneuss on the Occasion of His Sixty-Fifth Birthday,* ed. Michael Korhammer, with Karl Reichl and Hans Sauer, 293–303. Cambridge, 1992.

———. "Poetic Words in Late Old English Prose." In *From Anglo-Saxon to Early Middle English: Studies Presented to E. G. Stanley,* ed. Malcolm Godden, Douglas Gray, and Terry Hoad, 87–107. Oxford, 1994.

Frantzen, Allen J. *The Literature of Penance in Anglo-Saxon England.* New Brunswick, N.J., 1983.

Fulk, R. D., and Christopher M. Cain, with Rachel S. Anderson. *A History of Old English Literature.* Oxford, 2003.

Gatch, Milton McC. "Eschatology in the Anonymous Old English Homilies." *Traditio* 21 (1965): 117–65.

Gittos, Helen. "Is There Any Evidence for the Liturgy of Parish Churches in Late Anglo-Saxon England? The Red Book of Darley and the Status of Old English." In *Pastoral Care in Late Anglo-Saxon England,* ed. Francesca Tinti, 63–82. Anglo-Saxon Studies 6. Woodbridge, 2005.

Godden, Malcolm. "Anglo-Saxons on the Mind." In *Learning and Literature in Anglo-Saxon England,* ed. Michael Lapidge and Helmut Gneuss, 271–98. Cambridge, 1985.

Gorst, E. K. C. "Latin Sources of the Old English *Phoenix.*" *Notes and Queries* 251, new series 53 (2006): 136–42.

Gransden, Antonia. "Cultural Transition at Worcester in the Anglo-Norman Period." In *Medieval Art and Architecture at Worcester Cathedral,* 1–13. London, 1978.

Grant, R. J. S. "A Note on 'The Seasons for Fasting.'" *Review of English Studies,* new series 23 (1972): 302–4.

Grein, C. W. M. *Sprachschatz der angelsächsischen Dichter, unter Mitwirkung von F. Holthausen, neu herausgegeben von J. J. Köhler.* Heidelberg, 1912.

Griffith, Mark. "Old English *bræd,* 'flesh': a Ghost Form?" *Notes and Queries* 240, new series 42 (1995): 7–8.

Harper, John. *The Forms and Orders of Western Liturgy from the Tenth to the Eighteenth Century: A Historical Introduction and Guide for Students and Musicians.* Oxford, 1991.

Heningham, Eleanor K. "Old English Precursors of *The Worcester Fragments.*" *PMLA* 55 (1940): 291–307.

Hennig, John. "The Irish Counterparts of the Anglo-Saxon *Menologium.*" *Mediaeval Studies* 14 (1952): 98–106.

Hill, Thomas D. "The Kingdom of the Father, Son and Counsellor: Judgement Day II, 290–300." *Notes and Queries* 220, new series 32 (1985): 7–8.

———. "The *Syrwarena lond* and the Itinerary of the Phoenix: A Note on Typological Allusion in the Old English 'Phoenix.'" *Notes and Queries* 221, new series 23 (1976): 482–84.

Holsinger, Bruce. "The Parable of Cædmon's *Hymn:* Liturgical Invention and Literary Tradition." *JEGP* 106 (2007): 149–75.

Houghton, John William. "The *Old English Benedictine Office* and its Audience." *American Benedictine Review* 45 (1994): 431–45.

Johansen, Jan Geir. "The Cohesion of the Worcester Fragments." *Papers on Language and Literature* 30 (1994): 157–68.

Jones, Christopher A. "Performing Christianity: Liturgical and Devotional Writing." In *The Cambridge History of Early Medieval English Literature,* ed. Clare Lees. Cambridge, forthcoming.

445

———. "Wulfstan's Liturgical Interests." In *Wulfstan, Archbishop of York: The Proceedings of the Second Alcuin Conference,* ed. Matthew Townend, 325–52. Studies in the Early Middle Ages 10. Turnhout, 2004.

Kabir, Ananya. *Paradise, Death and Doomsday in Anglo-Saxon Literature.* Cambridge Studies in Anglo-Saxon England 32. Cambridge, 2001.

Karasawa, Kazumoto. "A Note on the Old English Poem *Menologium* 3b *on þy eahteoðan dæg.*" *Notes and Queries* 252, new series 54 (2007): 211–15.

———. "Some Problems in the Editions of the *Menologium,* with Special Reference to Lines 81a, 184b and 206a." *Notes and Queries* 254, new series 56 (2009): 485–87.

Keefer, Sarah Larratt. "In Closing: Amen and Doxology in Anglo-Saxon England." *Anglia* 121 (2003): 110–37.

Ker, N. R. *Catalogue of Manuscripts Containing Anglo-Saxon.* Oxford, 1957.

Klinck, Anne L. "*Resignation:* Exile's Lament or Penitent's Prayer?" *Neophilologus* 71 (1987): 423–30.

Lapidge, Michael. "Bede and the 'Versus de die iudicii.'" In *Nova de veteribus: Mittel- und neulateinische Studien für Paul Gerhard Schmidt,* ed. Andreas Bihrer and Elisabeth Stein, 103–11. Munich, 2004.

Leclercq, Jean. *Études sur le vocabulaire monastique du moyen âge.* Studia Anselmiana 48. Rome, 1961.

Lendinara, Patrizia. "Translating Doomsday: *De die iudicii* and its Old English Translation." In *Beowulf and Beyond,* ed. Hans Sauer and Renate Bauer, 17–67. Studies in English Medieval Language and Literature 18. Frankfurt am Main, 2006.

Leslie, R. F. "Textual Notes on *The Seasons for Fasting.*" *Journal of English and Germanic Philology* 52 (1953): 555–58.

Letson, D. R. "The Poetic Content of the Revival Homily." In *The Old English Homily and its Backgrounds,* ed. Paul E. Szarmach and Bernard F. Huppé, 139–56. Albany, N.Y., 1978.

Lindström, Bengt. "*The Phoenix,* lines 240–2 and 407–9." *Notes and Queries* 241, new series 43 (1996): 13–14.

Lockett, Leslie. *Anglo-Saxon Psychologies in the Vernacular and Latin Traditions.* Toronto Anglo-Saxon Series 8. Toronto, 2011.

Mellinkoff, Ruth. "Riding Backwards: Theme of Humiliation and Symbol of Evil." *Viator* 4 (1973): 153–76.

Meritt, Herbert D. *Fact and Lore about Old English Words.* Stanford, 1954.

Milfull, Inge B. "Formen und Inhalte lateinisch-altenglischer Textensembles und Mischtexte: Durham Cathedral B. III. 32 und 'The Phoenix.'" In *Volkssprachig-lateinische Mischtexte und Textensembles in der althochdeutschen, altsächsischen und altenglischen Überlieferung,* ed. Rolf Bergmann, 467–91. Heidelberg, 2003.

Mize, Britt. "The Representation of the Mind as an Enclosure in Old English Poetry." *Anglo-Saxon England* 35 (2004): 57–90.

Moffat, Douglas. "A Case of Scribal Revision in the Old English *Soul and Body*." *Journal of English and Germanic Philology* 86 (1987): 1–8.

O'Donnell, Daniel Paul. "Fish and Fowl: Generic Expectations and the Relationship between the Old English *Phoenix*-poem and Lactantius's *De ave phoenice*." In *Germanic Texts and Latin Models: Medieval Reconstructions,* ed. K. E. Olsen, A. Harbus, and T. Hofstra, 157–71. Mediaevalia Groningana 2. Leuven, 2001.

———. "*Hædre* and *hædre gehogode* (*Solomon and Saturn,* line 62b, and *Resignation,* line 63a)." *Notes and Queries* 244, new series 46 (1999): 12–16.

Ogawa, Hiroshi. *Language and Style in Old English Composite Homilies*. Medieval and Renaissance Texts and Studies 361. Tempe, Ariz., 2010.

O'Keeffe, Katherine O'Brien. *Visible Song: Transitional Literacy in Old English Verse*. Cambridge Studies in Anglo-Saxon England 4. Cambridge, 1990.

Olson, Aleisha. "Textual Representations of Almsgiving in Anglo-Saxon England." Unpublished PhD diss., University of York, 2010.

Orchard, Andy. *The Poetic Art of Aldhelm*. Cambridge Studies in Anglo-Saxon England 8. Cambridge, 1994.

———. "The Word Made Flesh: Christianity and Oral Culture in Anglo-Saxon Verse." *Oral Tradition* 24 (2009): 293–318.

Orton, Peter. "Disunity in the Vercelli Book *Soul and Body*." *Neophilologus* 63 (1979): 450–60.

Pakis, Valentine A. "A Note in Defense of 'The Partridge' (Exeter Book 97v)." *Neophilologus* 92 (2008): 729–34.

Pulsiano, Phillip. "*The Phoenix,* lines 199b–207 and Psalm 101.7–8." *ANQ,* new series 2 (1989): 3–7.

———. "Prayers, Glosses and Glossaries." In *A Companion to Anglo-Saxon Literature,* ed. Phillip Pulsiano and Elaine Treharne, pp. 209–30. Oxford, 2001.

Randle, Jonathan T. "The 'Homiletics' of the Vercelli Book Poems: The Case of *Homiletic Fragment I*." In *New Readings in the Vercelli Book,* ed. Samantha Zacher and Andy Orchard, 185–224. Toronto, 2009.

Richards, Mary P. "Old Wine in a New Bottle: Recycled Instructional Materials in *Seasons for Fasting*." In *The Old English Homily: Precedent, Practice, and Appropriation,* ed. Aaron J. Kleist, 345–64. Studies in the Early Middle Ages 17. Turnhout, 2007.

———. "Prosaic Poetry: Late Old English Poetic Composition." In *Old English and New: Studies in Language and Linguistics in Honor of Frederic G. Cassidy,* ed. Joan H. Hall, Nick Doane, and Dick Ringler, 63–75. New York, 1992.

Robbins, Rossell Hope. "Signs of Death in Middle English." *Mediaeval Studies* 32 (1970): 282–98.

Robinson, Fred C. "Notes and Emendations to Old English Poetic Texts." *Neuphilologische Mitteilungen* 67 (1966): 356–64. Reprinted in his *The Editing of Old English,* 116–27, Oxford, 1994.

Rosier, James L. "Addenda to 'Instructions for Christians.'" *Anglia* 84 (1966): 74.

Sauer, Hans. "Die 72 Völker und Sprachen der Welt: Ein mittelalterlicher Topos in der englischen Literatur." *Anglia* 101 (1983): 29–48.

———. "Die 72 Völker und Sprachen der Welt: Einige Ergänzungen." *Anglia* 107 (1989): 61–64.

Schabram, Hans. "*The Seasons for Fasting* 206f., mit einem Beitrag zur ae. Metrik." In *Britannica: Festschrift für Hermann M. Flasdieck,* ed. Wolfgang Iser and Hans Schabram, 221–40. Heidelberg, 1960.

———. "Zur Interpretation der 18. Strophe des altenglischen Gedichts *The Seasons for Fasting*." *Anglia* 110 (1992): 296–306.

Scragg, D. G. "Napier's 'Wulfstan' Homily XXX: Its Sources, Its Relationship to the Vercelli Book and Its Style." *Anglo-Saxon England* 6 (1977): 197–211.

Sisam, Kenneth R. *Studies in the History of Old English Literature.* Oxford, 1953.

Stanley, E. G. "Studies in the Prosaic Vocabulary of Old English Verse." *Neuphilologische Mitteilungen* 72 (1971): 385–418.

Swan, Mary, and Elaine M. Treharne, eds. *Rewriting Old English in the Twelfth Century.* Cambridge Studies in Anglo-Saxon England 30. Cambridge, 2000.

Thompson, Victoria. *Dying and Death in Later Anglo-Saxon England.* Anglo-Saxon Studies 4. Woodbridge, 2004.

Tolhurst, J. B. L. *Introduction to the English Monastic Breviaries.* Publications of the Henry Bradshaw Society 80. London, 1942. Reprint, Woodbridge, 1993.

Torkar, Roland. "Textkritische Anmerkungen zum altenglischen Gedicht 'Instructions for Christians.'" *Anglia* 89 (1971): 164–77.

Tristram, Hildegard L. C. "Stock Descriptions of Heaven and Hell in Old English Prose and Poetry." *Neuphilologische Mitteilungen* 79 (1978): 102–13.

Upchurch, Robert K. "For Pastoral Care and Political Gain: Ælfric of Eynsham's Preaching on Marital Celibacy." *Traditio* 59 (2004): 39–78.

Walther, H. "Versifizierte Pater noster und Credo." *Revue du moyen âge latin* 20 (1964): 45–64.

Whitbread, L. "Notes on Two Minor Old English Poems." *Studia Neophilologica* 29 (1957): 123–29.

——. "The Old English Poem *Aldhelm*." *English Studies* 57 (1976): 193–97.

——. "The Old English Poems of the *Benedictine Office* and Some Related Questions." *Anglia* 80 (1962): 37–49.

——. "Text-Notes on the Old English Poem *Judgment Day II*." *English Studies* 48 (1967): 531–33.

——. "Two Notes on Minor Old English Poems." *Studia Neophilologica* 20 (1947–1948): 192–98.

——. "'Wulfstan' Homilies XXIX, XXX and Some Related Texts." *Anglia* 81 (1963): 347–64.

Wilcox, Jonathan. "Ælfric in Dorset and the Landscape of Pastoral Care." In *Pastoral Care in Late Anglo-Saxon England,* ed. Francesca Tinti, 52–62. Anglo-Saxon Studies 6. Woodbridge, 2005.

Wrenn, C. L. *A Study of Old English Literature.* London, 1967.

Wright, Charles D. "More Old English Poetry in Vercelli Homily XXI." In *Early Medieval English Texts and Interpretations: Studies Presented to Donald G. Scragg,* ed. Elaine Treharne and Susan Rosser, 245–62. Medieval and Renaissance Texts and Studies 252. Tempe, Ariz., 2002.

Zacher, Samantha. "The Rewards of Poetry: 'Homiletic' Verse in Cambridge, Corpus Christi College 201." *SELIM: Journal of the Spanish Society for Mediaeval English Language and Literature* 12 (2003–2004): 83–108.

Index

All references are to page numbers. For the primary texts, references are given to the Modern English translations only.

Abraham, 147

Adam, 239, 251, 325; and Eve, 45–47, 384

Ælfheah (Elphege), Saint, 265, 428

Ælfric, ix–x, xxxviii, 265, 386, 427–28

Æthelstan, King, 406

Æthelwold, Saint, 265, 428

Aidan, Saint, 265, 429

Alcuin, 265

Aldhelm, xi, xxiii–xxiv, xxvi, xxxix, 126–27, 358, 395–97

Aldhelm, xi, xxiii, 127, 265, 428

Alfred, King, 386

All Saints, 187

alms, xxiii–xxvi, xxxix, 49, 119, 131, 133, 141, 147, 151, 159, 169. *See also* tithing; wealth

Almsgiving, xxiii–xxiv, 118–19, 357, 394

Andreas, xi

Andrew, Saint, 189

Anglo-Saxons, 127. *See also* English (people); Saxons

Apostles' Creed, The, xvii–xviii, 82–87, 285, 290, 301, 353, 388–90

arrows, of the devil, 167, 219, 407

ascension, Christ's, 85, 389

Augustine of Canterbury, Saint, 181, 412

Augustine of Hippo, Saint, 404

baptism, 167, 175, 197, 229, 410, 421

Bartholomew, Saint, 185

Bede, the Venerable, ix–x, xx–xxi, xxxiii, xxxviii–xxxix, xl, 265, 371, 392, 409–14, 427

bees, 121

Benedict, Saint, 177, 411

Beowulf, ix, xii

Bethlehem, 85, 107

bilingual *Office,* 284–343, 375–76, 430–40

Birinus, Saint, 265, 428

"Bretons or Franks," 163, 406

Britain, 127, 161, 175–77, 181, 185, 189. *See also* England

Cædmon's Hymn, xi, xx–xxi, xxxix, 100–101, 354–55, 392

Caesarius of Arles, 403

chastity, xxiii, xxvi, 142–43, 397

Christ (III), xl, 424

Christmas, 161, 175, 189, 409

Chrodegang of Metz, 435

circumcision, Christ's, 175, 409

Clement, Saint, 189, 413

contrition and penance, xix, xxi–xxii, xxv, xxix, xxxiii–xxxiv, 17, 109, 139, 149–51, 169, 223, 237–39, 243–49, 286, 311, 329, 411, 425, 434

corpse, decay of, xxix–xxxi, 55, 75, 199, 205–7, 211, 219, 227, 231, 281, 364, 416. *See also* worms

cross, appearing at Judgment Day, 239, 283, 423, 430

Cuthbert, Saint, ix, xxviii, 265, 428

David, King, 145–47, 293, 329, 341, 343, 394, 402

divine office (liturgy of the hours), 284–90, 293, 393. *See also* bilingual *Office;* liturgy

Dream of the Rood, The, xi, xxiv

drunkenness, 133, 135, 237, 257. *See also* gluttony

Dunstan, Saint, 265, 428

Easter, xxvii–xxviii, 161, 169, 179, 411

Ecgwin, Saint, 265, 428

Elene, xi

Elijah, xxvii, 165–67, 407

Ember Days, Ember Fasts. *See* fasting; *Seasons for Fasting*

England, 163

English (people), 187, 265. *See also* Anglo-Saxons; Saxons

English (language), 145, 265, 427–28. *See also* Old English

Epiphany (Twelfth Night), 175, 410

Exeter Book. *See* manuscripts: Exeter, Cathedral Library, MS 3501

Exodus, xi, 393

fasting, abstinence, xxvi–xxviii, 133, 139, 143–45, 149, 159–73, 201, 295, 404–8, 411. *See also* Lent

fire, at Judgment Day, xv, xxix, xxxii, 21, 51–55, 233–35, 241, 251, 273, 422–23, 426

flood, in Genesis, 21, 381

flood, on Judgment Day, xxxii, 233–35, 422

fornication, 133

Gabriel, archangel, xvii, 83, 137, 177, 398, 400

Gallican psalter, 289, 431, 434, 437

Genesis, xi

Geoffrey of Durham, 355

Gloria in excelsis deo, xviii–xx, 96–97, 391–92

Gloria patri (I), The, xi, xviii, xx, xxxiv, xxxviii, xl, 88–93, 284, 288, 290, 297, 353–54, 390

Gloria patri (II), The, xviii, 94–95, 354, 390–91

gluttony, 133–35, 171–73, 195, 217, 237. *See also* drunkenness

Godric's Hymn, xxi, 102–3, 355–56

Grave, The, xxxii, 230–31, 370–71, 418–22

Gregory the Great, Saint, xxvi, xxviii, 159, 163, 177, 181, 406, 408, 410, 412

Guthlac, xi

harp, 221, 419

harrowing of hell, xvii, 47, 85, 295, 325, 384

heaven, descriptions of, 259–61

hedgehog, xxxii, 222–25, 420

Helena, Saint, 179, 412

hell, descriptions of, 11, 233–35, 255–59, 281–83

Homiletic Fragment (I), xi, xxxiii, 120–23, 357, 394

Homiletic Fragment (II), xi, xxxiii, 124–25, 358, 394–95

Horeb, 165

Hrabanus Maurus, 285

Instructions for Christians, xi, xxiv–xxvi, 138–55, 359–61, 400–404

Isaac, 147

Isaiah, 151, 403

Israel, 99, 157, 295

Jacob, 147

James (the Greater), Saint, 183

Jeremiah, 149

Jerome, Saint, 418

Jerusalem, 382

Jews, 159, 275, 317

Job, 55, 385

John the Baptist, Saint, 183–85, 410, 412–13

John of Beverly, Saint, 265, 428

Joseph, patriarch, xiv, 3, 377

Joseph of Arimathea, 85, 239, 389

Judgment Day, the Last Judgment, xv, xvii, xxix, xxxi–xxxv, 21, 51–55, 75–77, 141, 195, 197–99, 201–3, 219–23, 232–63, 270, 272–83, 341, 385, 416, 419–20, 422–27, 429–30

Judgment Day (I), xxxii, 232–41, 371, 422–24

Judgment Day (II), xxxiii–xxxiv, xxxvii–xxxix, 242–63, 270, 371–73, 399, 424–27

Judgment of the Damned, The, xxxiv, 269–83, 374–76, 416, 424, 429–30

kenning, 378–79

Kent, 181

Kentish Hymn, The, xi, xviii, xx, 96–99, 354, 391–92

Kentish Psalm, The, xxxviii

Lactantius, xv, 380

Lament for the English Church, A, ix–x, xxxi, xxxviii, 264–67, 373–74, 427–29

Lammas Day, 183, 413

Laurence, Saint, 185, 413

learning and teaching, as Christian duties, 131, 135, 139, 143–45, 153, 165, 171, 265–67, 401, 428. *See also* wisdom

Lent, xxvi–xxvii, 158, 163–69, 406–7, 436–37

"liturgical verse," xvi–xx, xxii, xxxviii, 284, 288–89

liturgy, xv–xxii, xxiv, xxvii, xxxv, xxxviii, 376, 386, 391, 398, 405–6, 409. *See also* bilingual *Office;* divine office

Lord's Prayer (I), The, xvi, 66–67, 352, 386

Lord's Prayer (II), The, xvi–xviii, xxix, xxxiv, xl, 68–77, 288, 352–53, 386–88

Lord's Prayer (III), The, xvi–xvii, 78–81, 284, 290, 299, 353

lust, 253, 257

macaronic verses, 63, 127, 135–37, 385–86

manuscripts

Cambridge, Corpus Christi College: MS 26, 355; MS 201, xxxiii, 270, 288–89, 352, 358, 371, 374–75, 399; MS 326, 358; MS 419, 374

Cambridge, University Library: Ii.1.33, 359; Kk.5.16, 354; Mm.4.28, 355

Dijon, Bibliothèque municipale, MS 574, 354

Exeter, Cathedral Library: MS 3501 (The Exeter Book), xiv–xvi, xxx, xxxii, 349–52, 356–58, 363–64, 371, 414–16

London, British Library: Additional 43703, 361; Cotton Claudius A.iii, 358, 398; Cotton Cleopatra B.xiii, 374; Cotton Julius A.ii, 356; Cotton Nero D.v, 355; Cotton Otho B.v, 355; Cotton Tiberius B.i, 363; Cotton Titus D.xxvii, 354; Cotton Vespasian D.vi, 354; Harley 153, 355; Harley 322, 355; Harley 1620, 355; Royal 5.F.vii, 355

London, Lambeth Palace, MS 427, 356

Oxford, Bodleian Library: Bodley 343, 370; Douce 207, 355; Hatton 114, 374; Junius 121, 284, 353, 375; Laud misc. 413, 355

Paris, Bibliothèque nationale de France: lat. 5237, 354; lat. 8824 (The Paris Psalter), 288–91, 375, 411, 431–38

St. Petersburg, Russian National Library, Lat. Q.v.I.18, 354

Vercelli, Biblioteca Capitolare, MS CXVIII (The Vercelli Book), xii, xxx, 357, 363, 412, 414–17

Worcester, Cathedral Library, F.174, 366, 373

Martin, Saint, 189, 413

Mary, the Blessed Virgin, xxvii–xxviii, 83, 103, 125, 137, 175–77, 185, 261, 313, 388, 395, 400, 410, 426, 434

Matthew, Saint, 185

Matthew Paris, 355

Matthias, Saint, 177

Menologium, The, xi, xxvii–xxviii, 174–89, 363, 408–14

Michael, archangel, 187

monks, monasticism, 145, 284–85, 397, 402, 411, 431–32, 435, 438–39

Moses, xxvii, 147, 157–59, 163–65, 295, 406–7

Napier Homily XXIX, xl, 270, 372

Napier Homily XXX, xxxix, 270, 359

Napier Homily XL, 374

neorxna-wang, meanings of, 384, 413. *See also* Paradise, earthly

New Year's Day, 175

Noah, 147

Old English, use of in the Anglo-Saxon church, ix–x, xix, 265, 287–90, 427–28

Old English Benedictine Office, The. See bilingual *Office;* manuscripts: Oxford, Bodleian Library, Junius 121

Oswald of Worcester, Saint, 265, 428

Panther, The, xiv, 2–7, 349, 377–78

Paradise, after death, xxix, xxxix, 167, 185, 217, 247, 325, 329, 413. *See also* heaven

Paradise, earthly, 19–23, 45, 381, 383–84, 424

Partridge, The, xiv–xv, 16–17, 350, 379–80

Paul, Saint, xiii, 7, 147, 155, 183, 273, 343, 377–78

Paulinus, Saint, 265, 428

Pentecost, xxvi–xxvii, 161, 317–19, 406, 436–37

Peter, Saint, 163, 183

Peter Chrysologus, 403

Pharaoh, 295

Philip and James, Saints, 179

phoenix, physical description of, 37–39

Phoenix, The, xv, xxix, xxxv, 18–63, 350–52, 380–86

Physiologus, xiii–xv, xxxiv, 377–39. *See also The Panther; The Partridge; The Whale*

Pilate, 85, 389

pontifical (book), 129, 398

prayer, x, xv–xxii, xxxv, 49, 127, 131–33, 137, 139, 145, 147, 161, 209, 223, 245–47, 284–90, 295, 325–29, 335, 343

Prayer, A, xi, xxi–xxii, 104–9, 356, 392–93

priests, 145, 163, 169–73, 223, 401–2, 430–31

"prosaic" qualities and admixtures in Old English verse, xii, xxv, xxxiv, 269–71

Red Sea, 295

Reginald of Durham, 355

Regularis concordia, 435

Resignation (A), xxii, xxix, 110–15, 356–57, 393–94

Resignation (B), 357

resurrection, xv, xxviii–xxix, 7, 21, 32–35, 43, 46–47, 51–55, 61, 75, 85–87, 159, 163, 169, 179, 199,

resurrection (*continued*)
219, 235, 239, 275, 279, 317, 382,
384, 389
Rewards of Piety, The, xxiv–xxv,
xxxiv, xxxvii, xxxix, 130–37,
270, 358–59, 372, 399–400
Riddles, Old English, xxiv, 382
Rogation, Major or Greater (April
25), 179, 411
Roman psalter, 288–89, 393, 431,
434, 437
Rome, Romans, 85, 159, 163, 183,
389, 411, 413, 418

Sanctus (hymn), xvii, 69, 385–86
Saxons, 187–89. *See also* Anglo-
Saxons; English (people)
Seasons for Fasting, xi, xxiv, xxvi–
xxviii, 156–73, 361–63, 404–8
"seven creations, the" 225, 420
Simon and Jude, Saints, 187
slander, harmful talk, 121–23, 155,
227
Soul and Body, xxx–xxxi, 192–203,
363–66, 414–17
soul-and-body literature, xxix–
xxxii, xl
souls, origin of, 69, 93, 153, 195, 205,
414–15, 420
Soul's Address to the Body, The, xxxi–
xxxii, 204–29, 366–70, 417–22
soul's respite, apocryphal tradition
of, 193, 197–99, 414
Sunday observance, xviii, 91
swan, 27, 382
Swithun, Saint, 265, 428
Syria, 29, 382

Thomas, Saint, 189
Thureth, xxiv, 128–29, 358, 397–99
tithing, 139

Vercelli Book. *See* manuscripts:
Vercelli, Biblioteca Capito-
lare, MS CXVIII
Vercelli Homily II, 270, 374, 359
Vercelli Homily XXI, xxxix, 270,
374, 423

wealth, riches, xxiv–xxvi, 21, 45, 51,
129, 131–33, 141, 145–47, 155,
195–97, 209–13, 219, 227, 273,
401, 418. *See also* alms;
tithing
Whale, The, xiv, 8–15, 349–50, 378–
79
Wilfrid, Saint, 265, 428
William of Malmesbury, 395
wisdom, as a Christian duty, 143,
153, 401, 404. *See also* learning
and teaching
Worcester Fragments, ix, xi, xxxvi,
366, 373. See also *A Lament for
the English Church;* manu-
scripts: Worcester, Cathedral
Library, F.174; *The Soul's Ad-
dress to the Body*
worms, devouring the corpse, xxx,
55, 193, 197–203, 211–17, 227,
231, 281, 416, 418–19
Wulfstan II of York, x, xxxvii, 270,
285, 288, 398